RATIONALITY AND COGNITION: AGAINST RELATIVISM-PRAGMATISM

Cognitive science has posed some radical challenges to philosophy in recent years, particularly in the study of the cognitive activities and capacities of individuals. Many philosophers have taken up the challenge, and one result has been the emergence of a radical new wave of relativism, one that assaults the credibility of rationalist views. In this book Nenad Miščević defends naturalistic rationalism against these recent relativist attacks.

Miščević begins with an excellent introduction to cognitive science and goes on to create a searching defence of human rationality and of a traditional role for truth in epistemology. He presents a critical scrutiny of the relativism championed by Stephen Stich and Paul Churchland and their followers, showing that it not only exaggerates the subversive impact of science, but relies on its links with naturalism for much of its credibility. His careful dissection of relativist arguments establishes the main outlines of a positive rationalistic picture that is both original and convincing.

(Toronto Studies in Philosophy)

NENAD MIŠČEVIĆ is a professor of philosophy at the University of Maribor, Maribor, Slovenia. He is also the president of the European Society of Analytic Philosophy.

NENAD MIŠČEVIĆ

Rationality and Cognition: Against Relativism-Pragmatism

UNIVERSITY OF TORONTO PRESS
Toronto Buffalo London

Toronto Buffalo London

Reprinted in paperback 2014

ISBN 978-0-8020-4166-1 (cloth)
ISBN 978-1-4426-5770-0 (paper)

Printed on acid-free paper

Toronto Studies in Philosophy
Editors: James R. Brown and Calvin Normore

Canadian Cataloguing in Publication Data

Miščević, Nenad
Rationality and cognition : against relativism-pragmatism

(Toronto studies in philosophy)
Includes bibliographical references and index.
ISBN 978-0-8020-4166-1 (bound) ISBN 978-1-4426-5770-0 (pbk.)

1. Rationalism. 2. Cognition. 3. Relativity. I. Title. II. Series.

B833.M57 2000 149′.7 C98-932444-2

University of Toronto Press acknowledges the financial assistance to its publishing program of the Canada Council for the Arts and the Ontario Arts Council.

University of Toronto Press acknowledges the financial support for its publishing activities of the Government of Canada through the Book Publishing Industry Development Program (BPIDP).

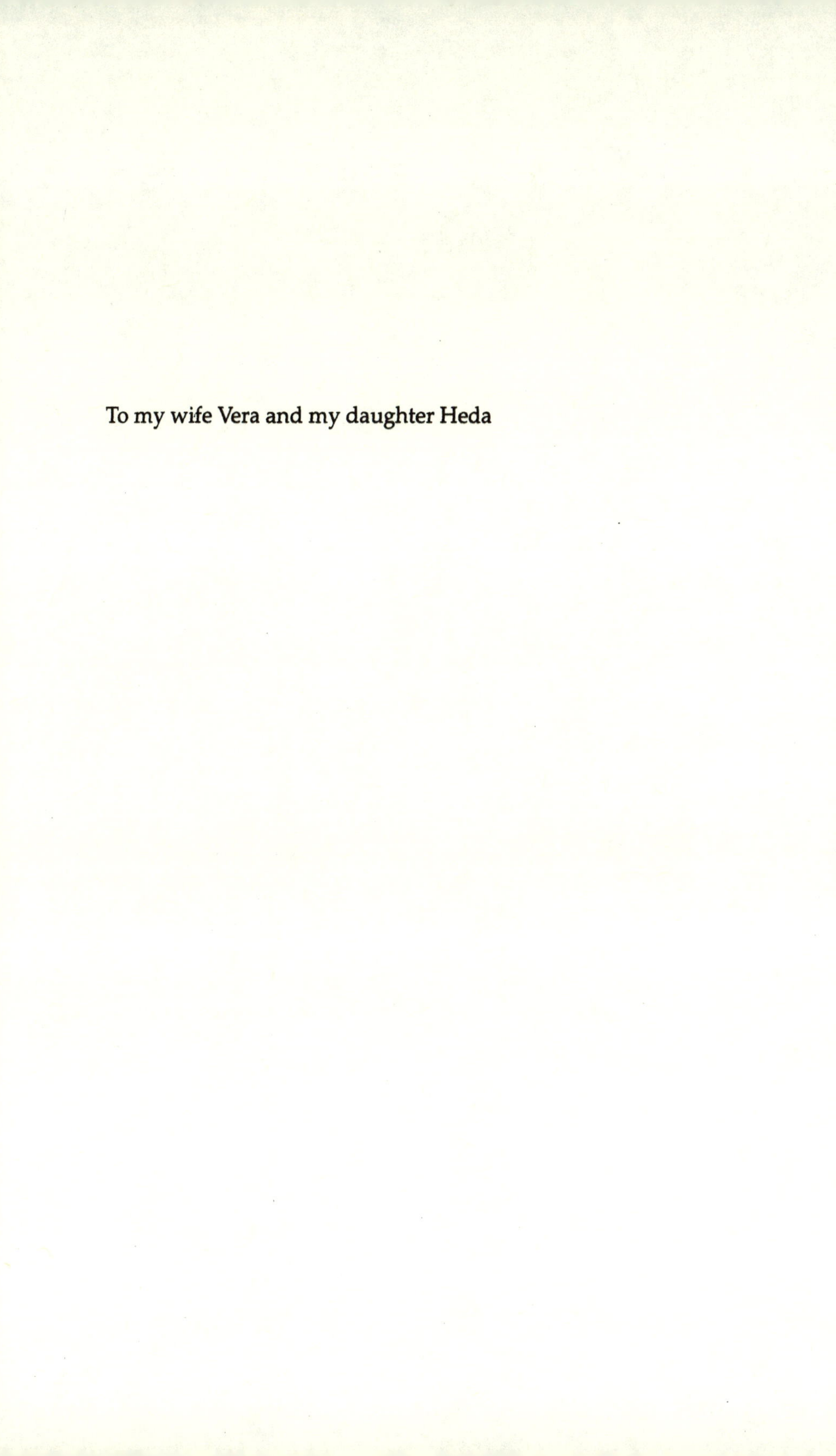

To my wife Vera and my daughter Heda

Contents

PREFACE ix

Part One: The Cognitivist Challenge

1 Philosophy and Cognitive Science 3
2 Epistemology: The Classical Picture 37
3 Relativism-Pragmatism 47

Part Two: Are Our Representations Truth-Tolerant?

4 The Idea of Truth-Intolerance 63
5 The Non-Sentential Media 75

Part Three: Truth and Rationality

6 The Value of Truth 135
7 From Truth to Virtue 186

CONCLUSION 227
APPENDIX: THEORY AND OBSERVATION 233
NOTES 277
REFERENCES 307
INDEX 319

Preface

This book is a defence of naturalistic rationalism against recent forms of relativism, forms inspired by a particular reading of the results of cognitive science and championed by Stich, Churchland, and their followers. The topic is formally introduced in the next chapter; here, I shall allow myself a few words of a more personal introduction.

The prehistory of the book is long and far from obvious. Almost twenty years ago, during a longer stay in Paris, I had begun to resist the temptation of a different kind of relativism, the French post-structuralist relativism of my older teachers, Derrida, Foucault, and their disciples. Having overcome that temptation, I turned to analytic philosophy and subsequently forgot about the whole issue. The discovery of Stich's book, *Fragmentation of Reason* – at that time still a manuscript – awakened my curiosity about the new brand of relativism. Its vocabulary showed amusing similarities to the French brand – terms like 'deconstruction' and 'fragmentation' rang a familiar bell – but more important were the deep similarities in philosophical stance. (I do not pursue this topic in this book; it would take too much space.)

In 1990 I produced a draft of a paper criticizing Stich's main argument. The paper was given to international analytic audiences in Bled (Slovenia) and Dubrovnik (Croatia). The reactions surprised me. Some of the most informed and astute participants – among them some well-known North American and British philosophers – dismissed the whole issue, refusing to believe that Stich could have claimed 'such a thing.' This would have been the end of the story, had it not been for Professor James Robert Brown, who persuaded me that the issue was worth pursuing. To him the book owes its very existence, and his kind encouragement and help have been crucial up to its very publication. So to him my warmest thanks go.

The bulk of the book was written during the war in Croatia. In fact, Jim Brown's suggestion came in April 1992 at the Inter-university Centre in Dubrovnik, during a wartime solidarity conference on the philosophy of science. In that period my home philosophy department in Zadar (Croatia) had been devastated, first by war circumstances, and then by the excesses of our own rightwingers from the ruling party, who had forced most of the active staff to leave simply because the department would not bow to their requirements. The writing of this book provided a stimulus, and a possibility of escape – at least for a few brief hours – from the sad realities of the period.

Preparation for the publication has taken a rather long time. Meanwhile, papers on the topic have appeared. My excuse for not dealing with them is that this book is not meant to be an encyclopedia of relativism-pragmatism: discussing them would lead us astray from the main line of argument. Also, both Stich and Churchland have published new books recently; however, they do not deal with relativism-pragmatism, at least not directly or centrally.

Different versions of various chapters have been given to audiences in Rijeka (Croatia), then at CREA, Paris, at Collège International de Philosophie, Paris; at the Philosophy and Psychology departments of the Universities of Trieste (Italy) and Klagenfurt (Austria); at the Congress of European Society for Philosophy of Psychology in Paris; at a Colloque de Cerissy in Normandy; and at a conference in Karlovy Vary (Czech Republic).

I have accumulated so many debts that I can hardly thank everybody, but here are the heaviest debts: to Nenad Smokrovic, with whom I have discussed the cognitive approaches to rationality, to William Ramsey for a long conversation about the book, to Georges Rey and Michael Devitt for intense questioning at the very early stage, to members of the brilliant philosophy group led by Hugh Mellor for their encouragement at a Dubrovnik conference, to Keith Lehrer for his comments at my talks at Collège International, Paris, to Marcelo Dascal, Miljenko Stanic, Boran Bercic, Dunja Jutronic, Martin Davies, and Karin Neander, for support and help at various stages of the work. Professor Stich has been sending me the offprints and preprints of his work, keeping me informed about the various turns of his relativism-pragmatism. Finally, to the readers for the Press, Ronnie de Sousa and Bill Seager, I owe a great deal for their comments, both of encouragement and of criticism.

N.M.

PART ONE
THE COGNITIVIST CHALLENGE

1

Philosophy and Cognitive Science

1. The Protagonists

Science has been challenging philosophy in various ways. It has often suggested metaphysical ideas shocking to the prevailing philosophical climate, it has suggested some unorthodox views on morality, and it has challenged received philosophical views of human cognition. In this book I am interested in the last, the challenge to epistemology that has taken many forms. One prominent form is the scientific success of methodologies neglected or looked down on by the philosophical establishment. The most radical challenge, however, has come from the scientific study of cognition. It enters a realm traditionally dominated by philosophers, and its results are bound to be of prime interest to them.

The scientific study of cognition encompasses both the study of the cognitive activities and capacities of individuals and the study of the social setting of cognition. In this book I deal with the former, individualistic part. On the one hand, the most prominent branch of study in this area is cognitive psychology. It shades into cognitive neurology; some authors even speak of 'cognitive biology' as the most general discipline encompassing both and augmenting them. Another branch is artificial intelligence, with its major contributions to the understanding of human cognition. All branches of this study are known by the common name 'cognitive science.'

Cognitive research has introduced numerous surprises, some of them quite spectacular and challenging. Philosophers ought to take science seriously, so that the option of rejecting the findings of cognitive science will not really be open. One should place one's confidence in its theories and results, accepting what are by now its standard claims. In cases of serious disagreement it is preferable to assume that at least one side is right and then to consider the epistemological consequences of each.

I shall consider two answers to the challenge and defend one of them. The first answer is somewhat anarchistic: one should abandon the very foundations of the epistemological enterprise and turn to relativism about cognition. The kind of relativism that emerges from this answer has some distinctive traits. Twentieth-century relativism about cognitive matters – from the beginning of the century to R. Rorty and the deconstructivists – has been associated largely with the humanities. Cultural history, linguistics, anthropology, and social sciences have fuelled the relativistic impulse and have provided evidence for and against relativism. Moreover, the history of science, with its cultural overtones, has become a battlefield of relativism about enquiry and knowledge. But the newest brand of cognitive relativism starts from the biological and cognitive sciences, including hard-science disciplines such as neurobiology. It is cognitive not only by its subject matter, but also through its reliance on cognitive science. Such a view has been propounded by Stephen Stich and Paul Churchland. The importance of this new wave of relativism resides precisely in its naturalistic, science-oriented perspective, which suggests that if one is a naturalist, one should end up being a relativist. Since many philosophers and linguists and most cognitive psychologists tend to be naturalists, the suggestion has a wide and sympathetic audience.

The other response to the challenge is rationalistic and anti-relativistic: epistemologists are free to pursue their task, but they have to modify some of their commonsensical assumptions about human cognition. This is the line I intend to defend. The tenor of the book will be critical. I hope to establish the main outlines of a positive rationalistic picture by dissecting the relativistic view, which I find wrong (although prima facie attractive and instructive in various ways). Rationalists have always learned from intelligent and resourceful relativists, and there is much in Stich and Churchland that is worth retaining, not least their uncompromising naturalism. I think, however, that one can be a naturalist without being a relativist; so I intend to subject their line to critical scrutiny in the hope of showing that it exaggerates the subversive impact of science. Similar discussions have been carried on in the face of similar challenges raised by the sociology of science and history of science. I find most congenial the books on philosophy of science of two rationalists fighting on the same front, William Newton-Smith and James Robert Brown (Newton-Smith 1981; Brown 1989, 1994).

A brief preview of the first, introductory part of the book follows. In the first chapter some relevant results from cognitive science are briefly recounted; in the second epistemology comes to the fore and the basic rationalistic picture of cognition is presented. In the third chapter relativism-pragmatism is introduced. A few words about terminology: I shall abide by the now standard use of 'cognitive' as a descriptive term, without any implications about further goals of cognitive items or any implications of success; a mechanism that produces only false perceptions or beliefs would still be 'cognitive' in this neutral sense. It will be the burden of discussion in this book to show that the goal of cognitive processes is knowledge, and it is an open question whether they actually attain it; so the outcome of the discussion should not be prejudged by the terminology. In order to underscore the tentative nature of cognitive effort, I use the term 'enquiry,' dear to classical pragmatists, and speak about the cognitive agent as an 'enquirer.' Finally, an explanation of my use of the pronouns 'he' and 'she': in the field of relativism-pragmatism, since Stich and Churchland are the most prominent figures, I use 'he' when referring to the 'relativist-pragmatist.' Otherwise, the pronoun 'she' will often be used for gender-neutral, unspecific reference.

2. Know Thyself: The State of the Art

We seem to know a lot about ourselves, and about our cognitive capacities. Part of this apparent knowledge is so routine and unproblematic that we scarcely take notice of it – you know that you are able to read English, that you can find your way to the entrance door of your apartment, and so on. People make quite accurate guesses about each other, and go about their business relying on such guesses and on the framework of assumptions about the way persons function. In recent times, researchers have begun to study this body of beliefs – 'folk-psychology,' or 'commonsensical psychology,' as it is called.[1] Beyond the needs of everyday life, folk psychology has supplied art, literature, and the cinema with the underlying framework for understanding human minds and actions, and it has been at rock bottom in the philosophical understanding of people, their cognitive powers and achievements. Philosophical epistemology has been built upon commonsensical assumptions about the human mind.

As I have already mentioned, however, the work of biologists, psychologists, and neurologists has produced many new insights and has extensively revised folk-psychological wisdom. They have concerned themselves with cognitive abilities, such as perception, the capacity to understand language and to produce new sentences, problem-solving abilities, reasoning, memory, and much more. Folk-psychology takes these abilities mostly for granted and has no clear account of how people manage to acquire perceptual knowledge, how they understand language, how they learn to add and multiply, and so on. Research in artificial intelligence has shown how difficult the questions are; when one tries to build a machine that will replicate even very modest human cognitive achievements, one becomes aware of the complexity of the tasks that human cognitive apparatus faces and successfully performs. The bulk of the research has been devoted to the most basic abilities. One can even argue that psychology became scientific with the recognition of the importance of the study of very simple abilities. To recall the most famous example, the German psychologist Hermann Ebbinghaus initiated the study of rote learning in this spirit about a hundred years ago, and it was such research that convinced the sceptical audience that scientific methods are applicable to higher mental processes. Since then, psychologists have persistently tried to answer deceptively simple-looking questions such as: How does one recognize the shape of the object in front of one? How does a child learn the past tense of regular verbs? Apparently there is a lot to be learned in the process.

It is this ground floor within the edifice of cognition that is still the preferred object of study in cognitive psychology and an interesting field for research in artificial intelligence. We shall briefly pass in review some central topics, starting with various cognitive abilities (perception, language processing, and reasoning) and ending on the more general question of the medium in which people think and reason. Warning: the brief selection offered here is incomplete and in itself is not a full introduction to cognitive psychology.

2.1 Perception: Does the Eye Know Geometry?

Ordinary perceiving does not feel like something we do: seeing and hearing are more like an effortless, involuntary intake than like an action. Except for careful, exploratory looking and listening, perception has been treated more as passive receiving than as an achievement, and philosophers (with some notable exceptions, e.g., Aristotle, Berkeley) have paid their homage to this felt ease by speaking about things and scenes as 'given' in perception.

A hundred years of research, from the pioneering work of Hermann von Helmholtz to the contemporary synthesis of David Marr, have completely reversed the picture. Seeing things is not simply effortlessly taking in; it is something that is done, but the doing pertains to mechanisms to which we have no introspective access and over which we do not exercise deliberate control. The task that these mechanisms face is daunting. From a mass of noisy sensory input they have to extract reliable information about the outside world. It is the recognition of objects in the outside world that is a vital guide for action, but the visual mechanism receives only patterned stimulation to work from.

The route from the stimulus to the full visual experience has often been likened to hypothesis formation and testing. We are invited to picture the visual mechanism by analogy with a detective trying to deduce, from scanty evidence and some general knowledge, what really happened. (Just how much general knowledge the mechanism can access is still a matter of controversy.) The analogy is part of the useful 'homuncular' picture: imagine a particular submechanism as 'a small man in the head,' a homunculus, receiving information, performing computations or inferences based on the received data, and passing the results to another homunculus. Each homunculus is more stupid than the whole system, so that the performance of the smart whole reduces to the interaction of less smart components. We can go further, and picture each homunculus as having in his head additional, smaller, and more stupid homunculi, and so on. The hierarchy of homunculi eventually ends with the most stupid ones, capable of performing only mechanical tasks. (This idea has been developed by D. Norman, D. Dennett, and W. Lycan.)[2]

David Marr has proposed a sophisticated theory of stages of visual processing.[3] According to his view, vision starts with an intensity array containing two sorts of information: intensity changes and local geometry. This information is then used by low-level mechanisms to produce a 'description' of an image in terms of simple, low-level symbolic assertion, called the raw primal sketch. The next representation is a full primal sketch that 'makes explicit object boundaries or contours, shadows, changes in texture, and specular reflexions, obtained by using geometrical reasoning on the earlier descriptions and some limited higher-level knowledge' (Vaina 1990, 54). Still further is the representation of the geometry of the visible surfaces, and so on, to the full, conscious, visual experience that tells us what the world is like. Each subsystem has access to a limited amount of stored knowledge – and the full store of memory is available only at the latest stage of processing.

Already at this juncture it is easy to see why such a picture would present a challenge to philosophers. The perceptual mechanism is performing tasks that are epistemologically Janus-faced: on the one hand, they are unconscious and must be done mechanically; on the other hand, they look uncannily similar to intelligent tasks. Again, the 'homunculi' performing the task are not conscious, responsible, and free epistemic agents, but their product looks like bona fide knowledge, and some segments of their activity (e.g., doing computations concerning visual geometry) seem respectable enough. How should we judge them? What do they know? One variant of these questions will be discussed in chapter 5.

2.2 Language Use: Does the Child Know the Theory of Syntax?

Discoveries about knowledge of language have provided the main incentive to the development of contemporary cognitive psychology. It started from the attempts to give a full description of the grammar of particular languages, not only didactic partial descriptions that rely on the intelligence and intuition of the reader, but a full story, told from scratch. These attempts have revealed the incredible complexity of grammars and have prompted the natural question: How can a naïve speaker possibly know her language?

The most prominent, but also the most debated, answer has been the Chomskyian one: people have unconscious knowledge of the grammar of their language. Although manifested as skill only, it is structured like any other knowledge. The language-processing subsystems (module, 'homunculus') of the cognitive mechanism have access to the internally represented grammars. Also, the acquisition of language is remarkably close to mature theorizing – the homunculus has some pre-wired, innate knowledge of universal principles of grammar, which he uses to form hypotheses about the linguistic input. This picture is extremely intellectualistic and is not shared by all theoreticians. Even less intellectualistic versions, however, admit that command of language involves an enormous amount of unconscious processing, which does resemble ordinary reasoning.

The intellectualistic picture has also featured an important idea known as the distinction between *competence* and *performance*. The motivation underlying the competence/performance distinction is very simple and can be stated by appealing to a common phenomenon – that people make more grammatical mistakes when producing and trying to understand very long sentences as opposed to very short ones. It would be odd to believe that the fact that their performance in these tasks is unequal has something to do with their grammatical skills as such, and particularly odd to suppose that people use different implicit grammars for long sentences than they do for short ones. The most plausible explanation is that the grammar is the same, and that the difference in actual performance is due to the limitation of memory. In terms of the homuncularist picture, the homunculus that processes grammatical information uses the correct grammar book, but his helper homunculus, who is supposed to pass him the data, is lazy or becomes tired too soon. The performance varies because of memory; the residue is fixed. Once the contribution of memory is factored out, a stable residue remains: it is the knowledge of grammar, called 'competence,' in contrast to 'performance.' Chomsky has persuasively argued that one of the main sources for a theory of competence is the speaker's intuitions about what is grammatical and what is not. The view that intuitions are the direct product of competence is appealingly optimistic, but recently it has been challenged.[4] (Many psychologists and linguists believe that a theory of linguistic performance must exhibit the structure of what is known by a competent speaker in purely formal terms. This belief has become a focus of much debate, which, fortunately, we can skip for our purposes.)

The competence/performance distinction has been generalized to other areas of knowledge. Two obvious candidates are the implicit mastery of rules of reasoning and simple arithmetical knowledge. The difficulties in surveying long chains of reasoning or of computation obviously are not a systematic characteristic of someone's knowledge, but are due to limitations of attention and memory. Thus, it would be reasonable to postulate the availability of logical and arithmetical competence, a stable underlying structure beneath the vagaries of performance. It can be reconstructed from reasoners' intuitions, as in the case of language: 'People have intuitions about all aspects of their cognitive functions. They 'know' many things without knowing how they know. Basic to the notion of competence is the belief that what is behind such intuitions is best characterized as a set of implicit rules or a procedure. If we can get a person to reveal his intuitions to us in sufficient detail we would then have the basis for inferring these rules – a basis much sounder than the record of his behaviour, since the latter are also strongly dependent on his other psychological faculties as well as on the conditions under which the behaviour was observed' (Pylyshyn 1973, 31). In the next section I discuss concepts and reasoning. In Part Three I shall appeal to the performance/competence distinction in matters of reasoning.

2.3. Concepts and Reasoning: The Good News and the Bad

The investigation of reasoning has also brought several surprises. The first is closely related to matters already noted in connection with perception and language – namely, the amount and the importance of unconscious processing. This is more surprising in the case of reasoning than in the case of perception, because reasoning has for two millennia played the role of paradigm of conscious rational activity. There are well-informed philosophers, for instance, John Searle (1990), who even nowadays reject the existence of non-conscious reasoning.

The other two surprises counterbalance each other: the first is the good news that people are very good at some reasoning tasks, whose very existence seems to have been unsuspected for a long time, and the second is the bad news that people perform very poorly at some elementary logical and probabilistic tasks, at which one would not expect them to fail. Sceptics and relativists tend to stress the bad news and to build upon it; so we have to devote some space to both kinds of news in order to present a balanced report of what one can expect from normal enquirers.

First, a few words about the ways people store conceptual information and then the good news. Psychologists have been paying increasing attention to real-life processes concerning conceptual information (as opposed to abstract logical and normative concerns).[5] When a child or a naïve cognizer in our culture thinks about birds, she has in mind animals that typically fly, have feathers, lay eggs, and often sing. She classifies actual items as birds, using this 'ideal type,' not using some definition or some exhaustive description. A set of criterial properties, or an 'ideal type' embodying them, is called a 'prototype,' and it is claimed that concepts are stored as prototypes. A definition of prototype by its inventor, the psychologist Eleanor Rosch, states: 'By prototypes of categories we have generally meant the clearest cases of category membership defined operationally by people's judgement of goodness of membership in the category' (1978, 36). Very often, prototypes are identified with typical members of the category (e.g., the robin is a prototypical bird), but most prototype-theoreticians define prototypes as 'clusters of correlated attributes that are only characteristic or typical of category membership' (Medin 1989, 1469). Prototypes are not specifically images or sentences.

Representation of concepts through prototypes is often contrasted with the classical idea of representing them through necessary and sufficient conditions. Also, the use of prototypes allows for graded judgment and for belief revision. A sparrow is a more typical bird than a dodo, and one can express this fact either in terms of probability (i.e., given the visible properties of the sparrow and the dodo, it is more probable that a sparrow is a bird than that a dodo is), or in terms of fuzzy membership (a creature with dodo-like properties only partly belongs to the category), but this second interpretation is highly contentious.

The evidence for the claim that everyday knowledge is stored in the form of prototypes comes from experiments probing subjects' readiness for and accuracy in categorization. A typical bird – say, a robin – is quickly, effortlessly, and without errors classified as a bird. For an atypical bird, such as a dodo or a penguin, response time (latencies) is significantly longer, and error rates are higher; also, people retrieve from memory the typical instances before the atypical ones. Children master the naming of typical instances before that of untypical ones, and typicality influences deductive and inductive reasoning.

The structure of prototypes has been the subject of intense research, which has uncovered some interesting features.[6] It is widely held that prototypes differ from more traditional representations along several dimensions:

a) They have a 'graded structure' and allow graded judgments of membership in the category. The members of the category 'vary in how good an example (how typical) they are of their category' (Barsalou 1987, 101). Sometimes the grading is taken probabilistically – a thing that flies, lays eggs, and sings is more probably a bird than a thing that does not act in these ways. Sometimes, it is taken in terms of non-strict membership – the concept-prototype itself is seen as fuzzy and admitting of graded membership.
b) They have built-in assumptions; so they allow revisions of ascriptions as the cognizer learns more about the item to be categorized.
c) They allow for representation in different media and are not limited to sentential description. 'Prototypes can be represented either by propositional or image systems,' according to Rosch (978, 40).
d) They can be coded holistically in a context-dependent fashion, or – according to some authors – in a fashion that allows ad hoc prototypes, constructed as the need arises (Barsalou 1987).

Research has also revealed some problems for prototype theories. The most important ones stem from the notion of similarity that has been taken as the unproblematic key to reasoning with prototypes. Lance Rips has shown that simple (perceptual) similarity to the prototype is not the only relevant feature in categorization – variability also counts. For example, pizzas are relatively variable (average of twelve inches), and U.S. quarters are relatively fixed in their diameters (one inch). Now, here is a circular object that has a three-inch diameter. Is it more likely that it is a pizza or a quarter? Only 37 per cent of subjects chose by the similarity criterion and opted for the quarter-solution – the great majority decided against similarity for the pizza-solution. Rips conjectures that 'in the pizza-quarter example, we conclude that the 3-inch object must be a pizza rather than a quarter because we can more easily explain how a pizza of that size could be created' (1987, 53). Of course, it can be claimed that a pizza is similar to a circular object of three-inch diameter, because both objects share some hidden, more important property than size, such as the ease with which it can be produced (I have heard this claim in discussion). But such a notion of similarity itself is in need of explanation and cannot play the role of a simple, obvious cue, which perceptual similarity was intended to play. These deeper features have been grouped under the name of the 'core' of the concept, and it has been proposed that a concept consists of two components – visible prototype properties, and more hidden core properties.[7] Let us now pass to the issue of reasoning.

Since the 1970s researchers in artificial intelligence (AI) have been preoccupied with the idea of designing a robot capable of coping with real life problems. Given that the robot will move things, which will then move other things, it must be able to foresee at least some effects of movements and changes in general. If the robot moves a plate with a cup on it, the cup will move simultaneously with the plate. The robot is supposed to know such facts.

This was the original frame problem – to specify, in a general and principled way, which (kinds of) things change together, and which remain untouched by some given change. It has turned out to be quite difficult. Various solutions have been tried: to break down the description of everyday knowledge into packages containing those items that change together, or to build programs that will ignore potential changes unless they are explicitly specified ('letting sleeping dogs lie'), or first to construct a logic of change and action. No solution was foolproof. Humans are very good at this (original) frame problem. What is it that they know and – more important – what is it that they can figure out so that they do not have to think about what will change with what when they are doing their usual work? The human achievement begins to seem quite impressive once looked at through the eyes of an engineer having to design a system to emulate it.

The original frame problem has since begotten the extended frame problem. The worry about knowing which changes go together has brought into focus the interconnectedness of everyday knowledge. Even rather immediate consequences of an action may depend on many things. How does the agent separate the relevant from the irrelevant in a very brief period of time? Everyday knowledge (belief system), mobilized in decision making seems to be much better structured than it was once thought, and its (unconscious) strategies of selection and of reasoning are quite impressive. This flattering conclusion then may serve to introduce the question about the organization of the human belief system and the strategies of reasoning within it.

How can one represent the knowledge of dependencies displayed by normal humans when they face the frame problem? Take, as an example, the falling of things. People know that unsupported objects (usually) fall, that there are exceptions (e.g., balloons), and that in situations of danger they can bring this knowledge to bear in split-second time. The quickness and ease with which they achieve this demands explanation. A good guess would be that people have at their disposal a prototype of 'heavy material object,' involving some rules of thumb, licensing the required inferences in given situations and admitting of exceptions, perhaps: 'If this object is unsupported, it will fall.' The rule has exceptions or 'defeaters' built in (e.g., 'unless it is a balloon'). Cognitive scientists have explored this avenue, and many find it quite promising. They hypothesize the presence of such rules of thumb in human minds and claim that a large portion of everyday knowledge is organized as a system of these rules. Others are sceptical and point out that the search through the library of rules takes time and skill.

A rule of thumb admitting of exceptions allows the reasoner to reach a conclusion 'by default,' that is, given the absence of any indication to the contrary.[8] Such reasoning is called default reasoning, and the rules are called default rules. Researchers have striven to describe default reasoning in detail, to test it on AI programs, to show that people really use it, and to give a formal logical reconstruction of it. There is some evidence that a kind of reasoning, broadly of the default variety, is also employed by perceptual- and language-processing units of the mind/brain.

One can think of default rules and reasoning in the following way: picture the 'reasoning subsystem' of the human cognitive apparatus as a homunculus receiving input information and then consulting the manual in order to figure out what will happen next. The manual is actually a pile of papers, each with a default rule written on it. One pile deals with one topic. Take 'falling,' for example. On the top of this pile there is the most general rule: 'If something is unsupported it will fall.' Below it are papers with more specific rules stating exceptions: 'If something is very light it will not fall,' 'If something is suspended it will not fall.' Further below are exceptions to the exceptions: A suspended object will fall if ... At the bottom of the pile are the bloodless and remote admonitions of science, brought home perhaps by space-exploration movies: 'Things do not fall in the absence of a gravitational field.' A pile structured in this way is called a default hierarchy (actually, the hierarchy of exceptions is only one kind of default hierarchy; I shall mention another kind presently).

Suppose a mild earthquake takes place, and the homunculus receives information that heavy things have started moving around. He first reads the paper at the top of the pile and concludes that unsupported objects will start falling. This conclusion can be used quickly and in its full scope. The possible exceptions might be taken care of later, because they concern the things that do not fall and so do not present a danger. The considerations about the behaviour of things in a gravitationless situation will never come to the fore. They pertain to physics exams, not to everyday situations. This example goes some way towards solving the frame problem, that is, accounting for the ease and speed of information retrieval and inference.[9] It also accounts for a certain conservatism of everyday knowledge – the focus on the typical and usual as embodied in the structure of prototypes.

From a logician's standpoint the most conspicuous feature of default reasoning is its sensitivity to additional information. In classical deductive logic, if a proposition follows from a premise, it follows from the premise plus any additional proposition (i.e., it will 'continue to follow' if you add additional information). The introduction of new information cannot invalidate old conclusions. Such a logic is called 'monotonic' (if the set of premises 'grows,' the truth value of the conclusion remains the same).

In default reasoning new information can 'subvert' old conclusions. To change the example to one from David Lewis (who uses it in a different context), suppose the following rule holds: 'If Jane comes to the party, the party will be fun.' You hear from Jane that she is coming, and you safely conclude that the party will be fun. However, the rule has a defeater: If Jane's jealous boyfriend comes, the party is not going to be fun at all. The additional information, that Jane's boyfriend is coming, will invalidate the old conclusion. There are ways technically to represent non-monotonic reasoning so as to bring the dependence on new information sharply into focus.[10]

Defaults and default hierarchies can be combined into larger units. For example, one can have all one knows about parties stored into one big chunk, usually called a 'script.' Think about a script as a mental text containing information about a prototypical topic, prominently an event-sequence. A script tells its owner what to expect, either unconditionally or consequent upon the owner's actions: 'If you insult the host at the party, there will be trouble'.

Reasoning with defaults and scripts has its shortcomings. Scripts are stereotypical, so they can sometimes support social prejudice. They are rather rigid, so they can obstruct creativity. At the level of detail, the default reasoning might seem too conservative and self-assured. Many methodologists think that the proper attitude to general rules (such as the rules about falling bodies or birds flying) is a more cautious one. The rule, for example, licensing the step from 'This is a bird' to 'This flies' should be replaced by some probabilistic rule, assigning a probability (lower than one) to the conclusion (better to be cautious beforehand than to repent and revise after having encountered an ostrich or a penguin). Other methodologists would object to the strategy of simply listing exceptions as they come along – they would see it as an ad hoc way to revise belief, amounting to a simple repair of an initial false assumption. They would encourage the enquirer to look for a genuinely true and more general rule, encompassing various possibilities (flying and non-flying birds) as special cases.

The strategies described and others of the same sort often are aptly described as cognitive 'shortcuts,' with the implication that there are other, more scrupulous ways of reasoning. We shall use the term without any value-implication, to cover all the strategies that are not either strictly deductive or strictly probabilistic – that is, do not follow a strict and foolproof algorithmic recipe. A near synonym to 'cognitive shortcut' in this context is 'heuristics.'

We have mentioned some of the advantages of cognitive shortcuts. There is a strong research tradition, however, which has focused on the shortcomings of heuristics, or on heuristics that have interesting shortcomings. The tradition (whose roots reach into the 1950s) was started by P.C. Wason (in deductive logic) and D. Kahneman and A. Tversky (in matters inductive), who were interested in testing the psychological role of normative prescriptions from deductive logic and probability theory. Their findings were negative: people often disregard normative theory and use heuristics.

A good example is the conjunction error – the tendency to judge the probability of a conjunction as higher than the probability of the conjuncts: it seems more probable to people that Linda is a bank teller and a feminist than simply that she is a feminist. Another fine example is the dramatic failure to search for the refuting instances of one's hypothesis, the so-called confirmational bias. The next step was made by researchers interested in more concrete and socially more relevant issues. How do people attribute responsibility and blame to agents? How do they reason about causes of socially salient events? This issue has been the province of so-called attribution theory, a research program that has started quite optimistically, with a lot of confidence in human reasoning abilities. R. Nisbett, L. Ross, and their colleagues, however, were able to show that people disregard the normative theory and use the same kinds of heuristics that were, on the more abstract level, investigated and criticized by Kahneman and Tversky.

An example follows. The subject watches a public discussion in which one participant is particularly salient (black among whites or vice versa, male among females or vice versa). Then she is asked who has contributed most to the discussion, exercised the greatest influence, and the like. Most subjects will pick up the salient participant, regardless of the salient participant's real contribution to the debate. Salient objects or features will figure more prominently in the causal story than ones that are non-salient, although perhaps the latter are more important. A similar example is offered by the so-called fundamental attribution error: the general and overwhelming tendency to attribute all the causal responsibility to the agent, and to minimize the impact of the circumstances. Fritz Heider very early on proposed the explanation of this error in terms of salience. Now this seems to be a variety of the 'availability heuristics,' which Kahneman, Slovic, and Tversky describe in more general and abstract terms: '*Availability.* There are situations in which people assess the frequency of a class or the probability of an event by the ease with which instances or occurrences can be brought to mind' (1982, 11). The reader will certainly be able to think of many illustrations for this heuristics.

Another kind of heuristics is called representativeness heuristics: A is taken to be causally linked to B if A is like B or somehow is representative of B. Nisbett and Ross (1980) illustrate the use of representativeness heuristics by ideas from ancient or primitive medicine: the lungs of a fox are a good remedy for asthma because the fox is known for its excellent respiration and so on. Contemporary classic theorists, Kahneman, Slovic, and Tversky state as a general description: '*Representativeness.* Many of the probabilistic questions with which people are concerned belong to one of the following types: What is the probability that object A belongs to class B? What is the probability that event A originates from process B? What is the probability that process B will generate event A? In answering such questions, people typically rely on the representativeness heuristic, in which probabilities are evaluated by the degree to which A is representative of B, that is, by the degree to which A resembles B' (1982, 4). Another example is as follows: 'In considering tosses of a coin for heads or tails, for example, people regard the sequence H-T-H-T-T-H to be more likely than the sequence H-H-H-T-T-T, which does not appear random, and also more likely than the sequence H-H-H-H-T-H which does not represent the fairness of the coin ... Thus, people expect that the global characteristics of the process will be represented not only globally in the entire sequence, but also locally in each of its parts' (ibid., 7).

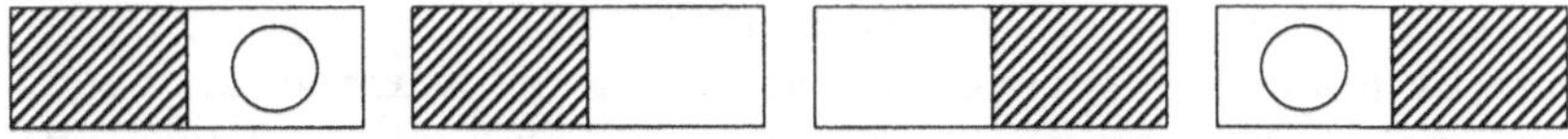

FIGURE 1.1
The four-card experiment

In the deductive reasoning task the most famous experimental paradigm is provided by Johnson-Laird and Wason's so-called four-card experiments, or selection task.[11] Subjects are presented with four cards; half of each card is masked (see figure 1.1). The task is to remove only those masks whose removal is essential to verify whether the following rule holds about cards: 'If there is a circle on the left there is a circle on the right.' People do very poorly on the task: less then 10 per cent give the right answer. (I have tried it on a group of graduate students, some of whom have had extensive training in logic; their results were almost as poor as those of the untrained subjects described in the literature.)

Apparently, however, people reason more successfully if the task is reformulated to include everyday practical knowledge. L. Cosmides has even found that a dramatic improvement takes place if the subject is put into the role of a detective who has to discover whether the rule has been obeyed by someone; people seem to be better at detecting cheaters than at abstract reasoning.[12]

Let me end this list of bad news items with the worst one of all, that concerning perseverance. In the experiments subjects are given evidence that is later discredited: they are debriefed and told exactly how they had been duped. Still, they tend to retain to a substantial degree the beliefs they formed on the basis of discredited evidence. The most spectacular examples concern belief strengthening in the face of recalcitrant data. People often stick to their theories come what may, and in the experiments the subjects have shown extreme meticulousness in searching for 'mistakes' in material that refutes their pet theories and extreme gullibility when materials support their pet theories. It seems that after criticizing the unpleasant, recalcitrant material, they are even more convinced in their initially held theories than before they were exposed to the material. Moreover, once the phenomenon has been identified, historians and philosophers of science have recognized it in the works of prominent scientists.[13]

The considerable evidence for such shortcomings can make one pessimistic about human rationality. On the other hand, the examples from science suggest some optimism: if one can make important discoveries by following imperfect heuristics, then the heuristics are not as irrational as they seem. Psychologists and philosophers have quite promptly registered the challenge and reacted to it. The basic move made by most theorists who question the pessimistic picture of irrational humans is to distinguish competence from performance. Performance is influenced by extraneous factors that have nothing to do with the subject's basic ability to reason. Further, the competence itself is not pictured as being perfect. Many theories of competence allow for the biases inherent in the structure of competence itself, but then point out how the competence can be de-biased. There are several kinds of competence theories.

Let me first mention a non-committal theory, which simply states that there is an 'analytic' competence without deciding about its internal workings. Such a theory blames most biases on the 'preparatory task,' of presenting the material in a form suitable for analytic processes. A typical formulation is as follows: 'reasoning and judgemental errors are very common in observed performance relative to the competence which people can be shown to possess. People can reason out the answer to syllogisms, for example, but frequently fall prey to syntactic or semantic bias ... People understand the essential truth conditions of conditional sentences but cannot apply this knowledge to solution of the selection task' (Evans 1989, 109). The biases concern the relevance of the particular material, not reasoning in the strictest sense. This relevance approach has been advocated by M. Bar-Hillel and by J. Evans: 'the major cause of bias in human reasoning and judgement lies in factors which induce people to process the problem information in a selective manner' (ibid., 19). It is a two-stage picture of problem solving: 'The theory essentially proposes that reasoning proceeds in two stages: (1) a heuristic stage in which aspects of the problem information are identified as "relevant" and selected for further processing; and (2) an analytic stage in which inferences are drawn from the selected information' (ibid., 25).

Let us illustrate the relevance approach by its account of the selection task. Evans has noticed that people tend to select those cards that match the explicit information in the task description, and he has called the phenomenon 'matching bias.' He claims that matching bias determines perceived relevance: 'An item named is likely to appear relevant whether asserted or denied (matching bias) but a proposition, including a negation is likely to appear relevant if it is the subject of a conditional sentence' (ibid., 33). Once the relevant items are selected, analytic reasoning proceeds correctly. There is no suggestion of profound irrationality: 'The human being, viewed as an information processing system, faces a massive problem of information reduction. Both the formation and manipulation of mental representations must be carried out in a highly selective manner using some form of heuristic process ... It is little surprising that such a system is vulnerable to bias and error' (ibid., 112).

Similar ideas and results are to be found in the field of investigation of inductive reasoning. Franca Agnoli and David Krantz (1989) have investigated the conjunction fallacy and the possibility of 'suppressing the natural heuristics by formal instruction.' They strongly oppose the original Kahneman-Slovic-Tversky view that heuristics is like 'perceptual illusions' in not being liable to be affected by the instruction any more 'than geometric courses affect geometric visual illusions,' that is, scarcely at all (Agnoli and Krantz 1989, 519) They admit that natural (biased) assessments are made automatically and strongly influence probability judgments, but they claim that these assessments compete with other problem-solving strategies. The errors and biases stem from 'discrepancies between the subjects' problem-solving *designs* and the (presumably correct) designs favoured by the experimenters' (ibid., 539). The 'design' explanation is very similar to the explanation given by Evans and quoted above for deductive errors: subjects make mistakes in estimating relevance and in selecting features of interest. In their experiments Agnoli and Krantz have simply pointed out to the subjects (in the so-called Training Group) that 'the size of a category is reduced when restrictive properties are added to its definition. (For example, adding the feature "20 to 30 years old" to "US born women" reduced the category size considerably.)' (ibid. 521). This simple training has produced a large and highly reliable reduction in conjunction error. We shall come back to the varieties of reasoning strategies in the main part of the book.

The pessimist about our reasoning capacities might also appeal to considerations from evolutionary biology. We are prone to think that we humans are basically different from other animals. Philosophers have been incessantly stressing the very special nature of our cognitive powers, and it is here that biology has reserved some surprises for us. Its challenge starts from the well-supported and well-argued thesis of continuity: Humans are in fact very much like other animals, and evolutionary continuity links human neural organization with its humbler forerunners. There is also ample evidence that human cognitive mechanisms and capacities are products of the same evolution that has shaped the lower animals. The optimistic hypothesis is that evolution favours rationality, but it is far from being generally accepted. Stephen Stich has systematized the challenges from evolutionary biology in an exemplary way. He appeals to the distinction between external fitness (fitness in relation to the environment) and internal fitness (the cost of the inner mechanism realizing the given feature or behaviour). As regards the internal fitness of cognitive systems, he claims that 'strategies of inference or inquiry that do a good job at generating truths and avoiding falsehoods may be expensive in terms of time, effort and cognitive hardware' (Stich, 1990, 61). A less reliable but less costly mechanism might be preferred to an expensive, reliable one. It might even bestow higher external fitness on its owner. The crucial type of example is the strategy 'better safe than sorry': if there is plenty of food, better believe that all white mushrooms are poisonous.

Other bad news concerns vagaries of evolution. Stich points out the importance of non-selectional factors, such as mutation, migration, and random genetic drift, and of limitations of evolutionary design – for instance, the limited availability of options, and pleiotropy, a genetic link between a very useful and a tolerably harmful feature – such that the harmful feature remains in the population riding piggy-back on the useful one.

The challenge then takes a particularly blunt form: why would such an evolutionary product exhibit virtues like rationality? What is rationality or truth to evolution? In what possible way could rationality increase the genetic fitness of its bearer? What would it be selected for?

I pass now to issues about the form and medium of cognitive processes.

2.4. *The Medium and the Message*

What medium do we think in? The writers of science-fiction have sometimes hypothesized that we think in 'thought-shapes,' whatever they are. Folk wisdom distinguishes conjectures that we think in 'thoughts' and perhaps also in 'images.' 'Images' are like pictures, whereas thoughts are best expressed by sentences. Early modern philosophers claimed that we think by having 'ideas.' Sometimes an idea is described as a picture, sometimes it is taken to be more like a sentence, or even a theory. Cognitive science has raised the issue of the medium of thinking in a serious spirit. For the first time there is hope that we might get a determinate and even definite answer.

For the moment we are offered a variety of theories. Some candidate media seem quite realistic. Again, as with 'ideas,' we are offered the choice of two kinds of media – the first kind, which is like words and sentences, only in some 'language of thought'; and the second kind, which is more like pictures. Recently, a third kind has emerged: so-called neural networks, which differ from both sentence-like and picture-like media.

2.4.1. Do We Think in Sentences?

Cognitive psychologists speak of the mind as handling scripts or as searching through default hierarchies, which are described as kinds of texts. We have spoken of the 'homunculus' reading a manual with rules. How should this be taken, metaphorically or literally? The most popular answer (at least till very recent times) has been to take the talk of mental text literally. There are representations, symbolic structures in our mind/brain, strings of symbols written in some neural code. They consist of sentences in the language of thought. To have the thought 'Grass is green' is to have the mental sentence 'Grass is green' in the proper place in one's head. To believe that grass is green is to have this same sentence stored in that functional part of our mind/brain that subserves belief states – call it (after Schiffer) the 'belief-box.' The belief-box is linked with some perceptual source of information, and to the decision-making unit.

Having a belief consists in standing in the right relation to the sentence (i.e., having it in one's belief-box). For example, when Sarah believes that the cat is on the roof, she has a sentence stored in her belief-box, and the sentence means 'The cat is on the roof.' In such a picture reasoning is described as mechanical manipulation of mental sentences, according to some rules, for instance, rules of logic, or recipes of a heuristics. The psychologists have investigated the hypothetical process of manipulation, whereas the philosophers have been especially sensitive to the issue of meaning or content of representation – what makes it the case that a certain representation means 'Grass is green.'

2.4.2. From Pictures to Networks

Some items of knowledge are hard to write in sentences. The spatial skills, which people share with animals, are a good example. To account for such skills, psychologists have hypothesized the availability of non-sentential media: maps, models, or pictures in the enquirer's head. The simplest kinds of spatial representation suitable for basic tasks like orientation and sensory-motor coordination are cognitive and neural maps. A cognitive map is a spatial-like representation of the outside world. A map can represent a town or a neighbourhood, and the cognitive system can consult it when faced with the question of how to guide its owner safely to its home in the late night hours, while another map can represent configurations in chess. (These are among the most explored cognitive maps.)

An interesting fact about cognitive maps is that some of them might have recognizable map-like neural correlates or substrata. Neurologists very early hypothesized the existence of map-like topographical representations in the brain, and subsequent research has confirmed their conjecture. The best known is the neural projection of the body surface. More sophisticated neural/mental maps have been recently studied by neurologists and introduced into philosophical discussion by Paul Churchland. As I shall later consider his views about epistemological implications of non-sentential processing, there will be ample opportunity to discuss them.

Another very popular kind of spatial representation involving the use of scripts and defaults is mental models. Take the understanding of a story, for example. When a reader encounters a description of a situation, she builds a quasi-spatial 'picture' of it. As new details are supplied by the storyteller, the picture gets updated. The background conditions are dictated by the reader's general knowledge about the world. The mental structure underlying the image of the situation is called the mental model of the situation. People seem to use something like mental models in planning and decision making and in many other reasoning tasks.

The idea that people use mental models for deduction stems from Philip Johnson-Laird. The subject confronted with a deduction task builds models of the premises and then derives a model of the conclusion. The appeal to mental models is one of the means by which the psychologists have tried to correct the pessimistic picture of human reasoning abilities, besides those mentioned in the last section. Johnson-Laird (together with Ruth Byrne) has tried to account for the subjects' failure on the selection task by blaming their models of the premises: 'The subjects consider only those cards which are explicitly represented in their models of the rule' (1991, 79). But in the selection task, only 'A' and '2' are explicitly mentioned, which narrows down the repertoire of the models considered relevant. Once the model is built by using the heuristics, the reasoning within the model proceeds in an impeccable manner. This suggests that people do possess basic logical capacities and are able to apply them. The view also predicts that the strategies the subjects use can be corrected by teaching them to make better models.

It is easy to extend the model-theoretic account to inductive biases. According to the account, bias emerges in the process of selecting the relevant aspects of the task and in the construction of the model. Once the model is in place, basic reasoning strategies are employed, which are logical, reliable, and rational. Three things should be emphasized: First, bias is explained by features of model construction (or design), whereas the reasoning within the constructed model is supposed to be bias-free. Thus, there is a kernel of general and common rationality that accounts for the possibility of de-biasing: 'There is a central core of rationality which appears to be common to all human societies' (Johnson-Laird and Byrne 1991, 209).

Second, biases concerning the construction of models are not incorrigible or, in principle, invisible for the subject. No principled stubbornness is predicted by the theory (or seems to have been found in the data). On the contrary, mental model-theoreticians offer concrete advice for the pedagogy of reasoning.

Third, Johnson-Laird and Byrne stress the importance of meta-cognition through models: 'Our theory postulates a capacity to think about thinking – to reflect on patterns of deduction and on the preservation of truth, to reflect on what one has deduced for oneself, and to reflect on the implications of what others can deduce. This general meta-cognitive capacity enables people to construct models of thought, and to construct models of those models, and so on, recursively. In this way, simple reasoning strategies can be invented by logically untutored individuals. The same ability can be used by logicians to create formal calculi for deduction, and then to reflect upon the relation between these calculi and their semantics' (Johnson-Laird and Byrne 1991, 164). In recent papers they have extended the use of mental models to the study of induction. Representations and operations on models have a quasi-spatial quality, even when the basic mechanism enabling the construction and manipulation of the representations is computational. This quasi-spatial quality has earned them their name.

We pass now to the most sophisticated kind of non-sentential representations, neural networks, that have become prominent objects of research in the last decade. First, I describe the elementary building block and then the way blocks are put together to form a network.

The initial idea is extremely simple and seems to have been used also by Mother Nature in building the human nervous system. Take two computing units, *A* and *B*, that can be in one of two states, an activated state and a dormant state, and link them together in an *A*-*B*-cell, so that they can pass their activation to each other. Let *A* get activated from the external source, and let its activation stand for the concept DOG. Let *B*'s analogous activation stand for TAIL. (If *A* and *B* were neural units in a living being, they might have received inputs from a perceptual module when their owner was confronted with a dog with a tail. In the artificial network it is the programmer who decides what information is coded by the unit.) We now try to mimic the 'learning' of simple relations. Here is a simple way, first worked out – in connection with neural units and with conditioning – by D. Hebb. We build the link between *A* and *B* so that its capacity to transmit activation, called connection strength or weight, can change over time, for example, in the following way: the more often *A* and *B* are activated together, the stronger the link is between them.

In the training period, *A* and *B* are often activated together, since the 'dog' input is often accompanied with a 'tail' input. (The inputs are often described as 'input vectors,' because of the standard mathematical format used for describing them.) After several trials, depending on how we have set the pace of change of weight, the mere activation of *A* will suffice to activate *B*. The cell has established an 'association' between DOG and TAIL. This is the basic pattern of 'learning' in connectionist networks: they are associative engines, as perhaps our brain is.

We have mentioned only the simplest possibility of two values for a state: activated or not activated. A more subtle cell would allow for change of activation values within some interval, usually presented ('normalized') as ranging from zero to one, and for activation thresholds: for example, *B* would become activated if *A* passed to it a positive activation of 0.7 units. Of course, the level of *B*'s activation level might be a continuous function of *A*'s level: thus, the changes become more smooth and the working of the network comes closer to the working of actual neural nets in the brain.

Let me briefly mention the simplest possible cell that would code for a logical relation: link *A* to *C* and *B* to *C* in a V-shaped pattern and ensure that *C* gets activated only when both *A* and *B* are activated:

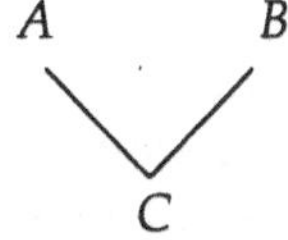

In this configuration *C* stands for *A*-AND-*B*. Assume, further, that the configuration is part of a larger system, that is capable of recognizing ('reading') the activation of *C* and reacting to it. Examples of this kind have been used in the literature to point to a most important feature of connectionist networks.[14] Consider the situation in which the system 'reads' *C*, and compare it with either the situation in which you read the formula *A*-AND-*B* or that in which a classical computer does the same. The system sees (or is sensitive to) the state of *C*, and if this state stands for *A*-AND-*B*, then the system does in a way access this information. The activation of *C* has no component parts, however, in contradistinction to the formula: activation of *A* is not part of the activation of *C*, whereas the letter '*A*' is part of *A*-AND-*B*. Therefore, the system cannot be sensitive to the compositional structure; *C* has none, and *A*-AND-*B* is not present to the system. This insensitivity imposes severe limitations on what the system can do. To judge their severity, take, for example, another state D, which is activated if at least *A* or *B* is activated, and take the formula it stands for, *A*-OR-*B*. When we read the two formulas, we immediately notice the similarity (both have the form *A*-something-*B*), and the difference (AND in the place of OR in the first one). The system, as described, sees only an activated node *C*, or an activated node *D*, no common structure, and no precise difference in composition. It cannot, simply by looking at C and *D*, recognize structural similarities and differences in information due to the way the formulas are composed. Human cognitive competence, on the contrary, seems to be very sensitive to structure. It is systematic in regard to combinations: if a child understands the sentence 'John gave a ball to Bill,' she will understand 'Bill gave a ball to John.' It is productive, capable of creating new items by combining in a regular way the old ones. It is sensitive to semantic compositionality, the way in which the meaning of a whole systematically depends on the meaning of parts. Considerable effort is currently being put into attempts to overcome limitations of connectionist systems deriving from insensitivity to structure.

Let us return to our two-unit cell. The connectionist network is put together from such elementary couples. One simple new possibility that emerges immediately when more couplings are available is the enrichment of the flow from one unit (or 'node,' as it is often called) to another by adding the possibility that deactivation is passed as well as activation: when one unit is active, it can block some of its neighbouring units. Simple networks are good at learning patterns: a pattern (say, *A-B-C-D*) is presented during the training period, and the network creates the right associations. It can then 'retrieve' the pattern from a truncated input (*A-C-D*), or from a noisy input (*A*′-B′-C′-D′). A more interestingly fact is that the networks can extract the typical (or prototypical) pattern from imperfect ('noisy') input, as long as the input clusters around the typical pattern. In this simple example one already notices an important peculiarity of networks: there is no firm distinction between software and hardware, and learning consists in actually altering the configuration of links.

The real advance, however, comes from using several layers of units. The simplest example is a two-layer network, where units of each layer themselves are connected to units of the other layer. Such networks are good at pattern association. To use an old example,[15] suppose layer-1 codes for visual shape and layer-2 for olfactory sensations. In the training period layer-1 learns the visual patterns of a rose and of a steak, layer-2 their olfactory patterns. For example, a single unit might code for colour (colour is then called a 'micro-feature' of the symbol ROSE-SHAPE and is described as subsymbolic in relation to the symbol). Moreover, the links between layer-1 and layer-2 then code for association rose-shape/rose-fragrance, and steak-shape/steak-smell. In the testing period, when presented with a rose-shape, the network retrieves the right aroma-pattern. (Layer-1 in this case receives input and is called the input-layer; layer-2 is the output-layer.) It should be noted that the learning rule mentioned is far from being the only one: there is a wide variety of learning strategies, including, prominently, ways of supervised learning, where the network is being 'told' about its mistakes.[16] Notice that the information concerning the covariation of smell and shape is not stored in any particular unit: it is *distributed* in the links between the two layers.

The situation becomes much more complex and interesting when one uses three levels: an input-layer, an intermediate or 'hidden' layer, and an output-layer. The real action occurs in intermediate, hidden units, which links them to input- and output-units. If we were to use such a network on roses and steaks, there would typically be no specific rose-shape or rose-aroma hidden units, nor steak-shape or steak-aroma units. The very same set of units and links would code for all four items ('concepts'), and several units and links would code for a feature. Of course, they would not be equally activated by every input, but most of them would participate in operating with most inputs.

A further crucial fact about networks is thus illustrated: various pieces of information are typically *superimposed* onto each other (so to speak). There is no way physically to distinguish the item that codes for rose-aroma from the item that codes for steak-shape; the information is spread over the same set of units and weights. The dormant network is highly opaque to us, whereas its activation states are clearly legible in terms of input and output.

To get a feel for the reality of connectionist representation let us take a brief look at two situations. First, a recent example – the connectionist system learning about diseases and symptoms (Neal 1992) – shows that in practice the cognitive scientists are interested not only in the performance (the behavioural output) of a system, but also in the ways and means it uses. Among the most important are precisely the representational links. When describing the system, its creator distinguishes several architectures; we shall focus on three.

The architectures are extremely simple. The only relevant feature is the order of the layers: changes in order change what the system is learning. The general picture is as follows:

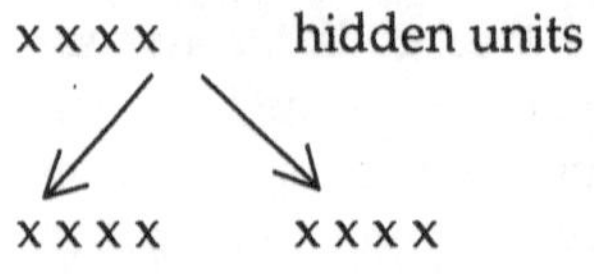

symptoms diseases

The hidden units feed into both symptoms-units and diseases-units: 'As a result of training, these units may come to model correlations among symptoms, among diseases, or between symptoms and diseases' (Neal 1992, 89). Let us distinguish two directions of information flow:

1. x x x x symptoms
   ↓
   x x x x hidden units
   ↓
   x x x x diseases

The hidden units receive information about symptoms and are being taught about diseases (in the process of supervised learning); 'This forces the hidden units to learn the model of conditional distribution of the diseases given the symptoms' (ibid., 189). The network thus becomes capable of performing diagnostic tasks, but is incapable of reasoning backwards: given a disease, it cannot predict the likely symptoms.

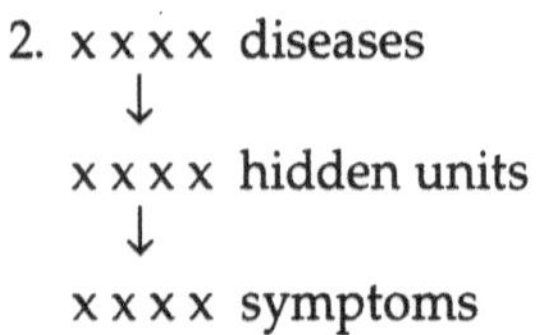

This network models the probabilities of symptoms, given diseases, and therefore, it comes closer to expressing 'the usual causal view that diseases cause symptoms, not the other way around' (ibid, 90).

Let me next mention almost everybody's favourite example, the mine-detecting network. (Since I have to discuss Churchland's ideas in detail, let me rely upon his presentation.) The task is quite difficult – the system should learn to distinguish mines from rocks or, more precisely, the sonar echo produced by mines from the echo produced by rocks. Echoes are quite varied, depending on different sizes and shapes of both mines and rocks. Consider a network equipped with thirteen input units, which code for energy levels each at a particular frequency interval of the incoming echo. The values obtained are coded as activation values. A given echo profile is thus transformed into a thirteen-place vector of activation values. The activation values spread through the network towards the output units. The users need a two-valued answer (either 'Mine' or 'Rock'), so two output units, one for mines and one for rocks, are just enough. The teaching procedure uses samples of genuine recorded mine and rock echoes. The teaching proceeds as follows: We then feed these echoes into the network, one by one, and observe the output vector produced in each case. What interests us in each case is the amount by which the actual output vector *differs* from what would have been the correct vector, given the identity of the specific echo that produced it. The details of that error, for each element of the output vector, are then fed into a special rule that computes a set of small changes in the values of various synaptic weights in the system. The idea is to identify those weights most responsible for the error, and then to nudge their values in a direction that would at last reduce the amount by which the output vector is in error' (*NP*, 166; emphasis in original). The procedure ('back-propagation of error') is repeated until the system learns to distinguish mines from rocks.

The reader will have noticed that even in this very brief introductory sketch one encounters a significant variety of ways that information is present in the network. Since this variation will be crucial in the sequel, we need some classification. Let me briefly summarize the one William Ramsey has offered in a conference paper.[17]

The classification distinguishes four main types, numbered as Type (1) to Type (4), in the increasing order of opacity, from those that are easily decipherable to those in which the method of coding particular information is impossible to deciphere.

Type (1): activation pattern = concept; single unit = microfeature. The individual units represent low-level properties and the overall activation pattern represents concepts. For example, the concept 'ROOM' is represented by the pattern of activation of units standing for features like 'bed' (positive, incitatory link to 'SOFA' and 'FLOOR'), or 'sink' (negative, inhibitory link to the same items). The result is the representation of a prototypical room (with a bed, a sofa, and a floor, but without a sink).

Ramsey notes that this type of representation nicely captures the empiricist view of concepts, reducing the prima facie simple concept of room to more elementary concepts.

Type (2): activation pattern = concept; single unit uninterpretable. Here the individual units – activated or not – do not admit of any semantic interpretation. The mine/rock network is an example: no single characteristic of mines or rocks is coded by a single unit, but the concept 'MINE' is coded in the pattern as a whole.

Type (3): activation pattern = proposition; single unit uninterpretable. Here the activation pattern of hidden units represents whole propositions, such as 'Dogs have fur' and 'Fish have scales.' The single units do not stand for semantic parts of propositions (for 'dog,') ('scales'), however, so the smallest unit that can be assigned to the activated pattern is the entire proposition. The non-activated, dormant set of units *has no semantic interpretation.*

Ramsey points out important differences between dormant and activated states of the network. The activated state manifests semantic structure: particular propositions can be identified with different activation patterns. The dormant state supports only the structural holism: the whole knowledge is present in the whole network, and the only relevant analysis is in terms of their dispositions. Dispositions themselves are to be construed globally, not in terms of isolated propositional attitudes. The dualism active/dormant presents an important challenge to folk-psychology and to philosophical theories of mind.

Techniques of statistical analysis still can yield some valuable data about the information stored. The most popular kind is cluster analysis, which considers similarity between units (e.g., *A* and *B*) in relation to their typical inputs or outputs (e.g., if *A* and *B* get activated by the same input units, and/or activate the same output units, they get grouped closely together.)

Type (4): series of activation patterns = proposition; activation pattern = concept; single unit uninterpretable. This is the most complicated and problematic type. In the simplest type, the syntactic role of a particular unit in the larger configuration is determined by its activity level. Since activity level differs from context to context, the representation is here extremely context sensitive. In Ramsey's words, we have not a representation of BOY or APPLE, but a cluster of representations of BOY-qua-(...),

APPLE-qua-(...), where the bracketed blanks are filled by an appropriate role from context to context.

Certain more sophisticated networks of basically the same kind, however, exhibit more structure and more context independence. Shastri and Ajjanagadde (1993) describe a family of networks that uses synchronization of activation as a way of building structures. Its simplest 'cell' performs the following task: given a node *G* for a predicate, for example, GIVES, with an argument place for the person that gives something (the variable for the 'giver') and a node *P* encoding a name of such a person ('Peter') the cell binds the name to the argument place. The binding is done by synchronizing: if *G* is activated at the same time as *P*, the temporal synchronicity encodes the fact that Peter gives something. Two such cells, synchronized with each other, can model a simple inferential step ('a directed inferential dependency graph' as the authors call it). Despite the fact that the finished proposition is expressed only in a transitory rhythmic activation, the activation is reliable enough to warrant the conclusion that the system has stored complicated facts in its memory.

Let me now list the properties of connectionist items that will play the crucial role in the debate and that we may call cognitive peculiarities (some of them have been introduced and illustrated above, some are added without illustration, since I shall discuss them at greater length in chapter 5):

a. *Non-sentential character.* Connectionist representations are not 'sentential,' unlike their classical counterparts. The representation with the content 'The dog barks' is not composed of a dog-representing part and a barking-representing part. This lack of 'compositionality' has been widely discussed in the literature (see chap. 2, n3). Further, they are 'subsymbolic' in the following sense: a given concept, say, DOG, can be represented simply by arrangements of microfeatures (links connecting features like 'barks,' and 'furry' without having an explicit syntactic symbol for dogs. In Churchland's words, 'there ... is a level of representation *beneath* the level of sentential or propositional attitudes' (*NP*, 155, emphasis in original). At this level the dynamics of learning is unlike the sentential.
b. *Distributed character.* The representations are typically non-local and 'distributed,' in the sense that a given representational content is coded by the pattern of activity pertaining to several, even many,

units, and a given unit contains piecemeal information about several representational contents. Representations are physically superimposed: the same physical configuration codes for several sets of representations. Therefore, the functional-semantic properties cannot be read from the physical structure.

c. *Holism.* In connectionist networks the information is coded holistically. A system that learns about cups and coffee starting from input concerning a cup filled with coffee will have not 'abstract,' 'atomic' representations of cup and coffee that can be recombined at will with any other representation, but a context-dependent representation of a pattern of dependence, presumably functional, linking cup with coffee.
d. *Prototypicality.* The three features (a)–(c) make connectionist representations ideal for prototyping: instead of rigid bivalent relations between elements, the representations work with similarities and similarity metrics, exactly as described by prototype theorists.
e. *Context-dependence and variability.* The connectionist representation is unstable in the following sense: if prompted with a vector, **G**, it gives one kind of answer, if prompted with another, **F** it might give an incompatible answer. This is the result of the holistic encoding in which each item is encoded together with its particular context.
f. *The essentially practical character of 'knowledge.'* The opacity of dormant states points to a further peculiarity: the 'knowledge' seems clearly to exist only in the activated state. Some philosophers have taken it to mean that it is knowledge-in-action and have appealed to the notion of knowledge-how as opposed to knowledge-that (Bechtel and Abrahamsen 1980, 225ff.). The network knows how to recognize a pattern with no propositional knowledge that the pattern is such and such. This characterization, however, might be too strong.

Not all connectionist representations need have the characteristics (a)–(d) to the same extent, which is why we needed a classification of networks.

Let me now briefly address the nature of standard descriptions of connectionist systems. The most important description is in terms of so-called state space. Since I shall need to mention it later, let me give a sketchy introduction to the bare notion. (I hasten to add that the exposition that follows is meant to help the reader innocent of state-space talk form a rough idea of what it means. If you are a state-space expert, you are invited to jump to the conclusion of the section.)

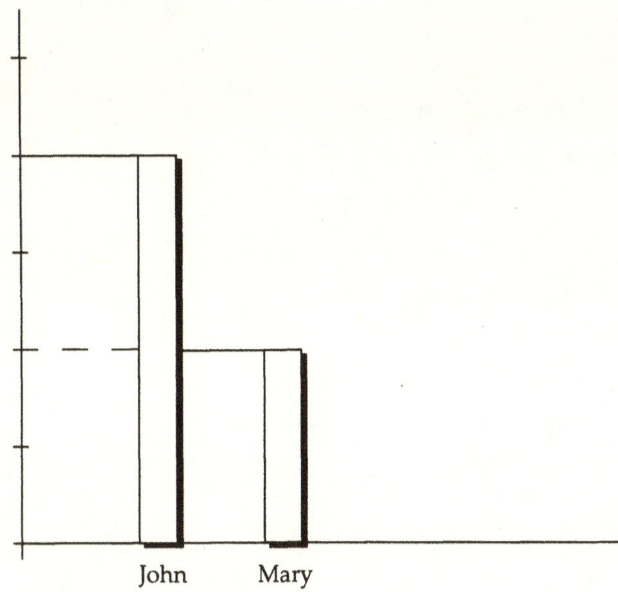

FIGURE 1.2
Histogram of John's and Mary's heights

In order to grasp the idea, consider the most simple case. A school physician collects data on height and weight of schoolchildren on New Year's Eve 1995. Imagine that she starts with only two children, John and Mary, and that she wants to represent their heights. She can draw a histogram placing John and Mary on the x-axis and representing their heights on the y-axis, as shown in figure 1.2.

However, she can use another representation. Let her represent John's height along the x-axis, and Mary's height along the y-axis (see figure 1.3). A point P with coordinate x_1 (for John's height) and y_1 (for Mary's height) will then represent the height of both on the given date. John-and-Mary form a 'system,' and their 'height-state' is represented by the representation point P. Now imagine a perpendicular being drawn from P to the x-axis. It will intersect the x-axis at the point x_1, which represents John's height. P 'projects' on the x-axis, so that its projection is x_1.

If the physician takes measurements at regular intervals, she can represent the successive results along the z-axis. The point P will 'move' in a definite direction (children grow over time, so their height coordinate will move away from zero at each step – John may start as 4 feet tall and

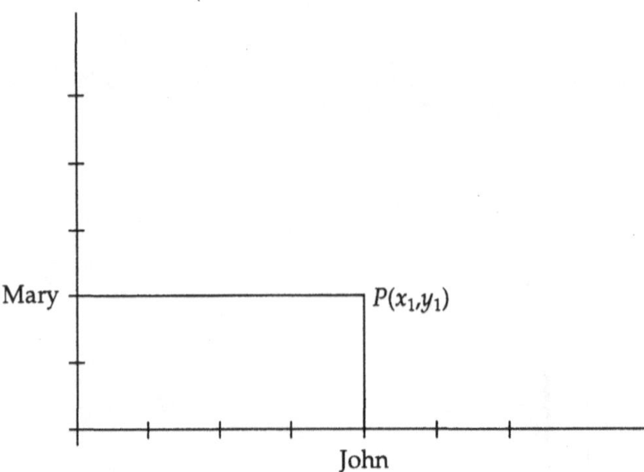

FIGURE 1.3
Alternative representation of John's and Mary's heights

then grow to be 6.3 feet tall). One may say that the movement of the point P represents the 'evolution in time' of the height of the 'system' John-plus-Mary.' Notice that similar heights and weights will yield similar positions of the representation-point.

The physician can now extend her representation to cover the heights of other children, say, thirty in the class. To each child a height dimension will correspond, so she will need thirty dimensions plus one for time. A point in thirty-one–dimensional space will represent the height-state of the class at a given time. She can then add weights, adding thirty more coordinates, one for the weight of each child. A point in sixty-one–dimensional space, with the coordinate system C, will then represent the height-and-weight states of the class at a given time. For example, the weight of Harry (say, fifty pounds) might be coded along the forty-fifth coordinate axis. The technical term for such coding is the familiar one – 'projection': the projection of point P on the forty-fifth axis yields fifty.

The projections of P will be listed in the specification of its position, for example, <New Year's Eve 1994, 4, 3.8, 43, ...>, where the first place stands for time, the second for the height of John, the third for the height of Mary, the fourth for the weight of John, and so on. The list is called a 'vector' associated with P, with the coordinate system C.

The height-and-weight representation is the simplest kind of state-space representation – so simple that a mathematician would consider it a caricature. Historically, such representations were introduced for the purpose of coding information about highly populated systems, for example, a system of particles of gas (imagine, for the sake of argument, that each particle moves completely independently from the others). Each particle corresponds to a school child in our example, and the physicist would be interested in coding three spatial coordinates of each particle and the particle's momentum. So for *n* particles one would need 3*n* position coordinates plus 3*n* momentum coordinates for each particle. The state of the whole system would be represented by only one point in the space of requisite dimensionality.

The beauty and elegance of state-space representation can be appreciated only when one has some knowledge of analytical geometry and advanced calculus, since complicated physical quantities can be given extremely simple and elegant analytical representations in state-space. The most important point for our discussion, however, can be grasped without introducing sophisticated mathematical techniques. Different parameters can be used to form a state-space. Let us look first at a descriptive representation and then at a representation embodying the assessment of success. In his rock mine example Churchland considers the state-space defined by the activation levels of units. First the hidden units: each unit is assigned a coordinate axis, and its values are given by activation levels of hidden units. Suppose we have only three hidden units, *H*1, *H*2, and *H*3; we assign a coordinate axis to each unit (*x*-axis to *H*1, *y*-axis to *H*2, and *z*-axis to *H*3). A point in the space describes the state of the system. Its coordinates form a list, or, mathematically speaking, a vector (e.g., *H*1 has activation level 0.3, *H*2 level 0.6, and *H*3 level 0.5). Different sorts of inputs will tend to bring the system into different states. A rock-input will tend to bring it into a certain state or family of states, which will be represented as a region in our space – call it the Rock-region. A mine input will carry it into a different region – call it the Mine-region. If the system has learned its job, the two regions will be distinct and separable. The story then generalizes for an arbitrary number of coordinates.

The epistemologist is interested in success and error in the performance of networks, so we should mention the way of describing the performance that reverts overtly to this parameter. In this representation we begin directly with weights of connections between units. Imagine that we start with only two synaptic weights, *W*1 and *W*2, and consider their reliability in a particular task. The strength of *W*1 will be plotted on the *x*-axis, and the strength of *W*2 on the *y*-axis. A point *P* in the plane will then stand for a particular combination of strengths, say 0.5 strength of *W*1 (= *x*-coordinate) and 0.7 strength of *W*2. Suppose that such a combination yields results in 60 per cent of cases, that is, makes errors in 40 per cent of cases. On the *z*-axis we may then represent the error percentage as 0.4 *z*-coordinate of *P*. Suppose that after some training the system hits at a better combination. It has 'travelled' to the point *P** representing a different distribution of strength, (e.g., 0.2 for *W*1, and 0.9 for *W*2) and a different percentage of error, say 20 per cent. In our coordinate space it has 'descended' the error slope (error gradient). Successful learning can be described in terms of such descent, which represents the procedure of minimizing error. The goal of the procedure is to attain the global error minimum, that is, to get as reliable a performance as possible.

The two-weights example is overly simplistic. One can represent hundreds of weights in a many-hundred-dimensional coordinate system, with one coordinate added for the error-success dimension. Such a system could possibly represent more complex learning. Churchland believes that such systems are embodied in our heads.

The challenges that connectionist networks pose to epistemology are various and important. I shall address them in detail in chapter 5 of the book.

Here we end the brief overview of relevant topics from psychology. We have sketched some of the (bona fide) features of the ground floor of cognition and have alluded to its neurological foundations. This will be the floor on which we shall dwell throughout the book. It is worth noting that cognitive research is beginning to inspire interesting work on sophisticated cognition as well, and one discusses cognitive models of science, hoping to paint a unified picture extending from the amoeba to Einstein (Giere 1992).

2

Epistemology: The Classical Picture

1. Introduction

How does the impact of cognitive science affect epistemology? In order to answer the question we have to take a look at the main topics and problems that epistemology is concerned with and at the main epistemological tradition, which is supposed to be challenged by the results of cognitive science.

In this book I shall be concerned mainly with the traditional province of epistemology – with goals and values of cognition and with the norms regulating cognitive processes. The evaluation of particular cognitive efforts and results is very common matter – witness the grading of students, or of participants in some knowledge competition. Already, in simple and banal cases, one can discern the general structure of issues concerning evaluation – the two-level structure that also is characteristic of epistemology.

On the first level is the evaluation of the relevant item – particular performance, kind of performance, kind of mechanism – according to given criteria (e.g., Does Sarah know enough history to get an A?). It is sometimes called the object-level. The second, or meta-level, is the level of discussion about the evaluation itself and the criteria used (e.g., Is it all right to tolerate slips and other mistakes due to carelessness at exams?). The first level is, of course, more concrete, humanly more relevant, and emotionally more exciting, whereas the second level is the domain of purely theoretical discussion.

Passing from particular issues, such as rating the performance of students, to more global, philosophical matters, one encounters first-level questions concerning the value of human (lay or expert) cognitive performances – perception, reasoning, and so on and second-level questions about what to value, and how to carry out the evaluation. I shall be particularly concerned with the second, or meta-level, asking questions about principles of evaluation, ultimate goals of cognition and the like. The first-level issues that I address will have a somewhat peculiar form, because I am dealing with very basic cognitive mechanisms: given that a cognitive process, strategy, or mechanism has particular features, is it subject to epistemological evaluation at all? For example, given that speech comprehension is involuntary, should we evaluate it epistemologically at all? If the answer turns out to be affirmative, a further question – how to evaluate the item – will arise.

2. The Classical Picture

A picture of the aims and values of cognition has dominated epistemology. From Plato and Descartes to contemporary epistemologists, it has dictated the general framework of the epistemological enterprise.[1] I shall call it the Classical Picture. It is this picture that now is being challenged by the theories and results of cognitive science.

The Classical Picture pictures the enquirer as a creature endowed with curiosity about the world. The curiosity is either a motive in itself, or stems from practical needs for accurate prediction. The enquirer wants to know what the world is like – she gathers information and then reasons further about the world (e.g., makes conjectures on the basis of it, and tests her conjectures). Knowing what the world is like is a specific epistemic or cognitive goal. Items satisfying the desire to know are cognitively valuable. The goal can be described in a more roundabout way: the enquirer wants to know the truth about things, and wants to avoid error. If she were to use belief-talk she would say that she wants her beliefs to be true. In order to value the moves made by the enquirer and to assess her cognitive capacities, one should fix one's eyes firmly on the ultimate goal of the enquirer. Very generally and roughly, the moves that further the attainment of the truth-goal are in general good, virtuous, or rational; the contrary ones are irrational (such a view is aptly called veritism). This is not always a simple matter: there are situations in which otherwise truth-conducive strategies generate error and vice versa, and we do not want to blame the enquirer for the inhospitality of circumstances. Further, there are unimportant truths not worthy of attention, so truth is not always enough, and so on; but the general thrust is veritistic – the closer a strategy brings the enquirer to her goal the better it is.

This is a general sketch. Many philosophers and scientists find it a completely natural and quite acceptable stance, and for my part, I agree with them. Consider, now, its components. The most important elements of the Classical Picture are summed up in the traditional definition of knowledge as true, justified belief, so we shall follow the lead of this definition.

The proponents of the Classical Picture have talked in terms of beliefs and belief states, claiming that the enquirer's beliefs are among the central items to be valued, together with her strategies of arriving at them. Traditionally, 'belief' meant full, conscious belief, which can be wholely expressed by a declarative sentence. Anything less than full, conscious belief was (with rare exceptions) banished from the province of epistemology. We can see that this is an obvious weakness if we attend to the message from cognitive science about the importance of unconscious processing and of non-sentential media. Think of our 'homunculus' in the visual system performing calculations to determine the distance of an object from data concerning retinal size and disparity. Does his mathematical skill come at all close to having 'beliefs'? Is his access to data correctly described as some kind of belief about retinal size and the like? On the one hand, his skill and his access to data seem to be too primitive and inflexible to count as belief-like; on the other hand, his data can be accurate or inaccurate, his math can be correct or incorrect and so evaluable in the true/false dimension. It seems profitable, therefore, to enquire about which properties of beliefs are essential for the epistemologist and which are optional. Maybe, some less-than-conscious states have enough relevant properties to enter the Classical Picture as its new denizens without subverting it.

If the goal of cognition is to acquire information about the world, then the essential property of the enquirer's goal-state will be that it can picture the world, or carry information about it. The common technical terms for such a state is 'representational state.' Any state capable of picturing the world will also be capable of being accurate or inaccurate, 'true' or 'false' in the widest sense. Call such states 'truth-tolerant.' It seems that truth-tolerance, the capability of being truth-bearer, is the crucial property of the relevant mental states of the enquirer.[2] We mean the perfectly ordinary notion of truth, as captured by familiar kinds of equivalence, for example, 'The sentence "Snow is white" is true if and only if the snow is white,' or, in general: '*p*' is true if and only if *p*. This equivalence points to a kind of 'transparency' of the truth predicate, which will play a very important role in the sequel: for most sentences, to enquire whether '*p*' is true is just to enquire whether *p* (forget here about the Liar paradox).

Since aiming at the whole truth and nothing but the truth has seemed overly ambitious to some philosophers, they have proposed notions akin to that of truth. The general idea can be thus summarized in a simple way:

The goal of the cognitive enterprise is truth or something akin to it.

Consider briefly these kindred notions, the 'truth family.' The notion of truth itself is cognizer independent. So are its poor cousins, such as truth-to-a-degree, partial truth, truthlikeness (verisimilitude), and high objective probability, all of them blood relatives of truth itself.[3] Often a philosopher claims that truth would be all right if attainable, but that there is nothing wrong with truthlikeness, or with partial truth. The in-laws of the notion of truth, on the more subjectivist side, include apparent truth, the best apparent truth, and perhaps verification.[4]

In what follows, I shall take truth *simpliciter* as representative of the whole family. In most contexts where I speak about truth, one can safely substitute its objectivist poor cousins (with somewhat diminished effect – partial truth fails at some tasks at which the whole truth succeeds). Why is truth supposed to be the goal of cognitive enterprise?

I confess that I cannot find much substantial discussion of the issue in the literature. Authors who are well aware of the importance of truth do not go out of their way to argue for it. For example, William Newton Smith, in his (otherwise excellent) *Rationality of Science*, tells the reader at the outset that 'the point of the scientific enterprise is to discover explanatory truths about the world' (1981, 14), and then he promises to discuss this claim in a chapter on truthlikeness. Unfortunately, in the chapter he limits himself to stating flatly that 'truth does play a regulative role in the sense that theories designed to solve a problem whose corresponding statement has been shown to be false ... are condemned for that very reason' (ibid., 190) and to making similar remarks, which I find very congenial but question-begging, against the opponent who does not think that truth is the point of the scientific enterprise.

The classical pragmatists initiated an interesting defence of the centrality of truth by its usefulness in the long run. Unfortunately, the best known among them simply identified the truth with 'what is useful in the way of believing.' This was then carried further, so that the notion of truth has been dislodged and replaced by usefulness-in-the-long-run.[5] We shall revert to this line of defence in the chapter on the usefulness of truth.

Another defence leans on conceptual analysis. The centrality of truth is defended in two steps: it is claimed that by definition the goal of the cognitive enterprise is knowledge and that knowledge is, by definition, simply true belief with some additional desirable features. Together, the two steps are then presumed to yield the desired conclusion.

This conceptual defence assumes too much. The first step heavily relies on the assumed normative dimension of the term 'cognition.' But many competent speakers, especially students of cognitive processes, use the term 'cognition' descriptively, like the terms 'belief-fixation' or 'inference.' From such use there is no purely logical or semantic route leading to the concept of knowledge in the normative sense. The second step similarly assumes that people generally accept the normative definition of knowledge, entailing the presence of the truth component. Many people, however, don't accept this definition; sociologists and anthropologists notoriously use the term 'knowledge' in the sense of 'corpus of beliefs accepted by a group' (and speak of 'astrological knowledge' without endorsing astrology). The worst mistake is to combine the two steps, ignoring the intentional character of aiming. Even if it were the case that people aim at knowledge and that knowledge, in fact contains a truth component, this would not entail that they aim at truth itself; they could aim at other components and take truth along as a part of a package deal. To see this, take 'schmoledge' to be like knowledge but without the truth component. Perhaps, people would aim at schmoledge if it were available separately; in aiming at knowledge they are, in fact, not interested in the truth component. Thus, the purely conceptual defence fails.

Why have rationalist philosophers been so high-handed and cavalier? Maybe because the centrality of truth has not been challenged in a sufficiently provocative way. The traditional sceptics, of course, accept the centrality of truth and then argue its unattainability; thus, in the confrontation with them the rationalists were motivated to avoid the issue and let sleeping dogs lie. On the other hand, those rare philosophers who have challenged the centrality of truth, most famously Nietzsche, have done so in a way that was not interesting enough for professional epistemologists.

It is to the credit of authors like Steven Stich (and, in philosophy of science, Larry Laudan) to have asked the question persistently and intelligently, so as to provoke philosophers to think seriously about the issue. I hope that in criticizing them I shall be able to defend the commonsensical answer that it is good to know how things are – and in this sense to know the truth – since such knowledge is generally useful, whereas ignorance is generally harmful.

Another important property of the goal-states is that they should be conveniently linked. Beliefs give rise to other beliefs, in an orderly fashion. The potential of these belief-transitions to preserve truth or high probability is valuable to cognizers, since it leads them from the obvious to the non-obvious. States incapable of such linkage would hardly be relevant for the enterprise of learning about things. Epistemology and logic have followed suit and offered sophisticated normative theories of belief-transitions. For the time being I shall suppose that representational character and the suitable linkage are essential for the cognitive architecture and that the rest is optional. (This choice will be argued more closely when we encounter the view of an opponent, Paul Churchland, and his counter-arguments.) Let me conclude with a discussion of a closely analogous tradition in the philosophy of science.

The Classical Picture in general epistemology corresponds very closely to what Newton Smith calls the 'Rational Image' in the philosophy of science (1981). The rational image involves specification of the goal of science and some principles or sets of principles for comparing rival theories with a given evidential background (referred to as methodological principles). Rationalists claim that the goal of the scientific enterprise is to discover explanatory truths about the world, so that methodology should specify means appropriate for achieving this goal. Therefore, both in what I call the Classical Picture and in the Rational Image the point of the enterprise is truth, and both ways of achieving knowledge are rated by appeal to justificatory principles, which are wholly or for the most part grounded in the point of the enterprise. This correspondence is most welcome, given that scientific knowledge is the paradigm of human cognitive achievement.

It is time now to describe the fatal encounter in which the Classical Picture meets cognitive science. The Classical Picture is mainly normative, but it rests comfortably on two kinds of factual presuppositions. The first concerns the availability of items mentioned in the norm. In order for the norms to be operative, there should be appropriate states and processes to which they could be applied. In order for epistemic virtues to characterize enquirers, the enquirers should posses the requisite cognitive capacities. As a matter of fact, people should have beliefs or states sufficiently akin to beliefs, that is, representational truth-tolerant states, and the transitions between these states should be enough like inferences or, at the minimum, be reliable or accurate. Finally, the goals set should not be hopelessly beyond human reach. 'Ought to know' implies 'Can know,' so that any realistic normative picture should seriously take into account enquirers' actual capacities.[6]

The second kind of presuppositions concerns people's normative intuitions and practices. The Classical Picture presents itself as a norm that is in a comfortable (reflective) equilibrium with people's intuitions and practices. In general, people do appreciate knowledge, prefer to be told the truth than to be lied to, disapprove of using unreliable methods at least in issues of some importance (also, most states use intelligence to get information about other states and use counter-intelligence to prevent others from learning the truth about them). Scientists harbour the same normative intuitions about the value of truth and of good methodology, but in a clearer form than non-scientists. The Classical Picture thus presents itself as a refinement of and a philosophical gloss on these commonsensical themes.

Both kinds of presuppositions are open to scrutiny with the help of cognitive science. Moreover, science should have the last word about whether or not they are actually fulfilled. Take, for instance, the importance of beliefs within the Classical Picture. Our commonsensical notion of belief seems simple and stable enough. It is part of a theoretical framework, however, with whose help people understand themselves, a framework that embodies substantial assumptions, for example, that beliefs have causal powers ('He apologized, because he believed that ...'). Are there really such states? It is a task for psychology to give a definitive answer.

The central problem is as follows:

Is the Classical Picture acceptable within the framework provided by cognitive science?

In other words, does the Classical Picture present a realistic view of our most general cognitive values, given what we know about human cognition and valuation? In order to motivate the search for an answer, let me mention some possibilities.[7]

It is easy to see that some results of research in cognitive science do pose a serious challenge to the Classical Picture, and it is understandable that some philosophers have denied that the Picture is compatible with what we know about the nature of cognition. For one thing, the bewildering variety of cognitive mechanisms and strategies, seemingly unrelated to each other, threatens to undermine the unity of the epistemological picture. Historians and anthropologists long ago started to question naïve assumptions of uniformity by presenting a landscape of heterogeneous cognitive practices – as if each culture and age had its distinctive set of cognitive practices. The additional normative message was the one of normative pluralism: each tribe should follow its own epistemic code. This time, with cognitive science, and with research on heuristics diversity is found in much closer quarters. Different people use different strategies and tend to persevere in the face of criticism. Neurology might find similar diversity even within the single mind/brain: the various 'tribes' of cognitive or neural units carry out their business, each in its own way. Of course (as is the case in anthropological discoveries), the variety of actual ways inspires the philosopher's imagination to seek even more exotic varieties of the imaginary and the possible. There is no end to possible cognitive strategies, each peculiarly consistent. Why should all these strategies have one common goal? If there is no common goal, how does one tell which tribe is more advanced or more virtuous; which strategy is more promising in absolute terms? Thus, it might be vain to look for common, tribe-transcending standards of rationality, epistemic virtue, or excellence. Furthermore, the evaluative intuitions of people might seem to be the offspring of mere ignorance, children of pre-scientific darkness. Introspection has been deceiving us about the complexity of our cognitive life, perhaps even about its very nature. Why should intuitions based on such cognition dictate our epistemic standards?

All these worries and many more, which I shall discuss in the following chapters, motivate the negative answer to the question – *the incompatibilist answer* – suggesting that the Classical Picture is incompatible with the dicta of science. However, this is not the end of the story. The incompatibilist – the philosopher promoting the negative answer – has a further choice: between a revolutionary, left-wing attitude and a conservative, right-wing one. The conservative attitude to the alleged incompatibility is to retain the Classical Picture and reject science, for example, to declare that descriptive scientific results have no relevance to the normative stance, or to claim that our basic cognitive processes are too primitive to merit epistemic assessment. Thus, the unruly tribes of the human mind/brain are to be relegated to a reserve and kept there. The revolutionary attitude recommends the opposite choice. The basic processes are relevant, but the Classical Picture is to be rejected: 'Power to the tribes, abrogate the epistemological Constitution!' This is the stance of relativism-pragmatism. As is the case in politics, the two extremes sometimes join forces. For instance, Alvin Plantinga has offered the following argument for supra-naturalism in epistemology: the relativists-pragmatists have conclusively shown that naturalism cannot ground rationality, but we do need and have rationality; therefore, it is plausible to ground rationality supra-naturally, in God's design (Plantinga 1993, chaps. 11, 12).

Since I am a compatibilist, I oppose both kinds of incompatibilism, but I don't find them equally interesting. The right-wing incompatibilism entices us to ignore the most interesting and the most accurate data, and the most interesting theories of cognition produced till now. It proposes an ideal of purity of epistemology, which is a purity of ignorance, not of heart and purpose, dissonant with the very spirit of the Classical Picture it professes to defend. The Classical Picture was inspired and formed by philosophers such as Descartes, Spinoza, and Russell, who were interested in the actual progress of human knowledge, deeply concerned about science, and anxious to bring the normative picture into harmony with what in their time was the most advanced view of the human mind.

The left-wingers, the relativist-pragmatists, are much more interesting. They have called attention to the results of cognitive science by dramatizing their relevance and importance for most perennial philosophical issues. This makes discussion with them engaging: to struggle against their arguments means rediscovering the exciting ways in which the deepest problems of epistemology mesh with the most recent laboratory data and scientific theories. Thus, among the two incompatibilist attitudes, both of which I reject, I choose for discussion and criticism the revolutionary attitude, relativism-pragmatism.

My final aim is to defend the compatibilist claim: The Classical Picture is broadly acceptable within the naturalist framework, so that the ground floor of human cognition can be assessed in the spirit of the Classical Picture. The tribes are not so heterogeneous or so unruly as they seem, and the Constitution leaves space enough for all of them.

Let me call the position I shall advocate *naturalistic rationalism* (later in the book, I shall refer to it simply as 'rationalism'). A few words about the term 'naturalism' are in order. The naturalist is the philosopher who thinks that philosophy should mesh with the scientific study of human beings (exactly how close the contact should be is an open question). Naturalism in this broad sense *does not exclude the issues of value and norm.* Some philosophers, most notably Quine (who apparently coined the term 'naturalized epistemology'), seem to think that normative philosophical thinking simply has to be replaced by descriptive scientific theorizing. This is not the sense of 'naturalism' that will be used here. My intention is precisely to show that one can build a respectable normative epistemology quite compatible with what we know about the evolutionary origin of humankind and about human mental life. Moreover, this epistemology will retain the basic traits of the Classical Picture. In a slogan: *Naturalistic rationalism is what the Classical Picture becomes when it is wedded to a broadly naturalist outlook.*

How does naturalism in normative issues fit into the general naturalistic framework? The naturalist about normative matters (cognition, morals, taste, art) tries to explain how they hang together with factual matters of human constitution and social organization. The naturalist about other problematic domains, such as mathematics or theology, tries to show how they might fit into the general story about the natural order of things, either as describing part of the order or as describing our fictions, explicable in terms of human constitution. The two endeavours form, so to speak, the moderate stage of naturalistic explanation, featuring a broad range of philosophers who have been engaged in it: Hume and Reid, Wittgenstein and Nietzsche, Strawson and Davidson, and many others. Finally, the more radical naturalists then try to reduce the human constitution to its physicalistic basis. In this ontological interpretation 'naturalism' is the claim that whatever exists is a part of the spatio-temporal world, unified by the causal cement of the laws of physics (Armstrong). This stage I mention only for the sake of completeness, but I shall not be concerned with it. We are ready now for the main task: the exposition and critique of relativism-pragmatism and the defence of the rationalist stance.

3

Relativism-Pragmatism

1. Introduction

Relativism about goals and values is an old and a familiar stance. To remind ourselves of its beginnings let us take a look at the following well-known passage from Plato's 'Meno,' where young Meno, recounting Gorgias's views, speaks about virtue in general:

> MENO: Then there is another virtue for a child, male or female, and another for an old man, free or slave as you like; and a great many more kinds of virtue so that no one need be at loss to say what it is. For every act and every time of life, with reference to each separate function, there is a virtue for each one of us, and similarly, I should say, a vice. (72a, transl. W.K.G. Guthrie, Penguin 1956)

The topic is cognitive value, excellence, or virtue. The relativist about it can appropriate Gorgias's general claim and turn it to his particular purpose. A new Meno would say something like the following: 'There is another cognitive excellence for a child, and another for a grown up intellectual, another kind of rationality for a politician and another for a mathematician, and there is not much in common between them. For every decision, and every time of life, with reference to each separate function, there is a specific virtue for each one of us, and, similarly a cognitive vice or defect.' More prosaically, *relativism is the view that cognitive goals and virtues, especially rationality, are relative to persons, situations, and purposes.* Value-for-John is different from and incomparable with value-for-Jane. A cognitive strategy that is rational in one kind of situation is irrational in another, and the situations are not comparable in any relevant respect. The notion of rationality and reason should be 'fragmented,' as the title of a relevant book suggests. Relativism-pragmatism adds an additional touch: value for each agent and for each situation is to be determined by *non-cognitive aims of the agent.* This is the content of the pragmatist doctrine to which Stich gives the innocent-sounding name 'Normative Pluralism.' In fact, 'pluralism' sounds not only innocent, but also attractive, and the rationalist has no reason to give up attractive-sounding labels; he, of course, acknowledges that there are many norms, as the words 'normative pluralism' suggest. What he does not accept is that these norms do not have a common ground and that there do not exist extremely general epistemic norms (such as those suggested by logic and probability theory). Thus, in what follows I shall distinguish the modest normative pluralism advanced by the rationalist from the relativistic variety, which I shall then take leave to dub 'Radical Normative Pluralism.' Let me briefly introduce both authors. Stephen Stich began his philosophical career under the influence of Quine, working on philosophy of language and mind or psychology. After publishing several ground-breaking papers on the philosophy of psychology, on subdoxastic states and on autonomous psychology, he has published a book on the 'syntactic theory of mind' in which he defends the idea of thoughts without content. His main relativistic work is *The Fragmentation of Reason* (1990), which hereafter will be referred to as *Fragmentation*, and a more recent programmatic paper, 'Naturalizing Epistemology' (1993).

Paul Churchland has been exploring the philosophical perspectives offered by neurology and by those trends in cognitive science that aim at modelling cognition in a way that is as close to neural reality as possible. He has proposed some original and daring ideas and has revived some older ideas in a new form, buttressed by neurological and biological considerations. In a recent programmatic paper (1992a, 341) he presents his views of science and cognition as a continuation of 'Feyerabendian themes in neurocomputational form.' He has published two books, *Scientific Realism and the Plasticity of Mind* (1979) and the one I shall focus on, *A Neurocomputational Perspective: The Nature of Mind and the Structure of Science* (1989), which hereafter will be referred to as *NP.*[1] Other relevant authors in the same current are W. Bechtel and A. Abrahamsen (1980), and the fashion seems to be spreading.

2. The Confrontation

It is easy to guess that the relativist-pragmatist will attack the Classical Picture as his main target. The Classical Picture presents a unifying rationalist ideal of cognition, diametrically opposed to the relativist fragmentation of reason. So the relativist-pragmatist program is in two parts: the critical or destructive part, and a constructive part. The critical part aims at destroying the Classical Picture; the constructive part proposes an alternative view of cognitive virtues and goals.

First, the critical part. The contemporary relativist-pragmatist aims at deconstructing the Classical Picture in its essentials. The deconstructor is to a large extent motivated by the idea that the Classical Picture is rendered obsolete by cognitive science (including neurobiology, evolutionary theory, possibly sociology of science, etc.) and sees himself as defending the only reasonable view of the facts and their normative implications, against an essentially conservative illusion. He might, however, use arguments of a more traditional analytical variety, having to do with conceptual issues, for example, with the definition of 'truth' or 'justification.' In his deconstructive enterprise he is mainly optimistic: the aim of deconstruction is liberation from the prejudice, not some depressing, sceptical insight into the impotence of the human mind.

The main thrust of the relativist-pragmatist attack on the Classical Picture is directed against the central position of truth and the whole truth family. Once the truth-family (truth, truth-centred verisimilitude, objective probability of statements being true, etc.) is demoted from its central place, the issues of epistemic virtue, justification, and norms become pressing; there is no fixed anchor left for these valuational items. As I noted in the introductory chapter on cognitive science, people reason in many different ways, using shortcuts and finding these shortcuts evidently correct. If the defender of the Classical Picture may not rate cognitive strategies by their truth-record, the Picture will be left without its main part. It then becomes much easier to demolish the rest of the Picture.

In *Fragmentation* Stich recounts the story of his conversion to relativism, which nicely illustrates the interdependence of relativist attacks on truth and on justification. He tells the reader how he started with an attempt to justify the standard procedures of sophisticated reasoning – logic, the use of probability and the like – in the face of a stubborn refusal of some reasoners to follows them. He began harbouring doubts about the possibility of justifying them by appeal to intuitions, consensual weighing, or the very concept of rationality:

a natural question to ask was whether there was any other paradigmatically epistemic feature of our cognitive lives that might be taken to be intrinsically

> valuable. And when the question was posed in this way, there was an obvious candidate: *truth*. However, from my earliest work in the philosophy of language, I had harboured a certain scepticism about the utility, indeed even the intelligibility, of the notion of truth. And in the process of polishing the argument against analytic epistemology, I came to suspect that there was a largely parallel argument to be mounted against truth. Thus I came to think that neither being rational nor generating truth would turn out to be an intrinsically valuable feature for cognitive processes to have. If the argument about the value of truth could be sustained, the natural upshot for the normative theory of cognition would be a thoroughgoing pragmatism which holds that all cognitive value is instrumental or pragmatic – that there are no intrinsic, uniquely cognitive values. And this indeed is the position I finally came to defend. (*Fragmentation*, 21; emphasis in the text)

This passage gives one a general idea of what the relativist-pragmatist wants, so I shall take the quotation as a guide. There are several lines of attack on the centrality of truth, some of them more conceptual, some relying more on facts or putative facts. One can gather them into two broad groups: those aiming to undermine the value of truth (or the truth family) and those aiming to show the cognitive unnaturalness of truth – that truth or falsity are not properties of our cognitive states. In the first group we place the arguments purporting to establish that it is pointless to care about truth; in the second, the arguments to the effect that truth is simply not a property of our beliefs.[2] Stich's strategy of attacking the centrality of the truth family differs from the strategy of the other prominent relativist-pragmatist, Paul Churchland, roughly along the lines just sketched: Stich is more inimical to the value of truth, Churchland to its naturalness and to the claims of independence of observation from theory. Notice that the attack is not only on truth itself, but on the whole truth-family, including truth-likeness and the objective probability of truth (and in the case of Churchland also explicitly on the degree of support). Many intelligent readers may side with the relativist-pragmatist in their rejection of strict truth, but part company with them when it comes to weaker notions from the truth family. Others may side with them on the truth of theories themselves, but part company on the importance of true observations and true predictions. Also, we shall see that relativist-pragmatists praise virtues such as accuracy or 'mirroring the deep structures of reality' in papers in which they deny the value of truth. Although trained and skilled philosophers, they sometimes seem to forget that these are mere varieties of truth. Everyday talk and scientific parlance do not often traffic in expressions like 'true belief,' the stock phrase of philosophers; so one is prone to overlook the fact that many terms of everyday epistemic praise – accurate, adequate to facts, factually correct, exact – most often commend the truth of beliefs, remarks, or theories. Having 'insight' or 'unerring intuition' is a way of having true belief, but the latter description is colourless in contrast to the former ones. Obtaining 'valuable information' or 'valuable data' usually entails obtaining the true items, and the words 'data' and 'facts' themselves are very often used for what philosophers call 'true propositions.' The antidote to confusion is then the following: when you read the phrase 'Truth is not useful,' simply translate it into one of the following:

- Accurate information is useless for you.
- (Factually) correct data are useless.
- Accurate predictions are of no use.
- Don't try to get data that reflect the situation!

This is what the relativist pragmatist is actually saying. Once he has argued for the worthlessness, cognitive awkwardness, and unnatural character of the truth family, he proceeds, to show first, that there are no special cognitive goals or virtues (Stich 1993, 8), and, second, that there is no way to compare the merits of various cognitive strategies or systems of strategies. He appeals to cognitive science to establish that people do use strategies with widely diverse structures. Stich calls this thesis descriptive cognitive pluralism: 'What it [the thesis of cognitive pluralism] asserts is that different people go about the business of cognition – the forming and revising of beliefs and other cognitive states – in significantly different ways' (*Fragmentation*, 13). Then he points out that people can be very consistent about their strategies, so that mere appeal to consistency or coherence will not diminish differences among them. If this contention is true, people's strategies are not moderate and revisable, but are unrevisable and thereby radically different in their structure. It is obvious why the relativist needs to insist that cognitive styles or strategies are radically different. If they were merely distinct, a person using a global strategy would not be *eo ipso* wedded to it; she could switch between strategies and compare them freely. If she were reflective enough, she would be able to find either an optimal pure strategy or an optimal mixture, and different cognizers could converge to a common reflectively chosen optimum. For his radical conclusion the relativist needs a radical premise that would block the possibility of convergence, a premise asserting a dramatic structural diversity of strategies.

The question then arises of whether there is any criterion independent of truth-generation that can be used for a comparative assessment of various strategies. It is prima facie very plausible that the answer is No. Once the truth-link is severed, it is hard to see what unique value could possibly replace truth as the goal and touchstone of cognition. Thus, strategies are not comparable with respect to their goal. Since they are also structurally diverse, the relativist-pragmatist has practically won the case. The essential strategy of the relativist-pragmatist may be summarized:

The irrelevance of truth together with descriptive pluralism entails the breakdown of the Classical Picture. Since descriptive pluralism is almost guaranteed by cognitive science, it is essential for the relativist-pragmatist to argue for the irrelevance (or unavailability) of truth.

Let me formulate the relativistic Main Argument in a succinct fashion. This will be a first version, to be enriched later by additional, pragmatic considerations:

The Irrelevance of Truth: There is no common goal of cognition, because truth is irrelevant.

Radical Descriptive Pluralism: There are many radically different cognitive strategies and styles. Therefore,

The Incomparability Thesis: Since there is no common goal, the strategies are mutually incomparable; and

Radical Normative Pluralism: There is no single norm valid for various cognitive styles or strategies.

I shall spend the most time upon the first and central premise. Two ways are open for the relativist to show that truth is irrelevant: first, to undermine the value of truth and, second, to demonstrate the cognitive unnaturalness of truth, that truth or falsity are not properties of our cognitive states. Stich pursues the first way. Churchland pursues the second way, arguing from some strong assumptions about connectionist processing that the human neural organization is inhospitable to any states capable of being true or being false, so that human representations cannot be assessed for truth. He proclaims himself 'entirely willing to let go' of the notions of classical truth and reference (Churchland 1992b, 422) and to replace them with success-oriented criteria. We shall be concerned with this main argument in the whole of the third part of the book. No matter how strange the claims about irrelevance of truth may sound, we have to give them a fair hearing and assess them in detail.

Let me now briefly present the constructive proposal of the relativist-pragmatist. Since he does not wish to saddle us with scepticism or to deplore imperfections of human reasoning, he wants to replace the Classical Picture with a constructive, naturalistically respectable alternative, in accordance with his preferred scientific outlook and with the data of the relevant sciences. Finally, like Meno and Gorgias before him, he intends to preserve a normative commitment, to keep giving advice and valuation and not to limit the talk about cognition to descriptive scientific talk. Unfortunately, in recent relativist-pragmatist publications one finds that much more space is devoted to the destructive rather than the constructive task. This might be just a tactical decision, first to clear the ground thoroughly, but it might also be a reflection of a deeper attitude – that once the Classical Picture is demolished, there is nothing more to do, and that Radical Normative Pluralism and Relativism do not demand any further careful philosophical grounding. It is pity that it should be so, since not even the basic tenets of relativism-pragmatism are clearly set out in the literature. We shall encounter some lacunae presently.

What is a relativist-pragmatist going to put in the place of the Classical Picture? To begin, what is to be the goal of cognition in general? Second, what is to be the goal of specialized cognizers, above all scientists?

First, the general goal. One would expect that a pragmatist will recommend the pursuit of practical goals, and, indeed, the relativist-pragmatist does so. From the irrelevance of truth (and the truth family as a whole) plus absence of other candidate epistemic goals or values he concludes that 'there are no special cognitive or epistemic values. There are just *values*' (Stich 1993, 9, emphasis in the text). Values then turn out to be simply 'what we value.' As a consequence, however, the relativist-pragmatist asks us to distinguish different ways of pursuing a practical goal and to choose those that do not rely on truth. For example, consider physical health as a candidate goal of cognition (most pertinently, of the study of medicine). The simple, straightforward, and (to many people) natural view would be the following. We value research concerning the human body because it helps us to remain healthy by producing true (or roughly true) ideas about the causes of diseases, the ways to prevent and cure them, the ways of acquiring and retaining physical fitness, and the like. These true ideas (beliefs) then guide the physician's action, and help us to remain healthy. This is not what the relativist-pragmatist has in mind. For him, the truth of beliefs is not relevant to their usefulness: they are useful or harmless regardless of their truth or falsity. Thus, *he urges us not to get true beliefs and then harness them in the service of practical goals, but somehow to use our cognitive capacities for achieving practical goods regardless of their truth-generating powers.* (Notice that this is not the advice given by classical pragmatists). Having his disregard for truth in mind, consider his advice:

> Cognitive processes, pragmatists will insist, should not be thought of primarily as devices for generating truths. Rather, they should be thought of as something akin to tools or technologies or practices that can be used more or less successfully in achieving a variety of goals. The consequences that may be considered in deciding whether to adopt a given technological innovation are as rich and varied as the things that people find intrinsically valuable. Some of these things, like health, happiness, and the well-being of one's children, we are probably biologically disposed to value ... If, as I am urging, we view systems of cognitive processes as analogous to tools or technologies, then they too are to be evaluated by appeal to the rich and varied class of things that people take to be intrinsically valuable. (*Fragmentation*, 131)

The advice is to replace one goal, truth, with a plurality of goals. *These goals are seen as alternatives to truth, not as further goals besides truth.* The right way to understand the relativist-pragmatist's advice is, then:

Don't seek usefulness through truth, but employ your cognitive powers directly for your practical purposes.

Let me call the recommended policy 'The Truth-Ignoring Pragmatic Policy.' Stich thinks also that, as a matter of fact, people are concerned not about truth, but about usefulness, so the policy seems natural to him: 'Though it's hard to see why anyone but an epistemic chauvinist would be much concerned about rationality or truth, we can count on people caring about the pragmatic evaluation of their cognitive processes because that evaluation is tied to goals that they themselves take to be intrinsically valuable' (*Fragmentation*, 135). I admit that I do not fully understand the import of the recommendation. It seems to enjoin the enquirer to form beliefs without regard to their truth, but with regard only to their usefulness. A very coarse statement of the advice might be as follows: 'If you are sure that believing that such-and-such is the case will make you happy, just go on and believe it!' On the other hand, I am not sure that Stich would endorse such advice, so I leave the question open.[3] Does our relativist-pragmatist have to recommend the Truth-Ignoring Pragmatic Policy, or might he advise the enquirer to seek true beliefs because they are at the same time useful? He cannot do so; if it turns out that the truth of beliefs is their useful-making property, truth is reinstalled as a cognitive value, perhaps as the central one, and the Classical Picture is reinstated.

The next step leads from pragmatism to relativism. According to Stich: 'The account of cognitive virtue I have come to defend is floridly pluralistic. Moreover, it is relativistic as well, since it entails that different systems of reasoning may be normatively appropriate for different people'; and 'An account of cognitive evaluation is relativistic if the assessment of cognitive systems it offers are sensitive to facts about the person or group using the system' (*Fragmentation*, 14, 136). Thus, an account of cognitive virtue is relativistic if it yields significantly different assessments of cognitive systems depending on the users of the system. For example, a norm to the effect that Bayesian probabilistic reasoning is better for timid people and Popperian bold conjectures are better for more outgoing persons would be relativistic by this criterion. In general, different strategies are not comparable across persons and situations. This is the 'Incomparability Thesis.'

Surely, a qualification should be added here: strategies are incomparable provided that the norm-giver does not further compare the users for their epistemic worth, or, more precisely, that he prohibits any such comparison. If I accept as epistemically relevant the timid/outgoing divide, but then claim that a good scientist is never timid, I endorse an anti-relativist stance (rationalism), claiming by implication that it is best to be outgoing (Popperian). This point is even clearer in a completely elementary example. If we discuss a mathematical problem, and you say that for a high-school student the best way of solving it is to use method A, but the best way for the professional mathematician is B, you have not thereby endorsed relativism about methods A and B, because you could have clearly implied that professional mathematicians are generally more competent in solving such problems, so that B is in absolute terms better than A. Call the crucial relativist qualification that insists that persons (and situations) be epistemologically non-comparable the 'Isolation Assumption.' Unfortunately, Stich is not explicit at this point. The very definition of relativism proposed by him is extremely sketchy, so sketchy that it is unclear whether, in fact, he accepts (as he should) the Isolation Assumption or whether he thinks that any mention of users in the assessment of cognitive systems is sufficient to make the assessment relativistic. It is clear that relativism cannot do without the Isolation Assumption (about users and situations), since it is the implicit groundwork on which the Incomparability Thesis about strategies rests. Thus, in order for an account to be relativistic, it should relativize the assessment to groups or persons and refrain from further comparing (ranking) these groups or persons in epistemic terms.

One additional complication is needed. Both Stich and Churchland insist on the incomparability of reasoning strategies and methodologies, and it is most often clear from the context that they mean incomparability with respect to some assumed goal. Sometimes, however, Stich is better construed as claiming, in addition, that actual reasoning strategies are so diverse that they lack any common denominator. The two claims should be considered separately.

How does one then pass from pragmatism to relativism? Stich answers: 'Given this characterization of relativism, a pragmatic account of cognitive evaluation is going to be relativistic for two quite different reasons. The most obvious source of relativism is the plurality of values to which a pragmatic assessment must be sensitive. A somewhat less obvious source is the consequentialist character of pragmatic evaluation' (*Fragmentation*, 136). First, he considers the plurality of values: 'The pragmatic account urges that we assess cognitive systems by their likelihood of leading to what their users value. If, as I have been supposing, people can and do intrinsically value a wide variety of things, with considerable variation from person to person and culture to culture, then pragmatic assessments of cognitive systems will be sensitive to highly variable facts about the users of those systems' (ibid.). I think the attractions of such a view are obvious. Instead of preaching a unitarian methodological doctrine to a largely indifferent audience, the epistemologist can address the interests of various people and various groups and make himself useful in the way they themselves acknowledge. His advice will be user oriented on principled grounds and will have a hypothetical form: 'If you really value this-and-this goal, you should form your beliefs in such-and-such a way!' One should not forget, however, that the recommendation is based on the questionable premise that forming true beliefs is of no clear use.

Second, he examines consequentialism: 'Epistemic pragmatism urges a consequentialist account of inferential virtue – the goodness or badness of a system of cognitive processes depends on the likelihood of the system leading to certain consequences. And consequentialist evaluations will typically be relativistic, since the likelihood of a given system leading to certain consequences will generally depend on the environment in which the system is operating' (ibid.). I would like to note that this criterion could be emended, by adding a suitable version of the Isolation Assumption: environments should not be further comparable. (For example, assessments of the following kind are forbidden: 'Palpation is all right if you have to make your medical prognosis on the spot in a bombed town, but if you could take your patient to a decent hospital, I would recommend giving him the test X.' Such advice implies that the test X gives better grounds for prognosis than palpation simplex, and the advice is thereby non-relativistic.) Let me call the recommended policy 'Situational Policy.' It assumes that what counts as the best strategy varies with situations, and that this is a kind of fundamental fact. This assumption yields a kind of radical situational picture of the epistemologist's task. He has to take into account not only the non-cognitive interests of agents directly and on a case-to-case basis, but also the varying circumstances in which they find themselves. Allow me to speculate further. Any branch of study that concerns itself with very general patterns of reasoning would feel the impact of the relativist-pragmatist revolution. Philosophers would never again teach simple logic; they would teach logic-for-small-business, logic-for-big-business, logic-for-people-in-love, logic-for-the-disillusioned, and so on (financially not a bad prospect, after all). The ideal would be logic-for-John, logic-for-Jane, even different logics for each time of the day. Logic would go the way applied ethics did, but without any unifying principle. Mathematics might completely change its outlook and revert to its Babylonian servitude to concrete and particularized goals without a unifying theory.

Is the relativist-pragmatist committed to such a perspective if he is consistent enough? Of course, since if he admitted that there are general methodologies, general canons of reasoning, valid and useful across a wide range of situations, he would have to admit the relative autonomy of such strategies – they are less situation bound, agent bound, and interest bound than particular rules of thumb. Then, he would have to place such general strategies higher than particular ones in the absolute sense and to abandon his stance altogether. The Situation Policy together with the Truth-Ignoring Pragmatic Policy make up the core of the relativist-pragmatist's methodological offer. We can now formulate the full version (of our reconstruction) of the relativist-pragmatist Main Argument:

1. *The Irrelevance of Truth*: There is no common goal of cognition, because truth is irrelevant.
2. *The Radical Descriptive Pluralism:* (a) Cognitive styles and strategies are environment and user relative, and (b) they are structurally radically diverse. (1) and (2) entail the following:

C1. *The Incomparability Thesis:* The strategies are mutually incomparable (both with respect to goals and to their internal structure).
C2. *Radical Normative Pluralism:* There is no single norm valid for various cognitive styles or strategies.

So much for the general goal. What about those specialized cognizers, the scientists? Is practical success, regardless of truth, recommended here also by the relativist-pragmatist? It seems that it is, if judged by the programmatic paper (Stich 1993). Stich begins by stressing the normative force of epistemology and asking how descriptive psychology could help with formulating normative advice, thus bridging the is/ought divide. He brings in a chess example: if you want to learn to play excellent chess, study the strategies of the best players. Analogously, if you are interested in reasoning, study and emulate the best thinkers. The program consists of four steps: first, determine the goal; second, locate the actual (historical) goal-achievers; third, discover the strategies they have used; fourth, explore the possibilities of improving on them. Stich dubs the project 'Normative Human Epistemology.' Such epistemology would respect the limits and idiosyncrasies of human cognition, as well as the fact that human cognizers are embedded in a social context. Stich also particularly stresses the importance of experimental technology for the development of science. How does one pick out the best thinkers? Not by the truth of their products, since many great thinkers did not produce true theories. Nor by any other epistemic or cognitive standard: there are no special cognitive or epistemological values, and what counts is simply *'achieving what we value'* (Stich 1993, 9; emphasis added). The good cognitive strategies for a person to use are those that are likely to lead to the states of affairs that she finds intrinsically valuable. Therefore, one should look at the thinkers and reasoners who have achieved the goals they have set for themselves. This would lead to an epistemology based on cognitive virtue, with rules derived from virtue. Unfortunately, Stich does not explicitly propound a line of research beyond very brief and programmatic remarks. He simply helps himself to the notion of 'a good scientist,' saying we should do what 'good scientists' do.

In the next step Stich declares that he has found an ally in Herbert Simon. For more than two decades the polymath and Nobel prizewinner has been practising, together with his collaborators, what Stich has recently started to preach, claims Stich with characteristic modesty. Simon is, in fact, studying historical scientific discoveries, trying to reconstruct them in a programmable way, and Stich gives a brief sketch of his methods and results. According to Stich, the epistemologists should join such studies and derive normative rules of reasoning from the practice of the successful scientists. The main issue, then, is the criterion for picking up the paradigm reasoners.

Stich also offers his choice of the list of successful reasoners as the part of the argument for the unimportance of truth. If we adopt the strategy of locating good reasoners by assessing the truth of their best products, we shall miss obvious stars like Aristotle, Dalton, Newton, and Mendel, he thinks; much of their best work has turned out to be not true, as has much of the best work of other great scientists. He then simply refuses to name any criterion but the fact that they are widely recognized as great scientists. It seems that, for him, the fact that Aristotle, Dalton, Newton, and Mendel count as successful reasoners is merely a brute fact, answering to no rational norms. How, then, does one pick up the paradigmatic reasoners? Stich appeals to a half-joke of Simon: go to the library and get a collection of widely used textbooks in the domain you are interested in and then make a list of people whose portrait appears in the textbook. To be considered a successful scientist is to be famous enough to get one's portrait in a textbook. This is all: Aristotle and Darwin are to be studied, ultimately, because their pictures appear in textbooks. I shall endeavour to show, in chapter 7, section 4, that this is not simply an oversight but the consequence of the relativistic position.

My introduction of the relativist-pragmatist concludes here. In the following pages I shall take a closer look at his deconstructive work, his arguments against the value of truth and rationality and against the unity of epistemic virtue. Since I take the notion of truth as central to the rationalist Classical Picture, I adopt the veritist view of cognition. Therefore, I argue against the relativist-pragmatist by concentrating on the issue of truth. Since ought implies can, I first have to show that our beliefs can be true at all. In Part Two I discuss the naturalness of truth, showing against Churchland how our representations – be they sentential or pictorial or distributed – are hospitable to truth and to falsity. In Part Three I discuss the main relativistic argument: first, the thesis that truth is cognitively irrelevant and of no value, then, radical descriptive pluralism together with the incomparability assumption; and finally, I endeavour to show that all three are false. This completes our defence of the Classical Picture.

PART TWO: ARE OUR REPRESENTATIONS TRUTH-TOLERANT?

4

The Idea of Truth-Intolerance

1. The Problem of the Representational Media

In this part of the book I shall defend the central assumptions of the Classical Picture: that human cognitive states can be true or false, that is, can represent the outside world correctly (true beliefs, true percepts, true schemes or prototypes) or incorrectly, and that one can value the transitions between such states classically with respect to their capacity for truth-preservation (or truthlikeness- or plausibility-preservation). Further, I shall defend the view that human cognitive processes can be judged to be rational or irrational by the usual criteria. I defend the view indirectly by criticizing the opposing relativist-pragmatist contention and, in particular, the most important line of attack that gets its impetus from a problem concerning our representational media: sentential (language of thought), or perhaps pictorial (mental images) or map-like or network-like. The essence of the problem is simple: Some representational media, for instance, the sentential medium, are capable of being true or false; they are 'truth-tolerant.'[1] The problem of the medium is as follows:

Is the natural medium (or media) of human thought and cognition truth-tolerant?

The problem gives some hope to the relativist-pragmatist: the negative answer to the question would vindicate his crucial thesis that the notion of truth is unimportant for the enquirer and unavailable to the epistemologist. Indeed, at first blush the general physicalist framework seems to support the negative answer. If our mental states are simply neural states, how can they be true or be false? However, matters are not quite that simple. Most physicalists have come to accept that some states of mind/brain do have representational content. Thus, our relativist-pragmatist must argue from some more specific evidence that the actual representations in the mind/brain are not truth-tolerant.

The relativist-pragmatist then appeals to a view that is popular in recent cognitive science, that mental representations do not have the form of sentences – not even neural sentences – but are more like maps, diagrams, or states of a neural network. Churchland suggests that the very numerosity of possible brain configurations speaks for the vast variety of representational possibilities: 'Consider a typical brain sub-population of something like 10^8 neurons. Its abstract activation space will have 10^8 dimensions. Clearly a space of such high dimensionality can support an extraordinarily intricate hierarchical system of similarity gradients and partitions across that space ... Now to demand that all possible conceptual frameworks must be somehow translatable into our current conceptual framework is just the demand that each and every one of the billions of possible configurations just alluded to must stand in some equivalence relation to our current configuration' (1992, 357). Now, assuming that neural configurations are representational, why would they have to be truth-hospitable? Is it not more probable that most kinds of configurations do not have this rather specific property? This is the line taken by Churchland, who tries to derive truth-intolerance from such a representational format.

In addition to arguments for the Irrelevance of Truth, the diversity of media seems to offer to the relativist-pragmatist a welcome support for Radical Descriptive Pluralism. If representational media are structurally diverse, they might couch incommensurable representations. Thus, Churchland claims (1992a) that connectionism gives new life to Feyerabendian relativistic themes. I shall address both issues in this part of the book, privileging the first one. Churchland also addresses the issue of the relation between theory and observation, which is indirectly but strongly relevant for the debate; I address this topic in the appendix.

Churchland offers no detailed statement of how the irrelevance of truth is supposed to follow from or be supported by the non-propositional character of human representations, nor is he entirely clear about the status of truth. Fortunately, W. Bechtel and A. Abrahamsen have offered a summary of the relativist-pragmatist view concerning the medium. They discuss the traditional picture of knowledge and the reason a philosopher committed to such a picture might have to reject the states of a non-sentential representational system as candidates for epistemological appraisal. 'Consider first the idea that knowledge requires belief. Belief is typically construed as a propositional attitude (Russell: *An Inquiry into Meaning and Truth*), where a proposition is the object of the attitude. If Sarah believes that the cat is on the roof, her belief is about the proposition "the cat is on the roof." According to the analyses of folk psychology, she could also have other attitudes towards this proposition, some epistemic (e.g., doubt), some emotional (e.g., fear). All require the existence of a proposition (although proponents of this approach might not be committed to the idea that a proposition is somehow represented in the head of the individual)' (Bechtel and Abrahamsen 1980, 225). In short, to have a belief is to have an attitude to a proposition; but people have all kinds of representations that are not propositional, and having such a representation (no matter what its functional role is) does not amount to having a belief. The authors then go on to show that the notions of truth and justification are tied to the 'propositional paradigm' and, by implication, should be abandoned (or drastically revised) if the paradigm is abandoned. We can now reconstruct the argument for the unavailability and irrelevance of truth in its full generality. It might run as follows:

The Argument from the Medium:

1. Most or all of the cognitive media are non-sentential.
2. Only the sentential medium is truth-tolerant.
3. Theories are (in their original form) couched in some non-sentential cognitive medium.

Therefore,

C1. Most or all of the cognitive media are truth-intolerant.
C2. The largest part or the whole of cognition has nothing to do with truth.
C3. In particular, theories (in their original form) have nothing to do with truth.
C4. It is completely unrealistic to take truth as a cognitive goal or epistemic value.

Let us first try to get a more detailed picture of the framework of the argument. The continuation of the summary by Bechtel and Abrahamsen is as follows: 'The requirement that knowledge be true also seems to require that knowledge is propositional. Although there are different theories about what truth consists in, truth values are generally held to accrue to propositions or sentences. It is not clear what other kinds of entities could be counted as true or false' (ibid.).

The authors are not quite explicit about what they mean by 'propositional,' but they use the locution 'propositions or sentences,' which has already begotten some confusion in the literature. The term 'proposition' has several meanings besides 'sentence,' the prominent ones being:

a. 'the thought or meaning expressed by a (declarative) sentence,'
b. 'state of affairs,'
c. 'sentences' themselves (including the hypothetical sentence-like representations in the head).

Propositions such as (c) sentences in the head are presumably in the head. Propositions in the sense of (a) meanings are God knows where, if they have any location. The (b) state of affairs are in the outside world. Suppose a philosopher says simply that belief is a relation or attitude to a proposition, for instance, Sarah's belief that the cat is on the roof is a relation to the proposition 'The cat is on the roof.' His words can mean any of the following:

Sarah's belief is her relation to (a) the meaning of the English sentence 'The cat is on the roof.'
Sarah's belief is her relation to (b) the state of affairs, comprising the cat and the roof.
Sarah's belief is her relation to (c) the mental sentence token in her head.

The meanings (a)–(c) often become conflated. In a debate, a philosopher declares herself an enemy of 'propositionalism' – it turns out that she has nothing against states of affairs, but a great deal against mental sentences. Another enemy of 'propositionalism' hates states of affairs, but gladly accepts mental sentences. The use of the same term creates the illusion that both reject the same thesis.

Fortunately, we can follow Churchland's own terminology, which is more uniform, adverting to sentences only. Consider the Argument from the Medium. Churchland argues at great length for thesis (1), that the principal representational media are non-sentential. He takes for granted thesis (2), that the applicability of the notion of truth to our representations heavily depends on the nature of the representational medium: No sentences – no truth! He also argues for thesis (3): Theories – as represented by the brain – are literally identical with brain configurations: 'Plasticity aside, any configuration of weights constitutes a speculative *theory* in its own right, since it imposes one taxonomy upon the inputs at the expense of trillions of other taxonomies that might have been imposed instead' (Churchland 1993, 316; emphasis in the text). Why focus upon neurally represented theories, theories-in-the-head, instead of verbally represented ones? Churchland is interested in the dynamics of human cognition, in particular, the dynamics of sophisticated scientific cognition and the resultant scientific theories. He believes (correctly, in my opinion) that the dynamics of cognitive processes that take place in scientists' minds/brains is very important, in the sense not only of merely causing the existence of verbally represented theories (call them 'theories-in-the-book'), but also of accounting for their internal structure. This idea is crucial for the whole debate, so we shall give it a name:

Relevance Thesis: Internal cognitive processes are crucially relevant for understanding the dynamics of theories.

Theories-in-the-head are the most important ones for the epistemologist because their dynamics accounts for the theory change, for the growth of knowledge, and for the origin of theories-in-the-book.

In contrast to theories-in-the-book, which consist of sentences, assessable for their truth-value, theories-in-the-head are non-sentential, Churchland claims, and therefore are not amenable to traditional assessment as to truth-value. He implicitly makes the same move that Bechtel and Abrahamsen make explicitly, the step from non-sentence-like in syntax to non-propositional in semantics. In his opinion the prominence of truth in the traditional view is due to the wrong idea that theories consist of sentences: 'Finally, if theories are just sentences, then the ultimate virtue of a theory is truth. And it was widely accepted that an adequate account of rational methodology would reveal why humans must tend, in the long run, towards the theories that are true' (*NP*, 153). Combining this argument with (3), he concludes that the neurological account of learning and cognition frees us from the (allegedly) antiquated notion of truth: 'Throughout this chapter we have been exploring causal accounts of the learning process – accounts moreover that are uniform for successful and unsuccessful cognitive configurations alike. And we have found it neither necessary nor useful to fall back on the language of observation statements, logical inferences, rational belief or truth' (ibid., 249).

Consider the conclusions reached. Churchland is not explicit about the notion of truth. We may guess that he is not insisting on a narrow characterization of truth, according to which only sentences can be true, while simultaneously admitting another notion of correspondence to reality for non-sentential representations. This would leave room for letting correspondence to reality still count as the ultimate virtue of theories and defeat Churchland's obvious purpose. He certainly does not worry about details, being after much bigger game: a restructuring of our whole cognitive enterprise.

What does he mean by claiming that truth is not a proper goal of cognition? First, whatever his exact meaning, it is clear that Churchland is highly critical of the notion of truth, and that he takes his reasons for criticism to be non-traditional ones, based on the sciences of cognition. The most prominent reason for criticism is that truth is tied to sentences: 'The traditional view of human knowledge is that the unit of cognition is the sentence or proposition, and the cognitive virtue of such units is truth ... I think the move away from the traditional conception is entirely correct ... Specifically, if we are to reconsider the truth as the aim or product of cognitive activity, I think we must reconsider its applicability right across the board, and not in some arbitrarily or idiosyncratically segregated domain of "unobservables." That is, if we are to move away from the more naive formulations of scientific realism, we should move in the direction of *pragmatism*, rather than in the direction of a positivistic instrumentalism' (*NP*, 150; emphasis in the text). The further question is what, in his eyes, is the exact status of truth? Truth does not rank highly at all: 'it is far from obvious that truth is either the primary aim or the principal product of this [i.e., cognitive] activity. Rather, its function would appear to be the ever more finely tuned administration of the organism's *behaviour*. Natural selection does not care whether a brain has or tends towards true beliefs, so long as the organism reliably exhibits its reproductively advantageous behaviour. Plainly, there is going to be *some* connection between the faithfulness of the brain's world model and the propriety of organism's behaviour. But just as plainly, the connection is not going to be direct' (*NP*, 150). 'The notion of truth is suspect on purely metaphysical grounds anyway' (ibid.). The idea of truth should not guide our view of science: 'Truth as currently conceived might cease to be an aim of science ... because we had *raised* our sights, in pursuit of some epistemic goal even *more* worthy than truth' (ibid.; emphasis in the text). With respect to truth (and verisimilitude), Churchland seems to oscillate between at least two different positions, the less radical one, which takes truth as a subordinate goal of enquiry, and the more radical one, which denies it the status of a goal. Let us consider first the less radical one.

A. Subordinate goal position: Truth is a (realistic) goal of cognition and science, but a subordinate one, in relation to goals 'even more worthy than truth.'

The position implies that truth is worthy and attainable, but states that it is not the ultimate goal of cognition. Churchland seems close to this position when he says that truth is not the primary goal of cognition, which seems to imply that truth is a secondary goal. The position allows two alternatives, the first of which is uninteresting for our purpose.

A1. Necessary condition position: Truth (and truthlikeness and kindred properties) is not the ultimate goal of cognition, but is a necessary condition of attaining the ultimate goal.

We have no quarrel with such a position. No matter what further, mainly practical, goals might be attained through attaining truth, the Necessary condition position amounts in practice to an injunction to scientists to search truth. The task of attaining the truth is so arduous that it would keep scientists busy for the rest of their lives, no matter what further goals they might seek through their search for truth. So, the Necessary condition position offers no consolation to the relativist-pragmatist and stands in contrast to the main thrust of Churchland's argumentation.

A2. The trade-off position: Truth (and truthlikeness, etc.) is subordinate to other goals, since it is less important, so that it can be sacrificed to these other aims.

Taken literally, the position dictates counter-intuitive and probably impossible trade-offs: accept a theory that you know to be false (and non-truthlike) to further your more worthy aims. (Note that we are judging not methodologies or strategies, but theories themselves, and here the only trade-off in view is the one proposed.) We have said enough about similar ideas in chapter 3 on Stich; we consider the position to be totally indefensible.

Churchland's pronouncement that truth may cease to be a goal of science, however, can be taken to stand for a stronger position, which we now state.

B. The No-goal position: Truth is not a realistic goal of cognition and science.

Truth is not attainable and is not worth striving for. Since the Subordinate goal position is untenable for theories, the No-goal position is the only interesting relativist-pragmatist proposal in the field. Moreover, since it is to this position that Churchland has made some original contribution, we have good reason to concentrate on it.[2] I assume that Churchland endorses (B) and claims that truth is not a realistic goal of cognition and science.

The position is worthy of consideration. The sheer novelty of Churchland's approach, the weight of the new material he brings to bear upon methodological and epistemological questions, and the brilliance of his style are apt to create the impression that he has somehow proved the irrelevance of truth from 'the most recent discoveries' of cognitive science. I shall argue at great length that this impression is false. In what follows, I shall first offer a brief principled answer to the Argument from the nature of the medium, which I shall then develop in detail and supplement by considerations from cognitive science throughout Part Two. I conclude by arguing that Churchland's anti-truth stance is incompatible with his endorsement of realism, and that his position is ultimately incoherent.

2. Truth without Sentences

Let me first present my reaction to the Argument from the Medium as a whole. Churchland devotes the bulk of his relevant writing to establishing (1), that is, the non-sentential character of our cognitive media, showing the powerful nature of non-sentential media and concluding that there is no need to postulate the existence of sentential media. He says almost nothing about (2), which seems to carry an equally heavy burden in the argument. I shall not question the thesis (1), granting Churchland – for the sake of argument – his view that even sophisticated scientists represent their complex theories in a non-sentential form, and accepting, in broad outlines, his account of the specifics of this non-sentential form. The crucial question is whether the destructive conclusions follow from that premise, and I shall argue that they do not.

The unsupported premise (2) reveals the main weakness of the argument. Why should sentences have a monopoly on truth? Beliefs were held to be true long before we had sentential theories about the cognitive medium supporting them. Great scientists have been able to find geometric-spatial solutions to physical problems without being able to put them into propositional (e.g., analytic) form, and no one doubted that their solutions were either true or false. In addition to this weakness, there is a loophole concerning the step to the first conclusion (C1). Granted that most human cognitive processing is non-sentential, it still might happen that cognitive output is ultimately transformed into a sentential medium (e.g., that we think in pictures but write in sentences). Then, one might take truth as the most valuable property of the output and plausibly claim that it is still the point of the whole enterprise.

Let me address the two components in order: first, the general issue of truth in a non-sentential medium; second, the issue of the causal powers of non-sentential representations, in particular their disposition to produce truth-tolerant verbal representations.

Traditionally and generally, not only sentences are held to be truth-tolerant. The philosophical tradition has taken beliefs as important bearers of truth/falsity, and these were often taken to be quite unlike written or spoken sentences (being either *sui generis*, or 'images' or 'mental acts'). The sentential view of thought has been only one of many. In folk-psychology there is no presumption as to the medium of believing (as Bechtel himself is at pains to argue in his 1990 publication). Similarly, in recent analytical work it is quite common to find theories about belief-states combining the view that belief-states are truth-tolerant with a non-sentential or agnostic view of their form or implementation.[3]

How can a representation in a non-sentential medium be true or false? A representation carries information about a state of affairs. A picture or a belief-state can carry accurate information about some state of affairs (e.g., the cat's being on the mat) and thereby can be true in a wide sense. The convenient semantic format for understanding this idea and making it explicit is that of possible situations (even 'possible worlds').

A representation R with content C (representing, e.g., a cat sitting on a mat) divides possible situations in two classes: those that exemplify C and those that do not. For example, the cat-on-the-mat-representation divides situations into cat-on-the-mat-situations and situations in which the cat is not on the mat. Such a representation corresponds to reality, and in this sense it is true if and only if the intended actual situation is in the set of cat-on-the-mat-situations.

The proposal is easily extended to cover beliefs and other propositional attitudes. In our framework the object of a propositional attitude is the state of affairs, or the situation, or a set of possible worlds. If Sarah believes that the cat is on the roof, she is related to the-cat-on-the-roof-situations. She is related to something in the world, expressible by talking about actual or possible worlds. Call the proposition in the sense of a possible situation or of a set of possible worlds, *w*-proposition ('*w*' represents 'world'). The notion of *w*-proposition is a semantic notion. Sometimes 'proposition' is used to mean a syntactic item, a sentence, or any string of symbols (e.g., neural tokens) similar to a sentence. One might call such a syntactic item an *s*-proposition to distinguish it from the semantic *w*-proposition. In principle, there are several ways in which Sarah can become intentionally related to a *w*-proposition. She might have a sentence-like or a non-sentence-like representation in her head. The essential thing is that her belief-state classifies possible situations into two groups: situations in which the cat is on the roof and those in which the cat is not on the roof. This partition of situations is the content of Sarah's belief, the *w*-proposition in question.

Robert Stalnaker, one of the most distinguished proponents of the view that beliefs are attitudes to (what I called) *w*-propositions, summarizes the motivation for the view in the following way: 'The picture suggests that the primary objects of attitude are not propositions [my *s*-propositions] but the alternative possible outcomes of agents' actions, or more generally, alternative possible states of the world. When a person wants a proposition to be true, it is because he has a positive attitude toward certain concrete realizations of that proposition. Propositions, the picture suggests, are simply ways of distinguishing between the elements of the relevant range of alternative possibilities-ways that are useful for characterizing and expressing an agent's attitudes toward those possibilities' (1984, 4). We do not need to go all the way with Stalnaker and claim that all beliefs are nothing but attitudes to *w*-propositions. Some beliefs might be attitudes to *w*-propositions plus something else.

One can use the semantics of *w*-propositions for any kind of representation that aims at representing the ways things are. Such representations partition the set of situations and are not immune to appraisal for truth and falsity or to correspondence correctness that conservatively extends the classical notion of truth. Most of what we need for the epistemological purposes at hand is captured by the relation of representation to *w*-propositions. Thus, *representations that are not sentential-propositional are truth-tolerant if they purport to represent the ways the world is and thereby stand in relation to* w-*propositions*. Call this line of reasoning in favour of truth-tolerance the Semantic Argument.

A brief comment. The argument does *not* claim that any item that one can get information from is thereby true or false; smoke is not true about fire. It claims only that *items that are representations* – that is, at least intended or selected to carry information for standard users, in particular, intended or selected to *guide their users by conveying the information* – are true or false.

How does one actually ascribe truth or falsity to human mental representations? Roughly, one does so by attending to their role in producing recognizably truth-hospitable items, utterances and statements. According to the Relevance Thesis the representation of a theory in the enquirer's mind/brain (the theory-in-the-head) has to account for verbally represented theories. The latter are true or are false. Even if their ancestor in the head does not have a truth value literally, therefore, it is at least a stable disposition to produce true or false sentences. If the representation in the brain has no connection with truth, it will be useless to explain how humans manage to produce true theories-in-the-book. Finally, if the alleged theory-in-the-head is not a representation or anything remotely like a theory-in-the-book, not even only functionally analogous to it, it is uninteresting from the viewpoint of methodology and epistemology of science.[4]

One can freely ascribe truth-values to mentally represented theories. Since in doing so the ascriber is interested primarily in the capacity of mentally represented theories to generate true sentential theories, a quick strategy of truth-value ascription would be the following dispositionalist one, limning this very capacity. Take the representation in the mind/brain as a machine producing a theory-in-the-book, in abstraction from all its other features, and assess its ability to yield true theories. Then take a system that has a stable pattern of answers, that is, the system in a state *S* that has a unique disposition to produce a response pattern *P* when suitably prompted. If *P* is a theory-in-the-book, estimate the truth value of *P*. *S* is (derivatively) correct or right if it has (or is identical with, whatever ontology of disposition one prefers) a disposition to produce a true response (true theory-in-the-book).

Call this general scheme of answer to the question about ascription the 'Argument from Disposition.' In my opinion it already settles the issue of truth-tolerance. The relativist-pragmatist might counter, however, that the dispositionalist strategy is merely a trick that offers a standard of assessment without yielding an understanding of actual cognitive processes in line with the Relevance Thesis. If one aim of the epistemologist is to understand, he might say, then she should get to the nitty-gritty of neurological argument. A closer look must be taken. Since Churchland discusses various kinds of neural representations, I shall analyse these kinds with respect to their truth-tolerance, taking a closer look at the maps, connectionist networks, and prototypes and processes in connectionist networks, most centrally the process of learning.

5

The Non-Sentential Media

1. The Information in Maps and Diagrams

In this chapter I begin to examine the truth-tolerance of particular kinds of non-sentential representations. The Semantic Argument and the Argument from Disposition generally favour truth-tolerance, and we need to test their applicability to particular kinds of representations.

I start with the simplest non-propositional medium, that is, maps or diagrams. They are common, familiar, and well-studied items from the cognitive-psychological standpoint. Churchland discusses a particular kind, neural maps: map-like representations in the mind/brain. If all maps are truth-(in)tolerant, so are the neural ones. I begin by asking about the truth-hospitality of common maps, where our intuitions are of greater help, and then transfer the answer to more recondite neural maps. I shall argue for their truth-tolerance from their role in carrying information and in reasoning. Maps are like beliefs – they help us to steer. They represent for us our environment, to which they are related by projection-rules, particular semantic rules for maps. They can be correct or incorrect, and their correctness is important for our steering. Suppose that you ask someone about the geography of the United States, and she draws a picture, as shown in figure 5.1. You will probably say that the picture correctly represents the shape of the United States, but that it incorrectly represents the position of Chicago relative to the whole territory (and to New York). Further, it misrepresents the relative distance from New York to Chicago. Obviously, you assume the usual projection rules for maps, the same way you assume that English words have their usual meanings.

Notice that your reaction to misrepresentation is roughly the same as it

FIGURE 5.1
The incorrect map

is when you are confronted with the false statement 'Chicago is south of New York.' In both cases you complain about being misinformed, since the message does not 'correspond to reality.' The communicative goals are the same: a person can deceive you by drawing a misleading map, and if the deceit is intentional and malevolent, it clearly amounts to lying, so that the pragmatics and ethics of the two situations look much the same.

At this juncture, encouraged by the sameness of the communication framework, we simply rerun the Semantic Argument. The intuitive view about correctness of maps suggests its applicability, and nothing speaks against it. A map, together with a projection method, divides situations ('worlds') into those that match (or resemble) it and those that do not. If the actual situation is among the former, the map is correct in the sense of corresponding to reality; if not, it is incorrect. In this way the map carries information about the world, much as a description does. Its correctness consists in some kind of correspondence with the object represented. Allow me a barbarous expression, 'correspondence correctness,' for this rather commonsensical property. A defender of Churchland might protest and claim that his views have been misinterpreted; the correctness of maps and photos is usually not called 'truth,' so Churchland is right after all in claiming that maps are simply not true.[1] Taken this way, however, the issue becomes one of terminology; no changes in epistemological norms, let alone a revolution, are needed to bring the correctness of reasoning with the help of maps into line with the usual ways of epistemic justification.[2]

The intuitive view, that messages in the visual medium are capable of correctness and informativeness, finds confirmation in the work done by psychologists on the processing of visual and verbal information. Psychologists routinely speak about information coded in pictures. An issue of *Memory and Cognition* contains a plethora of articles dedicated to the interaction between pictorial and verbal information; A typical statement runs as follows: 'The structure of language provides but a small set of propositions to encode the vast number of spatial relations that we can perceive. Thus to understand a situation that a speaker or a writer is conveying, the listener or reader must combine linguistic information with (perhaps metric) spatial information derived from pictures, the environment or memory' (Glenberg and McDaniel 1992, 458). The authors stress the relative ease and accuracy with which subjects switch from extracting information in a sentential medium to extracting it from the picture medium and vice versa. H. Taylor and B. Tversky (1992) investigated the two-way processes by letting one group of subjects draw a map after a description and another group describe the map (I am ruthlessly simplifying their sophisticated experimental design). The results of the two groups converged. The (educated) guess of the authors is that the similarity and convergence of the results derive from the similarity of the communicative goal.[3]

Now consider the neural maps, which represent various portions of an organism's sensory surfaces, or the distal environment and were discovered by sophisticated neuroscience.[4] Topographic representations within the cortex of proximal sensory surfaces – such as, for instance, the representation of a hand – can be found in nearly all sensory and motor areas within the brain, in the visual, auditory, and somatosensory fields, and in the motor cortex.[5] Some authors hypothesize that similar maps with more abstract features could play a role in higher processing. It is interesting to note that many maps are organized functionally, to bring together functionally close areas.[6] Churchland notes that these maps usually preserve not distances, but only neighbourhood relations (e.g., the image of a finger is a proper part of the image of the hand, etc.). This seems to imply that they are accurate about what is part of what and what is close to what: the map of the hand simply gives true information about fingers being parts of the hand. Obviously, such representations can be correct or incorrect in the usual sense.

Much more sophisticated are 'cognitive maps' of the distal environment. The best-known case is the spatial cognitive map hypothesized to reside in the nucleus called the hippocampus. One of its discoverers (or perhaps inventors?), John O'Keefe, describes the basic hypothesis in the following terms: 'The cognitive-map theory of hippocampal function postulates that the hippocampus and associated areas ... provide the rat with a spatial representation of its current environment. It locates the animal's position within the environment, and it contains the information that will allow it to calculate the behaviour necessary to move from its current location to a desired location (e.g., one containing a reward)' (1989, 225). This looks like any ordinary map, representing a given layout and containing information about it. Even more interesting is the issue of motivation: 'The motivation for building and modifying maps is a purely cognitive one. A mismatch system calculates disparities between the sensory input and the current stored representation of an environment. If the disparity is large enough ... exploration is triggered. Exploration is the systematic acquisition of information to build and modify maps' (ibid.).

The most spectacular maps are those for distant orientation. It is hypothesized that a migratory bird finds its way by first fixing its location within a coordinate map (Schoene 1984, chap. 2.8). The grid of the map may consist of 'two transecting gradient fields, which do not have to be at right angles to each other.' The gradients can be for instance odour gradients carried by the wind.[7] Gallistel in his monumental work (1990) has produced a wealth of similar examples, worked out in detail. He considers in particular, the cognitive maps in insects and the working of the 'geometric module' in the rat. He proposes a succinct definition: 'A cognitive map is a record in the central nervous system of macroscopic geometric relations among surfaces in the environment used to plan movements through the environment' (Gallistel 1990, 103). Churchland's own examples include sensory and motor maps in the crab's nervous system. He explains at some length how the coordination of movement is effected by simple superposition of the two maps (*NP*, 90 ff.). In the example the map is described as mapping the states of the retina, and it is claimed that the coordination is quite successful. Churchland routinely mentions maps 'mirroring some straightforward aspect of the physical world,' without noticing that this process introduces correspondence relations.

How about theories, Churchland's main area of interest? Pictures and diagrams are of great help in doing science and can code at least parts of theories. One can have a (true) theory without being able to couch it wholly in propositional terms. For example, Eudoxus's theory of proportions appealed to quantities that were algebraically inexpressible for him – only in geometrical representation did the theory make any sense. Still, his theory is as true as a mathematical theory might be, and this is not a small matter at all. Moreover, Galileo appeals to Eudoxus's representation – he finds it more reliable and perhaps is able to manipulate only this kind of representation with real virtuosity. Galileo's theory of free fall couched in these terms is considered to be nearly true, more true than its predecessors. Should we say that it was incapable of being true or false because it was not couched in the purely propositional medium?

James Robert Brown, a Canadian philosopher of science, has analysed various uses of pictures and diagrams in science (1991). One use is to capture the essentials of some interesting type of situation, for example, an artist's drawing of a situation in a Wilson chamber abstracts from irrelevancies (scratches on the photographs, etc.) and gives us a purified picture of the phenomenon itself. Brown even goes so far as to claim: 'Theories in high energy physics only try to cope with the phenomena as represented in the artist's drawing' (ibid., 8). Even more important is his analysis of proof through diagram. He concludes: 'Those who hesitate to accept the picture as a proof might think that the picture merely indicates the existence of a "real proof," a standard proof by mathematical induction ... But consider: would a picture of an equilateral triangle make us think there is a proof that all triangles are equilateral? No. Yet the above picture makes us believe – rationally believe – that there is a verbal/symbolic proof of the theorem. The picture is (at the very least) evidence for the existence of a "real proof" (if we like to talk that way), and the "real proof" is evidence for the theorem. But we have transitivity here; so the picture is evidence for the theorem, after all' (ibid., 4).

Psychologists H. Simon and J. Larkin have offered some explanations for the usefulness of diagrams for problem solving in science, in a paper with a telling title: 'Why a Diagram Is (Sometimes) Worth Ten Thousand Words' (1987). One reason for the usefulness might be that 'diagrammatic representations ... typically display information that is only implicit in sentential representations and that therefore has to be computed, sometimes at great cost, to make it explicit for use' (ibid., 65). The relevant information is about topological and geometric relations among the components of the problem to be solved, relations that are much more difficult to code sententially. Further, the diagrammatic information is 'indexed by location,' that is, all the data concerning the 'same spot' all presented at the spot itself. Therefore, when one location is attended to, all information at that location is given to the viewer, and the viewer can switch attention at will if directed by the current information to do so. They conclude: 'Therefore problem solving can proceed through a smooth traversal of the diagram, and may require very little search or computation of elements that had been implicit' (ibid.).

In relevant respects maps are similar to spatial mental models, which we briefly presented in the introductory chapter. Remember that the structure of mental models is not arbitrary, but plays a direct representational role, since it is analogous to the corresponding state of affairs in the world. A typical classification of models would distinguish simple static 'frames' representing relations between a set of objects, temporal models consisting of sequences of such frames, kinematic models that are temporal models with continuous time, and finally dynamic models that model causal relations. Several researchers have investigated reasoning in mental models (the best known is P.N. Johnson-Laird), and the following seems now established wisdom. Mental models are highly specific; they purport to represent concrete situations, with determinate objects and relations; their structure is not arbitrary, but 'plays a direct representational role since it is analogous to the corresponding state of affairs in the world' (Johnson-Laird 1983, 157). Reasoning in mental models demands rules for manipulation. Some constraints on manipulation come directly from the geometry of the model. It is essential that manipulation of elements mobilize the spatial skills of the subject, his 'knowledge how,' which generally is not verbalizable. Other constraints on manipulation concern the consistency and coherence of the model. Johnson-Laird hypothesizes the existence of general procedures that add new elements to the model, and 'a procedure that integrates two or more hitherto separated models if an assertion interrelates entities in them.' The integration of models is subject to consistency requirements: if the joint model is logically impossible, some change has to be made.

The point of building a mental model and working within it is to provide a medium that adequately represents the task and is convenient in being easily manipulable and 'mobilizing.' Let me quote:

The notion of *mental model* is central to our analysis of problem solving and induction. In common with many recent theoretical treatments, we believe that cognitive systems construct models of the problem space that are then mentally 'run' or manipulated to produce expectations about the environment. (Holland et al. 1986, 12; emphasis in text)

Although mental models are based in part on static prior knowledge, they are themselves transiently dynamic representations of particular unique situations ... mental models are the major source of inactive change in long-term knowledge structures. The reason is simple. Because mental models are built by integrating knowledge in novel ways to achieve the system's goals, model construction provides the opportunity for new ideas to arise by recombination and as a consequence of inductive model based prediction. (Ibid., 14)

The construction and use of models mobilize the everyday knowledge of the user. When you read a story beginning with 'Mary entered the room,' you suppose that the room has a door, that a person normally enters the room through its door, that she walks on the floor, not on the walls, and you use this knowledge in constructing your model of the situation. A very popular proposal about the microstructure of everyday knowledge is that it is stratified in a default hierarchy. The default rules with defeaters and alternatives, stratified into more and less readily accessible solutions, make up the default hierarchies.

The building of default hierarchies is usually presented as inductive learning, in a very broad sense of 'induction.' Alternatives are tried and rejected, rules (conditionals) are recombined and transformed, their 'credibility' being subject to empirical checking. In this way the finished default hierarchy embodies results of a long learning process. When a reasoner builds her model, she can use such stratified knowledge to reach swift and effortless cognitive decisions.

To summarize, mental models allow for reorganization of experiential knowledge, and the medium they provide can be heuristically superior to the purely verbal medium. There is no reason at all not to consider such models as hospitable to truth or to falsity. A kinematic model representing movement of an object is obviously truth-tolerant: if the object actually moves the way represented, the model is true; if not, it is false. For example, a kinematic mental model can represent the idealized behaviour of the pendulum and thereby represent ('depict') the classical theory of a pendulum. Both models – the theory and its mental 'portrait' – are empirically true about this chandelier if the chandelier behaves like the classical pendulum. Both models are icons, capable of being true or false. A mental model is true if it depicts a true theory.

Let us return to the main line of argument. Representation in a non-sentential medium can be correct or incorrect in the sense of correspondence correctness. Usually, correspondence correctness is the most useful dimension for the assessment of a map-like representation. It is structurally very much akin to the dimension of truth for sentences. Most important, for all epistemological purposes *the correspondence correctness is simply truth*: having a pictorial representation that correctly represents – under the relevant projection relation – the piece of reality it is meant to represent is simply *to know what the piece of reality is like*, and that is the right epistemic goal for the cognizer that is captured in the idea that truth is the goal of cognition.

Let me try to forestall some misunderstandings.[8] The semantic argument as applied to maps assumes that they are representations, that is, that they are produced – by nature or by people – in order to carry information and to guide their users. It is not only the fact that they carry information that counts for truth-hospitality, but also the fact that they are representations specifically meant to represent the environment. Further, although the understanding of maps can be tested by asking the subject to describe what is represented by a map, *the representational function and truth-hospitality of maps do not depend on any links with a verbal-sentential medium*. Maps are true or false independently, in virtue of the projection rules alone. A creature steering with the help of a map alone, without translating its content into sentences, is relying upon its reliability, that is, its property of representing things as they are, and this is the epistemologically most important point.

I have often heard the conjecture that projection rules are somehow more 'relativistic' than meaning-rules for language. I don't see why this should be the case, and I have never seen a convincing argument to this effect.

To this point we have considered relatively 'concrete' maps, diagrams, and models. Now, we have to discuss the truth-tolerance of more abstract, map-like representations, in terms of state-space. Consider our simplest example of the school physician, who represents the height and weight of n schoolchildren through time by a point P in $n + 1$ dimensional space. At a given moment, the state is represented only by this one point. It might seem that this fact gives some grist to the relativist-pragmatist's mill, and he may be tempted to argue as follows:

Being a point, *P* has no structure; it is an unstructured carrier of information. However, an unstructured representation cannot be true or false. Therefore, we have a (powerful) representational medium that is truth-intolerant.

The argument is wrong and its conclusion false. The blame should be placed upon the assumption that the carrier of information lacks structure. The carrier is not a point considered in isolation, but a point in the coordinate system, and the information is carried not by the intrinsic properties of the point, but by its position in the coordinate space. In our example, *P* has definite projections on the *x*- and *y*-axis, which stand for John's height and Mary's height.[9] This position bestows upon the point a host of relational properties, which guarantees the availability of the structure.[10]

Please notice that we do not need to appeal to the Semantic Argument or the Argument from Disposition. State-space representations are directly translatable into the sentential format, coordinate by coordinate, and this is largely without the indirect evidence provided by the two arguments. Let me generalize the conclusion:

State-space is in principle truth-tolerant. Minimally, the projections of the state-representation onto the coordinate axes carry propositional information capturable also by statements detailing the value of the state along the dimension projected upon. If such statements are truth-tolerant – and they obviously are – then the whole state-space representation is also truth-tolerant.

Consider now Churchland's stance. Churchland mentions, as one example of a state-space map, a map that represents colour features by distinguishing wavelength properties along three dimensions. A given patch of uniform colour will then be represented by a point in such a three-dimensional state-space. Similarity between colours is reflected as similarity between representation-points (*NP*, 103). Assuming that colours – or the corresponding surface or light properties – are represented, not invented, by the organism, the abstract state-space map 'reflects' the reality of colours. The arguments in favour of truth-tolerance mentioned above also apply here.

We have already seen that state-space representations are truth-tolerant. State-space maps and, in particular, state-space neural maps are then also truth-tolerant. A point in a state-space map projects on any given coordinate, and the value of its projection is the value ascribed to the relevant parameter.[11] Churchland himself comes close to confessing that these maps are truth tolerant: 'Consider first the abstract three-dimensional "colour cube" ... Each axis represents the eye-brain's reconstruction of the *objective* reflectance of the seen object at one of the three wavelengths to which our cones are selectively responsive' (*NP*, 103; emphasis in the text). The representation here is not just a coding of the state of the retina, but represents objective features: reflectance of the object. Such a description implies a positive answer to our question: a representation of an objective feature either matches this feature or does not. Churchland is very much impressed by the accuracy of discriminations that such state-space representations allow: 'the variety of discriminable smell sensations is larger still [than the variety of taste sensations]. Such variation reminds us further of the presumed variation across species, as instanced in the canine's extraordinary ability to discriminate, by smell alone, any one of the 3.5 billion people on the planet' (ibid.). The remainder of the story praises the systems' representational capacities. Churchland describes them as 'prodigious' (ibid., 109), and downplays sentential representations as arbitrary projections of deep, global information coded in state-space representations. I assume that Churchland himself is aware, in his more scientific moments, that 'prodigious representational powers' also do involve accuracy as an important virtue, and that accuracy concerns the way the exemplification of objective features (such as reflectance of colours or the really distinct, specific smells of individuals) is represented. Such an 'accuracy' in representing the exemplification of objective features, however, is simply another name for truth.

We are ready for an important step. First, remember the mathematical example in Brown's paper (1991). It is particularly valuable, since it shows that diagrams can stand in inferential (or at least quasi-inferential) relation to other cognitive states. Consider, now, the cognitive state of the person who 'accepts' the diagram as a true representation of the world. The state is exactly like 'sentential' belief, except that the sentential representation is replaced by a diagrammatical representation. The state stands in the right kind of relation to the outside world, to its *w*-proposition. But a person having an appropriate attitude to *w*-propositions is in a belief-like state. Most important, such a belief-like state can be true or false. A belief-like attitude to a *w*-proposition with the suitable functional role is simply a belief, or is simply a belief as far as the purpose of the epistemologist goes. What about the

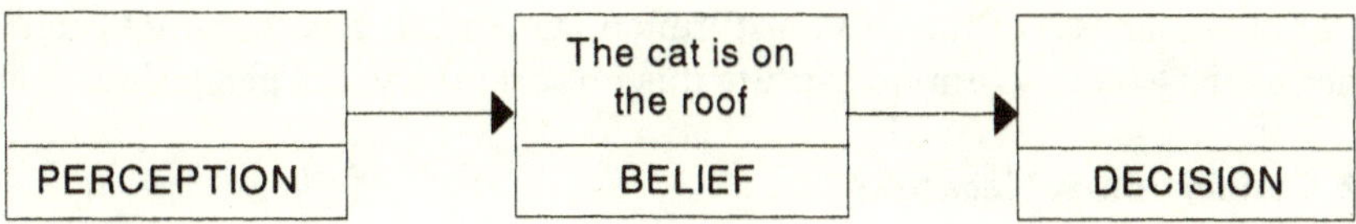

FIGURE 5.2
The belief box

appropriate functional role? The state of accepting the diagram is linked to perceptual stimuli and to action and seems capable of standing in inferential (or quasi-inferential) relation to other cognitive states.[12]

Let me abbreviate 'sentential-belief' as *s*-belief. A creature that steers through its environment by activating a non-propositional cognitive map is, in many respects, similar to the creature who does the same by activating a propositional data structure. If we are prepared to ascribe primitive-beliefs to the latter, we should ascribe a primitive belief-like state, call it *m*-belief ('*m*' stands for 'map,' not for 'murder') to the former. Take your favourite theory about the functional role of primitive *s*-beliefs. This theory will define an *s*-belief-box for you. Now, imagine a box that is functionally analogous to an *s*-box, differing only in its use of a non-propositional representational medium. Inputs and outputs will have to be differently 'phrased' (or drawn), but the global functional architecture should be the same. That box is an *m*-box. The creature stands in relation to the contents of its *m*-box in an attitude analogous to *s*-believing. Figure 5.2 demonstrates belief-boxes.

It is a technical question within cognitive psychology whether we have genuinely spatial representations (as the reader might have guessed, I am inclined to the affirmative answer). Of course our relativist-pragmatist opponent not only accepts that we have them, but is quite enthusiastic about them. One may wonder how one can be sure that the *m*-belief-box will be able to perform a role comparable, or even sufficiently similar, to that of the *s*-belief-box. The neurologists tell us that non-propositional cognitive maps are both powerful and ubiquitous and propose detailed theories of how they mediate inputs and outputs at the primitive level we are concerned with (Gallistel 1990). Non-sententialists are usually so busy stressing the contrast between sentential and non-sentential representations, that they overlook the similarity (if not sameness) of their (widest) functional role. It has therefore been necessary to coin a term to capture this important level of generality.

2. Connectionist Networks

2.1. The Form of Connectionist Representation

Maps are only a warm-up; the real paradigm for the relativist-pragmatist is connectionist networks. Churchland claims that with connectionism, 'a new door has opened in normative epistemology' (1992a, 361). In this section I shall consider connectionist networks, and their features.

Let us start with Churchland's favourite example of a connectionist system, the mine detecting network. Churchland praises this network and a related one called NET: 'both networks have contrived a system of internal representations that truly corresponds to important distinctions and structures in the outside world, structures that are not explicitly represented in the corpus of their sensory inputs. The value of these representations is that they and only they allow the networks to "make sense" of their variegated and often noisy input corpus, in the sense that they and only they allow the network to respond to those inputs in a fashion that systematically reduces the error messages to a trickle' (*NP*, 177). Note that Churchland is praising the internal representations for 'truly correspond[ing]' to the structures of the outside world (praise unexpected from someone who does not find truth important, or internal representations truth-tolerant). Remember the properties of connectionist items that play the crucial role in the debate: they are specific representations beneath the level of sentential or propositional attitudes; thus, their distributed character and holistic nature. Finally, recall the instability: the readiness of the network to modify its output according to the context of the input.

How do networks represent reality? Churchland's view is that connectionist systems typically learn 'dependence patterns,' by coding them in holistic ways. People, being connectionist machines, are particularly good at activating patterns of the kinds listed, he claims. What is a 'dependence pattern'? In stead of a general definition, Churchland lists several general types of such patterns, which he further characterizes as 'prototypes' (we shall discuss this characterization later) – property-cluster patterns consisting of 'typically co-occurrent properties,' etiological patterns depicting 'a typical temporal sequence of event types,' practical patterns coding 'complex means-end relations,' superordinate patterns used in mathematical reasoning, social-interaction patterns, and, finally, motivational patterns coding folk-psychology (*NP*, 212). All kinds of knowledge are supposed to be coded in dependence prototypes. This leads Churchland to the idea of a super-network, representing the relevant features (model) of a big domain and its associated state-space. A point in such a state-space codes the network's knowledge about the domain. In a case where the knowledge is systematic enough, the point will stand for a whole theory. Churchland believes, as we might have expected, that the possibility of such coding of theories introduces spectacular changes in epistemology: 'What we are confronting here is a possible conception of knowledge or understanding that owes nothing to the sentential categories of current common sense. An individual's overall theory-of-the world, we might venture, is not a large collection or a long list of stored symbolic items. Rather, it is a specific point in that individual's synaptic weight space. It is a configuration of connection weights, a configuration that partitions the system's activation vector space(s) into useful divisions and subdivisions relative to inputs typically fed the system. "Useful" here means "tends to minimize the error message"' (*NP*, 177).

The system could represent hundreds of weights in a hundreds-dimensional coordinate system, with one coordinate added for the error-success dimension. Such a system might be capable of sophisticated learning. Churchland thinks that such systems actually are embodied in our heads. Our folk-notions of belief barely scratch the surface of the actual representational powers of our brain: 'a specific image or belief is just an arbitrary projection or "slice" of a deeper set of data structures, and the collective coherence of such a sample slice is a simple consequence of the manner in which the global information is stored at the deeper level. It is not a consequence of, for example, the busywork of some fussy inductive machine applying inductive rules for the acceptance or rejection of discrete slices taken singly. Which means that, to understand learning, we may have to understand the forces that dictate directly the evolution of global data structures at the deeper level' (*NP*, 109). This idea might encourage a further step. As philosophers, we might extrapolate to a kind of super-process of learning, and think of the growth of human knowledge in terms of its state-space representation. What would be the goal of such a process? The best thing to hope for would be a global error minimum, optimally a point in a zero-error plane. Such a point would represent the most reliable combination of weights. Although Churchland is quite optimistic about the performance of networks in particular cases, he is pessimistic about the attainability of such a global error minimum:

> For one thing nothing guarantees that we humans will avoid getting permanently stuck in some very deep but relatively local error minimum. For another, nothing guarantees that there exists a possible configuration of weights that would reduce the error messages to *zero* ... And for a third thing, nothing guarantees that there is only *one* global minimum. Perhaps there will in general be many quite different minima, all of them equally low in error, all of them carving up the world in quite different ways ... These considerations seem to remove the goal itself – a unique truth – as well as any sure means of getting there. Which suggests that the proper course to pursue in epistemology lies in the direction of a highly naturalistic and pluralistic form of pragmatism. (*NP*, 194; emphasis in text)

We are invited to imagine the network attempting to minimize the tension between various constraints (given by the input and by the distribution of weights), and finding a path that is appealing but misleading. Like a shortsighted hill climber descending from a mountain, who is simply following the line of steepest descent, the path can end in a hole (local minimum) instead of reaching the foot of the mountain (the global minimum). Churchland here makes some very quick steps to a very strong conclusion. Starting from the premise that nothing guarantees the availability of global truth, he concludes that truth in general is unattainable, and from this that truth is not the proper goal of cognition. Not only is truth unimportant, consistency and coherence also should be jettisoned: 'A new door has opened in normative epistemology, and it concerns the comparative virtues and capabilities of alternative learning algorithms, algorithms aimed not at adjusting sets of propositions so as to meet certain criteria of consistency and coherence, but aimed rather at adjusting iterated populations of synaptic weights so as to approximate certain input-output functions or certain dynamic behaviours' (1992a, 361).

Churchland lists several 'Feyerabendian themes' that he sees re-emerging in neurocomputational form. Four of them are directly relevant for the issue of relativism, and the fifth is the eliminability of folk-psychology:

1. The inseparability of perception from knowledge or observation from theory.

2. The incommensurability of theories: given the vast dimensionality of the activation space of our brain, we may assume that it supports a vast system of similarity gradients. Possible configurations within this space are the actual mentally represented theories, and they are mutually incommensurable: 'But there is not a reason in the world to think that there is any such relation that unites the vast diversity of frameworks: not in their internal structure, or in their relations to the external world, or in the input-output functions they sustain. On the contrary, they are all in competition with one another, in the sense that they are mutually incompatible configurations of the same activation vector space' (1992a, 357).
3. The need for proliferation of theories: since the global error minimum is unattainable, and since various local minima can block initially promising paths, learning in networks should start from multiple and diverse starting points, 'in the attempt to find a descending path toward a genuinely global error minimum' (ibid., 360).
4. The need for proliferating methodologies, that is, learning algorithms. Regardless of coherence, consistency, and truth, one should explore diverse learning algorithms: 'the alternatives are certainly there and we will not appreciate their virtues unless we explore them.' The goal of exploration is to 'find those learning algorithms that make the system 'approximate certain input-output functions or certain dynamical behaviours' (ibid., 361).
5. Connectionism gives support to eliminative materialism in the philosophy of psychology – the doctrine holding that our commonsensical or folk theories about ourselves are radically false and should be replaced by neurological theories, couched in terms completely different from the common ones. Notions like 'belief,' 'memory,' or 'intention' are empty and will become obsolete, replaced by neurological terms that will have nothing in common with our commonsensical scheme of self-understanding.

We address (1) in the appendix, and leave (5) aside. The three remaining themes, (2)–(4), are centred around the issues of descriptive and normative pluralism. Their cogency depends heavily on the issues of representation and truth. For instance, the incommensurability thesis (2) is premised on two assumptions: first, that configurations can be incommensurable regardless of their truth-hospitality; and, second, that representational relations to the world do not constrain the choice of configurations to be realized in the brains of cognizers.[13] The appeal to the proliferation of theories (3) in order to reach 'a truly global error minimum' depends on what 'error' means outside the context of truth and falsity. Finally, the appeal to explore alternative methodologies (4) demands a clarification of the point of exploring them: how are they to be compared, what are the 'input-output functions or certain dynamical behaviours' that should be approximated by the cognizer, and what do we want them for if not to tell us what the world is like?

This brings me to the main topics. After the brief overview of Churchland's views on connectionism we can better judge their rationale and the cogency of the idea that connectionist representation precludes truth, consistency, and coherence. I shall divide what follows into three parts. In the first part I shall discuss the truth-tolerance of connectionist systems and processes. In the second part I shall discuss the contents of connectionist representations and their relation to truth/falsity. In the third part I shall tackle the issue of epistemological evaluation of connectionist items.

2.2. *Representation and Truth*

Churchland's official position is that connectionist representations are not truth-tolerant, this being an important, even revolutionary, feature. Sometimes he seems to endorse the opposite view, for instance, when he praises networks for their ability to learn representations that truly correspond to structures in the outside world. On these rarer occasions he seems to contradict his considered judgment, but I shall try to argue that he must do so, on pain of misrepresenting the facts about networks.

Let me note at the outset that I am conceding to Churchland much more than the rationalist would be obliged to do. I concede to him, first, that connectionist systems can represent, learn, manipulate, and even discover theories; and, second, that by doing so the connectionist processing remains *sui generis* and does not collapse into the mere implementation of classical processing. My motivation in conceding the two assumptions is to learn something on the positive side: if connectionist systems are as powerful as Churchland takes them to be, what are the epistemological consequences?

By the first concession I overlook the evidence pointing to the limitations of network capacities: networks are much better in pattern recognition and similar tasks than in manipulating abstract information. They model superbly the perceptual and action-guiding abilities of the nervous system, but they make dramatic mistakes in elementary arithmetic and parsing. Perhaps this is merely the infant stage in the development of the artificial networks; perhaps it is a deep handicap derived from insensitivity to structure, which I mentioned when introducing networks (see chap. 1, 2.4, above).

By the second concession we turn a blind eye to the difficulties in combining the two aims: preserving the peculiarities of connectionist processing and enabling networks to handle syntactically complex data. Some recursive strategies handle complexity well, but they bring connectionist processing too close to the classical one to make it relevant for the Churchlandian agenda. Others preserve its specificity, but at the cost of power. An important line of criticism, initiated by J. Fodor and Z. Pylyshyn and continued by G. Rey, B.P. McLaughlin, and others, insists that the difficulty is insuperable.[14] Other prominent philosophers, for example, A. Clark, T. Horgan, and J. Tienson, argue for a middle way, much more truth-hospitable than Churchland could consistently accept.[15] Paul Churchland himself does not address the difficulties in his published work, and even if one takes into account the cognate endeavours of Patricia Churchland, it is hard to cobble together a coherent picture of the Churchlandian response to them.

In what follows I shall ignore most of these difficulties of Churchland's project and grant him his most problematic factual assumption, that connectionist networks have specific means, powerful enough to handle advanced scientific theories. I shall first rehearse our earlier general arguments, applying them to connectionist networks, and then proceed to more specific arguments, tailor-made for the networks (in chapter 6 I shall discuss in more detail the semantic issues).

It is a part of the framework of the discussion that configurations in the connectionist network are representations. The assumption generally is not thought to be problematic, and in the context of Churchland's views it is clearly accepted. The scientists freely talk about distributed representations (of course, 'distributed' is nothing like 'alleged' or 'fake'), and Churchland enthusiastically praises the 'prodigious representational and computational capacities' of the networks. More important, his own description of the learning process draws heavily upon realistically construed notions of error and success. Remember the mine/rock-network, which learns by backpropagation. The input is *actual profiles* of mine-echoes and rock-echoes. The output is then tested for its accuracy and 'what interests us in each case is the amount by which the actual output vector *differs* from what would have been the correct vector, given the identity of the specific echo that produced it' (*NP*, 166; emphasis in text).

Further teaching weeds out the sources of discrepancy from the correct answer: 'the idea is to identify those weights most responsible for the error' and change them. Global correctness results from such steps. In Churchland's description itself it is shown how the representation can become increasingly global, still preserving the causal powers of the original one. In assessing the performance and the causal powers of the network and its patterns Churchland himself and the connectionist researchers talk about error and success, not only to characterize the performance of networks, but to characterize what the system has learned (e.g., 'my system has learned the correct pattern in ten of billions of attempts'). Most important, their vocabulary of 'error,' 'correctness,' 'match,' is vital for their assessment of the systems they build and study, and there is no indication that it has changed its meaning or become metaphorical. Remember that for Churchland himself, when he describes the learning done by a connectionist system, the appeal to correctness provides the purpose of the description. The system is designed to move 'down the error gradient,' in other words, to make fewer and fewer errors and come closer to a steady state, which should be as error free as feasible.

On the one hand, Churchland claims that learning algorithms should not maximize truth but 'approximate certain input-output functions'; on the other, his vocabulary of representation and error comes very close to the truth-dimension. Consider the mine detector. What is 'the correct vector, given the identity of the specific echo that produced it'? If the echo is produced by a mine, the correct vector is 'Mine.' So the input-output function is simply the function that for mine-like input gets the correct output, namely, 'Mine.' Here, the correctness is straightforward truth. Learning consists in coming closer to truth and avoiding falsity.

Churchland attempts to specify what error consists in without appealing to the notion of falsity (*NP,* 220ff). Suppose, he says, that we have a well-trained network with prototype vectors of some 'integrity.' Take two of them, *A* and *B*. Now, the network can misjudge the situation, and activate *A* when *A* is inappropriate. For example, a coyote, upon noticing 'a small tapered appendage disappearing into a tuft of long grass,' might activate its prototype of retreating desert rat (*A*), when the item is the tail of a poisonous snake. Now, the coyote's activation of *A* is wrong, but we should not assume that this is because the rat prototype falsely represents the snake-situation. Churchland takes a very complicated line about the wrongness of the activation of *A*: 'It may be wrong because the situation confronted is not a member of the class of situations that will reliably activate A from almost any perspective, even though it happened to activate A on this occasion' (ibid., 220); and 'It can occur if the agent apprehended only a misleading part of the problematic situation, a part that led to the activation of A because that unusual part was relevantly similar to A's typical activators' (ibid., 221). This is Churchland's only pronouncement as to what it means for an activation to be wrong and to misrepresent the situation (and there is no explicit story about being right). As an account of what it is for a network to go wrong, it is not much to go by. The appeal to 'almost any perspective' and to the 'low input ambiguity' ties the account to the cases of perceptual error, leaving no place for errors in theory-building, the most relevant ones in the epistemology of science. The use of the term 'misleading' is usually tied to falsity: an item is misleading if it typically prompts a false belief, so Churchland owes us an explanation of what else 'misleading' could mean.[16] (One might be tempted to claim that error is what well-trained networks do not commit. Unfortunately, since the only description available of training and of being well trained is couched in terms of decreasing error, the specification is not independent of previous understanding of the notion of 'error,' and all the examples point to the assumption that error is plain falsity and its absence simple truth.)

Finally, let me address one possible line of defence suggested to me by an anonymous referee, whose query I paraphrase here:

Query: First, the phrase 'error signal' in connectionist parlance is used to indicate the difference between an actual output and an output desired by the researcher and carries no normative epistemic force. Second, in living systems the error signal is not measured against truth, but against just another signal that somehow serves the organism better to achieve its current goals.

Answer: Notice that this is *not* Churchland's line. As for the first point, his examples of error signals are examples of genuine epistemic error, and also his examples of correctness are examples of genuine correspondence with the structures of the outside world. As for the second point, he is not arguing from the assumption that truth is not useful, and he does not address or mention the issue at all. He is arguing from the view that truth is not available as the property of representations. Further, and more generally, the connectionist talk of error does not reduce to mentioning 'error signal': connectionists are interested in how well their systems reconstruct actual patterns and how they guess at actual structures underlying the input (e.g., phonological or syntactic structure of English sentences), and they take error to consist in a mismatch with such target items. In such talk, error is a lack of fit to the given 'piece of reality,' in a most classical sense. Further, it is something to be avoided, and that is normative enough for the purpose of a truth-centred normative epistemology. End of the answer.

In order to understand how a non-sentential representation in the mind/brain can be truth-tolerant, I revert to the Semantic Argument. It is a truism that any representation represents its representatum and carries information about it. This should hold for connectionist patterns as for any other representation purporting to carry information about the world. (One may liken the pattern to a map, e.g., the map of the United States with which we started. Maybe, more information is coded in the pattern than in any pair of sentences, but such is the case with the map. The information is coded holistically in both cases. Most important, they exhibit the same pattern of right/wrong response).

Churchland's interest in the representations of theories adds a particular touch to the general idea. Theory-building deals with representations that aim to represent the world. Any such representation either succeeds in doing it, by representing things the way they are, or fails. Churchland is well aware of this fact, and in the text we quoted he comments on the performance of two relatively simple networks, saying that it 'truly corresponds to important distinctions and structures in the outside world' (*NP*, 177). Also, he is in no position to advocate the view that scientists should not be interested in what the world, including its unobservable portion, is like, given his staunch anti-instrumentalist stance. But a representation 'corresponding to important distinctions and structures in the outside world' is either true or false. Then theories do have truth value. The revisionist could, of course, claim that his idea of representation is a non-standard one, that representation in his sense does not really represent, but this is not Churchland's line.

Sometimes, the representational processes are entirely opaque (I discuss the opacity below). In these cases I fall back on the Argument from Disposition. Remember that the Argument is very global – whatever produced a true theory has the 'disposition towards truth' it claims, so it can be applied to connectionist representation: the representation of a theory in the brain (pattern or data-structure) must account for the verbally represented theories. Now, the latter are true or false; their neural/mental ancestor is, then, either true or false, or can be judged along the truth dimension indirectly, as having a stable disposition to produce true or false sentences. Further, if sentences in the written book correspond to a 'slice in the state space' of the network, then this slice is truth-tolerant if and only if the sentences are. The assumption that the whole state-space has many other qualities as well, and that the slices do not exhaust them, does not militate against the minimal demand that at least 'slices' are truth-tolerant and can be assessed accordingly. Finally, if the representation in the brain has no connection with truth, it is useless for the explanation of how humans manage to produce true verbal theories and therefore is uninteresting for the methodology and epistemology of science.

In this subsection I have presented a general overview of the two strategies. Now I proceed to apply them to the particular features of networks.

2.3. *Cognitive Peculiarities*

What are the special characteristics of connectionist networks, which may seem to entail the truth-intolerance of connectionist representations? The obvious candidate characteristics are those cognitive peculiarities listed in chapter 1, 2.4.2:

a. Non-sentential character
b. Distributed character
c. Holism
d. Prototypicality
e. Context-dependence and variability
f. The essentially practical character of 'knowledge.'

Taken together, these characteristics suggest a certain opacity of the connectionist structure: one cannot read the semantics off the syntax. I have in the general discussion shown the unimportance of (a), so I shall treat (a) together with (b) here, not reserving for it any special section. Prototypicality (d) is a semantic feature, so I reserve for it the whole of the next chapter. Here I concentrate on (a) together with (b), (c), (e), and (f).

2.3.1. The Distributed and Holistic Character of Representations

We can picture the relativist arguing in the following way for truth-intolerance: 'The connectionist representation is distributed, non-local and holistic. For example, the item representing the planet Venus does so only in the context of the whole system – it has no isolated meaning.

Moreover, some representations cannot be broken down into smaller significant units: the meaning resides only in the representation as whole.' A general answer would question the relevance of holism. There are two distinct issues. First, how does a system *S* get its meaning or representational content? Second, once *S* has meaning or content, is it true or false? How an item acquires its meaning is irrelevant to the issue of whether what the item means is true or not. (An extreme example might be the following. Suppose that a dot '·', by some crazy convention, stands in some code for the General Theory of Relativity. Then, drawing the dot during a debate going on in the code commits one to the truth of General Relativity. The ultra-holistic character of the representation does not absolve one from responsibility.) The compatibility of holism about semantics with a truth-oriented semantic theory has been a commonplace in analytical philosophy in the tradition of Quine and Davidson. Churchland enthusiastically agrees that distributed and holistic representations have meaning, and code for theories. Therefore, nothing should preclude the possibility that some of them are true.

On the more concrete level, the danger is even smaller. To start with a peripheral issue, the specific nature of a mathematical model of distributed representation does not in itself represent an obstacle for truth-valuation. Churchland discusses two ways of modelling distributed 'theories': as points in the weight space or as partitions of a hidden-unit vector-space. Of course, both can be assessed for their goodness-of-fit to the items represented by 'theories.' Also, the state-space model preserves truth-tolerance (if the theory modelled is truth-tolerant, usually, so is its correct state-space representation). Vectorial representations are used in physics and in econometrics to code true or false information, which often also can be coded in sentential-propositional fashion. (Prices of various items in a given currency on a market are represented as vectors. One can perform the requisite operations on them, e.g., multiply them by a scalar, say, by two, if the value of money halves overnight.) The use of vectors enables one not only to code propositional information that one already has, but also to derive new propositional information. In physics, all the way into the quantum-mechanical formalism, vector spaces enable one to do the same thing. Thus, it is well known that there is nothing in the nature of abstract spaces (vector-spaces, state-spaces) that would preclude the information coded with their help from being accurate or non-accurate, more probable or less probable, true or false.

In passing from mathematical models to networks themselves,

remember the classification of various pairings of network features and semantic features in chapter 1, 2.4.2. Let us briefly review them.

Type (1): activation pattern = concept; single unit = microfeature. The example was the concept 'room,' as represented by the pattern of activation of units standing for features like 'bed' (an excitatory link to 'sofa' and 'floor'), or 'sink' (a negative, inhibitory link to the same items). The pattern is holistic, and its single 'concepts' of room and of bed are not freely usable in other contexts. They are assembled on the spot from subsymbolic feature-representations, when the system is suitably prompted, and only then. The causal powers of the pattern are such, however, that it gives the right answer when prompted. The 'knowledge' coded by the network is unproblematic: the network 'knows' that rooms typically contain beds or sofas, and its knowledge is not only true, but transparent in its structure.

Type (2): activation pattern = concept; single unit uninterpretable. The example is the mine/rock detector. One should distinguish between the activated state and the dormant one. In the activated state the network represents a state of affairs as being such that this particular item is a mine (alternatively, a rock), and I have already noted why the activated state is truth-tolerant. Its dormant state admits of a more direct and of a less direct interpretation. The later appeals to the Argument from Disposition: the dormant configuration that enables the network consistently to give true output, codes for a quasi-theory (Churchland would say simply 'theory') that is dispositionally true. The more direct interpretation views the dormant configuration as coding for an implicit theory about mines, which either captures their characteristics and is then true, or does not and is then false.

Type (3): activation pattern = proposition; single unit uninterpretable. The activation pattern by stipulation is here truth-tolerant. The dormant configuration has no direct semantic interpretation. Notice that in this sense it also *does not code for a theory.* It is interpretable dispositionally, however, and in that sense is truth-hospitable.

Ramsey, Stich, and Garon (1990, 519) have pointed out some problems for dispositional interpretations, which concern individuating beliefs. Since the dormant state is not directly semantically interpretable, there is no telling which particular feature of the configuration produces a given response, that is, no telling which 'dormant belief' has led to the response. To use their example, when Clouseau says that the butler did it, commonsensical psychology assumes that there are distinct ways in which he could have come to the conclusion, starting from distinct stored belief (that the hotel is closed, that the train is out of service). Since such items are individuated and recognizable only when the network is activated on the particular issue ('Is the hotel closed?'), not in the dormant configuration, nor when some other issue is being decided, they are simply not available as the distinct ancestry of the activation corresponding to 'The butler did it.' Important as the problem might be, it is not relevant for the discussion here. Our Churchlandian has started with the assumption that dormant states do code for theories. He is in no position to scoff at the dispositional interpretation if he abides by this crucial tenet. He cannot reject the dispositionalist ascription of truth as being unserious or Pickwickian, since he himself needs the dispositionalist standards in order to ascribe the theory to the network. To spell it out fully, if our ascription of truth to the dormant configuration – on the grounds of its disposition to enter the right activation state – is unserious, so must be his insistence on ascribing the possession of the theory to the dormant configuration on the same ground, its disposition to enter the right activation state.

The impression is strengthened by the relative success of cluster analysis. It does manage to capture some of the informational structure of the hidden units. Moreover, it is interesting that the analysis follows the pattern of what I have called the Dispositional Argument. One kind of analysis groups those hidden units that are most responsible for a given output: in our terminology, it detects their propensity to give rise to the output (compare Hanson and Burr 1990). Another kind takes the reverse direction and identifies clusters similarly activated by a given input, thus detecting the propensity to react to the input.

Churchland is no friend of cluster analysis; he thinks that clusters have no causal power, and that all the causal power resides in microstructure. This viewpoint, however, sits ill with the Relevance Thesis: if the stored theories explain the practices of scientists (including their talk and writing), then some representation of theories must have enough causal power to figure in the right explanation.

Therefore, the holistic character of representation enters the picture elsewhere. It accounts for the particular pattern of strength and weakness of connectionist systems (being bad at symbolic reasoning, good at pattern recognition etc.). Being good or bad at a cognitive task, however, is most often linked to the correctness or to the error rate of the performance and is hardly separable from the assessment along the true-false dimension.

Type (4): series of activation patterns = proposition; activation pattern = concept; single unit uninterpretable. The meaning of the activation pattern is highly context dependent. In the simple networks alluded to by Ramsey the propositions expressed are relativized to the content, for example, 'THE APPLE (as-edible-fruit) IS HEALTHY (-for-humans).' Once the context is fixed, they obviously are truth-hospitable. The situation with the dormant state of the simple kind-four network is not, in principle, different from the one with the kind-three network, but the dispositional ascription should take the context into account.

This is the most difficult case for everyone interested, including Churchland. How does such a network code for scientific theories, invariant with respect to a wide range of contexts? For example, how does it code for the idea that momentum as such, not momentum-of-metal-bodies, not momentum-of-falling-stones, is proportional (absolutely) to the velocity, not only to the velocity-of-my-car, or to the velocity-of-his-airplane? It must develop some less relative way of coding if it is to serve the purpose Churchland is interested in; only then will it be capable of expressing propositions that are true or false in a less relative sense.

Therefore, the right type of kind-four network for coding theories seems to be sophisticated networks of the kind investigated by Shastri and Ajjanagadde (1993) (see chap. 1). Such networks, however, exhibit rich conceptual and semantical propositional structure and are described by their creators as coding for complex 'facts,' so that the relativist-pragmatist can find there no support for his theses.

Our discussion would end here but for one possibility. The relativist-pragmatist can try to strengthen his objection by appealing to eliminativism and arguing that the holistic representation does not carry any determinate content (along the lines of the radical proposal by Ramsey, Stich, and Garon 1990).[17] If it is not the representation that enables the system to output the theorems of some theory, then the system has not represented the theory, contrary to the initial relativist's assumption. Let us consider the issue in more detail. The eliminativists claim that there are no representations in connectionist systems: the relevant activation values are simply continuously varying magnitudes of activation and are not syntactically structured representations (compare Hatfield 1991, 95; Graham 1991). They argue that the appeal to representations within the system does no explanatory work, since they are not structured, causally efficacious carriers of semantic content. Take, for instance, some weight configuration *M*, which mediates between a representational input and representational output and is sometimes said to 'represent the distributed knowledge stored in the system.' W. Ramsey (1994) has argued in the same vein that internal configurations simply transform the input into the output, in way as devoid of representations as the way our digestive system transforms food. He claims that one can call states of the digestive system 'representations,' but calling them so does not explain what they do. Analogously, calling the internal configuration 'representation' does not add anything to our understanding of the functioning of the system. Here is the application of the view to the current issue:

Relativist: The problem arises only for a weak-kneed pragmatist, who wants simultaneously to have identifiable cognitive substructures in the head and to eliminate the notion of truth from the cognitive enterprise. However, let me opt for a radical variant of holism: there is no identifiable theory-encoding substructure in the head; all I have is the global state of the neural network and its outputs. The system does not, in fact, store theories. It behaves as if it had stored a theory, in the sense that it derives valid predictions from the observational input. What there is is a grey box with units and links, but no contours of a stored theory.

Answer: This line is self-defeating. Remember that Churchland wants to give a psychology-based account of theories and theorizing. He is committed to the Relevance Thesis, which says that internal cognitive processes are not only causally efficacious, but can also serve to explain the internal dynamics of scientific theories. (The appeal to such processes should help us to understand why, e.g., Ptolemy decided to neglect some of the astronomical evidence he had – if the story is indeed true; why Euclid preferred to put his mathematics into an axiomatic instead of a procedural form; why Maxwell changed his opinions about ether, etc.) The Relevance Thesis forces the relativist-pragmatist to admit (even to postulate) the existence of some entity in the mind-brain that corresponds to theories-in-the-book in such a way that the entity can account for theory-change. The mere 'passing of activation values' does not give him the right explanatory level, the one at which the entity becomes visible. The only level he can appeal to is some kind of representational level, which commits him to the view that there are neurally/mentally represented theories and that they produce and explain the sentential theories-in-the-book. If he accepted the radical view, he would be left with no identifiable neurally/mentally represented theories, that is, with nothing to do the explanatory work. If there is no meaning (content) to the states of mind-brain, then there are no theories of any kind, and there is no science to teach us *all this*. Alternatively, he can retreat to square-one accepting that the only science left is theories-in-the-book, and they certainly are sets of sentences. Then Churchland's sentential view of truth would apply: if theories are merely sentences, then the ultimate virtue of the theory is truth. The radical loses. End of the answer.

Let me finally (and only briefly) mention a thoroughly instrumentalist line claiming that one does not need any kind of theory; one needs only input-output correlation. Instrumentalist line is not available to Churchland himself. He is anti-instrumentalist in regard to theories, and he believes that theories are what they purport to be – descriptions of unobserved reality (which can, in principle, become observable; see the appendix). A system that has learned a theory has not simply established the relevant input-output equivalences; it has learned the theory as it stands. If the theory does not mediate between the input and the output, then the system has not stored the theory and does not qualify for epistemological assessment.[18] Let us take stock. Of four kinds of distributed representations, three are straightforwardly friendly to the truth-dimension: all the activation states are truth-tolerant, and the dormant configurations have standing dispositions for truth-tolerant activation. For two among the three a direct truth-oriented interpretation of their dormant configurations is possible. In these three cases the rationalist is right, while the fourth case is equally problematic for both Churchland and the rationalist and cannot decide between them.

2.3.2. Instability and Context Dependence

Beliefs are supposed to be relatively stable and context invariant. Some connectionist representations lack both characteristics. Ramsey, Stich, and Garon (1990) have explored the instability and context-dependence of connectionist representations of type (3): activation pattern = proposition; single unit uninterpretable. A relativist might try to exploit their ideas to buttress the thesis that networks are truth-intolerant.

Relativist: The connectionist representation is unstable. (as mentioned in chapter 1, 2.4). If prompted with a vector A it gives one kind of answer, if prompted with another, B, it might give an incompatible answer. So, there is no firm belief that the network 'holds,' nothing is to be assessed for its truth.

Answer: Note that instability alone does not preclude truth. An opinion held for a brief period is as true or false as a long-standing one. Therefore, the activation patterns are in the clear; they express truth-hospitable contents. Further, even if instability does threaten the identification of dormant representations, this is irrelevant for the debate. The idea that connectionist representations are inherently unstable is contrary to the initial assumption that the network is capable of learning definite theories, prototypes of 'some integrity' in Churchland's words, and of settling in a state that is stable in the long term, a so-called attractor state. Take, as an example, the learning of Kepler's laws. A system that gives correct responses about Venus, but incoherent ones about Mars, has not learned Kepler's laws. The enthusiast for connectionism cannot have it both ways: Either the state of the system concerning Kepler's laws is an attractor, at least as stable as the opinions of the average working astronomer, and in this case the argument from instability fails, or it is not and cannot be so stable, in which case connectionism cannot explain what is going on in working science.

There is one further point about the degree of stability of connectionist systems. Although such systems may appear volatile in that their answers might be context bound, in another, more basic respect they are more stable than classical systems. Classical systems often react to local damage with a global breakdown in performance. Connectionist systems, including our brain, possess, on the contrary, the property of 'graceful degradation,' a stability through time that contrasts with the first appearance. Thus, neither holism nor context dependence and alleged instability is of much help to the relativist.

2.3.3. Practical Knowledge

Relativists appeal to the notion of knowledge-how as opposed to knowledge-that to prove the alleged truth-intolerance. For example, Bechtel and Abrahamsen (1980) argue that the propositional paradigm should be at least supplemented, if not replaced, by an account of knowledge that stresses knowledge-how at the expense of knowledge-that. Churchland writes in a similar vein, but with more insight:

> Our best (Kuhn 1962) and most recent (Churchland 1989, chap. 9) accounts of

what learning a theory amounts to portray the process as much less the memorizing of doctrine and much more the slow acquisition and development of a host of diverse *skills* – skills of perception, categorization, analogical extension, physical manipulation, evaluation, construction, analysis, argument, computation, anticipation and so forth ... Sustaining enhanced practice is what theories typically do, at least for those who have internalized the relevant theories.

Once they have been internalized, of course, they no longer seem like theories, in the sense of the false stereotype here at issue. Yet theories they remain, however much they have become the implicit engine of intricate mundane practice. (1993, 218; emphasis in text)

We have no quarrel with Churchland over the 'skills' displayed by a connectionist network. A network can perhaps have knowledge-how to recognize rocks without having any true representations. It should be noted that this knowledge is tested by considering the truth of the system's verdicts ('rock' vs. 'mine'), so the assessment is not truth-independent.

It is implausible, however, that simply by being encoded in connectionist networks, some piece of knowledge becomes a piece of knowledge-how in the sense of opposed to knowledge-that. The network giving information about flight schedules tells the customer that there is a flight from New York to Chicago at 7 p.m. No matter how the network has arrived at its answer, the activation sustaining the answer is more a piece of knowledge-that than simply a manifestation of skill.[19]

What is more important, cognitive scientists are interested not only in the performance of the system, but also in the means it uses, including, prominently, the representational links. Remember the example concerning hidden units – the connectionist system learning about diseases and symptoms (Neal 1992). When describing the system, its creator distinguishes several architectures and shows how the differences in performance are due to the differences in what is represented, in the kind of (mini-) theory the system has learned.

The trouble for the relativist becomes more extensive with his ambitious claim, central to the whole project, that actual science is done by connectionist systems (the brains of scientists being such systems). In order to discover and learn theories, the system has to represent them. Remember Churchland's praise of connectionist networks: 'Taken jointly, the prodigious representational and computational capacities of a system of state spaces interacting by coordinate transformations suggest a powerful and highly general means of understanding the cognitive activities of the nervous system' (*NP*, 109–10). Representing theories is not simply having knowledge-how. According to Churchland, in the passage quoted at the beginning of the section, a theory remains a theory, no matter how useful it is and how much skill it supports. Knowing a theory is to a great extent knowing that such-and-such is the case.

We can now see how our connectionist fan got himself into trouble. He started with an account of connectionist systems adequate only for tinker-toy systems, and indeed very primitive and unstable ones. Such systems are dramatically different from our brains, which might make them exotic and interesting. He might also have been attracted both by eliminativism in respect to content or meaning and by the idea that connectionist states carry no determinate content. So far so good. But our relativist is also a naturalist and an epistemologist wanting to enlist his connectionist insights for understanding science as it is, a corpus of relatively stable theories with rather determinate content and controllable consequences. This puts him in a predicament: his picture of connectionist systems simply lacks the explanatory power to account for the dynamics of science. If he suggests that connectionist networks can do science, then he has to accept stability and determinacy, two handmaidens to truth. Alternatively and implausibly, he can claim that science is unstable and indeterminate in the dramatic fashion in which his pet connectionist representations are. Such an unstable science would carry no conviction. It is certainly not the science the epistemologist is supposed to account for.[20]

What qualities must a connectionist system capable of doing science have? First of all, it must have means of producing novel outputs by combining old elements, in order to meet all the different kinds of novel contingencies a scientist must be prepared to take into account. Productivity implies that the system must be sensitive to the way the new whole is (to be) built from its parts, that is, must exhibit sensitivity to syntax. In order to cope with complexity, the system has to use recursive procedures, reminiscent of the classical, non-connectionist ones.[21] Such a system has structured representations, and its processing is structure sensitive. Nothing short of such sensitivity can result in the flexibility and compass that actual scientific practice displays. But structured, or even recursively organized, representations make the answer about the truth-dimension obviously affirmative – the represented theories are just as true (or false, or truthlike) as the sentence-based theories-in-the-book-are.

Moreover, the structured representations are wholes in which parts support each other and the whole. Such a relation of support is surely similar to classical inductive support or deductive consequence and is to be judged by analogous criteria.[22]

The same considerations show up in the developmental perspective. Clark and Karmiloff-Smith (1993) have investigated the constraints a connectionist network has to satisfy in order to mimic the actual cognitive development of a child. They stress the assumed ability of the human cognitive system to switch between different representational formats to 'redescribe' in various formats its own representations.[23] In order to do so, networks must have three capacities: first, to treat their own representations as objects for further manipulation and do that independently of prompting by training inputs; second, to retain copies of the original configurations (earlier 'networks'); third, to form new structured representations of their own knowledge, which are not encapsulated, that is, can be accessed by other computational processes.[24] The three capacities are certainly closer to knowledge-that than to mere knowledge-how. The inner states must have rich and structured content. This brings us to the next topic: theories-in-the-head and prototypes.

3. The Content of Connectionist Representations

3.1. Prototypes and Their Virtues

After having discussed the 'how' of non-propositional representation, I now need to bring in the 'what.' Churchland opts for prototypes as the key cognitive contents for networks, and with good reason. As mentioned in chapter 1, 2.3, it is a common idea in contemporary cognitive science that concepts are implemented in the form of prototypes. The prototype format is suitable for connectionist representation, and it seems to be the best alternative candidate. Remember that prototypes differ from more traditional representations in that (a) they have a graded structure together with (b) built-in default assumptions, (c) they allow for representation in the non-sentential media, and (d) they are coded holistically so as to allow for context-sensitive adjustment and reorganization. The concept is not always there, but 'emerges from the interaction of large numbers of connected nodes' (Thagard 1990). Connectionist systems are good at pattern-recognition, and prototypes are often represented as specific patterns. For instance, assume that the prototype for 'bird' encompasses (default) properties of flying, singing, having feathers, and laying eggs. Then it will be realized in a connectionist system by an arrangement of units coding for these features and ready to activate themselves together.

Suppose an input-vector for item *A* has following values:

locomotion: flies
communication: unknown
external covering: unknown
progeny: eggs.

Now, the vector will activate the units for 'flies' and for 'is laying eggs.' These units might activate the relevant prototype arrangement for 'bird' (or for 'insect,' for that matter). The system concludes that *A* is a bird (or that *A* is an insect). Such a process of co-activation stands in marked contrast to the classical model of a concept defined through sufficient and necessary properties.

P. Thagard draws a summary of further elective affinities between connectionist systems and prototypical representations: 'The connectionist view of concepts appears promising for accounting for subtle categorization effects. A network could, for example, acquire the concept of a whale by being trained on examples of whales, learning to identify blobs as whales without acquiring explicit slots or rules that state typical properties of whales. No single unit corresponds to the concept whale, since information about whales is distributed over numerous units. Work in progress is investigating how concepts as learned patterns of activation can even be organized into kind and part whole hierarchies' (1990, 263).

The alliance of connectionism and prototype view brings us to Churchland's story. There is no a priori limit on the size of prototypes, and in exploiting this circumstance, Churchland has gone farther than most prototype fans. He claims that people represent whole theories, and sophisticated ones indeed, as prototypes. We have already met his 'dependence patterns' – patterns coded in prototypes. He classifies dependence-representing prototypes into several groups: First, cluster prototypes consisting of 'typically co-occurrent properties' – we may suppose that our bird example would belong to this group. Next come the etiological prototypes depicting 'a typical temporal sequence of event types' (notice a somewhat Humean picture of causality implicit in the description). Then we have practical prototypes coding 'complex means-end relations.' More complicated are 'superordinate prototypes' used in mathematical reasoning. Churchland explains the idea with the help of geometrical examples: prototypical properties of triangles can be understood in terms of the superordinate prototype of two parallel lines intersected by a third line.[25] The two last groups have to do with actions and interactions. Social-interaction prototypes govern ethical, legal, and social-etiquette matters. Finally, motivational prototypes code folk-psychology. (All terms in quotes are from *NP*.)

Humans, being connectionist machines, are particularly good at activating prototypes of the kinds listed. Prototypes are responsible for explanation and understanding: 'Explanatory understanding consists in the activation of a specific prototype vector in a well-trained network. It consists in the apprehension of the problematic case as an instance of a general type, a type for which the creature has a detailed and well-informed representation' (*NP*, 210). The brain should command, Churchland goes on say, 'intricate prototype representations of such things as stellar collapse, cell meiosis, positron-positron collision,' and many others of the same ilk (ibid.). This idea could be seen as a promising answer to the question of how connectionist systems that are typical pattern-recognizers can do any scientific explaining. The answer claims that scientific explanation has to do with patterns and pattern-recognition: it consists in finding the right general pattern for the event to be explained.[26] Such prototypes are not sets of sentences, although they guide people in producing theories-in-the-book which are sets of sentences. Churchland seems to think that prototypes should not be judged in terms of their truth, of how well they correspond to reality.

3.2. *Prototypes and Truth*

Let me now consider the specific feature of prototypes and ask whether these features make them truth-intolerant. Remember the arguments used before for the truth-tolerance of connectionist representations in general. Does the prototype format change anything in respect to their validity? Remember that prototypes differ from more traditional representations in several respects in that (a) they allow graded judgment of membership in the category; (b) they have a default structure, so that they allow revisions of ascriptions; (c) they allow for various representations, not being limited to sentential description; and (d) they can be coded holistically in a context-dependent fashion, or even produced on the spot as the occasion demands.

Do any of these features undercut the presumption of truth-tolerance?

Take, first, Churchland's practical prototypes encoding means-ends relations. Here the answer in favour of truth-tolerance is immediate: given the role of practical prototypes in guiding human planning and behaviour, it would be strange indeed if they were not subject to evaluation in terms of truth. For example, a practical prototype suggesting that eating cyanide-laced food is a good way to remain healthy, would be fatal to its owner simply because it is false about a matter of life and death. Similar reasons hold for etiological prototypes.[27] Notice that this point is independent of any of the features of prototypes listed and generalizes to other kinds of prototypes (as taxonomized by Churchland).[28] Concerning folk-psychology prototypes, one can remark that Churchland himself is the best-known proponent and defender of the claim that folk-psychology is a false theory, which could hardly be the case if folk-psychology were incapable of having a truth-value. There seems to be nothing in Churchland's own characterization of prototypes that excludes valuation in terms of overall truth and falsity, and there is much that suggests precisely this kind of valuation.

We are left with only one possibility for saving Churchland from outright error. As in the case of maps and networks, his defender might interpret him as propounding a mere terminological change: although the prototypes coding mentally/neurally represented beliefs or theories are correct or incorrect in the correspondence sense of correctness (which is as important in their case as it is in the case of theories-in-the-book), still, given the special non-propositional nature of these representations, one should not call this correspondence correctness 'truth,' but should reserve the term 'truth' only for correctness of sentences. With such a proposal the rationalist should not have any serious quarrel. The proposal itself is far from being revolutionary, since this wider notion of correspondence is an extension of the notion of truth, not its replacement. The correspondence is all the classical epistemologist needs, so that the details concerning representational format can be (and in my opinion should be) accommodated within truth-centred epistemology. (As mentioned above, I do not believe that Churchland intended to put forward the mere terminological proposal – to me he sounds more like a revolutionary than like a pedantic philosopher propounding a linguistic convention and a mere broadening of a well-entrenched concept. I am afraid, however, that he must choose between such pedantic irrelevancies and the interesting but ultimately untenable thesis of truth-intolerance.)

Let me now document and develop my claim about the truth-tolerance of connectionist prototypes. I shall use evidence from the literature, showing that the practitioners themselves judge the performance of their connectionist networks in terms of criteria from the truth family: correctness, accuracy, or downright truth.

P.G. Schyns (1991) presents a typical experiment concerning a system that can learn prototypes from cases that are not clearly prototypical but that cluster around a given prototype. His network shows a series of more or less typical dogs (i.e., uses a noisy input-vector), more or less typical cats and birds, in a considerable number of learning trials. By a process of self-adjusting through readjusting of weights, the system has come to extract the typical features of dogs (features representative of 'central tendencies' in the category of dogs), cats, and birds. Schyns describes the outcome of such a process: 'In particular, we can notice that after 40 iterations, a distinct region of weight vectors is already dedicated to *bird*, whereas *cat* and *dog* are not yet clearly separated, as they will later be. We can also see that as the weight portraits get sharper – as concepts are learned distinctively – the conceptual interpretation of prototypes becomes more distinct too. After 1,000 iterations of learning, each weight vector maps nearly exactly the prototype of one particular category. This effect is quite interesting because the prototypes were never presented during the training phase' (1991, 476; emphasis in text). Note the accent put on the near exactness of mapping. The author is interested in how accurately the system reconstructs the unseen prototype (the noiseless prototype-vector that has never been presented to it). Three things are taken for granted: that there is in reality such a prototype (indeed, Schyns reproduces a photo of the prototype he used), that the system can accurately represent it, and that the task of the system is to find a matching representation. The system is tested for accuracy achieved and is implicitly praised for it. (There is a mathematical expression for the degree of accuracy: the cosine between the output vector and the prototype vector. Further, there is no trace of the Churchlandian suggestion that because the measure of accuracy is a property of vectors, the measure does not measure the accuracy of fit to reality).

The faithfulness of a prototype kind (type as opposed to token) to reality gives us a first way of judging prototype representation in the sense of correspondence truth. A stored prototype is true (to reality) if it captures the actually typical features of a category (the actual central tendencies). The degree of truthlikeness admits of simple measurement, and there is no problem, let alone a deep problem, about this central truth-dimension of prototype storing.

Next, we look at another kind of assessment in terms of truth. In the model we are describing, categorization is separated from naming; the naming is done by a separate module, a concept-name associator. Its details are not important for us. After having learned the prototype and its name, the system can reflect on problems such as: Is this new item a dog or not? Suppose that the system is confronted with an animal, Alfred, that is, in fact, a wolf. It will produce the answer 'Alfred is a dog.' Schyns's account is as follows: 'Because the prototype of *wolf* is more similar to the prototype of *dog* than to any other, a wolf is interpreted as an instance of *dog* at the beginning of the relearning ... Because the new category has not yet been represented in the system's conceptual knowledge, all of its exemplars are regarded as instances of the closest concept that can interpret the new category' (1991, 486; emphasis in text). The answer 'Alfred is a dog' is false. At the beginning of the relearning, the system misclassifies Alfred. There is no doubt that this move has resulted in falsity – it has a wrong picture of Alfred. This example, then, shows the second way in which truth/falsity enters the story. A particular move – categorization-classification or characterization – can result in an accurate representation, or in a misrepresentation.

Thus, the classical idea of (correspondence) truth might need some extending and polishing in order to be applicable to a wider range of representational media, but the core of the classical idea seems irreplaceable – any useful proposal will have to deal with the dimension of the match with reality, no matter in what medium the content to be matched with reality is encoded.

Until now, I have dealt with cognition in general. Let us consider the implications of Churchland's ideas for science. In the preceding chapter I mentioned the view that connectionist systems support only knowledge-how, not knowledge-that, and I briefly registered disagreement. For the full discussion of the view, however, the idea of a prototype is needed. First, notice that Churchland is not quite explicit about the issue. I shall reconstruct and consider a line on science he *might* take, relying on (his own version of) Thomas Kuhn's views, which he believes are vindicated by connectionism. His summary of Kuhn is as follows:

> Mastering a theory, on this view, is more a matter of being able to perform in various ways, of being able to solve a certain class of problems, of being able to recognize diverse situations as relevantly similar to that of the original of paradigmatic applications ... Of central importance is the manner in which one comes to perceive the world as one internalizes a theory. The perceptual world is

> redivided into new categories, and while the theory may be able to provide necessary and sufficient conditions for being an instance of any of its categories, the perceptual recognition of any instance of a category does not generally proceed by reference to those conditions, which often transcend perceptual experience. Rather, perceptual recognition proceeds by some inarticulable process that registers *similarity* to one or more perceptual *prototypes* of the category at issue. (*NP*, 158; emphasis in text)

The view suggests, first, that scientific knowledge is only knowledge-how, and second, that it consists in quasi-perceptual recognition of similarities. Both suggestions point away from the truth-dimension, the first more than the second.

The suggestions, however, do not add up to a good reason to support the Churchlandian position on the irrelevance of truth. First, the view of classification and categorization stated at the end of the quotation is already invalidated. We have mentioned the pizza-quarter experiments carried out by Lance Rips, which show that categorization with the help of prototypes is not a matter of simple recognition of perceptual similarity. Either perceptual recognition is a bad model of categorization, or perceptual recognition itself goes far beyond similarity. In both cases the view expressed at the end of the quotation is wrong. (The case might be even worse: if concepts are at least partly determined by theoretical knowledge, then so are prototypes, and one then needs an antecedent notion of theoreticity to account for prototypes. The order of explanation is then reversed: it is not the prototypes that explain theories, but the other way around).

What is more important, I may run a variant of the argument from the explicitness and complexity of science to its truth-tolerance, and I shall do it against the central example adduced by Churchland. He is interested in accounting for science, and the prototypes he talks about are prototypes held by scientists. It is precisely here, however, that his assumptions are particularly inept. The typical task of a scientist working in mature science is not perceptual recognition. The theory she holds must enable her to perform purely intellectual (non-perceptual) tasks. Even if some of these tasks could be understood as analogous with perception, many could not. Physicists work on problems that cannot be, or at least are not, visualized in advance; the visual-perceptual model often follows the decisive step in science, which itself is performed by means of calculations or abstract reasoning. Such tasks suggest that the representations of theories (in the heads of scientists) are not simple perceptual or quasi-perceptual items and that the talk of 'perceiving the world' is in this context highly metaphorical and non-committal.

Furthermore, if science is coded in prototypes, then obviously these prototypes code scientific rather than everyday knowledge.[29] I mentioned in the previous chapter the complexity and explicitness of science as features that must be preserved in any representation of scientific theories, and here I add some illustrations. Suppose, for the sake of the argument, that an artificial connectionist system has managed to 'induce' Kepler's laws, and to store their representation. The representation of the First Law, for instance, concerns the links between the features relating to planets and the features relating to elliptic trajectories. Such links will have decisively stronger weights than those linking 'planets' to 'straight lines' or 'hyperboles.' Suppose, further, that the system gives all the usual behavioural evidence of having learned Kepler's laws: it solves successfully the standard problems, predicts the apparent position of planets, and the like. Grant, further, that Kepler's laws as formulated in the textbook are true (or truthlike enough). Now, it is obvious that the representational content of the connectionist system is also true. The representations link the right features (planets and trajectories) in the right way. They initiate the correct output. What else could be required?[30]

Churchland seems to be a victim of the same illusion in the case of prototypes as he was in the case of networks. He considers everyday prototypes and declares that prototypes code for science. The declaration sounds revolutionary if one forgets that one cannot code science except in scientific prototypes. The dilemma is as follows.

a. If prototypes are like scientific theories as we know them, then the usual descriptive and normative claims about theories apply to such prototypes; the revolutionary relativist-pragmatist goal is missed, and we are on familiar territory (of course, people may have both scientific and everyday prototypes, and the prototype theory might account for their relations and interactions, but this is basically an extension, not an overturning, of the standard views on science).
b. On the other hand, if prototypes are not like scientific theories as we know them, and a revolution seems to be in the offing, then they cannot account for the key features of science, in particular not for its complexity, accuracy, and explanatory and predictive success.[31]

Consider the horn (a): in general, if science is coded in prototypes, then these prototypes will look like science. After all, they must have explanatory and predictive power, in the sense of yielding precise quantitative predictions, and they must have the complexity required by such predictive power. But then they represent their 'representata' in sufficiently rich detail and with enough stability and structure to be judged by their accuracy and correspondence with what they represent. This is simply the rationalist proposal of judging theories by their truth. Now consider the horn (b): if prototypes are incapable of such articulateness, accuracy, and stability, they cannot code mature scientific theories.

The dilemma leaves open which alternative is correct – are prototypes both truth-tolerant and theory-tolerant, or are they incapable both of representing theories and of being true? Cognitive science does succeed in modelling some areas of knowledge through prototypes, however, and we have good evidence that such prototypes are accurate and true. Therefore, the facts point to the first horn: prototypes are suitable for coding theories, capable of being true or being false, and apt to be judged along this dimension.

3.3. True Theories without Sentences – the Semantic View

Which view of theories accords with the result tentatively endorsed at the end of the previous section? The sentential view, claiming that theories are essentially sets of sentences, sits ill with prototype representation. We should suppose that prototypes comprise various non-sentential components – reminiscent of maps, diagrams, or pictures – and that the connectionist medium in which they are couched is somewhat inhospitable to sentential representation. But are there really no plausible non-sentential views on theories that still ascribe truth-tolerance to them?

We know in advance where to look. The semantics of non-sentential representation is best seen as situation- or world-directed. A representation is true if it represents the way things are; more specifically, if it partitions the possible situations into two sets (i.e., *w*-propositions), a set of those that 'agree' with it and a set of those that do not, and the actual situation is among the 'agreeing' ones. This was the core of the Semantic Argument. Thus, we should look at the corresponding view of theories, which sees theories as world oriented, not medium oriented or even medium bound.

There are such views that allow for theories' being non-sentential but at the same time faithful to reality and true in the correspondence sense.

The most prominent is the semantic view advocated (in various versions) by Ronald Giere, Frederick Suppe, Philip Kitcher, Joseph Sneed, Wolfgang Stegmueller, Patrick Suppes, and Bas Van Fraassen. Churchland himself mentions and briefly discusses the view in his *NP*. According to this view, theories are not sets of sentences, but semantic entities modelling a domain. To use the example adduced by Giere, the classical theory of the pendulum is given by the abstract structure or theoretical model common to many systems (that can be characterized in various ways with various representational means): any system consisting of a suspended weight is a classical pendulum if and only if its period is given by a certain formula (specifying the period of oscillation in terms of its length and the strength of the uniform gravitational field). To quote a succinct characterization by one of the founders of the view, F. Suppe: 'In essence a theory is a general model of the behaviour of the systems within its scope. The model is a relational system whose domain is the set of all logically possible occurrences in the systems within the theory's scope ... A scientific theory is an iconic model' (1988, 141). The model is true of a given entity (situation, system) if the relevant elements of the model can be identified with the relevant parts of the situation so that all the relations are preserved. 'According to this semantic conception of theories, then, scientific theories are relational systems functioning as iconic models that characterize all the possible changes of state that the systems within their scopes undergo in idealized circumstances. And the theory will be *empirically true* if and only if the class of possible state occurrences determined by the theory is identical with the possible behaviours of systems within its intended scope under idealized conditions' (ibid.; emphasis in text).

Churchland himself characterizes the semantic view in the following way: 'This approach attempts to drive a wedge between a theory and its possibly quite various linguistic formulations by characterizing a theory as a *set of models*, those that will make a first-order linguistic statement of the theory come out *true* under the relevant assignments. The models in the set all share a common abstract structure, and that structure is what is important about any theory, according to the semantic view, not any of its idiosyncratic linguistic expressions. A theory is true, on this view, just in case it includes the actual world, or some part of it, as one of the models in the set' (*NP*, 157; emphasis in text). Churchland rejects the semantic view on the grounds that it says nothing about the way such theories are represented. He seems to think that mere silence about the medium makes the view psychologically/neurologically unrealistic: 'In particular, I think it strange that we should be asked, at this stage of the debate, to embrace an account of theories that has absolutely nothing to do with the question of how real physical systems might embody representations of the world, and how they might execute principled computations on those representations in such a fashion as to learn' (ibid.). This is an unfortunate move. Churchland overlooks the most important point: precisely because the semantic view is silent about the details concerning the 'embodiment' of theories, it is compatible with a wider range of psychological/neurological data than the sentential view. If theories-in-the-book are characterized by what they 'mean' (by theories-as-classes-of-models), not by a particular medium, then what they mean could be represented by different representations couched in various media. What is important is the suggestion that theories need not be sets of sentences and that they can be iconic. Once they are understood as semantic models, the natural possibility arises that these semantic models are represented, in the heads of enquirers, by various means. Furthermore, a theory that is true on the semantic view, retains its truth-value no matter how it is represented. (Note that Churchland does not dispute that a semantically conceived theory is truth-tolerant.)

We therefore can find within the philosophy of science a framework that preserves those features of theories we need. It allows for various semantically equivalent representations of a given theory, some of which might not be sentential. It shows that variously coded representations of the same theory can be true or be false if and only if the theory is. Let me then close this section with an idea about how one can use the semantic framework. We might envisage a synthesis of two components: *the prototypes as format (or syntax) for theories, and semantic models as the content.* A prototype would then encode the semantic model. This can be done by various means: for example, the semantic model for the pendulum can be encoded as description-plus-formula, or in a diagrammatic way, or through some distribution of weights in the neural network. All these representations of the prototype have one thing in common: they partition (possible and actual) situations into pendulum-situations and no-pendulum-situations. There will be some borderline cases, for instance, my (overhead) room light is not quite a classical pendulum, but it comes close enough to being one. If an actual system behaves like a classical pendulum, then the model corresponds to it, and the prototype is true of it. This (modest) proposal shows, in principle, not only that there is more than one way to preserve rationalist principles in the face of the evidence from cognitive science, but that the rationalist principles themselves (such as the centrality of truth) suggest some novel solutions in keeping with the most recent developments in cognitive research.

Let me come back to the main issue. I have tracked a path leading from propositional truth to the general correctness of fit. This is a well-beaten track, but historically it was used for travel in the opposite direction. The picture theory of meaning, as presented in Wittgenstein's *Tractatus* (and in some writings of Russell), starts from the general idea of representation and match, and takes pictures as its paradigm.[32] It relies on our intuitive view of what it is for a picture to be correct or accurate and generally what it is for non-propositional representations to match reality, and it characterizes propositional truth as a special case, the one in which a 'logical picture,' or proposition, corresponds to some state of affairs. I have brought the story to its source, so to speak, and underscored the applicability of correspondence correctness – truth in the relevant wide sense – to a wide range of more 'picture-like' representations.

4. Connectionism and Epistemic Virtue

4.1. *The Issue of Epistemological Assessment*

In the preceding chapters I have argued that connectionist representations are truth-tolerant in the hope of establishing a wider claim – that information processing done by connectionist systems falls within the scope of the Classical Picture. Before turning to this wider claim, however, I must briefly discuss Churchland's pronouncements on the issue.

It is rather difficult to reconstruct Churchland's stance. In his programmatic papers (e.g., 1992a) he seems a full-blooded relativist-pragmatist. When criticizing others, in particular, the instrumentalists, he unreservedly praises some of the traditionally accepted virtues of scientific theories – explanatory power, unification, simplicity – and is at great pains to show that connectionist networks possess such virtues. There is no mention of the possibility that such virtues might be relative to users and situations: 'Let me now try to address the question of whether the theoretical virtues such as simplicity, coherence, and explanatory power are *epistemic* virtues genuinely relevant to the estimate of a theory's truth, as tradition says, or merely *pragmatic* virtues, as van Fraassen urges ... I remain inclined toward the traditional view' (*NP*, 146; emphasis in text). In this passage Churchland diagnoses the problem and proposes his answer: genuinely epistemic virtues are those that contribute to a theory's truth and our estimate of it. A few pages later in the same book, Churchland will urge us to move away from truth, retaining the same set of epistemic virtues. Moreover, he tries to reconstruct a coherent story about these virtues, eschewing truth/falsity, entailment, and inductive support. It is entirely unclear whether he wants to justify this set by appeal to success and to cost-benefit considerations. Such a justificationary strategy would lead him into the narrow realm of empirical adequacy to which he does not want to be confined. How can he disparage 'merely pragmatic' virtues and in the same breath advocate a move in the direction of pragmatism? If one does not care about truth, why endorse realistically conceived explanatory power and unification as ideals? Why bother about simplicity, except on purely neutral – aesthetic or bookkeeping – grounds? What is it for a cognitive output to be correct (incorrect, wrong) if not to be true (false)?

Churchland is quite right in being absolutist about some of the fundamental virtues and values of theories. Unfortunately, his rejection of truth (together with his rejection of inductive support and entailment) leaves him in a very awkward position: he defends a truncated rationalist ideal, deprived of its logical, scientific, and historical motivation and hastily transplanted into a relativist-pragmatist context. The transplant simply cannot survive in these extremely inhospitable surroundings. I shall return to this point, below, in the section on the reliability of connectionist processing.

Let us now pass to the main topic, the epistemological status of connectionist processing. I have discussed the Cognitive Peculiarities of connectionist representations, their non-sentential and distributed character, holism, prototypicality, context-dependence, variability, and the practical character of the knowledge of the network. I have considered them statically, in relation to their semantic content and truth properties. It is now time to consider them in action, in the processing itself.

Connectionist processes are very unlike sentential reasoning; it is difficult and perhaps even impossible to identify particular 'premises' from which the connectionist process proceeds, and it is practically infeasible to distinguish particular token steps leading from the given initial state to some (global) final state, although there is a clear taxonomy of the types of steps employed. Rules of procedure are not explicitly represented in the system or for the system, and the patterns of activation may be highly context and problem dependent. Not only Churchland and his followers but also rather conservative rationalists deny that connectionist systems and processes, being bearers of Cognitive Peculiarities, can be judged by classical epistemological criteria and assessed for epistemic virtue and vice. The classical criteria are taken here to encompass the usual truth-linked ones proposed by various forms of foundationalism, coherentism, and reliabilism.[33] What can be said from the classical rationalist viewpoint about the rationality or justifiedness of connectionist processes?[34]

Ironically, Churchland's own all-out connectionist stance invokes the alternative most easily handled by classical epistemology. If human minds/brains are thoroughly connectionist systems, as he apparently thinks they are, then a connectionist system can do what humans do: invent logic, use it to check its (his, her?) own reasoning, discover Pythagoras's Theorem and the general theory of relativity. But then, of course, it can be rational in the most traditional sense. In this case, in order to judge how rational the advanced connectionist system actually is, we do not have to consider its internal workings – we can study its fruits: master-works, such as Ptolemy's *Almagest*, or Newton's *Mathematical Principles of Natural Philosophy*, or Frege's *Foundations of Arithmetic*. The minds/brains that have produced such works were presumably as rational as a mind/brain can be, since these works have set our standard of rational cognition in any case.[35] What advanced neuroscience could perhaps do is make us understand better how such achievements have been produced. Consider the psychology of invention in science: the folk-psychological data and guesses on which the Classical Picture had to rely have supplied meagre and purely anecdotal material, such as, for instance, the story of Kekulé's dream about the structure of the benzene molecule. Folk-psychology has occasionally thrown in some metaphor, 'flash of insight,' for example – and that was almost all. There is some hope that advanced connectionist modelling might contribute to our understanding of scientific creativity.[36] Suppose it were true. What would this mean for the epistemologist? Would it widen or restrict the area of what can be assayed in terms of rationality? The reasonable guess is that such a result would widen the domain of assayable processes: a mechanism hidden in the darkness would have been brought to light, laid bare, and dissected, its working described in detail. But then the classical epistemological questions spring immediately to the epistemologist's mind. The mechanism and the process that have led to the discovery of *X* are of such-and-such kind. Obviously, they have proved to be valuable in this case. But are they generally reliable, or was the discovery of *X* by means of such a process just pure luck? Further, does the process of discovery resemble anything already known and can it be approximated by more classical means, which have already passed the test of rationality?

We may not, however, have primarily to judge the full panoply of sophisticated cognitive strategies. We need to consider a (hypothetical) human endowed with both lower connectionist modules and a symbolic central processor – a design that is gaining popularity in cognitive research – and then reach a verdict on the connectionist part. Further, we may have to judge a simpler creature, whose cognitive apparatus is exclusively connectionist, but is incomparably poorer in its achievement than the sophisticated human one. Such connectionist systems can perform only a very limited number of tasks. The question then is whether the limitations of what they can do impose such severe limitations on what they ought to do (or, better, on what their epistemic value is) that a normative-evaluative viewpoint becomes inapplicable. Are living connectionist systems so stupid as to fall out of the province of epistemology? We need a principled way to judge connectionist processing in its less familiar facets. Fortunately, the discussions about connectionist processing have, in fact, already brought to light various ways of appraising connectionist systems, some of which are clearly principled and epistemological, so that we need only systematize them in order to rise to the challenge.

4.2. Sententialism

Let me first dispose of an argument that can be distilled from Churchland's and Bechtel's remarks. It is an extension of the sententialist argument for truth-intolerance. The argument has the familiar form.

1. Only sententially coded contents can be true or be false.
2. Traditional epistemology operates in terms of truth/falsity, and of other notions wedded to the sentential format, for example, inductive support.
3. Connectionist representations are non-sentential.

Therefore:

C. Connectionist representations cannot be judged within the framework of classical epistemology.

Call this the sententialist argument. It rests upon the premise that among representations it is only sentences plus operations on them (yielding arguments, proofs, etc., built from sentences) that can be epistemically rational or justified in the traditional sense. Is the premise tenable? Notice that in (1) 'sentential' is used literally, to mean 'syntactically like a sentence.' It is not a semantic notion. If, however, it were taken in (some odd) semantic sense, meaning 'being semantically like a sentence,' then (3) would become very difficult to establish.

Epistemic virtue, as traditionally conceived, concerns truth-related qualities of belief transitions, in particular apparent or real preservation of truth (or apparent truth) or plausibility. Now, some processes and operations on non-sentential representation certainly preserve truth, plausibility, high probability, and support. Remember doing Venn diagrams when teaching elementary logic, or using diagrams with 'possible worlds' when testing a formula for validity in modal logic. One can generate many examples by using well-known representation theorems, such as Stone's theorem, which assures us that the Boolean algebra of propositions is isomorphic to the algebra of the subsets of any given set. The theorem explains why one can do propositional logic using Venn diagrams – the semantics of the two representational formats is the same, although the syntax differs. In the same vein, Bas Van Fraassen has recommended the use of modified Venn diagrams in doing inductive logic – simply heap onto the usual Venn diagram a certain amount of mud, placing it on the areas that represent this or that proposition. Let the share of mud stand for the probability of the proposition and the total amount given will represent unit probability. The play with the muddy Venn diagram faithfully reproduces elementary probabilistic reasoning.[37] Thus, the elementary – and in this sense basic – logical and probabilistic steps can be done in a non-sentential medium, provided it has the right semantics. Such steps are the foundation of the whole epistemic enterprise and can certainly be assessed for their epistemic merit. Sententialism is wrong.

As before, I shall supplement the quick argument with a longer disquisition. Of course, throughout the rest of the book I shall appeal to knowledge about artificial connectionist systems, whose workings are perfectly understood, and I invite the reader to picture corresponding or analogous systems embodied in living creatures – the cognizers we are primarily interested in.

4.3. Applying the Classical Picture

Cognitive processes taking place within connectionist systems can be and are epistemologically assessed. Let us consider this statement.[38] The first kind of evaluative question that can be and has persistently been put to creators and investigators of connectionist systems concerns the *correctness of the global performance of the systems*. It is proposed to judge them in consequentialist terms, by the outcome of the overall performance, isolating the what, not the how, in abstraction from the micro-features of particular state-transitions. The resulting assessment is a global, goal-oriented one, of the kind promoted by reliabilism.

The second kind of question is less general: *Does the global performance bear any significant resemblance to those processes that we antecedently recognize and value as rational*? The affirmative answer to this question would lead to an indirect justification of given global strategies. It would imply that the performance is in its structure, as opposed to in results only, comparable to classical and well-understood processes. This assessment is a structure-oriented one, of the kind I have just used in connection with operations on Venn diagrams.

There is yet a third kind of normative question. It concerns particular moves a connectionist system makes: *Can the given move be justified by similarity to some already justified procedure*? It suggests a local justification by appeal to micro-structure.

Securing an affirmative answer to the first question would be sufficient to promote living connectionist systems to the status of epistemologically relevant cognizers. This is a bare minimum, and one would like to have something more recognizable. An affirmative answer to the second question would do. The third question is the least important in our context; we do not expect a new technique to mimic the details of the old, but expect it only to yield a recognizably similar overall result.

4.3.1. The Global, Goal-Oriented Assessment

The global consequentialist assessment is firmly rooted in the view that the general aim of cognition is reaching truth and avoiding error. It involves a quite traditional normative epistemological stance (although the term and the detailed analysis of its meaning are recent), but in virtue of its global reliabilist character, it leaves a lot of elbow room for assessing exotic and non-conventional strategies.

Remember that Churchland supports his Feyerabendian creed by his appeal to the diversity of connectionist configurations ('theories') and learning strategies ('methodologies'), and his view that 'there is not a reason in the world to think that there is any such relation that unites the vast diversity of frameworks (1992a, 357). Reliabilism allows one to accept the premise, that is, the factual diversity, but to reject the relativist conclusion: what unites epistemologically diverse frameworks is their function. They are taken by the reliabilist as so many means of finding out what the world is like. Here I assume that finding out what the world is like is the proper epistemic goal, and I argue for it in detail in chapter 7.

To show how reliabilism handles structural diversity, by appeal to the unity of purpose, let me briefly mention one non-conventional but understandable procedure, the so-called genetic algorithms (I am following very closely Booker, Goldberg, and Holland 1989). They operate in the twilight zone of hypothesis generation about which traditional normative disciplines are silent. The system starts with a set of initial complex hypotheses decomposable into building blocks, called 'schemes.' The hypotheses are ranked according to their previous performance. The genetic algorithm first selects pairs of hypotheses according to their record – the better the record of the hypothesis, the more likely its selection. Then, 'genetic operators' are applied, creating 'offspring' hypotheses. The most popular operator is a so-called cross-over, which simply exchanges a randomly selected segment between the pairs. Finally, the least successful hypothesis is replaced with a newborn-baby hypothesis. This procedure is borrowed from biology and does not look like any familiar cognitive process. Still, it is assessed by AI-judges in terms of its fertility in producing reliable hypotheses and, in particular, hypotheses reliable over a wide range of situations.[39]

Similarly, thanks to its consequentialist thrust, reliabilism is usable for exotic processes, which are (unlike genetic algorithms) hard to understand. Imagine that you are faced with a completely new connectionist process, which is technically so complex that you cannot (at least as yet) quite understand how it functions. Imagine, further, that the process yields excellent results (by our lights); it rediscovers laws of classical physics and of chemistry and makes novel predictions that upon observation turn out to be true, performing such feats in quite a regular fashion. Then, the global consequentialist, that is, reliabilist, criterion decides in favour of the process. No matter what its structure is, we have to presume that the process is cognitively virtuous.[40]

This proposal shows the narrow path between the right-wing and the left-wing excesses. The reliabilist criterion is traditional, but it is robust enough to justify quite revolutionary ways of thinking, and it should not be thrown away merely because there are non-conventional strategies, as the left-wingers suggest, since such strategies are conveniently assessed for their reliability. The reliabilist criterion is not wedded to particular strategies and procedures, in particular, syntactic or notational variants, as the right-wing sententialists think. Connectionist items are actually routinely assessed for their reliability. The creators of connectionist architectures and programs, as well as their professional judges, routinely praise the product in terms of its reliability: networks are said to be able to answer questions correctly, to recognize and sort (correctly), to be reliable over a wide range of input vectors, and the like. Very often the very term 'learning' is employed with connotations of reliability: when a researcher states that her network has 'learned a prototype,' or 'learned to assign a spatial tag to a non-spatial feature,' this is to be taken in the sense of learning how to perform the task correctly, with a very high rate of correct answers, which in a realistic setting is simply synonymous with reliability. Thus, not only are connectionist systems and processes capable of being judged by their reliability, they are produced and tested in view of their reliability and are routinely assessed in terms of it. The possibility of judging the cognitive achievements of living beings is then open if their cognitive apparatus is of a connectionist cast.

Ironically, Churchland himself seems to endorse a criterion of epistemic warrant that comes very close to a simple version of reliabilism, limited to perceptual input (see chap. 2, n3). His idea of the notion of warrant is as follows: 'High warrant is a matter of low ambiguity in the input. We need to ask, Is the input vector closely similar to any other possible input vector that would activate a different prototype. If so then the ambiguity of the current input is high and the warrant of the prototype vector activated is correspondingly low' (*NP*, 221). The idea is well known from the reliabilist literature (Goldman 1986). The input has to be capable of excluding all relevant alternatives, by being dissimilar to 'any other input vector that would activate a different prototype' (e.g., a percept of a barn has to be such as to exclude the activation of any prototype other than the barn-prototype). It is quite startling, however, to find such a definition in the work of a staunch anti-foundationalist. 'Low ambiguity' seems to be, first of all, a local property of input itself, not of the whole theoretical network. So, it is the local property of input that confers warrant upon the cognition. Worse still, 'low ambiguity' is only traditional 'clarity and distinctness' as warrant for reliability – put precisely into the semantic jargon that is supposed to be avoided. Further, 'low ambiguity' in the context entails at least the following: if the input has low ambiguity in relation to a prototype *A*, then the input points strongly towards *A*'s being the case (or being instantiated). This does not differ much from the notion of inductive support, which has been banished from Churchland's epistemology. Epistemic virtues seem to form a package deal, so that in reaching for some, Churchland is forced, implicitly, to buy all of them.

4.3.2. Global, Structure-Oriented Assessment

The next two criteria are more conservative and may be more parochial, as they measure the target process against the background of precedents of what is already *res judicata* – the well-known and assessed strategies and moves. They contribute to our understanding of why the target process is virtuous or vicious, by showing its relevant similarities to the familiar.

The second question was whether the global performance of connectionist systems bears any significant resemblance to those processes we antecedently recognize and value as rational. The prime candidate for a common denominator is the process of maximizing the coherence of one's set of beliefs (stored data), or the coherence of the stored prototypes (remember that coherence is of vital importance for prototypes). Classically, coherence is one of the prime indices of rationality and justifiedness. (The coherentists claim that it is not only a sign or condition of rationality, but synonymous with it.) The coherence-oriented picture of rational procedure follows.

The Enquirer starts with a set *K* of beliefs (presumably non-contradictory). She may be then prompted to consider some candidate proposition *p*, that her beliefs might lead her to the question of whether *p*. In deciding whether to accept *p*, she should concentrate on the following questions: 'Does *p* cohere with *K* better than with its competitors?' For example, if the only competitor to *p* is *not-p*, she should ask: 'Which proposition coheres better with *K*, *p* or *not-p*? The rational procedure is to choose the answer that coheres better with *K*, and thus maximizes the overall coherence of the set of beliefs. A popular candidate for the explication of '*p* coheres with *K*' is the notion of probabilistic support: '*p* coheres with *K* more than *not-p* does if *p* is more probable given *K* than *not-p* is.' The Enquirer is supposed to know the probabilities of propositions within *K* and have the associated conditional probabilities, most importantly, those that enable her to compute how probable *p* and *not-p* are, given *K*. There are ways of refining and constraining the relation of probabilistic support, but the basic idea is the simple one just mentioned. Given a probability distribution concerning *K*, the method singles out the answer that is most likely, given the distribution. The Enquirer who maximizes the coherence of her beliefs (i.e., the amount of probabilistic support within the set of her beliefs) is certainly rational in the classical sense. This is precisely what many connectionist networks are doing, and what some of the leading theories in the field recommend as the thing to be done. Consider the so-called constraint problems, for example, to select colours for a map with the constraint that adjacent countries are to be coloured differently. In the neural network the possible assignments of colours to countries are represented by neuron states. The switching of states is controlled so that a finally reached stable state fulfils all constraints (see Schaller 1990). Consider Smolensky's characterization of the activity of such connectionist networks; they activate all the constraints at once, thus initiating a descent into a balanced state: 'That is why the natural process for using this kind of knowledge is *relaxation*, in which the network uses all the connections at once and tries to settle into a state that balances all the constraints against one another' (1989, 57; emphasis in text). The balance sought is characterized in terms of best fit: 'Best-Fit Principle: Given an input, a connectionist system outputs a set of inferences that, as a whole, give a best fit to the input, in a statistical sense defined by the statistical knowledge stored in the system's connections' (ibid., 58).

Smolensky gives an example of a system seeking the solution to a simple problem in physics. The system learns that the resistor in an electrical circuit has increased. It has to mobilize its background knowledge and answer the question about the current and the voltage. 'Harmony theory analyses systems that confront the following statistical-inference task: If we give the system some features of an environmental state, it should infer values for unknown features. An example ... concerns reasoning about a simple electric circuit: Given the value of some circuit feature (say that a resistor has increased), what happens to the unknown features (the current and the voltage)? This general task is what I call *the completion task*' (Smolensky 1989, 59; emphasis in text). Suppose that the questions require simple yes/no answers (e.g., 'Did the voltage increase too?'). How does the system search for an answer? 'In response to the completion problem, the system is supposed to give the maximum-likelihood set of inferred values with respect to a probability distribution maintained internal to the system as a model of the environment. In other words, the system maintains a probability distribution that represents the likelihood of events' occurring in the environment, and it should give as its output the maximum-likelihood set of values for the unknowns' (ibid., 59). To illustrate the point from the simple example, if the question is the yes/no kind, the system selects the answer that has the maximum likelihood given the structure of the 'beliefs' already in the network's 'model of the environment.' The answer 'The voltage decreases' has maximum likelihood, given the information that the resistance has increased and given that some equivalent of Ohm's law is stored in the prototype or model-in-the-network.[41] The harmony theory comes with a numerical measure of consistency called *H*, and promotes this measure into the single most important function determining the description of the system. '*H* measures the internal consistency of a set of inferred values with respect to the constraint parameters' (ibid., 60). The system maximizing *H* is actually maximizing the coherence of its constraints and thereby maximizing the coherence of its system of internal representations. This is a good example of structural similarity and of the common structural goal (coherence in addition to reliability or in the service of the latter) for propositional and connectionist reasoning. Its special importance resides in the fact that learning by settling into an equilibrium state is usually taken to be a specifically connectionist procedure, closely tied to the essential peculiarities of design and an excellent example of connectionist innovations.

Remember Churchland's claim that he has given a causal account of cognition without having recourse, among other things, to the notion of degree of inductive support. We can now see that this is merely an empty piece of rhetoric; the notion of degree of support has been present all along in the story, under the very transparent guise of strength of connection and the soft constraint. It plays a most important role in determining the goal-states (attractors) of connectionist systems and in setting the measure of internal consistency. The reverse side of the coin is that the connectionist modelling is plagued with the well-known problems of inductive logic: how to figure out prior probabilities, how to treat probabilities equal to one, and how to find the optimal rate of inductive generalization. It is ironic to see Churchland riding roughshod over various suggestions in inductive logic: 'even the best of the rules proposed failed to reproduce reliably our pre-analytic judgements of credibility, even in the artificially restricted or toy situations in which they were asked to function' (*NP*, 154). Worse, in the same breath he claims that learning must extend all the way to the beginnings of perceptual organization. If this is true, then the problems with which the connectionist epistemologist has to cope will include all the traditional worries in inductive logic plus some that promise to be even less tractable.

The more conservative critic here might appeal to her argument from the externality of norms: the ideal of coherence, says she, is in the mind of the beholder, not in the workings of the network. The advocate of connectionism has several lines of response. First, he can argue that the ideal of coherence is built into the architecture of the network, but it is not explicitly represented for the network. Second, most people in updating their belief systems presumably use some technique of enhancing the system's coherence without having the slightest inkling of the rules or principles that summarize their epistemic behaviour. This does not exempt their moves from epistemological assessment. The system of rules should be represented primarily in the mind of the judge, and the judge should assess what the agent is doing, not how well she is representing her doings to herself. Third, it is possible, in principle, to construct a connectionist system that can monitor its own states; such a system could monitor the behaviour of its own harmony function and search for ways of maximizing its values.

To summarize, some of the crucial and specifically connectionist processes are quite accessible to the most traditional epistemological assessment in terms of the Classical Picture. If such central items are actually epistemologically friendly, one may believe that others will not be more recalcitrant.

In closing, let me briefly mention the elementary steps. It is not surprising that in many learning procedures such steps do look quite reasonable when measured by usual standards (in some they do not, as 'The butler did it' example mentioned above in section 2.3 on cognitive peculiarities shows).

The simplest example is inductive learning. For example, a two-node network cell can learn that *A* is a probabilistic consequence of *B*. In the learning period the *A*-node was activated conditional on the activation of the *B*-node, and the system has learned, by the use of a Hebbian rule, that *A* and *B* go together. Smolensky summarizes the possibilities under the heading of a principle: 'The Statistical Connection: The strength of the connection between two units is a measure of the statistical relation between their activities' (1989, 57). This is a most reasonable principle for learning by sampling. (If you are not impressed by it, please notice that it is at worst much more reasonable than the inverse rule: strengthen the ties between the representations whose representata do not go together.) The attendant rules (delta-rules, etc.) are merely the implementation of classical rules of inductive learning. It would be too much to claim that the single step is 'rational' or that its performance is 'justified.' Still, it is an element within a proto-rational reasoning process.

If the network is a part of a functioning system, such that the states of its nodes stand for or represent some states of affairs or carry information about them, then its inductive move is *a correct transition from one representational (informational) state to another.* If the network were part of the nervous system of a living creature, selected for its reliability, and if the states of its nodes were to stand for more belief-like states, the move would have been proto-rational. Semantically, it is plausibility preserving, and functionally it would be analogous to rational moves performed by more sophisticated creatures. After all, if neurological research is right, our own thinking might at some very basic level be done by such networks.[42]

4.4. The Hurdle of Explicit Representation

It seems plausible to conclude that the connectionist representations and processes can be assessed within the Classical Picture. However, there are objections in the literature that I still have to consider. In particular, I should confront a line of reasoning coming from more conservative quarters, appealing to the fact that rules of reasoning typically are not explicitly represented in connectionist systems and that such systems normally do not command notions such as 'evidence' or 'support,' although *we* (the theoreticians) may appeal to these notions when judging connectionist process. I shall use as my foil Jay F. Rosenberg's paper (1990) dedicated especially to connectionism. The argument starts with the idea of reasons' being essential for epistemology: 'The essential point is that characterizing a state or transaction or condition or episode in epistemic terms is not providing an empirical, matter-of-factual description of it, but rather locating it within a "logical space" of *reasons* and *justification*. A creature properly in this "logical space" of justification is one capable of having, giving and responding to reasons, and that means, *inter alia,* capable of recognizing and acknowledging the superior (epistemic) authority of some representings *vis-à-vis* others' (Rosenberg 1990, 41; emphasis in text). Only a creature properly in the logical space of reasons is epistemologically interesting; others are below the level of normative epistemology. Let me formulate what I see as his first premise:

A. Epistemology deals only with systems capable of having, giving, and responding to reasons.

He proposes some terminology distinguishing two kinds of systems: 'merely logic conforming or rational creatures and logic-using or *ratio-*

cinative creatures' (ibid., 42; emphasis in text). Merely rational creatures behave *as if* they were guided by reasons. Logic using or ratiocinative creatures are guided by reasons *as* reasons. Only ratiocinative creatures are fit for epistemological appraisal.

In order to unpack the metaphor of 'being in' the logical space of reasons and justification, Rosenberg considers a creature, a deer, and asks what capacities the deer should have in order to be in such a space, that is, to be a ratiocinative creature: 'That is, not only must the deer have the propensity to represent that the fire is nearby whenever it represents that smoke is present ... but it must also be equipped, so to speak, *in some way* to form a judgement that the presence of smoke is evidence that a fire is nearby' (1990, 42; emphasis in text). This is much stronger than the requirement of mere rationality: 'The stronger claim requires that the deer be capable of *representing* its evidence *as* evidence' (ibid.; emphasis in text). Let us formulate this as the second thesis:

B. Only systems representing evidence *as* evidence and *rules as binding* are systems capable of having, giving, and responding to reasons.

Thus, the primitive systems that, in fact, start from evidence and reach states representing what we describe as conclusions from evidence (but without representing evidence as evidence, and rules as something to be followed) fall outside the space of reasons. By (A) they are unfit for epistemological appraisal. All known connectionist systems are, as a matter of fact, such systems, so if (A) and (B) hold, then the critique applies to them.

Finally, Rosenberg invites us to contemplate the possibility of there being a ratiocinative connectionist system (far above the primitive ones mentioned): the adjustment of weights in such systems would lead to a 'homeostatic "web of belief" with interadjustments among representational and inferential commitments,' he claims (1990, 44). But, he immediately asserts, the story of such a system 'is not an alternative to a sentential epistemology, but to the *implementation* of such epistemology' (ibid.; emphasis in text). I am not sure of his rationale, but the ratiocinative creature is probably supposed to represent the rules it follows, and Rosenberg firmly believes that such rules must have the sentential format.[43]

I would like to offer some criticism. For the sake of argument I shall not question Rosenberg's idea that explicit rules must have the form of sentences, and consequently, I shall not question his move from (A) and

(B) to the thesis that the connectionist systems and processes are unfit for classical epistemological assessment in virtue of exemplifying Cognitive Peculiarities. Instead, I shall attack the conjunction of (A) and (B). It seems to me that (A) derives its apparent plausibility from a weak reading of 'reasons,' whereas (B) introduces an extraordinarily strong meaning. Rosenberg's whole argument trades on the ambiguity. A formulation of the weak sense is as follows:

WS: Believing that *r* is a reason for believing that *p* for the believer *B* if *p* is evidence for *r*, and *B* believes that *p* because *B* believes that *r*.

The strong sense requires that the believer herself should have the concept of evidence and the meta-belief that *r* is evidence for *p*:

SS: Believing that *r* is a reason for believing that *p* for *B* if (i) believing *r* is a reason in weak sense for believing that *p* and (ii) *B* believes that *r* is evidence for *p*.

(A) demands responsiveness to reasons. Since Rosenberg appeals (implicitly) to intuitions only, let us test our intuitions concerning such responsiveness. Imagine a cognizer who routinely forms the belief that *p* upon learning that *r*, and, when questioned why she believes that *p*, answers by pointing to *r*. Upon learning that *r* is no longer the case, the cognizer stops expressing belief that *p* and acting accordingly. Would not the change in talk and non-verbal behaviour show that the creature is 'responsive to reasons'? What else is responsiveness to reasons supposed to represent if not the readiness to change one's opinion, not through the impact of brute force, but because of learning new facts, possibly in a non-perceptual way. Such a readiness to change one's behaviour in response to new items of news certainly is a requirement for being suitable for the epistemological appraisal. It should also be sufficient. *There is certainly nothing in the Classical Picture to oppose the sufficiency of the requirement.*

Suppose, further, that our creature does not command the terms 'rule,' 'evidence,' 'proof,' and the like and is innocent of any logical theory. Moreover, it does not generalize about its own performance, and does not say things like '*r* stands to *p* in the same relation as *r′* stands to *p′*,' which would suggest that it has the general concept of evidence without having the word. Would that make the creature not responsive to reasons? Would her belief that *r* not be the reason for her belief that *p* simply because she does not have the concept 'reason' and is not able to generalize about the whole class of belief-pairs? Certainly not.

It is plausible to suppose that people were capable of changing their opinions under the impact of new data long before they were capable (in the same sense) of making generalizations about their cognitive behaviour, of systematizing their intuitions, and of proposing systems of formal rules. (If one thinks that the concepts of 'evidence' and 'proof' are innate, one might consider whether they have had to be activated in order for their owners to be responsive to reasons). Thus, the sense in which (A) is plausible is the weak sense of 'reason' captured by (WS). The thesis (B), however, legislates that only a very strong sense of 'reason' and 'responsiveness to reasons,' captured roughly by (SS) is acceptable. If we read the (SS) meaning of 'responsiveness to reasons' into (A), however, it will become quite implausible. It would deem not responsive to reasons any person (and any deer) who does not have the notion of evidence, of rule of proof, of rules of probability explicitly represented, and who is at least not capable of reconstructing her belief changes in terms of this logical apparatus.

Moreover, an important subset of rules for reasoning cannot be explicitly represented under the threat of regress. Therefore, our most important rules of reasoning are not explicitly represented, and, when reasoning, we 'use' basic, hardwired rules. We can come to represent them in due course, but we do not use them in virtue of being guided by the representation (except when doing exercises in textbook logic). But hardwired rules are exactly what primitive systems are 'using.' I am putting the quotes around 'use' because it is only a metaphor: the networks in our brain (and perhaps some others) operate according to a hardwiring that has a certain structure. This hardwired structure is what grounds the rest of our rationality.

The rigorous epistemologist who wants to deny rationality to the step performed by XOR-net solely on the ground that XOR-net is not following rules (in the normal sense of rule following, implying guidance by explicit rules) must bite the bullet and deny it to the basic step in our fundamental reasoning processes. The non-rigorous epistemologist, such as Pollock, who is ready to extend the intuitive notion of being justified to the operation according to hardwired norms, should be willing to grant the same status to the XOR-net performance (I assume Pollock would do so). I would welcome this as a gesture of justice, not of generosity.

I surmise that there is a third requirement implicit in the formulation of the other two. It is a requirement of reflexivity, of being able to monitor and assess its own states for their rationality, reliability, or generally epistemic authority. A rational cognizer should have a 'metamind.'

None of these requirements is beyond the reach of a connectionist system.

Of course, a determined critic of connectionism might simply stipulate that 'epistemology' should not be interested in persons who have no explicit notions of evidence, rules of proof, inductive logic, and whatever else he likes. He can banish the issues of cognitive development, of the epistemic virtues of unsophisticated enquirers, and all the cognitive qualities that we value but that do not fit the (SS) reading of 'reason.' In that case, simply invent the new term 'schmepistemology,' and let schmepistemology deal with assessment of cognition in general and of all cognizers that are responsive to reason in the undemanding sense of (WS). Schmepistemology will be more general than the narrow-based epistemology, will confront the new and exciting issues in cognitive science, will deal with a wide range of cognizers, and also will be capable of assessing connectionist systems and processes. This is all we need. So the 'conservative' argument poses no threat to the view that connectionism can be accommodated within the Classical Picture.

In conclusion, the connectionist processes are amenable to normative epistemological treatment along three dimensions of descending importance: first, the assessment of global reliability, second, the assessment of global structure, and third, the record of particular types of steps concerning their ability to preserve truth and plausibility. The first and most important dimension is quite unproblematic, and it has turned out that some typical connectionist strategies – deemed specific to connectionism – are very close to the most classical coherence-maximizing. Some of the most often-discussed types of steps and learning rules also appear familiar and reasonable. Therefore, cognitive peculiarities of connectionist items do not exempt them from epistemological assessment. One should reject the relativist-pragmatist criticism of epistemology and uphold the Classical Picture of cognition.

PART THREE
TRUTH AND RATIONALITY

6

The Value of Truth

1. Introduction

In the foregoing part I have endeavoured to show that the truth dimension is available for human cognizers, given their presumed cognitive organization. In Part Three I must go much further and defend the core ideas of the Classical Picture and, above all, the thesis that truth is an important, even central, epistemic value. Remember the strategy of our opponent, the relativist-pragmatist, in his Main Argument. He relies on two premises (1) and (2) and one intermediate conclusion (C2) for his ultimate deconstructive conclusion:

1. *The Irrelevance of Truth*: There is no common goal of cognition, because truth is irrelevant.
2. *Radical Descriptive Pluralism*: (a) Cognitive styles and strategies are environment- and user-relative, and (b) they are structurally radically diverse. (1) and (2) entail

C1. *The Incomparability Thesis*: The strategies are mutually incomparable (with respect both to goals and to their internal structure), and
C2. *Radical Normative Pluralism*: There is no single norm valid for various cognitive styles or strategies.

In the discussion I adopt critically the symmetrical line of argument, planning to organize my counter-argument by contrast:

a. Truth is the central goal of cognition.

b. Various cognitive strategies have a common epistemic goal (and perhaps a common structural core).
c. Cognitive strategies are comparable, at least in respect to their goal.

Therefore, there are single norms valid for widely different cognizers and situations.

Since I hold, in line with the Classical Picture, that the central question of the debate is that of the value of truth, I shall discuss premise (1) and its counter-thesis (a), concentrating most of my effort upon them in this chapter. Then, in chapter 7, I address more briefly (2) and (C1) and defend (b) and (c). I also address an important side-issue: besides being comparable in relation to their goal, are rational strategies also structurally comparable and commensurate? I tentatively defend the positive answer.

Thus, the central questions of this chapter: Should we care about the truth? Does truth have any value? You already know Stich's verdict: 'Now it surely is the case that many people, if asked, would profess to value having true beliefs. But most of the same people would be hard pressed to say anything coherent about what it is for a belief to be true and thus would be quite unable to explain what it is that they value' (*Fragmentation*, 22). 'Do people really value having true beliefs once they are offered a clear view of what having a true belief comes to? The result of the exercise, at least in my own case (and I don't think that my values are idiosyncratic here), was a consistently negative answer' (ibid.). This is a harsh judgment, and none too pleasant for its proponent. Suppose, first, that it is true. Then, its proponent should not care about its truth and should not rejoice about his judgment's being true. Second, suppose it is false. Then the proponent should care about its truth, and ought to regret endorsing a false judgment. In either case, the proponent loses. 'Well' the proponent might counter, 'if my judgment is true, it will have other liberating and generally pleasant consequences, which will largely compensate for the loss.' But if the truth of this judgment can have such good consequences, then truth is not entirely without consequence, at least not in this case. Then, we should care about truth, and the judgment is false. It takes a brave philosopher to defend the judgment, and Stich is certainly such a philosopher.

First, let me present my simple reaction to the central question. Consider the basic cases. People usually care whether some belief to the effect that *p* is true because they care whether *p*. I care whether my belief that Mary loves me is true because I care whether Mary loves me. I am interested primarily in Mary, not in my belief, but I can reformulate my interest so that it is now concentrated upon my belief: I wonder whether my belief that Mary loves me is true. The motivation, however, remains extroverted, turned to the state of affairs, not to what is going on in my head. To care about the truth of '*p*' is to care about *p*. The derived cases almost do not deserve special mention. I want a true answer about the date of Socrates's death from my student, because I want him to be reliable, because he will one day teach these matters and will have to transmit the truth about the date to others, and so on. People learn early in their childhood to appreciate the informational reliability of others and distrust sources that easily and dramatically turn out to be unreliable.

Secondly, why generally endeavour to have true beliefs and not to have false ones? Because of the role of beliefs in guiding our action. If my belief that *p* is true, this will help me in *p*-situations.[1] The interest in having true beliefs is primarily not introverted, directed to beliefs themselves, but extroverted, turned to the outside reality.[2] To use the well-worn analogy with maps, one can collect maps of a country for two purposes: for enjoying the aesthetic properties of maps themselves (attractive colours, fine drawing), in which case I would recommend old maps, inaccurate but beautiful; or one might have a tourist interest, wanting to find the way during travel, in which case one needs an accurate map. The latter is the primary purpose of maps, whereas the former is a secondary function. So it is with beliefs: the primary value is neither aesthetic nor antiquarian but action-guiding, and the valuation in terms of accuracy and truth is the relevant one. This simple answer seems so obvious to some people that they cannot believe that the relativist-pragmatist is rejecting it; 'He must have some sophisticated notion of truth on his mind and is critical of such a notion,' they guess. But if the relativist's objections were directed against only some semantic niceties concerning the definition of truth, they would hardly have revolutionary epistemological consequences. What the relativist-pragmatist endeavours to show is that enquirers should aim not at finding out objective matters of fact (since this is the core of the Classical Picture), but at arriving at any belief that happens to be systematically useful for them in a given situation.

Notice that by preaching his revisionary doctrine, the contemporary relativist makes himself vulnerable to a new variant of an old Socratic anti-relativistic argument.[3] Many people are curious, want to know the truth about things, and consider rational strategies to be good guides for their aim. The relativist-pragmatist cannot escape the requirement of uniform treatment of goals by discriminating against theoretical interests in favour of practical ones. He is in no position to legislate which goals are absolutely better, and he has to treat them equally. An invidious treatment of the truth-goal would introduce discrimination contrary to the very spirit of relativism. The relativist should not criticize the pursuers of truth for their choice, on pain of inconsistency. But if he gives to the truth-goal exactly as much credit as he does to any other, the rationalist has at least a part of what she needs.

The pragmatist would reply that preference for truth derives from a misunderstanding, and that at least some people find it obvious that truth is not particularly useful or worthy, and they do not rest content with the simple argument.[4] It is therefore necessary to probe much more deeply into the issue and to confront the relativist-pragmatist challenge on its own ground.

Stephen Stich – our interlocutor in this part of the book – mounts a forceful attack on the value of truth, which starts with the issue of the 'intrinsic' value of truth and proceeds to detailed semantic considerations about the definition of truth. Stich attempts to show, with the help of these semantic considerations that truth must lack any value – intrinsic and also instrumental. I shall not follow the order chosen by Stich, because I want firmly to establish the correctness of the commonsensical intuitions about truth and its usefulness before plunging into the technical debate about semantics. I shall therefore start with a relatively simple issue of the practical or instrumental value of truth, then proceed to the question about the so-called intrinsic value of truth, and end on technical semantic considerations. On principled grounds it is better for a naturalist to establish the practical value of the item he proposes to our attention. If truth is practically useful, then caring about truth is not a matter of some sophisticated epistemological attitude, but is firmly grounded in human needs, even in the needs of more humble non-human enquirers.[5] Further, it is important to show in the discussion with the pragmatist on dialectical grounds that truth possesses the quality he especially values, namely, usefulness.

Surprisingly, Stich has not argued in any detail his thesis that truth has no instrumental value. There are arguments to this effect in the literature, however, and the relativist-pragmatist can appeal to them. I propose that we give him the best run for his money and consider the most interesting arguments against the utility of truth to be found in the literature. These are the arguments of Michael Devitt, who is by no means a relativist-pragmatist, but whose attack on the practical usefulness of truth might give the relativist-pragmatist welcome support.[6] Let us start by rehearsing the commonsensical evaluation of truth and by proposing some arguments in its favour, so as to present from the outset elements of a positive alternative to the relativist-pragmatist attitude.

2. The Instrumental Value of Truth

2.1. Introduction: Defining the Issue

The question of value can be suitably divided into two: Does truth have any value independent of the practical consequences of true beliefs, that is, any intrinsic value? Is truth useful for practical purposes; that is, does it have instrumental value? In this chapter I address the second question. First, some terminology. Something – an object, property, or state – has instrumental value for an agent if it helps the agent to succeed in attaining her goal. In keeping with the relativist-pragmatist usage, only things having instrumental value will be considered useful here.

A belief is usually held to be capable of having instrumental value. When assessing the value of a belief, we may and should suppose that the agent is acting according to that belief, that is, rationally combining her beliefs and preferences and acting in conformity to her best resulting judgment. Two questions suggest themselves.

1. Non-comparative: Does truth, as such, have instrumental value, and if so, where does this value come from? In answering this question, one should hold all other parameters equal and, in particular, disregard the costs of cognitive resources.
2. Comparative: How does the instrumental value of truth compare with the value of other resources? (Is it better to be smart than to be rich and good looking?)

In this chapter we are concerned with the first question. Two related issues can be discerned in the present context.

a. Evaluative: Is it good (and important) to have true beliefs?
   The answer can be used normatively to give a prescription to the agent or to evaluate the agent's performance. (I share with the relativist-pragmatist this concern for normativeness.)
b. Descriptive: Does truth explain success?

The positive answer to this question leads to the positive answer to the evaluative question. There is also a derived, purely theoretical issue. Sometimes one explains the existence of an entity by its function, and, in particular, one may explain the existence of cognitive mechanisms – organs, strategies, practices, institutions – by the usefulness of beliefs that they produce. Does the truth of beliefs (or their implicata) enter such functional-teleological explanations? I shall concentrate upon the value of true beliefs for our actions, as the relativist-pragmatist also does.[7] The schedule is as follows: after having established, concerning issue (a), that true beliefs are, on the whole, useful in the literal and everyday sense, I address the more sophisticated issue (b) of explaining success. A reader unaccustomed to the intricacies of analytical debate might think that the positive answer to the direct question about usefulness entails that truth explains success; there are, however, matters about explanation that have to be discussed before the entailment is established.

2.2. *Why Is It Better to Know the Truth?*

An agent deliberating about what to do can evaluate the prospective goals and, choosing one, reflect about the ways of attaining the goal. If we leave aside the matter of goal evaluation where the issues about truth are obscured by our ignorance about mechanisms of evaluation, we are left with deliberation about means and with means-end-beliefs.[8] Let me call usefulness in relation to practical choice 'goal-based usefulness' or *G*-usefulness, because it comes from the role the belief plays in the agent's reasoning about attainment of her goal. We shall abbreviate 'valuable through the contribution to the reasoning about the goal' as 'goal-valuable' (*G*-valuable). Two kinds of beliefs can be immediately *G*-valuable: means-end-beliefs specify *the means for attaining the goal* that the agent has set to herself, whereas the *beliefs about the situation* inform the agent that the situation is such that some means-end-belief is applicable and that such-and-such action is within her power. Both enter practical reasoning and contribute to the achievement of the goal.

The second, less general source of instrumental value is the motivational contribution of the agent's belief concerning her estimate of herself and her powers. These beliefs are by themselves *G*-useful, but they might have additional motivational effect, independent of their goal-usefulness, and the potential to have such an effect we shall call motivational value (*M*-value).

Let us concentrate on *G*-valuable beliefs, since they form the vast majority. People generally hold that the true means-end-beliefs are, on the whole, useful and that false ones are harmful: it is good to know when one's train leaves, to have true belief about the state of one's bank account, not to be deceived about the intentions of one's enemies, and so forth. If the door is unlocked and one knows it, one can successfully attempt to leave the room by opening the door.[9] 'He succeeded because he had accurately estimated the situation' is a very common pattern of explanation of success. Another sign that people commonly take true beliefs to be useful and false ones to be harmful is the prudential recommendation of lying to one's enemies and the insistence of the moralists on not lying; if the untruth were not potentially extremely harmful, why worry so much? At a more elementary level, the usefulness of perceptual beliefs (many of them common to men and to more humble enquirers) is obvious. Although a true belief might sometimes be harmful, in being misleading or worse, that seems to be an exception; on the whole, it seems much better to have true beliefs than to have false ones.

Scientists tend in their practice to agree with the commonsensical judgment. The usefulness of science is commonly agreed to reside in its accurate predictions, that is, its true beliefs about future courses of events. The vast technique and methodology of measurement is geared to obtaining accurate observations – again, true beliefs about observable items. It is essential, therefore, that the input to theoretical science – observation data – be as true as possible, and it is essential that its output – predictions – be as true as possible. Many scientists also aim at true theories (and I think they are right in doing so). But even if one remained an instrumentalist about theories themselves, leaving the issue of the truth of theories in abeyance, accuracy of observation and prediction is so paramount for science that it justifies the claim that truth is a central value for it. We should now examine this common wisdom.

A handy example of a situation containing possible courses of action to which we shall refer in this chapter is the following. 'A captain of a submarine, call him simply 'Captain,' wants safely to reach the port in time of war. When the enemy ships are around, he has a more specific goal: to keep out of their sight. The best means for achieving this end is to (issue a command to) dive deeper. The contrary is the case if allied ships are around; then the appropriate action is to surface. Thus, there are two things to know: first, what is the situation like, and second, what is the best means to the proposed end?

A slightly regimented version of the conventional story about means-end-beliefs is as follows: Given a goal G, there will be good and bad ways of attempting to reach it. Some are so bad that they do not lead to the goal at all (surfacing in the face of the enemy ship), some are bad in that they involve high costs for the agent, and some are good. These ways can be represented by means of conditionals, which lead to success under given circumstances:

In the condition C the following conditional *Cond.* is true: If I perform the action *A*, I shall obtain the goal G.

For example, if C is the presence of enemy ships, then the following conditional is true: if we dive deeper we shall pass unnoticed and safe. Suppose that *G* is the agent's goal, that doing *A* is in the agent's power, and that conditions C obtain. Then, doing *A* will make the agent successful in obtaining her goal. Conversely, suppose there is an action *B* that hinders the agent from reaching her goal. If she believes falsely that *B* leads to her goal and chooses *B* over *A*, it will be to her disadvantage. Generally, in order to choose correctly under conditions C, the agent should believe that the relevant conditional *Cond.* is true. It is, of course, desirable that the agent believes roughly that conditions C obtain and that if C, then *Cond.* So the knowledge of *Cond.* and of the truth of the statement describing condition C is directly useful for the agent's practical purposes.

I shall defend this conventional wisdom by defending two fairly obvious claims: the first about beliefs concerning means for ends, such as *Cond.*, and the second about beliefs concerning the whole situation (circumstances C plus *Cond.*).

2.2.1. First Argument: The Logical Link

Generalizing and streamlining the conventional wisdom, I obtain a very simple but interesting argument to the effect that *the link between truth and usefulness in the case of means-end-beliefs in practical reasoning is a necessary link.* It is almost omnipresent but inconspicuous. Take any true means-end proposition, specifying the action (means) sufficient for the end, for example, 'If you surface, you will meet allied ships.' *If this proposition is true, the end will be reached by performing the specified action. The link is conceptual or logical.* If it were not the case that surfacing would bring one into contact with allied ships, it would not have been the case that the means-end proposition is true. A condition for the existence of the link is that the means are specified fully, detailing the required action.

I present the argument once again, this time in polemical form, as a *reductio ad absurdum* of the opposite, relativist stance. The relativist accepts that for a belief to be useful it should help the agent attain her goal, and that there are true means-end-beliefs. Let him pick out one particular such belief:

P: If the agent does *A*, then the state *G* (desired by the agent as her goal) will be realized.

Suppose the agent has *P* and, on the ground of *P*, does *A*. The state *G* results. The relativist knows that the agent's reason for doing *A* was the belief *P*. After learning about the occurrence of *G*, by accepting *P*, the relativist is committed to accepting its retrodictive transform:

P′: *S* has come about because the agent has done *A*.

Given that the agent has done *A* because she believed *P*, the belief in *P* has caused the coming about of *S*. This the relativist has also to accept (at the moment he is not questioning the explanation of action by reasons). At the same time, the relativist claims that true means-end-beliefs are useless. Thus, he must claim that *P* has been useless for *A* in attaining her goal. Now he is committed to accepting at the same time: The belief *P* is useless for the agent in relation to her goal *G*, and the belief *P* has brought it about that the agent has attained her goal *G*. By implication he has to accept: *The belief that makes you succeed is useless for you.* This is obviously out of the question, by the definition of instrumental value (= usefulness) given at the beginning. The relativist is contradicting himself.

We see that the logical link ties two elements together: the truth of the means-end-belief and the success of the action specified as means. How complete does the true means-end belief have to be? Minimally, it has only to specify the action that is in the circumstances sufficient to produce the goal. The hospitable world does the rest. End of the first argument.

2.2.2. Second Argument: The Whole Truth Is Always Useful

In addition to means-end-beliefs, the agent needs beliefs about the situation, which then interact with means-end-beliefs. (Given the goal of avoiding the enemy ship, the belief 'This is an enemy ship' interacts with 'If I issue the command to dive, we shall avoid the ship' to yield the intention to command diving.)

To see clearly the combined power of true beliefs about the situation interacting with true means-end-beliefs, consider the rational Super-Informed Agent. In every set of circumstances she finds herself in, she knows the following: first, the details of the circumstances; second, for every goal that she might have, all relevant means-end-truths and general truths supporting means-end-conditionals; and third, she knows (exactly) which actions are in her power. The Super-Informed Agent discerns, and being rational chooses, only goals attainable for herself. She never fails in attaining those goals for which there is a deterministic path starting from actions she can accomplish. She could fail only through not performing the initial 'basic action,' but she knows which basic actions are within her power. If there is only a probabilistic sequence leading to a goal, her success rate in the long run will be proportionate to the objective probability of the goal state, given the initial action.

It is obvious that true beliefs about the situation and regularities governing means-end relationships have high instrumental value. *The whole truth is always useful.* (In a decently deterministic universe a sufficient bulk of such beliefs would make the attempts of an agent failure proof.) This fact refutes the general claim that true beliefs have no instrumental value. For the converse, notice that complete falsity (if possible) is close to lethal, barring constant interventions of a good demon. It is plausible that the approximation to the whole truth generally will inherit some of the usefulness of the whole truth. Further, the dependence of certainty of success on 'kinds of determination' (deterministic versus probabilistic ties) reveals an important pattern. For the rational Super-Informed Agent the reliability of true beliefs is proportional to the 'degree of necessity' linking events themselves, because the agent exploits the nomic connections in nature. Thus, in the idealized case at least, the link between truth and success in the case of true beliefs about the situation is quite intimate, although not analytical (as it is in the case of true means-end-beliefs). End of the second argument.

How do particular kinds of belief contribute to the success of the Super-Informed Agent? The directly G-useful truths are singular truths about conditions of action, and about relevant means-end conditionals. Since conditions are present or future, useful knowledge will be either descriptive of the present situation or predictive. Also, the conditionals are cast in the form of predictions. Other truths can be G-useful by allowing the agent to derive the directly useful truths from them (or to have them derived by experts). Such truths are indirectly useful to the agent. Many general and law-like statements ('Cyanide is poisonous') are indirectly useful through their impact upon the practical conditional: they enable the agent to derive the practical conditional and support it. Indirect usefulness is transitive (if calculus is needed for physics, and physics for building bridges, then calculus is useful for building bridges).

True, general, and law-expressing propositions are of particular interest. Some such propositions purport to express metaphysically necessary truths, others physically necessary – 'iron' laws – and still others purport to express the ceteris paribus or 'oaken' laws. They entail predictions of various strength or 'firmness.'[10] The general pattern is also valid for less than Super-Informed Agents: Practical reasoning exploits the dependences in nature. With varying strength of dependence goes varying probability of success. In the case of a rational agent the usefulness of true beliefs thus inherits the modal strength of the proposition believed itself.[11]

What about rules of thumb with no nomic force (i.e., no force of natural law)? Although the general principle might be that the more one knows the more successful one is, there is a catch: a true proposition can become misleading if some further relevant feature of the situation is omitted. This does not show that truth is not useful, simply that you need more true beliefs in order to act successfully. 'The door is unlocked' by itself suggests 'If I press the handle and push, it will open.' 'The door is unlocked, but nailed to the frame' suggests 'If I press the handle and push it will not open.' To borrow the idiom of 'defeating,' the fact about nailing defeats the usefulness of our means-end proposition by defeating its truth. The weaker the general law or rule, the more defeaters – exceptions, ceteris paribus items – it has.

Lacking defeaters, true beliefs about the situation interacting with true means-end-beliefs behave as they do in the case of the Super-Informed Agent. (True beliefs, however, might be misleading. This does not thwart our general conclusion, since it concerns only the global utility of truth, but it does pose some interesting problems. We shall address them in the chapter on the explanatory value of truth). From the standpoint of the interested agent the fabric of knowledge consists of beliefs that are directly useful in the goal-based way, supported by others that are useful indirectly (also in the goal-based way), at one or more removes, and perhaps containing some beliefs that are of no practical purpose, not even a very indirect one.

2.2.3. Third Argument: No Policy Promoting False Beliefs

What about false beliefs? Many false beliefs are obviously harmful, for example, many false perceptual beliefs concerning the environment through which one moves and false positive beliefs about safety, edibility, and other positive affordances. Further, the idealization also yields the verdict of harmfulness: The Super-Misinformed agent would not survive for long. It seems, therefore, that it is, in general, better not to have false beliefs.

Some false beliefs, however, might prove useful. A benevolent demon might reward false beliefs in a systematic fashion.[12] Or a harmless false belief might bring a considerable benefit (e.g., one finds the treasure on the wrong way home); or there might be some systematic link between a given false belief and a benefit (e.g., the cases of 'better safe than sorry' variety advertised by Stich: If some white mushrooms are poisonous it will be advantageous for at least some agents to have the false belief that all are).

The question is then the following: Do these cases support any kind of truth-disregarding policy? Remember that the relativist-pragmatist is keen on advising enquirers. Therefore, do the considerations of cases of useful false beliefs add up to a consistent advice against truth? Let us look at particular cases.

The demon hypothesis is too far-fetched to ground an epistemic policy. It is, rather, a reminder of how difficult it is to imagine situations in which false means-end-beliefs massively and systematically lead spontaneously to success and speaks in favour of the usefulness of truth.

The pure coincidences (such as the wrong way home leads to treasure) by definition cannot ground a consistent policy; if longer walks were to bring big money once in a thousand attempts, the roundabout pathways would be crowded with poor or greedy people.[13] If coincidences were all we had to go by, they would suggest the advice to act randomly. The third kind (of the 'better safe than sorry' variety) involves impure coincidences. Take the belief about mushrooms. It is a coincidence that this mushroom is both white *and* poisonous. Thus, it is a coincidence that the belief *F* that all white mushrooms are poisonous leads to avoiding death by poisoning, that is, to surviving. It is not a coincidence that if *F*, all white mushrooms are poisonous, then *T*, this white one is poisonous (because it is an analytic truth), and it is not a coincidence that if I avoid eating this poisonous mushroom, I avoid death by poisoning (due to the mushroom). In such cases of impure coincidence the truth of *T* is a necessary condition of success. If *T* were accessible to the agent, its truth would also have been sufficient. In these cases, therefore, truth is at least as good as falsity.

We have seen that in all the examples adduced the success of false beliefs either is mediated by some truth implied by them or is purely coincidental. This suggests a generalization, namely, that there is a very strong link between truth and success: *Success without truth is merely coincidental.* The rationale for the conjecture is as follows: When we say that a false belief has led to success, we mean that there was something about the role of this belief in the agent's reasoning that has contributed to the success. This can happen only in two ways: either there is no link between the content of the belief state (the belief) and the circumstances in which action *A* has succeeded, or there is a link. In the first case, the success of *A* is independent of the belief content, so the fact that belief with such-and-such content has led to success is mere coincidence. Alternatively, there is a link. The only links that count in practical reasoning, however, are actual or potential inferential links. Thus, the only chance for a false belief to have contributed to success without coincidence is that there be an inferential chain in which a false proposition believed by the agent leads – given the laws of nature – to a true proposition that explains success.

To put it more precisely, in all cases we encounter the following regularity. If a false belief *F* is positively *G*-valuable, then either of the following cases holds:

1. *F* itself (alone or together with other beliefs activated by the agent in her reasoning) strongly supports a true proposition T that either is believed and *G*-valuable or, alternatively, explains the success, because it would have been *G*-valuable if entertained and included in the practical reasoning; or
2. *F* brings about the original goal in a roundabout way (through a deviant causal chain) or has a consequence that is independently valuable for the agent (in such a way that its usefulness compensates for the loss in respect to the original goal).

In case (1) there is a 'hidden truth' that does the job. It does not have to be part of the agent's beliefs, but it must be implied by them. In case (2) it is a pure coincidence that, given the original goal, *F* can be useful at all.

What about the policy to be recommended to enquirers in case (1) of impure coincidence, where the truth of *T* is a necessary condition of success? If *T* were accessible to the agent, its truth would also have been sufficient. Thus, in these cases, truth is at least as good as falsity. The only consistent policy that can be recommended to anyone interested in practical success is to aim at getting true information and avoiding falsehoods.[14]

Remember that we are still idealizing by taking cognitive resources to be almost free. The excessively pessimistic food gatherer forgoes perfectly edible food. Given that the training of discriminatory abilities is (by hypothesis about cognitive resources) cheap, the opportunity cost paid by forgoing food is unreasonable.[15] For vividness, suppose that our pessimistic gatherer lives on mushrooms. A change in sun radiation or a mutation changes the colour of all mushrooms in her habitat to white. The gatherer starves to death. The belief 'White mushrooms are poisonous' yields further false counter-factual generalizations: 'If this mushroom were white it would be poisonous.' Worse: 'If this Amanita (an extremely poisonous variety) were not white, it would not be poisonous.' Excessive pessimism does not help the agent to deal with a changing environment. It leads to the extinction of 'exploratory drive' and in more sophisticated enquirers creates intellectual laziness. Also, excessive scepticism cannot be generally and universally prescribed: 'Believe that everything is poisonous,' is not a good recommendation, but the more plausible 'Between two inductive policies always choose the more cautious one,' would, by transitivity of choice, reduce to the same bad recommendation.[16] All else being equal, it is better to rely on truth than to hope that falsity by coincidence brings a benefit. End of the third argument.

2.2.4. The Fourth Argument: The Only Alternative Available

The relativist-pragmatist thinks that he is offering a viable alternative to truth seeking. His first prescription is that one should not worry about the truth of one's beliefs, and we might call the policy recommended the Truth-Ignoring Policy. His second prescription is that one should use one's belief-forming mechanisms for satisfying one's needs and desires in the given situation: the Situationist Policy.

I want to show that the relativist-pragmatist's proposed policies are impossible to follow simultaneously, so that they are a false alternative to pursuing truth. Suppose John is in a predicament and asks for advice. The Situationist Policy (wisely) demands that one concentrate on the given environment, and the Truth-Ignoring Policy demands that one use the way of forming beliefs that will be useful, regardless of their truth. What procedure can the relativist-pragmatist recommend? Not that John gets as accurate a picture of his predicament as possible, because doing so would violate the Truth-Ignoring Policy; not that he should rely on true generalizations, for the same reason. The relativist can recommend to John that he form an optimistic belief about his own powers, because this will sometimes be better than a cautious pessimistic belief (unless John is sitting impatiently in a boat twenty feet from the shore and can't swim; then an overly optimistic belief that he can swim, would be fatal). Alternatively, John should simply rely on induction by enumeration – such and such belief-forming strategies have proved successful in similar situations, so they might be helpful now. This demand that he rely upon the truth of his beliefs about the past and his conditional beliefs concerning induction, however, violates the Truth-Ignoring Policy.[17] Any appeal to the record of past success relies on such assumptions of truth. If John were really to listen to the relativist-pragmatist, he would remain deprived of guidance and even paralysed, since the relativist-pragmatist is here worse than wrong. Given the facts, his prescriptions are mutually inconsistent. What should John do? It is more rational to flout the first prescription and abide by the second one, that is, try to satisfy one's needs and seek true beliefs about means for one's ends. Thus, the advice of the relativist-pragmatist turns against him; if you want to achieve the goals he is recommending, you should not do what he tells you to do.

The epistemic 'chauvinist' – as Stich calls her – wedded to veritism and the Classical Picture, has her answer. The best, and probably the only systematically reliable, way to satisfy one's needs and desires involves acquiring true beliefs about means for achieving one's goals. One cannot get all the true beliefs one needs simply by limiting oneself to the immediately relevant facts, so one often needs a lot of superstructure in order to arrive at the immediately useful belief. The veritistic advice relies on the epistemic structure of the human condition: different situations offer different opportunities to form a true picture of them, and different true beliefs accord with different courses of action. She gives the following banal but reliable advice to John in his predicament. First, try to form true beliefs about your situation. See which strategy is most likely to yield true singular beliefs about it. These particular or singular beliefs are supposed to take care of the environmental constraints. Then, ask yourself what kind of action will get you out of the predicament as you see it. In order to assess various courses of action, you should have a pool of true (or truth-like) general beliefs telling you which things depend on which other things. The more such beliefs you have and the closer to truth they are, the better it is for you. See which general beliefs apply. Put together your general beliefs and your picture of the situation and try to fit the two together in order to arrive at true beliefs about means for your end. You will obtain something like a practical syllogism. Act on its conclusion. End of the fourth argument.

2.2.5. Remarks about Motivational Value

Let us pass now very briefly to the other sort of instrumental value that a belief can have. As I mentioned earlier, some beliefs can and do predispose their holders *antecedently to means-end deliberation* to act in a certain way and thereby bring them success or failure. A belief, true or not, can bring its holder into a state that is advantageous or disadvantageous for attaining some end. Call this value *M*-based value and the belief *M*-valuable. *M*-based value of a belief does not come from its role in practical reasoning itself. Therefore, the content of the belief is less tightly connected to the aim the agent has set himself. True beliefs about one's powers are normally useful, and vast overestimation of one's powers are lethal, or at least very dangerous. Still, all sorts of deceptive beliefs about oneself can be extremely useful as well, and true but sad news can be extremely harmful. The following example is from Jon Elster: 'To the extent, then, that self-confidence has a positive effect on motivation and achievement, excessively positive self-perception due to cognitive bias may have good consequences, *even when it falls short of a complete self-fulfilling prophecy.* In many cases, I submit, the belief that one will achieve much is a causal condition for achieving anything at all' (1983, 158; emphasis in text). It follows that the same belief can have both goal-based value and *M*-based value, sometimes of opposite kind (e.g., John learns the truth that the only way to save his life is to submit to a very dangerous medical operation. The news obviously has high value in relation to his goal to survive, but it also completely paralyses him, bringing a high *M*-disvalue.)

In most cases, however – similar to the mushroom example with goal-valuable beliefs – some true beliefs can have the same beneficial effect as a false *M*-valuable belief (e.g., 'If I think that I can write the paper because I am put in a good mood by the false thought that I am handsome, then the same effect will be produced simply by the true belief than I can write the paper, period.'). More than that, in such cases the false *M*-belief works by producing the *true* belief 'I can do the requisite action,' in a similar way in which a false G-valuable belief ('All white mushrooms are poisonous') works by producing a true belief ('This white mushroom is poisonous'). One should notice that the trick works only if the agent is actually capable of performing the task, that is, if her belief that performing the task is within her power is true. This prompts the guess that the *M*-value of such false statements has a similar origin to the *G*-value of false statements that produce true ones, that is, that it is really a 'hidden truth' implied by the falsehood that is doing the work. A belief is *M*-positive because *it is itself true, or – being itself false – produces in the agent a true belief about her capacities* (the false belief 'I am good looking' in our example produces the belief 'I am capable of writing a good paper,' which is actually true).[18]

If the conjecture is true, therefore, there is a deep similarity between the two sorts of success discussed up to this point: the success of false *G*-valuable beliefs with true implicata and the success of false *M*-valuable beliefs! There is an asymmetry, however, concerning the relation between *F* and *T*: the deliberative character of the context in which a belief is *G*-valuable demands that the *F-T* relation be one of rational support, whereas the non-rational character of *M*-contexts allows for non-rational, purely causal *F-T* links.

I may now venture a general conclusion: (1) It is analytic that true means-end-beliefs are useful for attaining the goal and that false ones have negative utility for attaining the goal. Thus, in all cases in which the agent has hit upon a true means-end-belief that represents and suggests an action sufficient to achieve the end, the success is *guaranteed* by the truth. (2) The whole truth is always useful, and complete falsity is lethal, whereas a partial truth generally inherits some usefulness of the whole truth. (3) False beliefs can be useful either through pure coincidence or through entailing, supporting, or producing a true proposition that actually explains the success. None of these can ground a consistent policy for the enquirer. Therefore, it seems that the truth is on the whole quite useful, and it is certain that the only consistent policy to be recommended to enquirers is to search for it.

2.3 Rebutting the Counter-Arguments

What kind of counter-arguments does the relativist-pragmatist have at his disposal to shake people's confidence in the usefulness of truth? Let us begin with the most general arguments. I shall review the main lines of attack, starting with a simple, elementary remark that paves the way for the atrocities to come:[19]

1. A belief can be visibly useful for attaining a goal, but at the same time dramatically and in a hidden way harmful in relation to another goal.

Answer: The argument illicitly trades on the plurality of goals. It is like saying that a kitchen knife is not useful because one can kill oneself with it. The agent's goal has to be specified in advance, or else one does not know what one is arguing about.[20]

The naïve remark prepares us for the argument that does appear in the literature (Devitt 1987). In its general form (subsuming many variations) it is, perhaps, *the most popular philosophical argument against truth*:

2. Truth is neither necessary nor sufficient for success. It is obviously not necessary (e.g., ants are quite successful without having beliefs, so, a fortiori, without having true beliefs). It is not sufficient; true beliefs don't help against many contingencies.

Answer: Of course, truth is neither sufficient nor necessary for success. Truth, in general, is not conceptually tied to success, although, as we have tried to show, the truth of certain means-end-beliefs is. Usefulness for a purpose, however, requires neither: matches are useful for lighting cigarettes, being neither necessary nor sufficient in the philosopher's strict sense of the word (there are other means, and with the matches one needs the presence of oxygen, the cigarette should not be wet, etc.); cars are useful for travelling (although insufficient without roads and without gasoline), and so forth. Means are useful by contributing to success in achieving some end. In the same line, truth is useful by being *a contributory cause of success*, and true beliefs fill the bill: one can succeed without having true beliefs, but when one succeeds through correct practical reasoning and consequent trying, having relevant true beliefs is a necessary part of that process.[21] The confusion between sufficient/necessary conditionship and causal relevance appears in a great many variations in relativist-pragmatist arguments. As a case in point, an example from Stich, and the *only* example he gives against the utility of truth independent from technical semantic considerations, is the following: 'Consider survival. Is true belief *always* more conducive to survival than false belief? Clearly the answer is no. To see the point we need only reflect on the plight of poor Harry who believed that his flight left at 7:45 a.m. He wrote it down, ordered a cab the night before, and asked his wife to be sure he was out of bed by 6:30. Harry's belief was true, and he got to the airport just on time. Unfortunately, the flight crashed, and Harry died. Had Harry falsely believed that the flight left at 8:45, he would have missed the flight and survived. So true belief is sometimes less conducive to survival than false belief' (*Fragmentation*, 123; emphasis in text).

The example is irrelevant and confused on two counts. First failure: it is essential for its point that it concerns an exception. To see this, try to generalize and derive some good advice. The only candidate I can think about is 'Don't get reliable information about the airline timetable, so that you will often miss planes, which might save your life.' It sounds like a bad joke. Avoiding truth is not a policy that can be generally recommended. Second failure: the goal is not specified in advance – Harry did realize one goal, the immediate one of catching his plane, but he has failed dramatically on the most important goal, to stay alive. But this is analogous to the example with knives: the fact that one can fatally injure oneself with a knife (fail in realizing the goal of staying alive) does not entail that knives are not useful. Here the confusion about necessary/sufficient conditionship and usefulness is combined with the issue of the plurality of goals, and the results are dramatic. Does Stich imply that only foolproof means are useful at all? That planes, cars and ships are not useful because of the possibility of accidents, that fire, electricity, gas stoves, are not useful, that it is a superstition to believe that houses are useful (they are not always good for survival because in an earthquake they can tumble down and kill you)? *By this criterion nothing is useful* – certainly not screwdrivers, pressure cookers, rat poison, electric lamps,[22] bottles, window panes; potential danger deprives all of them of their alleged usefulness. Now, if this is a price to pay in order to show that truth is not useful, let it be paid by someone else. Our philosophers have confused the non-necessity and non-sufficiency of truth for success with the non-existence of a causal link tying the former to the latter.

The example illustrates a recurring feature of Stich's arguments: he successfully shows that an unpleasant situation sometimes occurs and then goes on to use the result as if he has established that the situation is frequent, typical, and central for the issue. A variant of the fallacy is establishing the bare possibility, and then surreptitiously jumping to the actuality. For future reference let me call these jumps Pessimistic Leaps.

Fortunately, we may now address a more sophisticated and interesting argument:

3. The epistemic competitors: Truth might seem successful, but so are its

> competitors. In the words of M. Devitt, who has championed this line of attack: 'True beliefs tend not to face recalcitrant experience. The problem is that warranted or justified beliefs tend not to either. A belief that is well-supported by past experience is likely to be also by future experience; so the expectations the belief gives rise to are unlikely to be disappointed.' (1987, 36)

How good are the epistemic competitors? Take justification, for example. Justification and truth presumably often go together, and then it is hard to guess which of them did the job. Therefore, we should separate the two, and consider the effects of truth without justification and of justification without truth. Remember the submarine example and its hero, the Captain. His success story is the story of truth plus justification: the Captain sees an allied ship and issues a command to surface, or he gets a reliable report that enemy ships are around and issues a command to dive deeper. In order to see which component of the two, justification and truth, is responsible for success, one should isolate each.

First, justification without truth. Suppose the enemy has, unbeknownst to the Captain, developed a way of perfectly masking his ships as allied ones. Through his periscope the Captain scrutinizes the ship his submarine is facing, and after scrupulous reflection decides that it is an allied ship. His belief is justified but false. If he acts in accordance with it, he will bring disaster to the submarine.

Second, truth without justification: Suppose the submarine meets the same enemy ship (which looks like an allied ship). The drunken Captain overlooks the appearance and decides out of the blue that it is an enemy ship. His belief is unjustified yet true. If he acts in accordance with it, he will succeed in saving the submarine. When push comes to shove, it is the truth that counts.

The moral: Success primarily depends on the world, that is, on whether the world is the way the belief represents it to be; it does not depend on the intrinsic virtues of the believer. Where the truth is successful, one cannot substitute justification alone *salva utilitate* (preserving the success), so justification is valuable as a guide to truth, but it is truth, not justification, that does the job.[23]

2.4. *Explanatory Value*

After the usefulness of truth has been established on both inductive and intuitive grounds, I pass to the more 'philosophical' question of whether truth explains success.[24] Devitt has argued that success can always be explained in two stages, neither of which requires appeal to truth. In the first stage the basic action that brought the benefit is explained by appealing to the internal process of practical reasoning, and in the second stage the route from the action to benefit is described in purely external terms, so that truth falls out. Let us illustrate his point using our submarine example and two very simple success stories. The first story is as follows. In circumstance *E* of the presence of the enemy ship the Captain recognizes the ship, forms the belief '*E*' ('The enemy ship is present'), uses his knowledge of the means-end-conditional 'If *E*, then dive deeper,' issues the command to dive deeper, and the submarine escapes unnoticed. The second story is as follows. In the presence of an allied ship – the situation *A* – the Captain forms the belief '*A*,' goes through analogous thought processes, and again saves the ship.

The explanation of both stories, recommended by Devitt, starts in its first, internal stage from a narrow characterization of the Captain's decision-making process, from his visual states, through the deployment of beliefs in reasoning, to the issuing of a command. The second, external stage takes him from the issued command to the escape. The internal part does not mention truth, since it deals only with the truth-bearer; the external part does not mention truth, since it deals only with the truth-maker; no part is concerned with the relationship of the truth-bearer and the truth-maker.

In criticizing, notice, first, that the bipartite explanation is incomplete. The first, internal part does not explain why, in the given circumstances, the Captain issued the 'Dive!' command. An essential ingredient is missing: namely, that he *saw* the ship. Only his visual experience is recorded, not its origin, that is, that the circumstance *E*, the presence of the ship, caused him to believe '*E*.' In order to incorporate this fact, the theoretician has to link the internal story to the external one at the beginning, not at the middle. ('But methodological solipsism allows one to skip the causal history!' our interlocutor exclaims. False: methodological solipsism allows one to separate the internal from the external, not to forget the external causes when explaining why the agent did something here and now.)

Further, perhaps as the consequence of this omission, nowhere in the explanation do we come across the following simple truths:

1. If *E* were not present, and everything else – in particular, the Captain's beliefs – were the same, the Captain would not have succeeded.

2. If the Captain believed that not-*E* and everything else were the same, the Captain would not have succeeded.
3. Given that the Captain believed that *E*, and *E*, he succeeded.

Of course, they are implicit in the explanation: If *E* were not present, the outside world would have been different, so the external part of the story would come out different, and analogously for the rest. (1), (2), and (3) form an implicit part of the explanation. They might have gained some prominence if the micro-explanation had started with the causal sequence *E*-belief that *E*, instead of starting with the Captain's internal states.

Do we need these truths? Let us look at both stories together. The bipartite explanations of the success in the two stories need not reveal any common traits: the narrow ancestry of the two decisions is different, and the external circumstances differ as well. Do the stories have anything in common? Is there any generalization to be gleaned from both? Yes, of course. In the first story, in the circumstances *E*, the Captain believed '*E*' and succeeded. In the second story, in circumstances *A*, Captain believed *A* and succeeded. In the first story, the three counter-factuals (1), (2), and (3) were true, and in the second story, very similar counter-factuals hold (with some implicit ceteris paribus clauses):

1′. If *A* were not present, and everything else were the same – in particular, the Captain's beliefs – he would not have succeeded.
2′. If the Captain did not believe *A*, and everything else, particularly the outside circumstances, were the same, he would not have succeeded.
3′. If the Captain believes that *A* obtains, and *A* does obtain, the Captain succeeds.

There is a common pattern, invisible in the bipartite micro-explanations, but perfectly transparent once the counter-factual dependences are taken into consideration. It is precisely this pattern that is captured by the following:

* If the Captain's beliefs were not true, he would not have succeeded.
** If the Captain's beliefs are true, he succeeds.

The generalization in terms of truth captures the common, general features of both situations, invisible in micro-explanation. Statements (*) and (**) legitimately can be used in answering the question 'Why did the Captain succeed?' What does the explanatory work is the notion of truth. The explanation of success by the truth of the beliefs involved is a higher-level explanation, showing regularities inaccessible at the micro-level of particular causal dealings. On the micro-level it is hard to see that it is some relationship of the Captain's beliefs to the circumstances that ensures his success. When counter-factuals (1), (2), and (3) are deployed, the fact becomes more visible. It is the generalization to other cases, however, that points to the need for a notion like truth.[25]

We have almost finished discussing the instrumental value of truth, except for Stich's master argument from semantics. As mentioned above, Stich argues from a sophisticated semantic theory and claims that this argument – which I dubbed the Semantic Argument – leads to the denial of all value of truth. His rationale for flouting common sense is that people are confused about the nature of truth: 'Now it surely is the case that many people, if asked, would profess to value having true beliefs. But most of the same people would be hard pressed to say anything coherent about what it is for a belief to be true and thus would be quite unable to explain what it is that they value' (*Fragmentation*, 22). In his writings subsequent to *Fragmentation*, particularly in his 'Do True Believers Exist?' (1991a), he draws further, metaphysical lessons from the Semantic Argument.[26] More important, his own original argument against the practical value of truth turns on the results of the Semantic Argument. In order to address the argument, we should make a detour through his critique of the intrinsic value of truth.

3. Intrinsic Value and the Semantic Argument

3.1. The Argument Recounted

Out of pure curiosity, people sometimes value knowing truth. The target value is then intrinsic in the sense of 'non-instrumental.' Of course, 'intrinsic' does not mean 'non-worldly'; on the contrary, the intrinsic value of truth seems to reside in what true beliefs tell us about the world. Against the assumption that truth is intrinsically valuable, Stich has invented his new and original argument, the Semantic Argument.

The strategy used in the Semantic Argument parallels that used in the Main Argument, taking the reader from the plurality of alternatives and the absence of common measure straight to the relativist conclusion. The form of the argument is roughly the following:

a. Show by using the semi-formal theory of truth and reference that there is not a single notion of truth, but a family of distinct truth notions (and predicates), our common notion being just one among them.
b. Assume that various truth notions are at odds with each other, possibly yielding different verdicts about the same situations and prompting conflicting courses of behaviour.
c. Show that our predilection for our notion of truth is ungrounded, and that there is no rational way of choosing among the members of the family, so that pursuing any one of many 'truths' is an idiosyncratic and irrational choice.

There is a naturalistic presumption against accepting the conclusion of the Semantic Argument, regardless of the detail of the argument itself. Human curiosity is such a widespread, species-endemic phenomenon, that any sophisticated semantic theory having a consequence that is completely misplaced is prima facie implausible (like a medical theory endeavouring conceptually to prove that health is unimportant). It is more probable that the sophisticated reasoning contains an error or does not capture the essential aspects of the pre-theoretical notion of 'truth' than that people massively misrepresent their valuations.

I think I have located the error: it is (b) that is problematic, and *various 'truth notions' are not epistemically in competition*, so there is no need to worry about which one to choose.[27] Stich, however, expends most space on (a) and (c). Let me first present and then examine the argument.

Stich's argument for (a) starts from the standard assumptions of the recent semantics for natural languages plus the Language of Thought hypothesis: people think in mental sentences and to believe that *p* is to have a mental sentence '*p*' in one's 'belief-box' (this apparatus will be not be questioned in what follows). Sentences have truth conditions (states of affairs, for convenience), and there exists a mapping from sentences to their truth conditions, called the 'interpretation function.' The mapping that maps singular terms onto their referents – the reference scheme – is a 'part' of the mapping of the whole sentence onto its truth-conditions. Of course, syntactically identical strings can figure in different mapping; for example, the phonetic string we get by pronouncing 'Empedocles leaped,' would yield in German a sentence that is true if and only if Empedocles is in love, that is, 'Empedocles liebt.'[28] Thus, the same phonetic string (or hypothetical neural-tokens) gets different truth conditions under different interpretation functions. Now, the reference schemes can differ not only in what individuals they pick up, but also in the ways they do it. Stich's paradigm contrast is the well-known one between the causal and the descriptive manner of picking up a referent: a word '*A*' may refer to the item baptised '*A*' in virtue of there being a series of speakers transmitting the word up to its present user by a causal chain; or '*A*' can be associated with a description and refer simply to any item that satisfies the description. Call the causal reference scheme REFERENCE-*c*, and the descriptive one REFERENCE-*d*.

Stich takes as central the reference of proper names. Suppose – along with him – that the name 'Jonah' (in object-language) was given to a person Jonah-*c* ('*c*' for causal) who never was in the belly of the fish, and of whom the biblical story is thus false. Call the reference scheme based only upon the causal origin REFERENCE-*c*. Suppose, further, that there was a person, whose name was 'Samuel,' who is the real doer of the famous exploits attributed falsely to Jonah-*c*; he was in the belly of a fish, and so on. Now, contrast the reference scheme that completely disregards the causal origin and rules that a name is to refer to the person of which the most descriptions associated with the name are true and call it REFERENCE-*d*. The difference between the reference schemes runs deeper than the difference between usual natural languages, since the assignment of the nominatum follows different principles: causal origin in the first case, descriptive truth in the second. Further, consider various schemes of reference for proper names that differ in the weight of the descriptive component of meaning – from zero (no description is relevant for the reference of 'Jonah') to the maximum (all and only descriptions determine the reference of 'Jonah'). There is a considerable wealth of alternative different reference schemes, REFERENCE*, REFERENCE**, and so on.

An analogous story can be told about predicate terms. Truth conditions of sentences are determined by the reference of sentence parts. In the simplest theory, a sentence such as 'Jonah was a Moabite' gets mapped onto the state of affairs in which Jonah-*c* – the REFERENT-*c* of 'Jonah' – was a member of the set denoted by 'Moabite' under REFERENCE-*c*. The mapping is called the 'interpretation function' and in this case is a causal interpretation function. With each reference scheme an interpretation function is associated, mapping the whole sentence onto some states of affairs. Such an interpretation function then determines a corresponding technical notion of TRUTH(*, ..., *): 'Each of these alternative interpretation functions provides an alternative specification of the truth conditions for beliefs. So while the interpretation function based on the intuitively sanctioned notion of reference might specify that a certain belief token of mine is true if and only if there is no H_2O on the sun, an interpretation function based on REFERENCE*** would specify that the same belief token is true (or, better, TRUE***) if and only if (iff) there is no H_2O or XYZ on the sun' (*Fragmentation*, 117). As an illustration, consider TRUTH-*c*:

'*a* is *P*' is TRUE-*c* (i.e., true under the reference scheme REFERENCE-*c* and the attendant interpretation function) iff the causally identified referent of *a* is *P*.

In our example,

'Jonah was a Moabite' is TRUE-*c* iff Jonah-*c* was Moabite.

The same syntactic string is used differently under TRUTH-*d*:

'*a* is *P*' is TRUE-*d* iff the descriptively identified referent of *a* is *P*.

For example,

'Jonah was a Moabite' is TRUE-*d* iff Samuel was a Moabite.[29]

There are many interpretation functions and attendant TRUTH(* ... *)-notions. Stich assumes – probably correctly – that people abide by some given reference scheme and interpretation function, probably the causal or causal-functional one (REFERENCE-*c* and TRUTH-*c*). This ends stage (a). It remains to be shown that members of the truth-family are mutually incompatible and enter epistemic competition.

Stage (b) is as follows. From the fact that TRUTH-*c* and TRUTH-*d* result from different reference schemes, Stich seems to conclude that they stand for competing alternatives. If TRUTH-*c* is our choice, Stich thinks that when we say 'truth,' we refer to TRUTH-*c* only. Other TRUTH(* ... *)s then stand for substantially different epistemic goals than our goal. The only argument he offers to support this extremely important step is that we spontaneously accept such a stance and condemn other choices. 'These alternative interpretation functions are not the ones sanctioned by our intuitive judgment. They strike us as wrong or inappropriate' (*Fragmentation*, 245). Call this line of thought the Argument from Intolerance. To get an intuitive feel of the implications of the

Argument, consider the Jonah example. Assuming that our notion of reference and truth are, respectively, REFERENCE-*c* and TRUTH-*c*, imagine that we meet a biblical scholar, call him the '*d*-scholar,' who is working on the legend of Jonah. He tells us that he is not interested in who did actually first carry the name 'Jonah,' but he works on the fellow who was in the belly of the fish and who preached in Nineveh, that is, the fellow for whom the name 'Jonah' is descriptively adequate and to whom it *d*-refers. The scholar has spent ten years of his life trying to find out in the historical record whether his Jonah (the referent of 'Jonah' by REFERENCE-*d*) was a Moabite. In Stich's parlance the scholar wanted to know whether the sentence 'Jonah was a Moabite' is TRUE-*d*. Given that TRUTH-*d* is different from TRUTH-*c*, which is 'our' truth, Stich's Argument would predict the following reaction of ours: we would normally say that our scholar is not interested in truth, and we would claim that he is interested in something radically different from truth, his interest being somehow perverse, 'wrong or inappropriate.'

Step (c) is as follows. There are many alternatives to the given scheme, and people ignore all these alternatives in preference to the given one. This one, of course, is not chosen deliberately and rationally; it is merely the traditional scheme we happen to be 'born into.' Abiding by one scheme is, to Stich's taste, 'highly idiosyncratic' and wrong.[30] By cherishing it, we waste the immense potential of semantically non-interpretable syntactic strings we have at our disposal – he does not say how. But worse, we miss all the alternative TRUTH(* ... *)s. Stich invites us to consider a set of belief tokens, say, S_1, ..., S_n (*Fragmentation*, 127). Interpreted according to the function TRUTH*, it will have a certain number n^* of positively valued ('true*') tokens. Interpreted differently, by two-starred TRUTH**, it will have another number, n^{**} positively valued ('true**') tokens, and so on for each TRUTH*, ...*. Now *n*s will differ, so if we abide by TRUTH*, we miss all the good things from the other ones and might get a smaller set of positively valued tokens than we would have had with some other alternative. Call this line the Argument from Omission.

His conclusion is as follows: 'But recall that, on the accounts of mental representation in question, a belief is true if and only if it is mapped to a true proposition *by the intuitively sanctioned mapping function*. If it is granted that there is nothing uniquely special or important about that intuitive function – that it is simply one mapping among many – it would seem to follow that there is nothing special or important about having true beliefs' (*Fragmentation*, 23; emphasis in text). Finally, Stich offers the reader an additional bonus. His semantic considerations also yield – in his view – an argument against the usefulness of truth. It relies on his assumption (b) that various interpretation functions yield mutually competing truth-predicates, so that the veritist faces a difficult choice:

So the fact (if it is a fact) that our intuitive interpretation function is the product of an extended process of biological or social evolution does not make it plausible that it is more conducive to survival or thriving (or anything else) than any of the nonintuitive functions that characterize alternative notions of TRUTH* ... * Moreover, even if it could be shown that using the intuitively sanctioned interpretation function is especially conductive to survival or success, this would still not be enough to show that *having true beliefs* is more instrumentally valuable than having TRUE* ... * ones. To show this, it would presumably have to be shown that the reason the intuitively sanctioned interpretation function is conducive to success is that it fosters believing the truth.' (Ibid., 122; emphasis in text)

This is his semantic argument against the usefulness of truth. If truth has no intrinsic value and has no usefulness, then it should be irrelevant. The major premise of the Main Argument holds, and relativism-pragmatism is rendered plausible. Or so it seems.

3.2. The Argument Citicized

I shall now try to show that the Semantic Argument is flawed. The counter-attack will focus on steps (b) and (c). Given that Stich never substantiates the idea that different truth predicates enter epistemic competition, except by appeal to our conservativeness about truth, first I shall argue against the idea and then question his contention that we are conservative and ready to discriminate against people who are seeking some kind of positive correlation other than TRUTH*, and that we do not see them as truth seekers (in spite of their being all right on other relevant counts, including honesty, dedication, etc.). An important by-product of the discussion will be the insight that our epistemic goal is not specifically TRUTH*, as opposed to TRUTH**, or TRUTH***, but something more general, namely, having beliefs that 'correspond' to how things are (i.e., believing that *p* only if *p*), TRUTH* being only a means to achieve the more general goal. The generality of function should then undermine the accusation that by pursuing TRUTH* we are untrue to wider Truth and should vindicate the usual strategy of reasonable enquirers: abide by the interpretation function that you have and try to get to know as much about the facts as you can. This will bring us back to the extroverted approach with which we began. First, the issue of competition. To see that various truth-predicates need not compete with each other, consider the simplest case: various natural languages (which presumably share the same scheme of reference). The traditional analysis of truth breaks the concept down into more specific notions of truth-in-*L* where *L* is a schematic letter for various languages: truth-in-English, truth-in-Croatian, and so on. Now, when I seriously utter an English indicative sentence, say, 'It is raining,' I intend to say something true by using it as a sentence with its usual English meaning. The analogous process goes on when I speak my mother tongue, Croatian. These truths-in-*L*, however, are not in competition for semantic value: if a Croatian sentence is true-in-Croatian, then its English translation is true-in-English (barring logical paradoxes in which the translatability is itself in question). Therefore, they cannot compete for practical value, in the sense of prompting different advice about same matters. Nor do they compete epistemically: my caring for truth-in-Croatian does not compete with my caring for truth-in-English, nor does it compete with the caring of a monolingual American friend of mine. His care for truth-in-English (and not for truth-in-languages-he-does-not-speak) does not make his love for truth idiosyncratic or conservative. Similarly, one does not become a better enquirer into truth simply by expanding the range of *L* and the true-in-*L* schemata that presumably capture one's epistemic concern. Commonsensical intuition says that all honest and serious speakers of various languages aim at the same goal, namely, the truth, the distinction between various kinds of truth-in-*L* being irrelevant to the determination of the goal. It does not consider as idiosyncratic or conservative the practice of a native speaker of English using her native language to state what she thinks is the case. No matter what language is used, the aim of the sincere speaker is that her statement should 'track' the state of affairs it speaks about (if she states '*p*,' then *p*). So, the analysis of truth in terms of truth-in-*L* does not attain the right level of generality to characterize with precision speakers' cognitively oriented goals, such as transmission of true information.

What about Stich's argument concerning the difference in the schemes of reference and truth for beliefs? Here there are no entrenched general views, so we should tread carefully. Stich seems to think that different types of mapping sentences onto states of affairs define mutually competing epistemic goals, and that common sense is wedded to a certain type, TRUTH*, which then dictates its epistemic goal, so that we regard other TRUTH(* ... *) seekers as enquirers who aim not at truth, but at some essentially different goal, or at least we should regard them as such. I shall argue that the case with different TRUTH(* ... *)s is analogous to the case of different languages. First, they do not compete for semantic value. If *p* is TRUE*, then, barring logical paradoxes, its 'translation' *p*, in the language using REFERENCE** and asserting that the same state of affairs obtains, is TRUE**. To see this, let *S* stand for the syntactic string 'The plane leaves at 7:45 a.m.,' let TRUE* map it onto its usual truth conditions, so that it asserts that the plane leaves at 7:45 a.m. under interpretation scheme *I**, and let *Q* assert the same under interpretation scheme *I***. Then *S* is TRUE* exactly in the circumstances in which *Q* is TRUE**. Other interpretation-functions and truth-predicates should differ from TRUTH* either in the referents of the referring expression(s) or in the extensions of the predicate expression and then cannot directly clash with TRUE*. Moreover, they cannot clash indirectly, since the state of affairs that the plane leaves at 7:45 a.m. makes false any sentence that implies that it does not, and the state cannot cease to obtain simply because of variations of interpretation-functions. Generally, in the model in which *p* is TRUE* a certain state of affairs *A* obtains and any sentence-under-interpretation that states (or implies) that *A* does not obtain cannot be true in the same model. Therefore, they do not compete for practical value and cannot yield or ground competing advice on the same matter (e.g., when to wake up in order to catch one's plane), *pace* Stich.

Do they compete epistemically? It does not seem so, both by analogy with various truths-in-language and by semantic considerations. We can still ask whether people would consider other schemes to be epistemic competitors, as the Argument from Intolerance maintains, and see whether commonsensical intuitions are as conservative and intolerant as Stich supposes. For example, would we condemn the colleagues who use different means of fixing reference for not being intellectually honest, or not being truth-seekers merely because of the difference in their interpretation functions? Consider the example of the *d*-scholar who – abiding by TRUTH-*d* – has spent ten years of his life trying to find in the historical record whether his Jonah (the referent of 'Jonah' by REFERENCE-*d*) was a Moabite. Remember that Stich's Argument from Intolerance predicts that we would normally say that our scholar is interested not in truth but in something radically different from truth, and that his interest is 'wrong or inappropriate.' But would we say so? The scholar, of course, intuitively speaking, is seeking the truth about a certain fellow, and his interest is of a completely respectable kind. The way he has of identifying the fellow is irrelevant to the question at hand. My intuition tells me that I would regard him as sharing his epistemic goal with us, and I expect that the reader will have similar intuitions.[31] The epistemic goal we seek, that is, to believe what actually is or was the case, is more general than particular TRUTH-and-REFERENCE schemes.

The following analogy might be helpful. Let the goal under discussion (and the analogue of truth) be health. Suppose that you have a detailed breakdown of the notion of health-for-humans, in short, HEALTH* containing a Health Chart, that is, a specification in highly technical medical vocabulary of what every organ 'should be doing' if its owner is to be healthy. This is our analogue of the Theory of Truth. Now, a person ignorant of the Chart, but careful about food, dedicated to jogging, and so on, aiming at not falling ill, at being fine, and so forth thinks she cares for her health. In fact, she directly contributes to such a state of her organism as prescribed by the Chart. When confronted with such a low-level description and asked: 'Do you really care about that?' however, most of us either would be puzzled or would answer in the negative. That does not entail that we don't care about our health. Further, take an intelligent extraterrestrial, built out of silicon, and the corresponding specification of her healthy state, specifying HEALTH***. Suppose she cares a great deal about being physically fit, but extraterrestrials do it by lying still, by continuous practice of telekinesis, and by reading comics. There is nothing in her specification that would even remotely resemble the human Health Chart. If she and our jogging human could communicate, they might engage in conversation concerning fitness, illnesses, and similar topics. They would discover that they care, intuitively speaking, about the same things. The human could be puzzled about the relation of telekinesis and comics to health, she might even laugh at the extraterrestrial, but there is no reason for her to doubt that the extraterrestrial is pursuing being healthy, though in odd ways. Conversely, nothing in the situation would license the following conclusions. 'The human is not interested in her health, because health is a very exotic thing described in the Health Chart, and if she read the Health Chart, she would not say that she cared about what was described there (the analogue of Stich's claim that people would stop thinking that they cared about truth if they came to understand the semantic Theory of Truth). The human is conservative and idiosyncratic in her attitude towards her health because she uncritically accepts a very specific notion of HEALTH*. The human could not possibly think that the extraterrestrial has the same goal as she has.' The health goal is the common goal variously described by various charts.

Similarly, the facts that we speak in a language given by tradition and that the semantics of our thoughts is shaped by our culture (on this point let us agree with Stich), does not make conservative our attachment to truth (to the particular TRUTH-scheme and to 'correspondence with reality'). Our choice of topics might be less liberal than would be desirable, our choice of relevant properties in the world might be arch-conservative, but once the choice is made, the fact that we prefer truth to falsehood is, itself, neither conservative nor liberal.

So Stich's hypothesis is wrong. Various TRUTH(* ... *)s do not compete with each other, and they are not intuitively seen as competing, so the choice between them is epistemically neutral and leaves the epistemic goal untouched: no matter how John's mental sentence '*p*' manages to stand for the state of affairs that *p*, John will typically wish to have it in the belief-box only if *p*.

Consider now the Argument from Omission. Is the proper way of enquiry the one Stich recommends to a truth-seeker: fix your uninterpreted sentences in the head, and then look for the mapping that makes most of them come out right? Is this really a matter of serious choice?[32] Take natural languages first. Suppose John wishes to assert that Empedocles was in love. Is the right way for him, first, to accept the phonetic string 'Empedokli:s l:pt' and then try to decide whether to speak German – asserting that he was in love – or English – asserting that he jumped? Or imagine the following situation. You answer yes-or-no questions at a quiz-show in English, and your answers come out false. A Hungarian friend criticizes you afterwards: 'How irrational of you that you did not speak Hungarian! All your "yes"s would have meant "no"s in Hungarian and you would have won! Next time apply only for quizzes where you can fix the meaning of your answers after the quiz is over!' Of course that would be 'highly idiosyncratic,' much more so than the practices Stich condemns; in fact no quiz could work that way.

With mental sentences things are much worse. One cannot simply decide to put an uninterpreted sentence in one's belief-box – can one? – and then go in search of a good interpretation function. In which interpreted meta-language does one perform the search? How does one decide in advance which sentence is TRUE(* ... *) under which interpretation (e.g., how do I know that the sentence 'Ti swons' will be TRUE*** under the three-starred interpretation function that assigns 'it' to 'ti' and 'snows' to 'swons' without knowing that the English sentence 'It snows' is TRUE under the usual interpretation)? The only language of thought we can think in either has some definite interpretation built into it, or it will never have any. This is all to the good. Suppose that the designer of our mental architecture wanted the sentences in the head to indicate the states of the changing world, for the benefit of its owner. Given that the world is changing, it would be reasonable for him to have proceeded compositionally – first linking words to things by suitable reference schema, and then letting the combinations (sentences) get their truth-value the way the world decides. There would be nothing intrinsically conservative or idiosyncratic about such a procedure. On the contrary, it would help our beliefs to track the situations they are about. The Argument from Omission criticizes us cognizers for not performing impossible and nonsensical tasks.

The impossibility of choosing one's interpreted language of thought also blocks one possible line of defence for the relativist-pragmatist: he cannot use the conceptual possibility that various schemes are mutually untranslatable and therefore in competition with each other. If that were so, then our being stuck with one such scheme for language of thought would be simply a biological limitation (like having so many senses and not more), not a personal idiosyncrasy.

My diagnosis is as follows: Stich's account of truth fails to capture the most important features of our cognitive aim, because it fails to attain the right level of generality. Our epistemic goal is to know what the world is like, and various reference-schemes and TRUTH(* ... *) predicates are merely means for describing this common goal. The deeper reason for the failure is the disregard ('oblivion,' one is tempted to say) of the ordinary motivation for attaining truth about pertinent matters and for its ascription to the assertions and thoughts of our informants.

What about the semantic argument against the usefulness of truth? Since the various TRUTH*s do not compete over the same matters, Stich's question is wrongly posed. Take Stich's Harry, who believes that his flight leaves at 7:45 a.m. There is no TRUTH*** or TRUTH**** about the flight that contradicts his TRUE* belief, either directly or by implication (if the plane leaves at 7:45 a.m., no amount of semantics can change its schedule). If 'flight' by REFERENCE*** had meant something else (e.g., 'wife'), Harry might have had some other belief (e.g., about his wife) unrelated to flights, but this has nothing to with his catching the plane. Had he used the three-star REFERENCE***, he would still – if all non-semantic facts are the same – have to look at the plane schedule or call the airport service, and he would have formed the three-star TRUE*** belief about his plane, with the same practical consequences as harbouring a modest, one-star TRUE* belief might have. Truths are unlike hotels – having more stars does not buy you additional services.

To recapitulate, the Semantic Argument is wrong on several counts: various TRUTH-predicates are not in semantic, epistemic, and instrumental competition, and all stand for the same higher-level epistemic goal, expressible in terms of 'fit' between sentences and reality (believing and saying '*p*' only if *p*):

- the choice among TRUTH-predicates for natural language is epistemically and instrumentally insignificant;
- the choice among TRUTH-predicates for (hypothetical) language of thought is not available to us, thinkers, since we do not choose in what interpreted language of thought to think;
- we are not to be blamed for not exercising choice where we have none.

The natural assumption that people are curious and want to know how things 'really are,' in part, simply for the sake of knowing it, can be upheld and with it the assumption that truth has intrinsic value. Notice that in criticizing Stich I did not appeal to any non-naturalistic considerations, nor did I tie the truth-goal to any particular aprioristic preconception about the nature of belief.[33] Since the central argument against the usefulness of truth hinges on the false premise (on the step (b)), it also should be rejected, and we may believe that truth is also useful. This vindicates the classical picture of truth as an epistemic goal.

Let us now return to the Main Argument for relativism (remember: first, since truth is of no value, there is no common epistemic goal; second, epistemic strategies are incommensurable; therefore, relativism about epistemic rationality holds). If my critique was successful, I have disarmed one group of arguments for the initial premise.

4. Truth, Reliability, and Evolution

4.1. The Relativist-Pragmatist's Arguments

Let us now address the issue of the biological plausibility of the truth-centred approach. It seems that the issue is quite clear: if the correct estimate of environmental parameters and contingencies does contribute to fitness, there should be a presumption in favour of reliability in selection, provided selection does favour fitness-enhancing traits. I hope to have shown that truth is, on the whole, more useful than falsity, and I assume that fitness-enhancing traits are, to a large extent (although not always and unconditionally), favoured by evolution. Thus, I think we may safely subscribe to the position that evolution does favour reliability (truth generation), and we may give our assent to Ronald N. Giere's general assessment of the situation: 'At the *ground level* is the evolutionary fact that human perceptual and cognitive capacities are the product of biological evolution. We are reasonably well adapted for survival in small groups of fellow humans dealing with the necessities of life here on Earth. There is, therefore, no *scientific* basis for doubting the general reliability or our perceptual and cognitive abilities' (1990, 21; emphasis in text).

Let us dwell on the topic, since much more needs to be clarified. We have considered the usefulness of truth only in a non-comparative way, that is, without taking into account the actual costs (and opportunity costs) of having truth-generating mechanisms and employing strategies with a high truth-record. All these matters become vital when biological plausibility is in question.

Stich dedicates a chapter to the evolutionary issues.[34] His aim is to 'challenge the idea that natural selection prefers "reliable" inferential systems' (*Fragmentation*, 59). He assumes that he has already shown that truth is, in general, neither useful nor a proper goal of cognition. The rationalist is then left with the task of accounting for rationality without appealing to truth. Stich then considers a very optimistic rationalist, who argues from the alleged optimality of natural selection that naturally selected cognitive strategies must be epistemically virtuous. (Such an optimist is often called a 'Panglossian' in the literature, after Voltaire's over-optimistic hero, Dr Pangloss, a caricature of Leibniz.) Against him the relativist-pragmatist easily wins.

Stich also argues, however, against the more modest veritistic assumption that reliability is central to cognitive processes. The pattern of the argument is again ambiguous. Stich officially argues for a weak and, in my view, correct thesis: If a genetically coded inferential subsystem is found in successful animals, this *does not guarantee* that the subsystem is reliable or rational. Survival does not guarantee rationality. (The fact that you are alive does not mean that you are smart.) But this weak thesis is not what he really needs, since it leaves space for the following conjecture: although selection does not invariably pick reliable systems over non-reliable ones, it does so quite often. Thus, although there is no guarantee of reliability, there may be *considerable support*: if you are alive you can't be completely stupid. What Stich and his fellow relativists-pragmatists really need is to defend a very strong and pessimistic thesis that leaves no space for even modest optimism. This is the just quoted thesis that selection is indifferent to reliability. Here we have another example of the Pessimistic Leap, the jump from the demonstration of mere possibility to the assumption of actuality. Let us give the thesis an official name, for further reference:

Indifference Thesis: Selection does not favour reliable information-processing systems over non-reliable ones.

Stich hedges a bit, saying that it may be the case that selection prefers less reliable systems (*Fragmentation*, 61), but this seems to be a mere rhetorical understatement, since he later flatly asserts that there is no chance to show that truth-generating mechanisms are the ones that have been selected for:[35] 'it would presumably have to be shown that the reason the intuitively sanctioned interpretation function is conducive to success is that it fosters believing the truth. And the "evolutionary" argument does not even begin to support that contention. Here, as before, the evolutionary argument for instrumental value is a hopeless nonstarter' (ibid., 122). It is obvious why he does it: he badly needs the Indifference Thesis. If this pessimistic thesis does not hold, then the naturalist-rationalist has strong leverage: if selection does support reliability to a considerable degree, a high epistemological evaluation of reliability is a natural and useful attitude, as the Classical Picture has always presented it. Thus, against the pessimistic view I intend to defend the moderately optimistic view that reliability has ranked very high among evolutionary priorities, especially in the case of our ancestors.

I shall only briefly rehearse here Stich's arguments for the weak thesis, that evolution does not strictly guarantee optimality – his 'coming attractions,' as he advertises them.[36] Stich appeals to the distinction between external and internal fitness. Regarding the internal fitness of cognitive systems, he claims that 'strategies of inference or inquiry that do a good job at generating truths and avoiding falsehoods may be expensive in terms of time, effort and cognitive hardware' (*Fragmentation*, 61). A less reliable but less costly mechanism might be preferred to an expensive reliable one: 'the unreliable, error-prone, risk-aversive strategy may well be favoured by natural selection. For natural selection does not care about truth; it cares only about reproductive success. And from the point of view of reproductive success, it is often better to be safe (and wrong) than sorry. What we have shown is that one inferential system might have a higher level of external fitness than another even though the latter, less fit system makes fewer mistakes and gets the right answer more often' (ibid., 62).

The next 'attraction' is a family of arguments against the optimality of evolutionary design. He first identifies the main theses of the evolutionary optimist (*Fragmentation*, 63) and then argues against each one.

1. Evolution is caused by natural selection.

Against this thesis Stich appeals to the importance of non-selectional factors mutation, migration, and random genetic drift.[37]

2. Natural selection will choose the best designed system available in the gene pool.
3. Over evolutionary time a huge and varied set of options will be available for natural selection to choose among ...

Against these assumptions Stich lists several considerations: first, the limited availability of options; second, pleiotropy – a genetic link between a very useful and a tolerably harmful feature, such that the harmful feature remains in the population riding piggy-back on the useful one; third, heterozygote superiority, that is, a situation of the following kind: people who are homozygous for the gene that carries sickle-cell anemia suffer severely from this illness, whereas heterozygous individuals have no symptoms but have a significant level of resistance to malaria. It would be fine to have a mutant combining resistance to malaria without anemia in homozygotes, and such a mutant would probably be a winner in the population. Unfortunately, such mutants simply did not appear. Stich's further arguments concern meiotic drive – the capability of certain genes to 'cheat' in meiosis and get over-represented in the sperm or eggs and the combinatorial considerations showing that in certain situations the suboptimal option might drive the optimal one out of the population.

Stich also lists the optimist's thesis that our inferential system was produced by evolution, and questions it on the grounds that 'it is entirely possible that the cognitive mechanisms subserving inference are similar in important ways to the cognitive mechanisms underlying language comprehension' – various inferential strategies might be simply a result of environmental diversity, largely independent of genetic factors: 'If inference is analogous to language in this way, then changes in the distribution of inferential strategies in a population might have little or nothing to do with the level of biological fitness that the strategies in question afford' (*Fragmentation*, 69). Finally, he presents the evolutionary variant of the Semantic Argument: 'So the fact (if it is a fact) that our intuitive interpretation function is the product of an extended process of biological or social evolution does not make it plausible that it is more conducive to survival or thriving (or anything else) than any of the non-intuitive functions that characterize alternative notions of TRUTH* ... *. Moreover, even if it could be shown that using the intuitively sanctioned interpretation function is especially conducive to survival or success, this would still not be enough to show that *having true beliefs* is more instrumentally valuable than having TRUE* ... * ones' (ibid., 122).

The arguments seem to me to be a mixed bag. We have already seen that the Semantic Argument fails, since different TRUTH(* ... *)-predicates do not compete with one another. Some of the other arguments are valid against the Panglossian, and I applaud Stich for bringing them into the epistemological debate. I accept his biological considerations – the point that evolution is not driven exclusively by selection and the fact that selection itself has limited options available. They are very efficient in establishing the weak thesis, that is, that there is no strict guarantee that the most reliable mechanism will be always and systematically favoured by selection. Barring the Pessimistic Leap, however, these arguments do not establish the strong Indifference Thesis that the relativist-pragmatist actually needs and for this purpose seem to be doubly beside the point. First, the rationalist needs not an evolutionary guarantee or optimality, but only high probability and sufficiently good strategies. Second, they are implausible in the case of a systematically interconnected cluster of features, which cannot develop by sheer coincidence. I shall endeavour to show that cognitive features are such. The relativist's argument from the possibly high cost of reliable strategies will be briefly addressed at the end of this chapter and the analogy between inferential systems and language in chapter 7 on the validity of inference.

4.2. The Biological Usefulness of Reliability

Let me again make clear that the rationalist need not be – and that I am not – committed to an unrealistic hypothesis about optimality; there is no guarantee that evolution will – even in the case of primates and humans – select the optimal strategies.[38] I am defending a more modest thesis:

Very probably, evolution in general favours more reliable strategies over less reliable ones among those available to it.

This thesis is sufficient against the general thrust of relativism-pragmatism. To see the difference from the Panglossian optimist, consider how the modest thesis fares against Stich's argument from non-availability of optimal solutions (the argument that is efficient against the Panglossian, who settles for a proof of optimality). The thesis asserts only that evolution will – in relevant cases – favour reliable systems over unreliable ones when both are available. Thus, it promises to secure for the naturalist the respectability of reliability and truth, without committing the naturalist to a panglossian adaptationism.[39]

The defence of the modest thesis is as follows. The most general rationale behind the thesis is, of course, that truth is useful and that falsehood can be lethal. Detecting accurately the ways things are is of paramount importance for organisms that are active in a changing, flexible environment. Let me merely note that the task of detection of how things are is not the prerogative of the central nervous system. Another system of detectors is the immune system. The task of reliably identifying invaders (viruses, bacteria, etc.) has the highest priority for any organism.[40] Recognizing an intruder is vital for bacteria, and they have developed mechanisms for detecting viruses (discovered in the early 1960s by Werner Arner, who received for his discovery the Nobel prize in 1978.) If one had to find some definite starting point for the line of 'cognizers' from amoeba to Einstein, recognition mechanism of this sort would be the most serious candidate. The central nervous system (CNS) performs, among other tasks, the analogous task of detecting environmental contingencies. The question confronting us is whether the cognitive apparatus as a whole, including inferential mechanisms, functions in the same line of work. If yes, then the accuracy-reliability of cognition will be very important. I shall endeavour to show that we can get what we need.

I first argue that cognitive mechanisms do have a proper function, for which they have been selected. The relativist might venture an argument to the contrary from the alleged coincidental pleiotropic origin of belief-mechanisms. – As we saw above, the argument would proceed from the mere possibility that belief-forming mechanisms give no contribution to fitness, so that it would be reasonable to suppose that they have evolved by coincidence (e.g., riding on the back of some useful property). Intelligence would be pleiotropic. If so, there would be no biological value in truth and reliability.

I want to argue for the proper function of cognition and intelligence and for its ties with reliability. The general plan of the argument is as follows. A pleiotropic trait is an isolated feature. Cognition is, by contrast, ubiquitous. The complexity of the neural bearers of cognitive capacities is systematically correlated with the sophistication of the capacities themselves, and these are correlated with diversity and complexity of behaviour. Such systematic, overarching correlations can hardly be due to random factors (e.g., pleiotropy or meiotic drive). More specific cognitive abilities are continuous with the general ones, however, and can therefore be hardly coincidental. Further, it is rather well known that the developed central nervous system is biologically very expensive, and that the sophistication of the CNS is correlated with growing abilities of its owner. I shall briefly document these well-known facts and use them as evidence that a sophisticated CNS – in particular, the cortex – is probably not a luxury: nature can tolerate idle wheels, but not super-expensive idle wheels. The main contribution of the cortex to the life of its owner is the cognitive control of action. A significant part of the control is finding out what the environment is like, so we are free to suppose that this is an important proper function of the cognitive apparatus, part of the reason why the expensive apparatus is maintained. It so happens that primates seem to be morphologically specialized in the direction of having large neocortices, so they might be specialized cognizers (I offer, below, a speculative guess, based on recent literature, as to why they need cognition and intelligence). Now, if a cognitive apparatus has a proper function to indicate what the environment is like, then its *biologically paramount virtue is reliability about relevant matters, its truth-record.* Reliability is thus the link tying usefulness, truth, and rationality, thereby offering a naturalist underpinning of the rationalist program.

In order to show this in more detail, let me borrow from the biologists. The main evidence for the thesis that intelligence is fitness enhancing (not pleiotropic) comes from three facts concerning the nervous system, in particular, the brain. First, having a central nervous system supporting intelligence is very, very expensive; second, we do have an expensive CNS; and third, a fancy CNS is the only fancy feature we do have. The third point is (unfortunately) obvious, so we shall devote most attention to the first two. First, developed brains are not an accident. It seems to be an established fact that the relative size of the brain is a rough indicator of the sophistication of behaviour control by its owner. Let me list some data from an overview compiled by Kathleen Rita Gibson (1990). She mentions the following groups of questions as relevant for the analysis of zoological and ethological descriptions (I omit the detailed questions from each group):

1. How many discrete movements of the mouth, hand, foot, and tail regions does a species possess, and how many actions can the species organize into one action directed towards a goal?
2. Do species members swallow food as a whole? Do they practise external sexual fertilization? What bring these questions under the same heading is that they have to do with manipulation – of prey, food, and sexual partners. The species members practising internal fertilization have to have some manipulators for that task, and the species capable of breaking prey into smaller pieces prior to ingestion also must have requisite motor skills.
3. Do species members identify relevant objects (prey, mates, etc.) on the basis of few stimuli, or do they construct 'object images'? Can they recognize relevant items, whether they are stationary or moving? Can they recognize individuals, or do they respond to simple group or kind characteristics?
4. Do species members actively search for food?
5. Do species members construct mental representations of relationships between several objects? Can they use tools?
6. Do species members predict the actions of their conspecifics or their prey?

The answers to the questions define a scale of sophistication of behaviours and systems of behaviour control. *The size of the brain is roughly correlated with the position on the scale*: small-brained fish and amphibians represent the least sophisticated extreme, the large-brain mammals the most sophisticated. Most small-brained fish recognize relevant items by key stimuli only, for instance, they identify food by movement and size. They lack manipulative skills. The large-brained sharks and rays possess sufficient motor skills to manipulate both food and sexual partners. Rays can crack mollusk shells and the like. Reptiles stand higher on the scale. They possess 'motorically complex aggressive and sexual displays' and exhibit more complex feeding patterns than most fish do.

Mammals have the largest neocortices, and they correlate with 'major advances in feeding strategies,' and other behaviour patterns. Among the mammals the most interesting for us are omnivorous or frugivorous extractive foragers: monkeys, great apes, frugivorous bats, and perhaps elephants: 'Primate extractive foragers derive their skills from two aspects of neo-cortical structure. For one, the sensory and motor cortices controlling the primate hand are particularly enlarged, as is the visual cortex. For another, the largest-brain primates exhibit differential enlargement of the neocortical association areas. Such enlargement reflects duplication or multiplication of sensory and motor processing areas ... The greater the duplication of sensory and motor areas, the more parallel processing ability, and in particular the greater the ability to construct relationships between multiple objects and multiple actions' (Gibson 1990, 112). Notice the parallel between increased cognitive abilities and increased motor skills. The two seem to complement each other, in a way that suggests high behavioural usefulness of cognitive functions. The following supports one suggestion, among many others. Why, for example, have the mammals living on great continents, like the Americas, Africa, and Asia, increased their brain size? Enters the intelligence. An educated guess was offered by biologist A. Jolly, summarizing the work of her colleague R.J. Andrew, who 'pointed out that the mammals of both America and Afro-Asia have, as whole, increased the brain size since the Eocene. He suggested that the increase was due to interaction between species: as prey species grew cleverer, their predators and competitors survived only by also becoming cleverer and vice versa. The mechanism works best with a large number of species and close competition: mammalian intelligence evolved faster and farther on the large, interconnecting continents than on Australia or Madagascar' (in Byrne and Whiten 1988, 30).

We are very far from the Indifference Thesis and the idea that intelligence is not selected for, since in this example the usefulness of cognitive apparatus explains morphological difference on a continental scale. This brings us to our ancestors, special among other terrestrial mammals only in that they have a better developed brain. The facts about the relative size of the brain are well known; the most important point is not the size, however, but the consumption of energy. Not only is the brain as a whole metabolically expensive, requiring large supplies of oxygen and glucose (its demand for these products is constant and unrelenting, regardless of the mental or physical state of the organism), but the grey matter, the locus of specifically cognitive functions, possesses a much higher metabolic rate than the white matter. *Cognitive apparatus is extremely expensive.* Let me quote the data from Sue Taylor Parker's paper 'Why Big Brains Are So Rare?' (1990). Among neonatal humans the brain uses 87 per cent of the oxygen and energy consumed (measured in terms of the so-called basal metabolic rate, the amount of oxygen and energy per unit time). Moreover, the high-sugar, low-fat composition of human milk seems to be designed to 'optimize brain growth rather than body growth' (ibid., 140). The brain of two-year-olds uses 64 per cent, and that of five-year olds 44 per cent of the available oxygen and energy. The metabolic rate of the human brain is higher than it is in other mammals, but more important, the cortex is the most active: the respiration rate of the cortex is 40 per cent greater than the respiration rate of the whole brain.

The leap in costs is so great that biologists spend their time answering the question 'Why?' not the question 'Whether?' as the relativist would have us suppose. Why did evolution give to primates such disproportionally large brains and such an expensive cortex? Why do monkeys have larger brains and why are they more intelligent than their less developed poor cousins, for example, the lemurs? In a well-known article Nicholas K. Humphrey states: 'It is not her (Nature's) habit to tolerate needless extravagances in the animals on her production lines: superfluous capacity is trimmed back, new capacity added only as it is needed. We do not expect, therefore, to find that animals possess abilities which far exceed the calls that natural living makes on them (1988, 13).

It is unlikely that humans would possess an extremely costly and delicate cognitive apparatus if it did not significantly contribute to their fitness. The relativist-pragmatist might agree that intelligence has a function, but still might wonder what this function has to do with rationality and the truth-goal.[41] The simplest way to connect intelligence with rationality is via the point of enquiry as dictated by the Classical Picture: it is overwhelmingly plausible that cognitive apparatus has the proper function of gathering information about the environment, which can then be used to guide behaviour. The simplest way to argue for that is from continuity with perception. It is clear that sense organs have not evolved by coincidence, because functionally very similar kinds of organs, prominently the eye, have evolved independently on different levels of evolutionary development (the insect eye has evolved independently from the squid eye, etc.). Thus, basic sense perception is not coincidental; it is obviously fitness-enhancing and informs the agent about its environment. However, perceptual beliefs are produced by mechanisms that refine basic sense-perception and make it more reliable, capable of more effectively tracking the events and objects in the outside world. For instance, the early warning perceptual system simply gives information that some middle-size object is approaching. A more sophisticated perceptual system will yield a more precise perceptual (quasi-)belief, that a predator is approaching or that a potential mate is approaching. If the availability of some basic mechanism is due to its information-gathering power, it is plausible that its refinement, which does the same thing better, has a similar function. But most of the belief-fixation processes on the level of perceptual beliefs presumably resemble higher belief-fixation processes and are developmentally continuous with the former. They do have a proper function, and informing about the environment is a most plausible candidate. But then, information-preserving (truth-preserving and high-probability-preserving) strategies will have a high price.

We hope to have shown that truth and reliability do have some value, but we have left the question of their comparative value untouched. Is it better to be smart than to be rich and good looking? Is it more fitness enhancing to have a somewhat more reliable inferential strategy or to have stronger teeth? Let us use the economist's jargon, and speak of marginal utility: call the usefulness of one additional 'unit' of cognitive virtue marginal cognitive utility, and the usefulness of one additional unit of some non-cognitive quality (speed, strength) marginal non-cognitive utility. There is no need for us to endorse the implausible idea that marginal cognitive utility is always higher than non-cognitive (i.e., that it is always better to be smart than to be rich, strong, and beautiful). We might instead suggest that different kinds *specialize* in different virtues and that specialization drastically constrains marginal utilities. Somewhat stronger teeth will not help a rabbit to engage in a battle with a wolf, but a little additional speed might save its life. Some animals will survive thanks to accurate perception, which is useful for early warning, for estimation of distances (jumping from tree to tree), and for other tasks. To such an animal marginal utility of perceptual reliability will certainly be greater than marginal utility of strength (bought at equal cost). Other animals might engage in more higher-level processing, and this would then enhance the marginal utility of cognitive improvements. Are primates and humans such specialized animals?

All the evidence that we have already adduced in discussing the proper function of the brain, points at the same time to specialization, since the only specific feature of primates and humans is their cognitive apparatus. It is so special in primates and humans, so disproportionate to their generally unimpressive morphological features, that we may safely conclude that intelligence is the human being's only specialization. Biologists (e.g., Chance and Mead in Byrne and Whiten 1988) claim that primates (including humans) generally represent a primitive mammalian condition, specialized in nothing but having an outstanding brain. It seems that the primates and, in particular, humans are 'specialized enquirers,' curious and equipped for satisfying their curiosity. If this is true, the case can be made for the rationalist claim: cognitive improvements have high marginal utility. Somewhat stronger teeth would not help apes or humans much, whereas an improvement in cognitive strategies might have disproportionally high value. The morphological considerations adduced speak in favour of this hypothesis. Still, a nagging question arises: where, exactly, does the biological value show itself in the case of primates, including early humans? Given a rather hospitable environment and low demands for technology in such environment, what was the intelligence good for?

Let me engage in a longish speculative interlude and present the essentials of one line of answer, which I (as a non-professional) find very promising and has, as mentioned, become prominent recently: the line stressing the importance of social interaction. Much of what is suggested here is somewhat speculative, so I am not using these ideas as arguments against the relativist-pragmatist, but rather propounding them as a potential answer to the question posed above. During the last decade, some prominent zoologists have been developing the hypothesis of Machiavellian Intelligence, claiming that the principal task to which the cognitive powers of primates have been harnessed is the task of social interaction. The anthology by Byrne and Whiten, *Machiavellian Intelligence*, from which we have already quoted, gives interesting and detailed evidence against the Indifference Thesis, presenting the situations in which the accurate (i.e., true) estimate of social circumstances and adequate forecast is directly relevant to the agent's fitness.

In social interaction an animal is trying to change the behaviour of its conspecific, who may also be trying to do the same thing to the first animal. Social interaction thus demands the accurate perception of the 'state of the game,' but also a flexible planning, taking into account various alternatives and various responses of the partner in the interaction. Such demands obviously concern intelligence, and coping with them might be essential for its development. Nicholas Humphrey, one of the first contemporary proponents of the idea that social intelligence is the root of all intelligence, writes: 'To do well with oneself whilst remaining within the terms of the social contract on which the fitness of the whole community ultimately depends calls for remarkable reasonableness ... It is no accident, therefore, that men, who of all primates show the longest period of dependence (nearly 30 years in the case of Bushmen!), the most complex kinship structures and the widest overlap of generations within society, should be more intelligent than chimpanzees, and chimpanzees, for the same reasons, more intelligent than cecropithecides' (1988, 21). In such situations, the fitness of the individual will crucially depend on the accuracy of its cognitive strategies: examples of intellectual prowess bringing social success are not limited to humans. The hamadryas baboons are described (by the Swiss zoologist Hans Kummer) as engaging in complicated social behaviour involving a male (the group leader) and two females, where females compete for the protection and attention of the male. In such situations, Kummer writes, 'the tripartite behaviour comes close to exploitation: a primate may learn to use for his own protection, or for increasing the effect of his aggression, another one who primarily is not involved in the events.' (Byrne and Whiten 1988, 121). Byrne and Whiten credit baboons with 'tactical deception,' which presupposes that the deceiver has some idea about how the other will react given the evidence he (the other) has.

Chimpanzees are said to be very good at deception. Here is a charming example, from the chapter by Frans de Waal (the heroes Yeroen and Nikkie are his animals at the Arnhem colony in the Netherlands, where he worked before moving to the United States):

> Yeroen hurts his hand during a fight with Nikkie. Although it is not a deep wound, we originally think that it is troubling him quite a bit, because he is limping. The next day a student, Dirk Fokkema, reports that in his opinion Yeroen limps only when Nikkie is in the vicinity. I know that Dirk is a keen observer, but this time I find it hard to believe that he is correct. We go to watch and it turns out that he is indeed right: Yeroen walks past the sitting Nikkie from a point in front of him to a point behind him and the whole time Yeroen is in Nikkie's field of vision he hobbles pitifully, but once he has passed Nikkie his behaviour changes and he walks normally again. For nearly a week Yeroen's movement is affected in this way whenever he knows Nikkie can see him. (Byrne and Whiten 1988, 123)

De Waal concludes that Yeroen was play-acting in order to placate his stronger rival, Nikkie, probably knowing by experience that Nikkie is less hard on him when he is limping.

Other examples come from mating behaviour. De Waal's chimpanzee Dandy, the youngest and lowest-ranking of four males, sometimes steals a chance to mate with adult females, after having made a 'date.' The female and Dandy pretend, after exchanging glances, to be walking in the same direction by chance and then meet behind a few trees. (Dandy's 'accurate judgment' concerning the complex situation is directly relevant to his fitness). He also mentions the example of a female, Oor, who learned to suppress a high scream (still adopting the facial expression that goes with screaming) at the point of climax when mating at 'dates' but still screamed normally when mating with the dominant male: 'Oor's noiseless scream gives the impression of violent emotions which are only controlled with the greatest of effort' (Byrne and Whiten 1988, 125). Jane Goodall (as quoted by de Waal) gives parallel examples from the observation of animals at large.[42] David Premack (Byrne and Whiten 1988) has asked the pertinent question: Does an ape like Oor know that the sound can be effective in creating in the dominant male the (true) belief about her doings, whereas the sight cannot? Three-year-old children do not understand that belief depends on perception. (When allowed to see what is in the box, and asked 'Do you know what is in the box?' they answer correctly. But when shown another child in the same experimental condition and asked if the child now knows what is in the box, they answer incorrectly). He points to the exploit of a four–year old chimpanzee, Jessie, who has done the right thing in the relevant context: when presented with the trainer who was blindfolded with several blindfolds and did not follow her as usual, she removed the blindfold over his eyes. In general, exploitation of the ignorance of others, manipulation of their attention, creation of alliances in contests, and taking care of the requirements of hierarchy exercise primates' social intelligence more than enough.

Moreover, as Byrne and Whiten stress, 'Machiavellian intelligence' demands a large knowledge base, since only extensive explicit knowledge allows flexible or intelligent action. Therefore, social intelligence will depend on curiosity – and indeed the primates exhibit more curiosity and exploration than any other animal.[43] We may end with yet another quotation from the pioneering paper by Humphrey: 'If intellectual prowess is correlated with social success, and if social success means high biological fitness, then any heritable trait which increases the ability of an individual to outwit his fellows will soon spread through the gene pool. In these circumstances there can be no going back; an evolutionary "ratchet" has been set up, acting like a self-winding watch to increase the general standing of the species' (1988, 21).

If the evidence is valid, we may conclude that intelligence has been useful to our ancestors. In particular, having true beliefs about the intentions of their conspecifics (and about states engendering the intentions) can be of crucial importance for reproductive success. Reliability is not an idle ornament.

After this speculative interlude I shall briefly address the relativist argument concerning the internal fitness of cognitive strategies: the relativist stresses the importance of the cost-benefit ratio in the case of expensive strategies. Cheap strategies are favoured in relation to costly ones, other things being equal. Some cheap suboptimal strategies are favoured over costly optimal ones: 'If the costs are very high, and there is an alternative available that does a less good, but still acceptable, job of generating truths, then natural selection may prefer it' (*Fragmentation*, 61). This is correct so far, but the relativist needs more to make us pessimistic; he needs the assumption that cheap strategies are rarely the good ones. But cheapness can often bring epistemic goodness. To see that cheapness may mean simplicity, and that simplicity may be an important virtue, consider curve fitting. Johnny and Mary are dropping bread crumbs, and you have to reconstruct their path. The cheapest way is to draw straight lines between the spots with bread crumbs. A much more expensive way would be to draw a sinusoid passing through each spot. The cheapest way is the simplest one, and in this case the most rational one. Is this merely a happenstance? Epistemologists tend to agree that simplicity is a virtue – not always, but very often. More important yet, if one errs by too much simplicity, one errs on the better side than if one errs in being too baroque. Simple and daring hypotheses are better than complicated ad hoc construction of epicycles, many epistemologists claim. Therefore, good things do not have to be terribly expensive and the cost-benefit analysis of cognitive strategies need not make us very pessimistic.

Cost-benefit analysis might give support to the rationalist in yet another way. The more general a strategy is, the greater its marginal utility, especially within a changing environment and within a flexible social context. An expensive general strategy might still be more cost-efficient in such contexts than a whole battery of singly inexpensive specialized ones. For example, the evolutionary designer can set up in us the capacity to recognize numerosity by giving us specific templates for each small number (one-detectors, two-detectors, three-detectors) or, alternatively, by giving the cognitive apparatus the ability to one-one correlate the members of relevant collections (or members of target collections, say, predators, with a given paradigm series, such as our numerals). The first, particularized strategy might be inexpensive for each small number, but less cost-efficient when it comes to counting up to thirty items, than the alternative, general strategy. The general strategy then wins. Finally, one should not forget the vicissitudes of intraspecific competition, given the intense social life of primates. A cheap-but-unreliable strategy might be tolerable in a non-competitive milieu in which the animal faces only less intelligent interactors. In a competitive milieu that puts a premium on intelligence, no cost can be too high for outwitting the conspecific. It remains to be seen what the detailed facts of life are in this domain, but the rationalist has no reason to be pessimistic.

Let us conclude by filling in the general framework discussed at the outset. The biological importance of reliability is all the rationalist-veritist needs for the biological plausibility of rationalism. The modestly optimistic non-Panglossian line of reasoning is as follows:

1. Natural selection is an important cause of evolution.
2. Natural selection in the long run favours better-designed systems (which are available) over less good ones.
3. Over evolutionary time, a set of options will be available for natural selection, and the items within the set will be comparable in respect to reliability.
4. Cognitive systems are the product of evolution and selection (witness their widespread and systematic links with behaviour). Very expensive but biologically inert cognitive systems are dramatically fitness decreasing and are not tolerated by selection.
5. Information-gathering and processing is what cognitive systems do. There is a correlation between cognitive prowess and the general sophistication of behaviour.
6. The primate cognitive system is extremely expensive. It has been maintained and it has developed in the course of evolution, so that probably the basic structure of our inferential subsystem is due to evolution.
7. Given (4)–(6), it is plausible that cognitive systems in general and primate cognitive systems in particular have been selected for what they actually do. Information-processing power is the main contribution of cognitive systems to the increase of fitness.

8. The reliability of the information processed and obtained is crucial for its usefulness.

Evolution probably favours reliability in cognitive systems.

To repeat, I agree with Stich that evolution does not guarantee (i.e., secure in a foolproof way) rationality or reliability, but I claim that the facts point to strong biological support for reliable cognitive strategies. It is at least more probable on evolutionary grounds that our cognitive system is reliable, than that it is not. Moreover, the reliability of cognitive strategies is a value supported by evolution, not by some idiosyncratic accident in our taste. The conclusion of this chapter is simply that truth is valuable on pragmatic grounds, including evolutionary ones. The relativist-pragmatist loses on his own ground, and veritism and naturalism go together. This suggests the following general picture of the enterprise of cognition.

Higher animals represent their surroundings. Some of them, including, prominently, the primates, actively search for information about the ways of the world. Such a search is extroverted, turned towards the object of beliefs, not towards beliefs themselves. Obtaining correct information is, on the whole, advantageous for such an extroverted enquirer. In terms of representing the world, it is advantageous to have true representations. For kinds of enquirers who have specialized themselves for cognitive tasks, the truth of representation is their crucial quality, and having truth-generating cognitive processes is an important fitness-enhancing virtue. Humans are probably such a species, specialized for survival through successfully predicting the values of environmental parameters. In order to fulfil such a task, an enquirer needs more than just true information gathered through perception. She needs means for figuring out what is non-obvious from more directly gathered information. This involves having belief-states (with transitions between them) that are broadly truth or probability preserving. The totality of structures supporting belief-transitions form a kind of cognitive architecture. When the states are sufficiently like beliefs and transitions are recognizably reliable, we speak about 'rational architecture.'

Correct representations – 'models' of reality – and reliable means of figuring out further facts support each other. The enquirer might start with a few basic facts and a few rough reliable rules of thumb and then proceed to more facts, which in turn allows her to refine her rules of thumb. Some strategies of figuring out demand sophisticated factual knowledge and are utterly unsuitable until such knowledge is acquired.

The way from the rough biologically based reliability to the panoply of actual rational strategies is a long and tortuous one, which is just beginning to be explored by naturalistically oriented epistemologists. Let me mention that Robert Nozick has pointed out that the primitive strategies probably instilled in us by evolution might correct themselves in the process: 'A group of *roughly* accurate reasons relations can shape itself into a more accurate group. One roughly accurate tool can detect and correct flaws in another; this second, now improved tool can do the same for a third; and this third then can examine the first tool and detect and correct some flaws in it' (1993, 124; emphasis in text).

This is the setting I take to be the proper factual framework for general epistemological purposes. I have argued against the relativist-pragmatist that all the essential traits of the Classical Picture can and should be preserved in this new setting. Within this setting, the proper goal of cognition is truth or something quite close to it. Its bearer does not have to be a full belief-state such as we know it (or postulate it in our folk-psychology), but it has to be a representational state. The notion of truth should preserve and underscore the essentially extroverted traits of the classical notion of truth in virtue of what-the-world-is-like. True representations – maps, models, sentences, beliefs – tell us how the world is, and it is this trait that is naturalistically relevant, both in explanatory and in normative contexts.

Finally, we may conjecture that the representational states and transitions between them are to be profitably judged in terms of their overall function of representing the world. The cognitive architecture underlying these states and transitions is the bearer of basic epistemic virtues and vices. To this conjecture I turn in the next chapter.

7

From Truth to Virtue

1. Introduction

In this part I complete my defence of rationalism and veritism. With the truth goal I return to the core of the Classical Picture and to the province of normative epistemology in the strict sense dealing with cognitive virtues, rationality and justification. Let me briefly give a word to the relativist-pragmatist. Understandably, on the very first page of his book, Stich tries to separate the domain of epistemic evaluation from the issues of knowledge and truth. He distinguishes between 'three interrelated projects that traditionally have been pursued in epistemology': first, evaluation of the methods of enquiry; second, of understanding what knowledge is; and third, of answering the sceptic. He recounts how he was interested in the first project, but has 'found the latter two projects to be somewhat dreary corners of epistemology' (*Fragmentation*, 3). This separation is hard to swallow (regardless of the autobiographical character of Stich's remark). The second project, understanding what knowledge is, is inseparable from the first project, evaluating the methods of enquiry, since by the traditional and widely accepted definition, knowing a proposition entails justifiedly (rationally) believing it, and the very notion of justification is at the core of the first project. Questions – such as: Which methods are rational and justified? When is the enquirer justified in using a belief-forming strategy? – are common and central to both evaluating the methods and understanding what knowledge is.

From the testimony of Stich himself there is a further hint, namely, that truth-generation or reliability would be a valid ground of rationality, of course, if truth were valuable: 'Another well-explored idea is that the rationality or justifiedness of a set of cognitive processes can be explicated by appeal to the success or failure of the processes in producing true beliefs ... But if the evaluative notion can be explicated along reliabilist lines, the situation is very different. For then processes that fall within the extension of the notion do a good job of producing true beliefs' (*Fragmentation*, 22). Thus, the paradigm relativist agrees that if truth were valuable, truth-generation would be the proper explicandum of the notion of justifiedness or rationality. I hope to have established that the antecedent holds: truth is valuable. The consequent then follows without much effort – simply follow the directions given by the relativist and explicate the notion of rationality in terms of truth-generation.

Remember the premises of the relativistic Main Argument:

1. *The Irrelevance of Truth*: There is no common goal of cognition, because truth is irrelevant.
2. *Radical Descriptive Pluralism*: (a) Cognitive styles and strategies are environment- and user-relative, and (b) they are structurally radically diverse.

(1) and (2) entail

C1. *The Incomparability Thesis*: Strategies are mutually incomparable (both with respect to goals and to their internal structure); and
C2. *Radical Normative Pluralism*: There is no single norm valid for all the various cognitive styles or strategies.

I hope to have refuted in the foregoing parts of the book premise (1). After a brief account of the link between truth and rationality I proceed to question ways of arguing for the incomparability of strategies. They fall into two groups: the general arguments from user- and situation-relativity (i.e., premise 2a) and arguments from the structural diversity of actual reasoning strategies (2b). They are supposed to support the crucial thesis (C1). Let us first address the general considerations (2b).

2. General Considerations: User- and Situation-Relativity

The defining tenet of cognitive relativism is that cognitive virtue is user-relative and situation-relative in such a way that cognitive strategies, methods, and singular moves cannot be compared and ranked across differences of users and situations. Remember the example of a mathematical problem, where for a high-school student the best way of solving it is to use method A, but the best way for the professional mathematician is to use B. The diversity does not by itself force one to endorse relativism about methods A and B; since professional mathematicians are generally more competent in solving such problems, B is in absolute terms probably better than A. Thus, both the rationalist and the relativist accept the commonsensical claim that the overall appropriateness of strategies varies with circumstances (modest normative pluralism). Where they differ is over whether or not this variation is ultimate. The rationalist claims that the comparability reaches beyond the diversity: there are ways to compare strategies in a non-relative sense. The rationalist-veritist takes some member of the truth-family as the ultimate basis. For the relativist, the variability in appropriateness is ultimate: strategies with differential appropriateness cannot be further compared in relation to some non-relative criterion. Most important, there is no further comparison of the users and of situations for their epistemic worth and adequacy. I have dubbed this crucial claim the Isolation Assumption about users and situations. It is the implicit groundwork on which the Incomparability Assumption about strategies rests, so it must be examined first. (A warning: The reader who is a professional methodologist and philosopher of science might find our examination insufficiently sophisticated. However, I intend to criticize the relativist-pragmatist assumptions in the formulation that their authors give them and that has the great merit of simplicity and clarity. If the formulations are not particularly refined, it is not the task of the critic to make the issues more complicated by introducing additional refinements).

Let us first consider the issue of user-relativity. The idea that it is ultimate strikes one as intuitively implausible if one considers its implications for widely different cognizers: would one really accept the claim that the elementary-school mathematical techniques and the sophisticated ones used in research institutes are epistemologically incomparable, only because the first ones are appropriate for children and the second ones for grown-up scientists? The sophisticated ones are vastly superior, in terms of range, yield, precision, and reliability. Therefore, relativism seems to run counter to simple and forceful intuitions and counter to considered opinion of practitioners in the field. Further, within actual social practices a hierarchy of expertise and sophistication is widely acknowledged: most educational systems are built upon the assumption that students should progress towards acquiring better cognitive techniques, so that teaching methods fostering epistemic sloth and blocking the access to better techniques are criticized and replaced. If the common practice of deferring to experts is to be rational, the methods they use should be better than the lay ones in a non-relative sense. Therefore, the burden of proof falls on the relativist.

Still, if there were no goal common to different enquirers-users, the user relativity would have some chance; there would be no point in a search for a common denominator shared by strategies that are appropriate for different users. Given some community of goal, however, the situation changes: the strategies become goal-comparable. If a goal *G* is common to John and Mary, John uses the strategy *SJ* and Mary uses the strategy *SM*, and Mary is, ceteris paribus, vastly better at achieving *G*, then *SM* is to be ranked as superior to *SJ* in absolute terms, not only in terms of being better for one agent than for the other. If John is unable to use *SM*, then *SM* is worse for him, but is still better absolutely. For instance, 'This is the most reliable way to perform a particular surgery; unfortunately, most surgeons are incapable of doing it properly.' The remark makes perfect sense: some way of performing the surgery may have the highest success ratio and be absolutely the best one, without being accessible to many, even to most, surgeons. Applied to cognitive value, if the principal goal of cognition is to come to know what the world is like, then strategies can be judged by the likelihood of yielding such knowledge. The Isolation Assumption is false.

Let us now apply this simple consideration to the historically oriented example used by Stich himself: 'It's not implausible to suppose that there are strategies of thought that will lead to a dead end in a community where geometry is unknown, others that will lead to a dead end without the calculus, or probability theory, or powerful computers, and still others that will be pragmatically powerful only in environments where the distinction between velocity and acceleration has been clearly drawn, where the basic idea of evolution by natural selection is widely accepted, or where the expectation that things have final causes has been rejected' (*Fragmentation*, 140). Since the factual claim is correct, the issue is whether it justifies the assumption of ultimate incomparability. Take, first, the dependence on calculus: if some calculus-dependent strategy *SC* yields correct and precise results, whereas another calculus-independent strategy *SI* (using, e.g., primitive approximation and exhaustion methods) yields only approximate and sometimes incorrect results, then *SC* seems to be better in the absolute sense. The dependence on calculus is not a vice or a liability, tainting the mathematics of

Euler and Gauss or the mechanics of Newton, Lagrange, and Hamilton. (Also, if there is a calculus-independent strategy that matches the success of *SC*, then the two are equally good, ceteris paribus).

What about their users? If Aristides the Greek uses *SI* and obtains the best results possible, then Aristides is epistemically in the clear. He has used the best method available to him, done his epistemic duty, and shown his epistemic virtues, and the rationalist is happy to congratulate Aristides. On the other hand, had Euler used *SI*, we would regard this as a lapse from his usually high level of epistemic performance. Complying with this intuition, the rationalist, at the level of principle, will distinguish between judging the cognizer and judging her method. The method (e.g., *CI*) can be second best, whereas the user may be at the same time a paragon of epistemic virtue (since she has used the best method available to her in an epistemologically commendable way).

Take, next, the dependence on the framework of final causes. Suppose that a teleological strategy gives an otherwise coherent explanation of a physical phenomenon in terms of final causes, for example, in terms of God's will, and a mechanicist strategy gives an otherwise equally plausible explanation without invoking final causes, in terms of efficient causes only. Stich seems seriously to suggest that our preference against teleological strategy is merely a parochial cultural phenomenon. He is probably bound to judge it so, since relativism-pragmatism commits him to accepting that the explanations stating that the stone falls because God wants it to, or because the stone wants to fall, are, absolutely speaking, neither better nor worse than the mechanistic explanations given by our physics. In that case he should give up scientific realism and should not appeal to the results of science (biology, psychology, neurobiology) to buttress relativism-pragmatism (for details see chapter 6). Thereby, he ceases to be a naturalist, and the discussion is over. Suppose, however, that he wants to remain a naturalist and to trust science in its most general claims. Then, he must admit that the theistic final-cause strategy simply makes its followers blind to the correct explanation; it is not incomparable, but comparable, to the mechanistic one; it is wrong and clearly inferior. This is what the rationalist claims. The fact that the better strategy is normally accepted only in the community that has given up asking about (preordained) goals of physical phenomena is an important sociocultural fact, and that is all.

To summarize, there is no denying that judging the quality of a cognitive strategy could be a daunting task, and that it is often difficult to come up with an acceptable set of standards for the task. The full story is going to be much more sophisticated than anything that can be offered here. The difficulties, however, do not add up to any principled user-relativity, as the relativist claims, nor do they support the Isolation Assumption, as he seems to imply.

Before passing to situation-relativity, let us distinguish two kinds of global framework: theoretical and practical. Within the theoretical framework the enquirer is guided primarily by curiosity, the wish to know what the world is like; whereas within a practical framework her primary interest is practical, and the truth is valued only in relation to the practical issue at hand.[1] The terms of cost-reliability trade-off are dramatically different between frameworks, and the availability of the theoretical framework in human affairs gives the rationalist an additional edge. Within the theoretical framework the absolute ranking of strategies in terms of reliability defines the cognitive ideal, period.[2] The issue of situation-relativity is important primarily in relation to the practical framework, to which I now turn.

Situation-relativity is largely analogous to user-relativity and is limited in the same way: although some strategies are more appropriate for some situations, the situations themselves can be compared with respect to their epistemic hospitability. With situations an additional issue arises, however, since some strategies are useful in all kinds of situations, whereas others are useful only locally, for one particular kind of situation.

The relativist-pragmatist aims at direct usefulness of cognitive strategies, recommending (what we have called) the Situationist Policy:

1. The proximate (direct) goal of a strategy is usefulness in the given situation.
2. Such usefulness is environment-relative.

3. There are no generally valid cognitive strategies, only the situation-bound ones.

The relativist-pragmatist's defence of (1) depends on his stance about truth: since that stance has no value, cognitive strategies are to be viewed as tools, supposed to yield immediate pragmatic returns. This commits him to the situationist view: for every kind of life situation and environment one should find a matching cognitive strategy among many mutually incommensurable candidates: one for war and one for peace, one for office and one for home, one for bedroom and one for living room, and so on, indefinitely. In contrast to this account, which ties usefulness directly to particular situations, the rationalist explains success in stages. (Remember our appeal to practical reasoning and the example of the Captain of the submarine [see chapter 6, 2.2]). The reasoner has to reach a true belief about the situation, which, together with the means-end-belief, yields a belief about what she should do. The process has two stages: first, the acquisition of true beliefs about the situation and contingencies (what causes what), helping one to form true means-end beliefs grounded on the beliefs about contingencies; second, the choice of the best means in the context of practical reasoning. The assessment of cognitive strategies concerns the first stage only. By thus breaking down the success story into two stages, the rationalist narrows down the range of situation types he has to deal with, and considers only the variations of cognitive opportunities. He does not have to recommend looking for special, mutually incomparable reasoning strategies for each kind of situation (war, peace, etc.) and is able to concentrate on general cognitive strategies, *reliable over a wide range of different environments. Particular cognitive strategies are often just general ones, adapted to circumstances.* The adaptation might require insight and talent, even genius, but it need not present special philosophical problems. In Quine's admirable phrase, it is the 'versatile yield' of general strategies that makes them particularly useful.

Against the relativist's first premise the rationalist stresses that cognitive strategies are useful indirectly by providing true input to the practical reasoning unit: general means-end-conditionals and beliefs about the situation. Against the narrow focus recommended in the relativist's second premise she stresses the availability of general strategies valid across a wide variety of situations. Such strategies are topic neutral. Consider, in descending order of generality: logic, arithmetic plus calculus, inductive strategies (such as Mill's methods), and statistics. Logic is, as Quine so aptly phrased it, 'handmaiden to all sciences,' and mathematics follows suit: 'We might say at the risk of marring the figure that it is their promiscuity, in this regard, that goes far to distinguish logic and mathematics from other sciences' (1970, 98).

Mathematics and logic are, at minimum, conservative, leading from true premises to true conclusions, without adding new 'facts,' and at maximum literally true. I have once heard a critical rejoinder that such strategies are empty. For mathematics, this is hardly credible. For instance, the calculus is certainly not obviously trivial, since it has been considered by some of the most brilliant philosophical minds (e.g., Berkeley) to have been false. It has allowed scientists to build mechanics and systematize electrodynamics, to mention the most spectacular and best known of its merits. If such a method is empty, one would like to be shown a non-empty, substantial alternative to it. Statistics is another obvious candidate for respect on pragmatic grounds. These strategies are applicable under extremely variable circumstances. The only exceptions that might even begin to threaten their application belong to Cartesian and Humean imaginary worlds: worlds in which demons change mathematical truths, or in which there are no law-like regularities. It is a serious question whether such a world can be imagined in any detail at all. This is a far cry from the relativist appeal to the actual, tangible variability of ordinary environments. Cartesian variations, although philosophically relevant, do not threaten the basic lines of epistemological assessment in the way relevant for the relativist-pragmatist. The bare imaginability of such distant possibilities does not require actual enquirers to use an irreducible plurality of criteria when making their cognitive choices.

In contradistinction to general cognitive strategies and to sophisticated methodology, the everyday heuristics is much more context-bound, and this is its weak spot, excusable on pragmatic grounds, but depriving it of a high degree and a high range of reliability. This is not news, and the relativist-pragmatist can derive no deep moral from it. Very briefly, the idea of the positive rationalistic proposal amounts to the following. Under the assumption that a goal from the truth-family is central, the reliability of a strategy is its main virtue. For inferential strategies, the ranking is largely independent of particular environmental features (in the next section I shall consider in more detail the importance of the truth-link for deductive and inductive logic). The next stage of evaluation is a more inclusive assessment that takes into account the costs of reasoning. Some strategies are more cost efficient, and in particular situations the trade-off between reliability and cost becomes important. The two kinds of comparison – the purely cognitive and the one in terms of cost efficiency – are complementary, and there is nothing about them to prompt relativist worries. In the next section I consider and defend this view in more detail.

3. Diversity and Comparability

3.1. The Relativist Argument

Let us now examine the relativist's arguments relying on the assumed vast diversity of actual strategies, diversity that is alleged to make them incomparable. Stich rightly distinguishes actualist descriptive pluralism about matters of fact, from a possibilist pluralism about (conceptual) possibilities, and he endorses both in respect to cognitive strategies. In his view it is both conceptually possible that people have vastly different cognitive strategies and a fact that there are significant differences among the strategies available. Following his naturalistic lead, let us focus upon the factual claim that different people reason differently, that they persevere in their respective styles of reasoning, and that styles of reasoning are mutually incommensurable. This claim entails that there is no reasoning competence common to all people: 'there are substantial individual differences in cognitive competence' (Stich 1985, 131). Stich draws comparison with languages: 'In grammar we expect different people to have different underlying competencies which manifest themselves in significantly different linguistic intuitions. The linguistic competence of a Frenchman differs radically from the linguistic competence of a Korean ... But why should we not expect that cognitive competence will vary just as much as linguistic competence?' (ibid., 130). One point of his discussion of evolution (which we did not address) was to show that 'there *may* be lots of diversity in the population, and for lots of different reasons' (*Fragmentation*, 73). Also, 'There is a great diversity among contemporary humans with respect to the language(s) they speak and understand ... the first step is to note that, in light of what little is known on these matters, it is entirely possible that the cognitive mechanisms subserving inference are similar in important ways to the cognitive mechanism underlying language comprehension' (ibid., 69); and 'The existence of innate inferential strategies is an entirely open, empirical question, as is the extent to which a person's inferential strategies are shaped by his or her cultural surroundings' (ibid., 72).

Besides using descriptive pluralism as a premise for the Main Argument, there is another auxiliary, but more sophisticated, way of using it against the rationalist. The rationalist needs to weigh cognitive principles, intuitions and expectations of truth-yield.[3] For example, Nelson Goodman has made the (famous) suggestion that we adjust our general inductive policies to our intuitions in single cases and aim at an equilibrium state, the so-called reflective equilibrium.[4] Stich harnesses descriptive pluralism against this rationalist proposal. He insists on the stubbornness of reasoners: some subjects adhere to principles that we deem erroneous, and they have intuitions in accordance with their principles. Their views are in equilibrium, and they cannot be talked out of their way of reasoning, Stich claims. If the inferences generated in reflective equilibrium differ widely from what we think is the rational way of inferring, this casts doubt on the claim that reflective equilibrium captures our intuitive idea of justification. He continues: 'In a paper published some years ago, Nisbett and I exploited the strategy just described to argue that the reflective equilibrium does not capture anything much like our ordinary notion of justification. On the basis of both controlled studies and anecdotal evidence, we argued that patently unacceptable rules of inference would pass the reflective equilibrium test for many people' (*Fragmentation*, 83).

The evidence for such irreducible descriptive pluralism allegedly comes from cognitive research. Remember, from chapter 1, 2.3, the sketch of the results in the tradition of Wason, Johnson-Laird, and Kahneman and Tversky, who were testing the status of normative prescriptions, and focus upon their negative findings. There was much bad news about deductive reasoning. On the inductive side we have mentioned the conjunction error – the tendency to judge the probability of a conjunction as higher than the probability of the conjuncts: it seems more probable to people that Linda is a bank teller and a feminist than simply that she is a feminist. Another fine example is the dramatic failure to search for refuting instances of one's hypothesis, that is, the confirmational bias. Remember, also, other shortcomings of everyday judgment, which were mentioned in chapter 1, 2.3. Salient objects or features figure more prominently as causes in the reconstruction given by the reasoner than ones that are non-salient, although perhaps they are causally more important. Next to be considered are the fundamental attribution error and the 'availability heuristic,' by which people assess the frequency of a class or the probability of an event by the ease with which instances or occurrences can be brought to mind. The representativeness heuristic suggests that one take *A* to be causally linked to *B* if *A* is like *B*, or is representative of *B*. For epistemological purposes the most important weakness is perseverance – the maintaining or even strengthening of belief in the face of recalcitrant data. Add to this the gambler's fallacy and ignore base rates in probabilistic reasoning for a fair sample of troublesome results.

Stich claims that the 'vast diversity' of human reasoning strategies *lacking a common epistemic goal* entails relativism. We first have to consider the very idea of diversity and incomparability. As mentioned before (at the end of chapter 3, 2, the first presentation of the relativist-pragmatist stance), there are at least two ways in which items could be comparable, or commensurate: first, as means for a common goal – in short, by being goal-comparable; and second, by virtue of having enough structure in common, that is, by being structurally comparable. For example, a camel and a helicopter, considered as means for crossing a desert, are certainly goal-comparable, but are not obviously structurally comparable. Both a camel and a horse are goal-comparable in relation to the same task and are also structurally comparable. For cognitive strategies, goal-comparability is central, since the primary epistemological interest concerns not their intrinsic features, but their ability to serve for a purpose. In line with the previous section, I shall first argue from the relevance and centrality of the truth goal that cognitive strategies are goal-comparable as means for attaining truth and avoiding error. Then I shall briefly argue that cognitive research suggests that there might also be structural similarities between various strategies, making them structurally comparable as well.

3.1.1. Goal-Comparability

I have tried to show that there is a common epistemic goal, and that it belongs to the truth-family. How does the relativistic conclusion fare *in its presence*? This issue has been severely neglected in the literature (in favour of discussion about a priori justifiability of basic strategies).

Let us momentarily grant for the sake of the argument that radical actualist descriptive pluralism is true, so that cognitive strategies are not structurally comparable (I shall question this assumption in the next section). Remember that the relativist-pragmatist has to concede a minimal agreement on inductive uniformities in order to ground his own recommendations. Imagine that human strategies are as diverse as the most pessimistic researches claim (excluding the worst possibilities of straightforward systematic counter-induction and the flouting of most norms of logic in simple cases – the nightmare that is not envisaged by even the most radical pessimists among scientists and is not open to the relativist[5]). This still does not entail, or even seriously support, relativism, since the availability of the truth-family goal makes strategies goal-comparable, so that the epistemologist would none the less be able to compare them by their expected truth-yield and recommend the ones with the best score. Admittedly, in the presence of a vast disagreement about the essentials of methodology, the comparison itself would be extremely difficult to negotiate, depending on how radical the disagreements are. With minimal agreement about the basic inductive uniformities, however, it is, in principle, allowed to expect that the good truth-record in the past promises a similar truth-record in the future. The truth-record of various strategies thus can be compared, meta-strategies of comparison developed, and a ranking of strategies made in principle acceptable to thinkers whose intuitions and practices were initially radically diverse.

At this point the relativist-pragmatist might be tempted to accuse the rationalist of circularity: The rationalist enjoins the enquirer (and the epistemologist) to assess cognitive strategies by their retrospective and prospective truth-generating capacity, that is, by their truth-record, and by the likelihood that they will in the future have the same truth-ratio as in the past. What about the rationality of this inductive assessment itself? asks the relativist-pragmatist. Does not the rationalist illicitly presuppose the rationality of induction? He does presuppose it, but not illicitly against the relativist-pragmatist, since they share the assumption. The relativist-pragmatist is in no position to question it, since he enjoins the enquirer to assess strategies in terms of how promising they are in practical matters. He accepts that they use the cognitive means at their disposal to assess the likelihood of success and claims that no vicious circularity is involved.[6]

The relativist-pragmatist is not a Cartesian or a Humean sceptic, and he has to grant to the rationalist the same techniques he himself uses. His own pragmatic assessment deals in likelihoods of attaining a practical aim and accepts some non-deductive strategy of assessment. If the enquirer's goal is truth, she must be granted the same licence – to accept and use those strategies that have the greatest likelihood of bringing her closer to her goal.

Similar considerations are relevant with respect to the following question raised by the relativist: Why choose strategies that we think are reliable under normal circumstances, rather than those that would be reliable under other circumstances? Is not our preference for 'normal' against 'exotic' simply a symptom of parochialism? Stich balks at the rationalist's use of the idea of 'normal world': 'What is important is to see that if he is even close to being right, then *our* concept of justification occupies a small and rather idiosyncratic region in a large space of more or less similar concepts that can be generated by altering the specification of possible worlds in which the reliability of psychological processes is to be assessed' (1991, 201; emphasis in text). The preference for normal strategies over the exotic ones is justified in relation to the truth goal, and it is additionally to be recommended on account of its flexibility and ability to correct itself. If one thinks one lives in a lawful world, so that lawfulness is essential to normality as one sees it, it is rational for one also to think that in such a world a lawfulness-tracking strategy will lead to more truths. Induction is such a strategy. Counter-induction (an exotic procedure), one conjectures, leads nowhere. Now, this is a means-end judgment. It is an expression not of taste, or of any deep-seated prejudice. An enquirer will follow induction only as long as she believes that she lives in a lawful world. Moreover, the use of a normal strategy does not condemn the enquirer to cognitive slavery. If induction turned out to be systematically unreliable, we would be hard pressed about what to do, but we would have good reason to think that our world is not lawful. In such cases the enquirer is free to use other strategies, but then again, she must make means-end judgments, not follow her taste or her whims. On the other hand, suppose that you opt for an exotic strategy, out of a love for the exotic. You believe in advance that such a strategy is not suitable for the world you live in, so you decide to use it on non-cognitive grounds. The failure of the strategy will not change these grounds, and you knew anyway that it was cognitively unpromising. Thus, there is not much you can learn from failure; the use of exotic strategies *is not self-correcting*.

Worse yet for the relativist-pragmatist, the whole line of attack is hardly available to him. In appealing to exotic possibilities, the relativist-pragmatist comes very close to classical scepticism, betrays his original naturalist stance, and gives up his characteristic commitments. First, let us examine naturalism. The relativist-pragmatist has called into question the Classical Picture by appealing to the facts about actual enquirers, their strategies, and track records, claiming that the actual variability of strategies and environments – not exotic Cartesian possibilities – dictates the overthrow of the Classical Picture. Second, he should give up his characteristic optimism about estimating the practical outcomes of using particular cognitive strategies; if there is no way of knowing that a strategy is useful, however, there is no point in recommending it. On the one hand, if the relativist-pragmatist is confident about practical inductive estimates, how can he be sceptical about the inductive estimates in this debate? On the other hand, if he proposes that the alien sceptical possibilities threaten the enquirer's judgment of her own reliability, should he not think that these same possibilities are relevant for the enquirer's judgment of the likelihood of her practical success? Either he should turn sceptic on both issues, or he should grant to the truth-seeker the use of the same means he grants to his happiness-seeker. The stick of circularity is not available for the relativist-pragmatist to wield.

Let us now briefly revert to the actual epistemological ranking and the priority of the general strategies and rules traditionally and widely held to belong to the core of rationality: the rules of deductive logic or inductive strategies based on probability calculus. We have already pointed out their 'versatile yield' and suggested that they are appreciated for their reliability. We have now to document the suggestion. If one can prove that these core strategies are traditionally held in high esteem because of their truth-preservation, one can claim that their rationality as traditionally conceived is linked to the independently and naturalistically valuable goal, the truth. But then, the two items support each other: the traditional preference for the core strategies is not a matter of parochial taste, but is derived from the naturalistically reasonable goal, and truth-generation asserts its place as the cornerstone of the edifice of rationality. One party to the marital contract, truth-generation, offers its naturalistic wealth, whereas the other, core strategies, offers its aristocratic lineage and respectability in academic circles.

The task is easiest for deductive logic. For a long time it has been held to be the canon of rationality and has retained an important place in shaping our ideal of rational enquiry. Almost no one questions its rationality, and those who are suspicious of its demands base their suspicion on the claim that its demands are too high, not too low. It is not that one would be irrational if one successfully followed its dictates, but only that one may be excused for not being quite able to live up to them.[7]

What are the credentials of deductive logic and logical consequence (and validity) that make it into the paradigm of rationality? Let me quote an expert opinion on the function of logic: 'There are two main sources of knowledge, one being perception in its various forms, the other reasoning as a process of transforming knowledge structures and creating new ones ... Thus logic is the study of *knowledge in action*. Another way of describing the field to be studied is as the process of manipulating *information*: extracting it, modifying it, transferring it. This is reflected in the various *functions* of reasoning: to prove a statement, to refute it, to correct it, etc. A deeper account of these functions turns out to involve a study of the possible *forms* of information, and a common assumption, also in logic, is that these forms can be found, or at least be represented in some kind of language, whether natural or artificial' (van Benthem 1989, 185; emphasis in text). The central characteristic of logical consequence is its truth-preserving character. Let me quote from John Etchemendy: 'The most important feature of logical consequence, as we ordinarily understand it, is a modal relation that holds between implying sentence and sentence implied. The premises of a logically valid argument cannot be true if the conclusion is false; such conclusions are said to "follow necessarily" from their premises' (1990, 81). He goes on to say: 'this is the single most prominent feature of the consequence relation.' The official definition of logical validity and logical consequence is framed in terms of truth: A sentence is valid if and only if it is true in all models: sentence *A* is the logical consequence of sentence *B* if and only if all the models that make *B* true also make *A* true. Thus, logical consequence guarantees that the truth of the antecedent is transmitted to the consequent. Translated into epistemic terms, this means that *logical consequence is a paradigm of reliable truth-transmission. Logic is ultra-reliable*: If one believes *B*, *B* is true, and *A* is the logical consequence of *B*; then one may safely go on to accept *A* – there simply is no chance of *A*'s being false.

Let us look at the other question: what is the rationality-bestowing characteristic of logic? What justifies it and makes it epistemically highly virtuous? In a simple formulation Wesley Salmon states: 'The aim of deductive logic, I take it, is to be able to draw true conclusions from true premisses. To achieve this aim we endeavour to adopt as rules of deductive inference only those rules which are truth-preserving' (1974, 3). Similarly, Michael Dummett has pointed out that if deductive logic is to have a justification at all, it must be in terms of properties from the truth-family (he starts with truth, but ends with verification). It is the semantic relation to the truth-family that distinguishes the logical consequence properly so called from one that is merely algebraic: 'At this stage, the only justification that would be possible would be ... semantic rather than syntactic justification' (Dummett 1978, 291). Further: 'Semantic notions are framed in terms of concepts which are taken to have a direct relation to the use which is made of sentences of a language; to take the most obvious example, the concept of truth and falsity' (ibid., 293). So, we have it from well-informed sources (Salmon, Etchemendy, and Dummett), that truth-preservation is the primary reason why logic is taken to be valuable. This is a widely held opinion, backed by the tradition from Aristotle onwards. Here, the naturalistic motivation coincides with the expert opinion that logic is justified by its ultra-reliability. The match of ultra-reliable deductive logical rationality and the truth-goal is no marriage of convenience, but the result of deep elective affinities.

These remarks, of course, do not even begin to do full justice to the complexity of the topic. Even within its own province deductive logic does not always give clear methodological advice – one person's *modus ponens* is notoriously another's *modus tollens*; logic is demanding, and using it might be too costly in actual problem-situations. Its ultra-reliability remains its most conspicuous virtue, however, and that is all we need in this polemical context.

We pass now to induction. What does one demand from a good inductive argument or a good inductive strategy? If one wanted to know, for instance, whether induction by simple enumeration is a good strategy, what should one look for? Consider the simplest pattern of enumerative inductive inference, illustrated by the following: 'The raven Alpha is black, the raven Beta is black, the raven Gamma is black; these are all the ravens observed so far; so the next raven, Delta, will turn out to be black.' What one wants to know is whether, given the colour of Alpha, Beta, and Gamma, it is reasonable to believe that Delta is black. This resembles very closely our interest in deductive judgment – we want to know whether it is reasonable to accept the conclusion if one accepts the premises. What is it about the conclusion, the statement 'Delta is black,' that attracts one's attention? The natural answer amounts to accuracy of prediction, that is, its truth. The cognizer asks: Do I have good reasons to hold that Delta is black, or, equivalently, that it is true that Delta is black? This is how 'the problem of induction' is usually stated:[8] 'in a correct inductive inference the premisses make it reasonable for us to accept the conclusion in the sense, very roughly, that they report the evidence favouring the truth of the conclusion, making it rational to believe the conclusion, making it likely or adding to the likelihood of its truth' (R. Swinburne, in Swinburne, ed., 1974, 3). Wesley Salmon writes in the same vein: 'A justification of induction must, I hold, hinge upon a relation between induction and frequency of truth-preservation or success. I do not deny, of course, that induction is rational; I claim that it is rational *because of* its relation to truth-preservation' (1974, 66). Please note that he gives a rationale for his claim in terms of 'frequency of truth-preservation,' and it would be easy to list many authors who write in the same vein (Braithwaite 1974; Kyburg 1970). This is one description of the truth-link. Other descriptions are in terms of 'likelihood of truth,' or 'expected truth.' Induction is centrally concerned with truth, and the measure of goodness of induction is truth-preservation, or preservation of likelihood-of-truth.

There are, however, some interesting philosophers who refuse to admit the existence of a direct link between induction and truth. David

C. Stove argues that the logical probability is independent of actual truth, and that the justification of inductively acquired beliefs has nothing to do with their being true, but everything to do with their being (highly) probable (1986, chap. 'Probability and Truth'). I shall not insist on the issue of logical probability (as analysed in the Carnapian tradition of Carnap, Hintikka, and his school, most recently Pollock). The standard accounts define it in terms of truth in possible worlds, or state-descriptions, enriching the garden variety, actual or 'absolute' truth, with a more technical variety. Therefore, Stove's claims do not sever the link with truth but only imply that high probability need not reduce to actual truth (as against the frequentist interpretation of probability, which reduces probability to actual or long-run truth). One can show it also without reverting to technical logical matters. Stove takes as his basic and important contention that, for instance, after seeing many black ravens and no white ones, the observer has excellent (logical) reasons to believe that the next raven (e.g., our Delta) is black. Now, what does the belief consist in? Does not believing that Delta is black commit the observer (equipped with the notion of truth and with sufficient mental ability) to the belief 'It is true that Delta is black'? Moreover, are not the *reasons* for both beliefs the same? Therefore, I do not think that Stove would object to the following truth-invoking formulation: Induction is justified if the belief that the premises are true gives a good reason for believing that the conclusion is true (and a good reason for believing that the negation of the conclusion is false). What he does explicitly reject is the frequentist claim that for *P* to be held with good reason, it must be the case that *P* is (sometimes, in the long run, etc.) actually true (or that some suitable weakening of *P* is actually true). But nothing in the truth-invoking formulation commits one to the frequentist claim. The truth-invoking formulation should be acceptable even to Stove, who at first glance seems inimical to the idea that truth-generation is a virtue of inductive strategies. Truth-links are central both for deduction and for induction. The use of heuristics and shortcuts points to no special goals, only to the importance of speed and efficiency, in addition to the truth-goal. In any event, cognitive strategies are goal-comparable.

3.1.2. Heuristics and Structural Comparability

Given the difficulties of reaching an agreement based on goal-comparability alone, without the help of common methodological assumptions, it is worthwhile to explore the additional question of whether cognitive strategies have enough structure in common to be structurally comparable as well. Does the work accomplished in the area of cognitive shortcomings support radical actualistic descriptive pluralism? Does it show that people reason in *irreducibly* different ways?

Stich has used the available evidence to argue that a human 'could be an irrational animal' (1985). Against the aprioristic optimism of philosophers like Jonathan Cohen he has persuasively shown that there is *no guarantee* that people are rational.[9] These cautious formulations using 'could be' and 'there is no guarantee,' however, express only a weak and inconclusive, and therefore plausible, thesis that it is *just possible* that radical pluralism holds. The weak thesis has been developed further (see Stein 1994), and it has found some merited approval among epistemologists. A warning is appropriate: the literally weak thesis can be misunderstood. The use of 'it is possible that' is often a rhetorical way of insinuating a firmly held but unpleasant view ('But isn't it possible that she has another lover?'). Therefore, when one reads that it is established that people *might* be irrational, one is tempted to jump to the conclusion that people *are* irrational. Remember, therefore, that what Stich does establish – by his own admission – is simply the bare possibility.

Is this bare possibility of radical pluralism sufficient to ground relativism? Or do we have another example of the Relativist Leap from demonstrated possibility to freely assumed actuality? Consider, first, Stich's starting point: the parallel with linguistic competence. Even concerning linguistics itself (which was presumed to give a clear example of irreducible plurality) Stich's claims are doubtful; many linguists follow Chomsky's lead in claiming that there is a common underlying competence, shared by the French, the English, Koreans, and so forth, which can be captured by a kind of 'universal grammar.'

The situation is much worse for the relativist in the matters of logic and reasoning. Stich writes as if the experimental data clearly and unequivocally point to irreducible descriptive pluralism of cognitive styles – as if everybody confronted with the data could only give up any hope in a unitary account, and as if most cognitive psychologists acquiesce in pluralism-relativism, acknowledging that there is no competence common to most reasoners.

This impression is, however, quite erroneous. Let me first mention the simple fact that people mostly make similar mistakes. There is no wide variety of wrong answers given at the Selection Task or the Conjunction Task. Biases seem to be uniform, so they do not, at least prima facie, support any kind of descriptive pluralism.

Psychologists seem to be aware of the uniformity of biases, and seek *uniform explanations that would accommodate the small number of kinds of biased heuristics.* An example is presented by Johnson-Laird, proposing his model theory of induction – people build models of the premises of the inductive argument and then generalize simply by adding new information (new assumptions) to the model: 'One final advantage of the models is that they elucidate the clues about induction that have emerged from the psychological laboratory. Because of the limited processing capacity of working memory, models represent only certain information explicitly and the rest implicitly. One consequence is that people fall into error, and the evidence shows that they make the same sort of errors in both deduction and induction' (1994, 25). Johnson-Laird goes on to account for the short list of common kinds of error by appealing to a *unitary mechanism* that produces them: in deduction and induction people focus on what is explicit in their models, overlooking, for example, negative instances, and reasoning on items that are easily available. This covers confirmation bias and availability heuristics. In induction and deduction they rely on the structure of the model; this makes them vulnerable to the way problems are framed. Background knowledge biases the reasoning in the same way in both induction and deduction.

Similarly, Cheng and Novick (1992, 367) praise their own model of heuristics – focused on covariation – for its uniformity: 'our assessments converge on a single normative mechanism that underlies this essential component of causal induction [i.e., covariation].' The tendency is widespread and understandable both from the empirical results and from the general tendency to find uniform explanations.

This uniformity is troublesome for the relativist-pragmatist. On the one hand, he needs it to show that people do systematically flout deductive and inductive logic – without systematicity the mistakes could be simply due to incidental defects. On the other hand, the more uniform, systematic, and widespread the biased heuristics is, the less support it gives to his views, First, and most important, if they are uniform, then the vast diversity of reasoning strategies is a myth. Second, if they are widely spread and to be found in competent and creative reasoners, then they do perhaps have a rational core (as claimed, e.g., by Gerd Gigerenzer and his co-workers in psychology, and by Hilary Kornblith in philosophy).[10] The situation of the relativist-pragmatist is thus inherently unstable: the more he insists on the importance of biased heuristics, the less support he can draw from it.

The *common overall structure of biased reasoning* is one essential element of uniformity. There is another, which might be even more important, the *uniformity of basic competence*. The experimental data have triggered an avalanche of theories, all aiming at accounting for the biases, errors, and shortcomings of intuitive judgment and inference. Most of the theories are precisely theories of competence. They aim to describe the *competence common to most (or all) reasoners*, in such a way as to leave space for the observed errors and biases in reasoning. This is precisely what Stich explicitly rejects, claiming, at the same time, support from cognitive science, that is, from the very research program that has generated competence theories.

Worse yet for Stich, many prominent theoreticians have opted for *a rationality assumption*, (the assumption that people are capable of rational inferences) only correcting an unlimited logicist optimism in the direction of *limited rationality*. There is little suggestion of any irreducible diversity of cognitive styles, and there is a clear consensus that errors and shortcomings are only that: anomalies to be detected against the background of correct thinking. Most psychologists do not call into question normative theories of rationality the way the relativist-pragmatist does. Note that the relativist is in no position to reject such moves. He has pledged fidelity to naturalism and to science, so he should not treat the work of psychologists selectively and invidiously. Stich himself relies on the studies of Ross, Nisbett, Johnson-Laird, and others as revealing and important. Barring special reasons (which he nowhere offers), he should then follow these studies to the bitter end, rather than shrinking from accepting their accounts as a whole, having already accepted those parts he finds suitable.

Let me now prove my claim by briefly sketching some explanations of shortcomings, offered within the theories of limited rationality. First, let me mention the attempt by Gigerenzer and his co-workers – foreshadowed by some remarks of Jonathan Cohen and Isaac Levi – to vindicate everyday probabilistic reasoning by pointing out the existence of several *correct inductive strategies, some of which agree with everyday responses.* Gigerenzer argues that some of the alleged biases are not biases at all, but instances of alternative inductive policies. For example, 'in everyday language words like *probability* legitimately have several meanings, just as "if ... then" and "or" constructions do. The particular meaning seems to be automatically cued by content and context' (Gigerenzer 1991, 262). The particular meaning triggers a particular inductive strategy, which might differ from what a particular set of norms condones. Of course, 'statisticians similarly have alternative views of what probability is about' (ibid.). As against relativism, he abides by a very limited plurality of traditionally accepted normative systems of probabilistic reasoning and of theories of probability.

The more common move is, as mentioned, to distinguish competence from performance. There are several kinds of competence theories. Remember from chapter 1, 2.3, the theory that simply states that there is an 'analytic' competence without deciding about its internal workings and that blames most biases on the 'preparatory task,' where they concern the relevance of the material, not the reasoning itself. Let us illustrate the relevance approach by its account of the selection task. Evans has noticed that people tend to select those cards that match the explicit information in the task description, and he has called the tendency 'the matching bias.' He claims that the matching bias determines what is perceived as relevant for problem solving: 'An item named is likely to appear relevant whether asserted or denied (matching bias), but a proposition, including a negation, is likely to appear relevant if it is the subject of a conditional sentence' (Evans 1989, 32). Once the relevant items are selected, the analytic reasoning proceeds correctly. There is no suggestion of profound irrationality: 'The human being, viewed as an information processing system, faces a massive problem of information reduction. Both the formation and manipulation of mental representations must be carried out in a highly selective manner using some form of heuristic process ... It is little surprising that such system is vulnerable to bias and error' (ibid., 112).

Similar ideas and results are to be found in the field of investigation of inductive reasoning. Franca Agnoli and David Krantz have investigated the conjunction fallacy and the possibility of 'suppressing the natural heuristics by formal instruction.' In a paper under a homonymous title (1989), they strongly oppose the original Kahneman-Tversky view that heuristics is like 'perceptual illusions,' in not being liable to be affected by instruction any more 'than geometric courses affect geometric visual illusions, i.e., scarcely at all.' (ibid., 519). They admit that natural (biased) assessments are made automatically and strongly influence probability judgments, but they claim that these assessments compete with other problem-solving strategies. The errors and biases stem from 'discrepancies between the subjects' problem-solving *designs* and the (presumably correct) designs favoured by the experimenters' (ibid., 539). The 'design' explanation is very similar to the explanation given by Evans and quoted above: subjects make mistakes in estimating relevance and in selecting features of interest. In their experiments Agnoli and Krantz have simply pointed out to the subjects (in the group that was receiving the training) that 'the size of a category is reduced when restrictive properties are added to its definition (for example, adding the feature "20 to 30 years old" to "US born women" reduced the category size considerably)' (ibid., 521). This simple training has produced a large and highly reliable reduction in conjunction error.

Let me note in passing that Tversky himself, in a recent paper written with Eldar Shafir on some fallacies in inductive reasoning, claims that the pattern of fallacies shows that people are not ignorant of the normative principle in question (the so-called sure-thing principle): 'These patterns, we suggest, reflect a failure of people to detect and apply this principle rather than a lack of appreciation for its normative appeal' (1992, 469).

So much for non-committal theories that simply distinguish a design or heuristic stage from a more analytical stage without specifying the mechanisms at each state. We now look at more demanding competence theories that propose a picture of the internal structure of the competence. They usually retain a two-stage format, including the use of heuristics at the first stage and of more analytic procedures at the second, but specify what goes on at each stage in more detail.

The first group are formal rule-theories, depicting competence as consisting of logical inferential rules, like those in logic textbooks (advocated by the psychologists Lance Rips [1983, 1989b] and John McNamarra [1986], and philosopher John Pollock [1989, 1992, 1993]). They account for shortcomings by postulating an additional set of rules – heuristic rules or cognitive shortcuts – which the naïve subject uses when confronted with a practical problem. Of course, some shortcomings can be accounted for by failure of memory, attention, and the like. On the other hand, the logical, high-quality rules account for the naïve subject's ability to recognize her own mistakes, to learn logic, and to recognize that it is right, and for the invention of formal logic in the first place.

Another kind of competence theory postulates the availability of mental models for deduction and induction. I briefly presented Philip Johnson-Laird's theory of models in chapter 1, 2.3. It attempts to account for the subjects' failure on reasoning tasks by blaming their models of the premises and allowing that after the model is in place, reasoning within the model proceeds in the logical manner. People possess basic logical capacities and are able to apply them. I mentioned three features of the theory: first, that the bias is explained by properties of models, whereas the reasoning within the constructed model is supposed to be bias-free; second, that the biases involved in the construction of models are not corrigible or, in principle, accessible to the subject; and third, the importance of meta-cognition that 'enables people to construct models of thought, and to construct models of those models, and so on, recursively' (Johnson-Laird and Byrne 1991, 164). Thus, there is a kernel of general and common rationality that accounts for the possibility of debiasing: 'There is a central core of rationality, which appears to be common to all human societies. It is the semantic principle of validity: an argument is valid only if there is no way in which its premises could be true and its conclusion false' (ibid., 209).

Let me add another example of how theories of limited rationality account for biases, where the experimental material itself suggests the improvements in reasoning to be made. The confirmational bias is remedied by a simple change in the formulation of the task. Instead of mentioning only one hypothesis, and thus letting its negation lie implicit in the shadow of the positive hypothesis, the experimenter explicitly mentions the alternative, under a positive (non-negative) name: 'Subjects were told that the experimenter had two rules in mind, one of which generated "DAX" and the other "MED" triples, and that 2 4 6 was an example of DAX. The DAX rule was in fact the usual "any ascending sequence" and the MED rule any other triple. Hence, the feedback on triples tested was in the form "DAX" and "MED," rather than "right" or "wrong." The result was a dramatic improvement in performance, with the majority of subjects announcing the correct rule at the first attempt' (Evans 1989, 52). Evans interprets the finding in terms of 'positive bias': creating a positive label changes the whole attitude of the subject. It seems that the underlying cause is not some deep irrationality, having to do with uncontrollable motivational factors, but a benign shortcoming tied to the preference for a positive formulation. This point blunts the polemical edge of descriptive pluralism. Remember that the relativist is committed to a kind of incorrigibility of cognitive styles in order to justify his rejection of reflective equilibrium, and here he has the opinions of the cognitive psychologists against him.

To return to the more general level, the two-phase-competence theories are able simultaneously to account for two phenomena: first, for the observed biases, and second, for the human ability to find correct ways of reasoning. Any over-optimistic view of reasoning is bound to fail on the first task. But a pessimistic view, claiming that people are inherently irrational, is unable to account for the complementary fact that we do have deductive logic, the theory of probability, and the rest of mathematics. Standard competence theories successfully steer between the two dangers.

Competence theories dominate the field. Still, the relativist might hope to find some consolation in the availability of a different kind of theory, postulating that the reasoning is domain-specific. The best known theory is the one proposed by Cheng and Holyoak (1985), claiming that people possess content-specific, or at least domain-sensitive, rules. In this approach the rules applied to a given problem are seen as dependent upon the meaning and context of the premises and hence can explain why people's reasoning is not simply a reflection of the logical structure of the problems. The content of a conditional rule cues one of several pragmatic reasoning schemes. A permission schema, for instance, is cued if the rule relates an action to a precondition.

The main piece of evidence supporting content-specificity is the interaction between knowledge (belief) and reasoning. People often make mistakes by treating a piece of reasoning as valid if the conclusion is (independently) believable and as invalid if it is (antecedently) unbelievable. Similarly, people give up valid inferences if premises are added, reminding them of additional conditions that, in their opinion, influence the truth of the conclusion (Byrne 1989).

The idea of content specificity is also linked to the fascinating research on the modularity of human cognition. For example, it seems that children's theories of other peoples' minds could be modular, so that a child lacking the specific theory cannot make up by using his general knowledge. Take, for instance, the following claims: 'autistic children have severe difficulties developing certain kinds of concepts but not others. We find that whereas autistic children perform very poorly on tests of the concept *believes*, they are at or near ceiling on comparable tasks that test understanding of pictorial representation ... These findings suggest that the concept, *believes*, develops as a domain-specific notion that is not equitable with "having a picture (map or diagram) in the head"' (Leslie and Thaiss 1992, 225; emphasis in text). Another theory of content-specific reasoning, the so-called social-contract theory (Cosmides) deals with the social domain. A typical statement of the main claims: 'This theory postulates (1) that we should think of reasoning as rational insofar as it is well designed for solving important adaptive problems, and (2) that there exist domain-specific cognitive processes for reasoning about social contracts' (Gigerenzer and Hug 1992, 129).

Theories of domain-specific reasoning, however, are by their nature limited. They cannot account for the simplest formal reasoning (e.g., with sentences containing schematic letters, say, 'All *A*s are *B*s'), or for the transfer between domains, so they have to be supplemented by some account of domain-general abilities: a theory of domain-specificity, claiming that there are no general strategies, would be doomed to failure from the outset. Moreover, most theories admitting of domain-specific styles also suggest that domain-specific schemes of reasoning have evolved through application of general principles (inductive and deductive) to the particular domain. Patricia Cheng herself, together with L. Novick, has proposed a completely domain-general account of basic strategies of causal induction. The moderately optimistic conclusion is worth quoting: 'It seems that causal induction is the proverbial elephant. Many researchers reported on various of the multiple facets of covariation computation, a component of causal induction that has been regarded as essential. These seemingly inconsistent, nonoptimal, shifting facets of this putatively essential component have led some to conclude that a coherent elephant of causality does not exist ... On the basis of our own work and our interpretation of others' reports, however, we believe we have put together enough pieces to suggest that an elephant is indeed there and that it shows signs of being an adaptive elephant' (Cheng and Novick 1992, 379). It seems that domain-specificity offers no lasting hope for the relativist.

Let us resume:

1. The available theories of human reasoning purport to *explain* bias and error, not praise it, and they seem to succeed. They do not acquiesce in relativism, nor do the most prominent theorists think that their findings point to an irreducible or irremediable bias, or to the non-existence of general rationality.

1a. Biases are uniform, shared by most reasoners. Nothing in the findings supports the idea of incommensurability in biased reasoning.

2. Another uniformity is to be found at the level of minimal logical core strategies, built into reasoning competence. Most psychological theories of reasoning are competence theories. They account for biases and errors by postulating a multi-stage process and by postulating several different abilities, all of which participate in reasoning tasks. Some of the abilities are central to reasoning and make up the competence of the reasoner; on most accounts, some basic logic and probability theory forms part of the competence. The explanation in terms of underlying competence does not seem to be problematic. It

accounts for the capacity for debiasing and at the same time leaves space for more specific theories about specific errors and biases. No competence theory supports radical descriptive pluralism.

3. Reasoning can be improved. The plain fact is that tens of thousands of people learn formal logical methods, and that many more learn statistics and improve their inductive reasoning.

In a word, the stubbornness or perseverance is more socially impressive than theoretically relevant. Perhaps Stich himself has used a heuristic – vivid and available in this case – and has overgeneralized on some handy examples of stubborn believers.

4. Successful Reasoners

To this point the discussion has been almost exclusively confined to the ground floor of cognition. The present issue concerns the assessment of sophisticated theories. We pass now to a specific positive proposal offered by Stich in his paper (1993).

In order to avoid repetition, I ask the reader to return to the summary of Stich's strategy in chapter 3, p. 58. Let me briefly mention several obvious problems before embarking upon the main topic. My main disagreements concern the first two steps; I agree wholeheartedly with the idea of studying good scientists' methods, but I disagree with the relativist-pragmatist's rationale. The relativist-pragmatist rejects the idea of specific cognitive success. Why does he then propose to study only scientists? Given the wide variety of people successful in their profession, thanks to their reasoning abilities, why concentrate on such a tiny and special group as scientists? A complacent accountant living a happy life thanks to his modest reasoning abilities is much more successful – under relativist-pragmatist criteria – than a typical active scientist perpetually in the grip of some new theoretical problem. Why, in particular, concentrate on 'great scientists'? A modest physics teacher who has managed to earn as much money as he needs, has secured the admiration of pretty college students, and is happy to see a good movie every now and then has secured his intrinsic goals in a much more solid fashion than a great, but socially unsuccessful, scientist, admired only by posterity, not by her contemporaries.

Generally, the step from the pragmatist idea that the goodness of a cognitive strategy is measured by the satisfaction of its actual user to the recommendation to take 'good scientists' as our paradigm is unclear.

The qualification 'good' for a scientist, as he uses it, is ambiguous between the everyday meaning – the fellow who does science of high quality – and the relativist-pragmatist's meaning – the fellow who has satisfied his goals, whatever they might be. The relativist should tell us which of the two he has in mind, since they fit very different scientists. Of course, the relativist cannot reply that he is interested in scientists who are good *as scientists*, because this introduces the rejected specifically cognitive virtues and standards by another name. It would betray a fatal failure of nerve on the part of the relativist-pragmatist.

Let us grant the relativist-pragmatist his appeal to everyday judgment, however, and agree to his list of good scientists (in spite of the fact that he is in no position to propose such a list by his own relativistic lights). He then faces the main issue.

The idea of studying successful reasoners, prominently great scientists for normative purposes, is not new, and it has been for some time part and parcel of the naturalist rationalist package. Rationalist philosophers of science from Popper to Glymour have been taking the work of great scientists as paradigmatic of rationality. The stress on cognitive psychological research is more recent, and again, rationalist authors, for instance, Ronald Giere, advocate the same kind of study.

The main issue between the relativist-pragmatist and the rationalist concerns the criterion of success. (Simon himself simply speaks of 'discovery' as his topic and concentrates his attention on successful discoveries. One chapter in his book is dedicated to Stahl's phlogiston hypothesis, however, so not only the clear success stories count for him.) The rationalist, claims that epistemic success is always truth-linked. The reasoner is successful if her theory is linked to truth in the right way. 'Theory' is here taken in the widest sense. Since rationalists disagree on the particular kind and strength of the link required, it is best to focus on the minimal rationalist requirement in spelling out in what the right way consists: Minimally, a theory has to yield *true predictions and retrodictions in a systematic manner* if it is to be considered successful. This minimal claim is the common core shared by realist and instrumentalist. The realist takes a step further and demands the truth not only of predictions and retrodictions, but of the very body of the theory itself. But both the realist and instrumentalist agree that theory has to be empirically adequate, that is, *true within the observational domain.*

Call the ratio of truth to falsity of propositions of the theory *T* the truth-record of the theory *T*. The ratio has to be established in the light of the best current knowledge of the domain. Then *T*1 is more successful than *T*2 if *T*1 has a higher truth-record than *T*2. (There will be some complications; e.g., the number of propositions entailed by theory *T* might be infinite, but these are slight technical matters that do not enter the general debate with the relativist – he is disputing not the determinacy of the truth-record, but its relevance). The instrumentalist (e.g., van Fraassen) restricts the set of relevant propositions to the observational ones entailed or supported by *T*1 or *T*2. The realist endeavours to judge *T*1 and *T*2 themselves and is concerned with their comparative truthlikeness, measured by their overall truth-record.

As mentioned, Stich's chosen list of reasoners that are successful regardless of truth or of falsity of their theories features the names of Aristotle, Dalton, Newton, and Mendel. Now why are they and why ought they be considered successful reasoners? Remember that success is comparative, in science, as much as in sport and money-making. The historians of science typically look at the progress made and at the contribution of the individual reasoner to that progress.

The rationalist answer reverts to the comparative truth-record of their theories and to their fertility, that is, their capacity to give rise to theories with an even better truth-record. Newton's theory of universal gravitation has yielded an unlimited number of true retrodictions and predictions (besides being approximately true itself and more truthlike than its rivals, the much earlier impetus theory and the contemporary Cartesian vortex theory). It has begotten more accurate and more systematic versions (in the hands of Laplace and Lagrange) and has prepared the ground for its own overturn. A similar story can be told about Dalton and Mendel. Aristotle has established his title of successful reasoner in at least two domains – logic is biology. The vast number of his claims about deductive logic are simply true, and he was the first one to make them; thus, his truth-record in logic compared with the nonexistent one of his predecessors is quite spectacular. (Do not compare him with Frege, but with Plato or Democritus). He discovered a great number of facts in biology, and probably initiated the field of study. Again, look at his comparative truth-record, which is equalled perhaps only by the Chios medical school. Finally, take his contribution to qualitative physics – the only one available at his time and for a long time to come.

Let me expand on the rationalistic-veritistic answer a bit more. William Newton-Smith (1981) offers a list of 'good-making features of theories' grounded in the truth-goal or verisimilitude goal of science. It is good to be reminded of these features:

1. Observational nesting: It is a virtue of a theory that it yields true predictions about observable matters. 'A theory ought to preserve the observational success of its predecessors ... Given that increasing observational success is our primary indicator of increasing verisimilitude, it will count against a theory if it is unable to replicate the observational success of the theory currently in the field' (Newton-Smith 1981, 226). Of course, to be able to gauge the observational success of a theory independent of the theory itself, one must be able to make independent observations. The relativist will typically deny this possibility. (These matters are considered in more detail in the appendix.)
2. Fertility: A theory ought to give promise for future development.
3. The track record: It is important to establish how many problems the theory has already solved, and how many tests it has withstood: 'The longer the theory is in the field, the more important its past track record becomes. Continuing observational success not only counts in itself for the theory, it is also an indicator of future fertility' (ibid., 227). Newton-Smith discusses at length the criterion according to which those theories are to be preferred that solve or promise to solve more problems, where solving a problem means giving a true solution to a problem, not proposing any old candidate solution.

Further items on the list are inter-theory support, smoothness in coping with failures, internal consistency, and compatibility with well-grounded metaphysical beliefs. Some of these items are more closely related to the truth-goal, some less.

The relativist-pragmatist typically underestimates the power of rationalist criteria. He would like us to focus exclusively upon the shortcomings of Aristotle's and Newton's physics or of Mendelian genetics, and the fact that their central theoretical claims are not strictly and literally universally true. From this examination we are supposed to conclude that truth does not matter. The truth of the theoretical core, however, is an ideal extremely unlikely to be achieved by immature science. A more charitable assessment is the global and comparative one: look at the true observational consequences of the theory and assess its success, comparing it with its rivals and predecessors. I assume that this is the informed intuitive criterion in the current historiography of science. Compared with the rationalist explanation of people's intuitions concerning epistemic success, the relativist-pragmatist has nothing to offer. He cannot appeal to the usual instrumentalist gambit about empirical adequacy, since empirical adequacy is nothing but truth in the empirical (observational) domain. He can only dig in his heels and proclaim that the fact that Aristotle, Newton, and Mendel were successful reasoners is simply a brute fact, inexplicable and irreducible. Stich appeals to a half-joke of Simon: go to the library and get a collection of widely used textbooks in the domain you are interested in, and then make a list of people whose pictures appear in the textbook. To be a successful scientist is to be famous enough to get one's picture in the textbook. This is all: Aristotle and Darwin are to be studied ultimately because their pictures appear in the textbooks (Pythagoras falls out, since we don't have his picture).

The difference in explanatory power between the relativist's view and the rationalist's view shows when the epistemologist confronts the actual history and its cognitivist reconstruction. Since Stich recommends, and with good reason, Simon's book (with collaborators), *Scientific Discovery,* as the major source for understanding the naturalist project, we may take a look at the relevant chapter, 'The Possibility of a Normative Theory.' There, one gets not only the brute fact that a scientist's picture is in the textbook, but also a detailed story, which shows what is the real stuff science is made of (Langley et al. 1987).

Simon's main example in the chapter is Planck's discovery of black-body radiation. Planck's goal was to find the right function relating the intensity of the radiation to each wavelength and the temperature of the cavity. The advances in experimental instruments over the last quarter of the nineteenth century had allowed increasingly accurate measurements of the intensity function, so that the theories thus faced increasingly stringent tests. (The story so far is well in line with Stich's insistence on the development of experimental technique as a major motor of theoretical progress.) Planck's work was a continuation of the work of German physicists Friedrich Paschen and Wilhelm Wien; he had initially worked on the theoretical justification (derivation from the known laws) of the formula proposed on purely empirical grounds by the former and elaborated by the latter. By the summer of 1900 new observations over the wider range of temperature and frequencies invalidated the formula. The very evening after obtaining the news about observational results, Planck guessed a new law, which was to become his revolutionary quantum theoretical law of black-body radiation. Only five years later Einstein and Ehrenfels pointed out that the formula really does subvert classical physics. Simon and collaborators commented: 'Planck's theoretical derivation, therefore, was in considerable measure driven by data (or, more exact, by a formula obtained inductively from the data). The solution to the problem that Planck posed for himself had to satisfy concerns imposed by the data as well as constraints imposed by classical theory. The latter were sufficiently ill defined that it was possible to violate them inadvertently, and thereby find a solution under the driving force of the given empirical formula' (Langley et al. 1987, 50).

The rationalist view of the story stresses Planck's insistence on conforming to the data. His first proposal involved a formula that gave good retrodictions concerning the intensity of radiation over an observed range of frequency and temperature. Obviously, the formula in the first proposal gave wrong predictions about the as yet unobserved range: low frequencies and high temperatures. When the news came in, the first formula was overturned and replaced with the revolutionary formula that gave better retrodictions and promised *eo ipso* better predictions. Indeed, the rationalist sees Planck's concern as being about true retrodictions and predictions – about how the things have turned out to be and will turn out to be, at least in the observable domain (and possibly in the unobservable domain as well).

For his part what can the relativist-pragmatist offer? How does he explain Planck's apparent obsession with the data, quite mysterious if the scientist is not aiming at truth at least in the observable domain? How does he explain the further development in the course of which physicists have given up the extremely well-entrenched global theory, that is, classical physics, in order to conform to newly found data? From the relativist's perspective this appears to be a quirk of irrationality – if one doesn't care about the truth, why bother about the predictions of one's theory?

The rationalist will do much better on the project of Normative Human Epistemology than the relativist-pragmatist will, and Simon himself seems to be a rationalist, after all, not a practitioner of the sermons that Stich is preaching. The general moral is that truth-generation is not only a virtue, befitting basic, simple cognition, but also an important virtue for mature, sophisticated science. Meno's and Gorgias's relativistic guess that there are different virtues for different positions in a hierarchy does not apply when general qualities such as truth-generation are at issue.

5. Realism and Relativism

Let me conclude by considering a very general issue of principle: the attitude of relativist-pragmatists to scientific realism. Scientific realism is the view that there is a mind-independent reality and that science, at least roughly and approximately, manages to capture important features of that reality. Anti-realism comes in different varieties, and in this context the most important one is the anti-realism of conceptual scheme(s). Again, one has a choice: one can claim that there is one ultimate conceptual scheme or that there are several different ones, and that science captures the reality-as-seen-through-the-scheme(s). On the unitarian alternative, the ultimate 'scheme of viewing things' is the point of convergence of the cognitive efforts of humankind; we should postulate such an ultimate, common scheme as an unavoidable idealization (e.g., Peirce 1955 and Putnam 1981). The pluralistic and relativistic anti-realist endorses a plurality of conceptual schemes.

Relativists-pragmatists, in particular Stich and Churchland, are realists and appeal to realistically construed scientific theories and results. Churchland is not only explicit but enthusiastic about realism. Stich, on the other hand, discusses and endorses realism in his first book and relies on the realistic construal of psychological theories in *Fragmentation*. Are relativists-pragmatists consistent in endorsing realism? Realism and relativism-pragmatism seem to be strange bedfellows, and the question is certainly justified. Moreover, there might be readers – philosophers or scientists – who are realists and are ready to accept relativism-pragmatism if it is compatible with their realist stance. When reading Churchland's panegyrics to realism, they might simply follow him and, without further analysis, assume that it is a routine matter to become a relativist while remaining a realist.

A malicious reader might claim that relativist-pragmatists are merely paying lip service to the realist fashion. Even if this were true (and I don't believe that it is true), and if fashion-following were the only motive for realistic declarations by relativist-pragmatists, it would still be important to find out whether the relativist-pragmatist can consistently endorse realism; for there might be sincere realists among their relativistically inclined readers.

Realism, however, is much more than a fashionable ornament of today's relativism; it is its essential ingredient. To see this, try consistently to imagine the contrary: relativism without realism. Picture a relativist-pragmatist, call him Landchurch, who endorses anti-realism and who is theoretically as close to Churchland (and to the Stich of *Fragmentation*) as an anti-realist can be to a realist. Landchurch claims that theories, in particular, neurological and psychological theories, are not true *simpliciter*, but are true only relatively to a scheme of viewing things and in a watered down sense of 'true.' In his opinion, theoretical terms of cognitive science (e.g., 'processing unit'; 'cognitive map,' 'stored prototype') do not refer to actual items (that humans carry around in their heads), but quasi-refer to quasi-entities of our making. Landchurch rejects the unitarian, absolutistic kind of anti-realism, and, since he is a relativist, endorses a plurality of conceptual schemes, so that the conceptual scheme of his preferred science of cognition (neurobiology, psychology, or other) is only one among many equally acceptable schemes.[11]

Landchurch is in *no position to argue for his relativism (and against the Classical Picture) by appeal to science.* The Classical Picture in its original form relies on folk-psychology, which is a highly successful and reliable view of people. Landchurch must view it as only one conceptual scheme, alternative to, and in principle equal to the scientific scheme. His theoretical entities, like 'stored prototypes' or processes like 'relaxation' have no bearing beyond a limited conceptual scheme and no edge over 'belief' or 'understanding' of folk-psychology.

Furthermore, he will be hard pressed to argue his position without appeal to the truth (or approximate truth) of his favourite scientific theories. Why should we trust his theory if it is not true or even approximately true? We might find some aesthetic satisfaction in it. If the theory requires us to abandon our common-sense understanding of ourselves, however, it is too much to ask that we believe it on grounds of aesthetic satisfaction alone. He might retreat to some very weak notion of rightness (a distant in-law of truth), having to do with entrenchment, or plausibility. But our folk-theory will certainly have as much claim to rightness in such a weak sense, if not more; it is certainly better entrenched, believed by many more people, and so on. Without appeal to the truth of cognitive theories, Landchurch is simply powerless.

Can Landchurch appeal to the empirical adequacy of his favourite theories – the fact that they predict the observable events better than the folk-theory does? No, for at least two reasons. First, he rejects the observation-theory distinction, so he cannot help himself to the theory-independent criterion of predictive success. Second, and more important, his epistemological conclusions are drawn from a theoretical guess about the structure of theoretical entities – presumed things in our heads. The Classical Picture is to be abandoned because of its alleged incompatibility with the structure of human cognitive apparatus. This structure is therefore essential to his argument and cannot be bypassed by appeal to mere empirical adequacy. The only route of escape for Landchurch is to admit to using science in a provisional and dialectical manner – accept the science provisionally in order to show that no cognition, including science, has any objective foothold. By doing so, however, he abandons naturalism and comes to the brink of classical scepticism.

Landchurch is not completely fictional. Steven J. Wagner has raised some difficulties for naturalism stemming from the prospect that our semantic notions might be eliminated in the ultimate theory *T* to which the naturalist appeals, exactly the way Churchland predicts. His worries nicely illustrate the plight of the naturalist realist who is sceptical of truth and reference: 'Even if any human enquirer must use a form of folk psychology, we have reason to think that ultimate theorists will proceed otherwise. And, not speaking of beliefs and other propositional attitudes, they would lose objects of which we predicate truth. Hence the semantic predications, too, would presumably disappear. A truth predicate will be of no use to an ultimate theorist who has nothing to apply it to. Why, then, should we give semantic discourse any distinguished status now? Why insist on preserving it, even should it lose empirical utility? More intelligent theorists would, anyway, not posit the mental states to which a truth predicate applies' (Wagner 1993, 152). The particular worry follows; maybe neural representations are semantically radically indeterminate: 'Although neural representations are analogous to beliefs in certain respects, they also differ crucially: in the units to which they are assigned and, above all, in the nature and determinacy of their contents' (ibid.).

Our critic insists upon the divorce and contrast of two domains: on the one side, the streamlined, successful and trustworthy ultimate physical theory *T* comprising neurology, on the other side the stagnating, prehistoric Jurassic Park of folk-psychology, with its superstitions and with the attendant semantics. The situation is as described by Churchland, but harnessed against naturalism.

Churchland, I think, is in no position to answer the challenge. By depriving himself of the vocabulary of truth and reference, he has also deprived himself of his theory of the adequate conceptual apparatus. Some of his defenders try the reasonable line of bringing back truth and reference; for instance, Adrian Cussins simply wants to invert the explanatory order: first, explain representations without appeal to truth, only from ecological adaptiveness, and then 'explain what truth and reference (the world!) is by means of an understanding of embodied animal activity' (1993, 248). Then relativism goes by the board.

The rationalist naturalist has a reply. If a theory represents reality *faithfully*, then it *represents* it. Thus, any evidence for the antecedent is also evidence for the consequent. More precisely, suppose that evidence *E* supports hypothesis *H* (claiming that *p*) to a considerable degree and that '*H*' states that *p*. Then *E* also supports the claim *C* that *H* is true, that is, that '*H*' represents reality *truly*. But then *E* also supports (although less directly) the semantic claim *SC* that '*H*' *represents* reality truly.

Take the well-worn example of the history of the atomistic hypothesis (and assume that the traditional story is right). Many scientists at the beginning of the century treated talk of atoms and molecules simply as a predictional and computational device, but with the work of Perrin and Einstein on evidence coming from Brownian motion, atoms become accepted as real.[12] The same evidence that has testified to the reality of atoms has also been taken to testify that the term 'atom' actually stands for an entity and that the atomic discourse is *about* atoms. The discourse of the atomic theory has been proclaimed to be (roughly) true, in virtue not of advances in semantics, but of those in physics.[13] If this line of reasoning is sound, the semantic claim that our (scientific) theories are roughly true and that terms therein actually refer is supported by the same body of evidence that supports the theories themselves. This is to be expected, given the disquotational property of truth and reference predicates. What is *not* thus supported are *the details of our semantic views* on the nature of truth and reference, and they might easily turn out to be false without putting the general theory into jeopardy.

Consider, now, the representational medium *M* and system *R* in which '*H*' is formulated. It seems that *E*, by supporting *H* and thereby the truth of '*H*' also gives some slight degree of support to the more general semantic claim *SG* that *R*-in-*M* manages to represent reality. The degree is slight because '*H*' is merely a drop in the ocean of possibilities open to *R*-cum-*M*, and its being true is only locally relevant to the issue of representational powers of *R*-cum-*M*. The cumulative weight of many confirmed hypotheses, however, would incline one rationally to place one's confidence in *R* and its semantic clout, that is, in *SG*. Conversely, a candidate-representational system that generates inconsistencies when confronted with data or, even worse, when left to run by itself arouses the suspicion that it is incapable of representing crucial features of the domain it should capture. The history of mathematical and physical notation offers many examples of how notational systems were modified or abandoned under the impact of practical or theoretical need.

The picture is then the following: human enquirers begin their enquiry having some innate representational system or systems. They are capable of translating representations from one system into another and of building new, auxiliary representational systems. Some representations couched in some of the systems are better confirmed than others, and some systems break down under the weight of discoveries that cannot be accommodated within them. The evidence favouring the truth of assertions couched in a given system indirectly also favours the assumption that the given system is representationally successful. The support given to the meta-level of semantics by the confirmation of object-level scientific discourse suggests that we have been lucky to have had a decent initial representational medium at our disposal and enough abilities to change and enrich it. There is no a priori guarantee for such possession; had our representational powers been different, we might not have ended with many true representations. (So the present argument is not the aprioristic argument against eliminativism discussed by Churchland 1993). That we have had good luck is something we can judge from the success of our theories; had our representational medium been hopelessly inadequate, we would have had no reason to believe theories couched in it. *The substantial truth of our theories and their representational powers form a package deal – one cannot get one without the other.*

At the start we have the idea of sentences describing how things are (it is the job of cognitive scientists and, in particular, of the researchers into cognitive development to tell us where the idea comes from). With the success of our theories we are encouraged to accept that the idea is right, that we have managed to come into epistemic contact with things in the world. Our theories somehow correctly represent their domains. The naturalist then extrapolates to *T*, the theory best supported by the ultimate total evidence that is ever available. This ultimate evidence, in supporting *T*, would also support its truth, truth in the minimal sense, sufficient for the purpose at hand, namely, that things stand as *T* says they do.

We can now see that the contrasting general picture of scepticism cannot be true, because of the package-deal effect: the core semantic hypotheses – those concerning the truth and reference of developed theories and the representational capacities of the medium-and-system in which they are couched – are supported by the same evidence that supports the theories themselves. The credibility of the basic semantics is part and parcel of the credibility of developed theories, not an unconnected and indifferent issue whose poor standing is to be invidiously contrasted with the status of Real Science. This credibility is an a posteriori matter, as is the credibility of developed theories, and it shares its fate. This high credibility of the general and basic semantics is to be contrasted with the problematic status of particular semantic theories aiming to explicate the ways in which our words and thoughts refer to reality. They will probably be replaced, within *T*, by some better theory. (Wagner himself seems to endorse the availability of the move, but he does not draw any consequences from it in the paper itself).

The same goes for the specific worry, the indeterminacy. In order to diagnose and pinpoint the indeterminacy, *T* has to be *more precise* than the folk theory. But then, the *T*-theorist will have beliefs exactly as precise and determinate as *T* is – there is no other way she can accept *T*.[14] (A foretaste of the situation of the *T*-theorist: in order to prove the indeterminacy claim the critic reverts to the well-known example of a frog and its neural state linked to the appearance of black dots on the frog's retina, normally caused by bugs flying in front of the frog: 'whether the content of the frog's state is taken to concern bugs, or black dots, or ... does not really matter to cognitive science' (Wagner 1993, 153). This makes sense only to those readers who distinguish bugs from black dots from ... so *their* content cannot be indeterminate the way frog's content probably is.[15]

The critic has one more argument to offer: that the semantic apparatus contained in the package-deal is too meagre to be of any use to the naturalist (Wagner 1993, 154). But is the apparatus really so meagre? It gives us minimally representational states, capable of being true/false, and of being as precise as necessary in order to accept *T*, which is rather precise and determinate (e.g., sufficient to get a Nobel prize in medicine). Further, we might reasonably hope that there is a subset of such representational states, which is suitably linked to perceptual input (how else would we ever come to have theories about the world, let alone true ones?) and somehow guides our action. The action-guiding role of inner states is currently assumed by all cognitive scientists, including most eliminativists, and there is little chance that any subsequent theorizing might overthrow the assumption. The representational content plus links to perception and action is more than enough for the naturalist. If this basic structure remains preserved by *T*, then naturalism is largely vindicated.

Let me now answer the initial difficulty: It is incredible that *T* will prohibit the minimal semantic discourse needed to formulate its own truth. For suppose it does so for a set of reasons *R*, and consider the would-be *T*-theoretician. Any reason from *R* is a reason to accept that no theory is true and that no theory stands for anything; it is thereby a reason to accept that *T* is not true, and that it does not stand for anything. *R*, being a subtheory of *T*, is also undermined by its own success. Therefore, *R* is not credible. A methodological remark: what might be a priori (if anything) is the structure of confirmation: how the confirmation of the whole and of its parts interact. What is a posteriori is that we have theories that are roughly true – with the package deal implied.

We see now that the half-hearted line exemplified by the opening quotation – accept the possibility of *T* and then argue against truth and semantics – is not open to the critic. On the contrary, he can rightly insist on the a posteriori character of all of our substantial knowledge and point to the possibility that there may be no *T* or *T*-like theory within our ken, even in the idealized case, because the very idea of truth and representation are misleading. Things are never such as any representation – any theory – states. The initial bases from which the naturalist extrapolates is misguiding; we have never represented anything or had any true beliefs (since there are no representations, beliefs, and truth). The possibility is, then, that the world is un-representable or, more precisely, that representation and truth are unavailable. This possibility, however, turns our critic into a radical sceptic, who is arguing not from any empirical failure of our theorizing, but from a rather outlandish possibility of epistemic groundlessness of cognition as such.

The moral of this *reductio* is simple and important: Realism is essential for relativism-pragmatism as we know it. The relativist-pragmatist is a naturalist, who argues largely by appeal to science, and only realistically understood science can offer the Archimedean point from which the relativist can hope to dislodge the Classical Picture from its base. The appeal to scientific theories as against commonsensical ones has force only if these theories are assumed to be true, or at least closer to truth than the commonsensical ones. Churchland is right: the relativist-pragmatist must be a realist.

But can a relativist-pragmatist consistently endorse realism? Churchland seems to hope to reconcile relativism with realism by proposing a dual picture: there is one objective reality and many schemes of representing it, many alternative ontologies. When it comes to realism about theoretical entities, however, the following problem arises. The realist is committed to the claim that theoretical entities are part of objective reality, not merely quasi-entities within the scheme. As we have seen, in the case of the theoretical entities of his preferred cognitive theories, the Churchlandian realist cannot simply assume that these entities are as good as entities postulated by folk-psychology; one of them must be real and one fictional.

To illustrate the point, consider natural kinds, that is, kinds that figure in laws. The quintessential argument for neurology as against commonsensical psychology is that the kinds and laws postulated by the one are incommensurable with the kinds and laws postulated by the other (no smooth reduction) and that the ones postulated by neurology are real (or at least 'more real' than the folk-psychological ones). In his programmatic and deservedly well-known paper Churchland states: 'From the perspective of the newer theory, however, it is plain that there simply are no law-governed states of the kind FP [folk-psychology] postulates. The real laws governing our internal activities are defined over different and much more complex states and configurations, as are the normative criteria for developmental integrity and intellectual virtue' (*NP*, 7). All the realist needs is here: the claim that there are real laws of our internal activities, and that they are directly relevant to epistemological assessment. Consider, then, the following disclaimer at the conclusion of another Churchland paper dedicated to natural kinds: 'The familiar multitude of putative natural kinds embraced by common sense, and by many derivative sciences, are at best merely practical kinds. Genuine natural kinds form a very small, aristocratic elite among kinds in general, being found only in the most basic laws of an all-embracing physics. And if there are no such laws, or if the human cognitive medium should turn out to be a representational cripple, then perhaps there are no natural kinds at all' (ibid., 295). Thus, the neurological kinds are merely practical, like the folk-psychological ones, and there are no real neurological laws. Why then should we opt for any single picture, to the exclusion of others, and why the neurological picture in particular?

It is easy to find local inconsistencies, even in the works of the best philosophers, and my intention is not to criticize Churchland for slips. I claim that examples like this one are symptoms of a deep instability of the whole relativist-pragmatist stance, arising out of the tension between relativism-pragmatism and realism. The picture becomes even clearer when one considers the notion of truth, since the appeal to truth or closeness to truth of scientific theories is essential for the credibility of the relativist-pragmatist appeal to science, and thereby of his naturalism. This clashes head on with the equally essential relativist claim that truth is simply not something theories have, and that it is unimportant for the cognitive enterprise. Remember Churchland's Argument from the Medium, starting from the Relevance Thesis (theories-in-the-head are the important ones, in contrast to verbally represented theories) proceeding with the help of the claim that theories-in-the-head are embodied in a medium that does not admit of a true/false dimension, and leading to the conclusion that epistemology should abandon the appeal to truth and falsity. To get the feel of the clash, concentrate on the claim that theories are not simply true nor false and that falsity and truth are unimportant, and then read the following passage from the book we are discussing: '2. Why Folk Psychology Might (Really) Be False: Since folk psychology is an empirical theory, it is at least an abstract possibility that its principles are radically false and that its ontology is an illusion ... We must consider what theories are *likely* to be true of the etiology of our behaviour, given what else we have learned about ourselves in recent history ... Thus the basic rationale of eliminative materialism: FP is a theory and quite probably a false one' (*NP*, 8, 9; emphasis in text). If theories cannot be false, it is hard to imagine how they can be radically false. It seems as though Churchland's writing wavers between two modes: the realistic mode and the no-truth mode. Claims made in one mode clash with claims made in the other, and no remedy is proposed.[16]

Churchland is aware of the problem: 'Finally, there is a question put to me by Stephen Stich. If ultimately my view is even more sceptical than van Fraassen's concerning the relevance or applicability of the notion of truth, why call it scientific *realism* at all? For at least two reasons. The term "realism" still marks the contrast with its traditional adversary, positivistic instrumentalism. Whatever the integrity of the notion of truth, theories about unobservables have just as *much* a claim to truth, epistemologically and metaphysically, as theories about observables. Second, I remain committed to the idea that there exists a world independent of our cognition, with which we interact, and of which we construct representations: for varying purposes, with varying penetration and with varying success. Lastly, our best and most penetrating grasp of the real is still held to reside in the representations provided by our best theories' (*NP*, 151; emphasis in text). Churchland's first reason is somewhat unclear. He finds it important to affirm that claims about unobservables are as true as empirical claims. What is the point, if truth is unavailable or at least is inappropriate and unimportant for the assessment of theoretical claims? Van Fraassen holds that the truth of theoretical claims is unimportant, Churchland asserts (in the same paper the conclusion of which we have just quoted) that the truth of any kind of theory is unimportant. His claim, therefore, does not contrast with Van Fraassen's, but it supports and extends it to all statements (their motivation is different, but that is not the issue here).

The second reason reveals the deep tension between relativism and realism. Churchland claims that our representations – the best theories we have – allow the 'most penetrating grasp of the real' we have. Now, if a theory is not true, not even approximately true, how does it allow the penetrating grasp of the real? To grasp the real with the help of a representation is presumably to have a representation that represents the real as it is.[17] Now, this is the content of the traditional notion of truth.[18] To revert to Stich and his question quoted above, it would be interesting to know whether he asked it about his own stance. Probably he did, and one day we shall know his answer. Structurally, he is in a position very similar to that of Churchland. Even if he lacks enthusiasm for scientific realism, his view of cognition is shaped by reliance on science: cognitive psychology and evolutionary theory. He can give up the realistic interpretation, but then his appeal to science would lose its credibility and its bite, and he would come very close to the unfortunate Landchurch.

It seems that the relativist-pragmatist is in a predicament: he cannot live with realism, and he cannot live without it. We may conclude that relativism-pragmatism is ultimately inconsistent.[19]

Conclusion

Let me first briefly summarize the discussion and critique of relativism-pragmatism. It has been organized around the main relativistic argument. The argument starts from

1. *The Irrelevance of Truth*: There is no common goal of cognition, because truth is irrelevant.

Next, it borrows from cognitive science the insight that people use various cognitive strategies and inflates it into

2. *Radical Descriptive Pluralism*: There are many radically different cognitive strategies and styles.

This thesis buttresses

3. *The Incomparability Assumption*: Since there is no common goal, the strategies are mutually incomparable.

(1), (2), and (3) entail Radical Normative Pluralism: there is no single norm valid for various cognitive styles or strategies.

I have discussed the ways the relativists-pragmatists defend (1) The irrelevance of truth and (2) The radical descriptive pluralism, and found them wanting. Moreover, it appears that the relativist-pragmatist use of his allegedly strongest weapon – naturalism and scientific realism – renders his position extremely vulnerable, if not downright incoherent. I have rejected the relativist-pragmatist conclusion and proposed the alternative, rationalist theses that fit the Classical Picture and extend it in a naturalistic direction:

Truth (or some related item from the truth family) is the goal of cognition, in a naturalistically respectable way.

Although cognitive strategies are diverse, they are goal-comparable, and they might be also structurally comparable.

Therefore, the criteria centred around the truth family can ground a common normative core for a naturalistic epistemology. The rest is a debate within the family: which subset of truths shall we single out as significant and which criterion from the limited set fits best our intuitions and brings us best to our goal? (I have not addressed the issue of radical scepticism, since the rejection of radical scepticism is the common ground between the relativist-pragmatist and the rationalist).

Truth-oriented epistemology can and should take into account the diversity of epistemic situations together with the variability of cognitive capacities, and all the complications that follow from that fact. Given that situations and capacities themselves are comparable in respect to epistemic goals, however, they pose not an obstacle in principle for the rationalist epistemology, but only a challenge to work out the right scheme of comparison.

Let me conclude by briefly sketching my answer to a question obviously related to the preceding discussion. What is the status of the basic rules of rationality? Where do they come from, and why do they seem obvious? The answer is not a part of my critique of relativism, but an attempt to go beyond the issues addressed in the main body of the book, in a way consistent with what has been suggested in it. Also, I shall only present the answer, not defend it, leaving the defence for another occasion.

A sophisticated cognizer typically learns some explicit rules of reasoning from others, and figures some out for herself. The most basic ones are probably not learned and are probably not explicitly known by most people. They are rules of transition between cognitive states – in particular 'belief states' in a very wide sense – that people can recognize on reflection. Following the moderate rationalist views, outlined in the chapter on cognitive strategies (chap. 1), the basic non-logical heuristics may be distinguished from the basic rules of deductive and inductive logic. My long discussion of representational formats has also produced an awareness that there might be transitions between non-sentential states that are also basic, complying with corresponding rules. People find some – if not all – of the basic transitions and rules compelling, often without being able to give a reason. Being compelling has two phenomenal components: the rule or the transition seems obvious (self-justifying), and it seems impossible to the cognizer to imagine a valid alternative to it. Let me concentrate on such 'primitively compelling' transitions and rules.[1] They are a mixed lot, encompassing simple logical rules (*Modus Ponens*), modal logical rules, simple arithmetical rules, intuitions about probability, simple heuristics, basic geometrical rules, and perhaps rules of folk-physics available in physical intuitions. (Let us leave out semantic rules on this occasion.) How should we think of them?

A promising naturalistic-rationalistic starting point is the assumption that such cognitive transitions and rules are means of extracting and manipulating information. The deductive logical rules and rules of probability calculus are perfectly reliable or ultra-reliable ways of manipulating information, the heuristics is less reliable (I am using 'ultra-reliability' to mean reliability in all possible situations). The rules of folk-physics seem to linger behind in respect to reliability (and it is an open question how compellingly obvious they seem to the folk). I assume that differences in representational format are not systematically correlated with variation in reliability: a rule coded in a non-sentential format can be as perfectly reliable as a sententially represented rule.

Cognitive psychologists are inclined to regard some basic patterns of transition as innate. Very probably such innate patterns are strengthened and enriched through successful application. Research in both classical and connectionist architectures might enrich our understanding of such processes in unexpected ways. Further, it is an open and debated question whether the external representational means (writing, speech, drawing) essentially modify the basic tool-kit of the human mind, or whether they only make its use more solid and its results more complex and durable.

Given the evolutionary importance of the extraction and manipulation of information, one may assume that some basic transition-patterns are innate and relatively rigid. If the transitions are governed by sentential representations of rules (at an unconscious level), then the rules are also innate. The innateness and rigidity might account for the phenomenology: the transitions seem obvious and compelling because we are so hardwired that we cannot but perform them. Some rationalists, most prominently Nozick (1993, 109ff), have speculated that the feeling of obviousness or self-evidence has also been selected for. It need not have been, however, since the evolutionary, selected hardwiring might produce the phenomenology without the phenomenology's being specially selected for. The basic hardwired transition-patterns and rules form 'the rails of the mind.' (The phrase is Wittgenstein's; he insists that we should not think of rules of thought as of rails of the mind; I think that the opposite advice is correct.[2]) The rails determine what is self-evident and yield the corresponding intuitions in particular cases. They account for the moderate structural unity of human cognitive strategies, which I defended in chapter 7, 3.2.[3]

Given the above assumptions, what is the epistemological status of the whole package comprising the basic patterns, rules, and intuitions they generate? My personal view of the matter is as follows. First and most important, being contained in the package does not guarantee infallibility; some obvious heuristic rules are not only logically invalid but often are simply incorrect, some geometrical and physical intuitions are misleading, and others are fraught with ambiguities (e.g., 'Proper part is always smaller than the whole'). Therefore, any justification that intuitions might have by virtue of their obviousness is only a prima facie, defeasible justification. The defeasibility is now widely accepted, even among rather conservative apriorists. (It is questioned only by the opponents of any kind of intuitive knowledge, such as Philip Kitcher and Michael Devitt; they try to make life hard for the defenders of intuitive knowledge by encumbering them with the implausible view that intuitions should be indefeasible).

Still, there are several ways in which the basic package is justified. Let us distinguish external justification by reliability (external, since it is not necessarily available to the cognizer) from internal justification through reasons had by the cognizer herself. 'Reliable' here means having a good truth-record), and 'ultra-reliable' means having an absolute truth-record, yielding truth under all possible circumstances. The first kind of justification that the package probably has is that most of its content is reliable; some items (logic, elementary arithmetic) are even ultra-reliable, and others are highly reliable, or at least reliable under the normal circumstance in the usual environment of the cognizer. This is an external justification, ascribed from the standpoint of impartial and knowledgeable observer (from God's point of view).

The internal justification is of two kinds, an immediate-intuitive and a wide, coherentist one. The first kind of internal justification derives from the compelling character of the package. The cognizers are justified in accepting it, because they cannot reasonably do otherwise. Even the relativist, who disdains the compelling character and denies any justificatory character to it, does have a strong intuition that two plus two equals four, that if p entails q and p then q, and the like. If he is honest, he will admit having the intuition, but he will try to undermine its cogency by denigrating its pedigree: our intuitions are all too human, produced by a fallible biological constitution (cognitive relativists) or by early social conditioning (social relativists). The compelling character and obviousness, however, should give some initial prima facie justification, if anything should – without such justification we would be irrational even to trust our perception (before having a perfect sophisticated theory of it, unavailable without a previous trust in perception).

The availability of the immediate prima facie justification allows us to consider elementary arithmetical beliefs justified in advance of rich experience. It also explains why we should distinguish calculating and reasoning from experiment even in rather simple-minded and mathematically unsophisticated persons. They do not ask themselves what the result of adding two to three is going to be next time, as if it were up to Nature to decide the result each time. Intuitively, they are justified in not asking the question, and their being justified is captured by the immediate prima facie justification of intuitive judgments. Admitting such prima facie justification does not land us in any kind of objectionable foundationalism. It is not infallible, not sufficient for sophisticated cognizers, and is, in our view, less important that external justification by reliability.

The second internal kind of justification is indirect, theoretical justification. Let us distinguish two kinds of coherentist considerations: the narrow and the wide ones. The narrow considerations concern relations between the items from the package together with their implicata, in abstraction from application to concrete, empirical cases. The basic package is certainly somewhat incoherent, but not hopelessly so: it can be made more coherent by confronting the items and attempting to reach some kind of reflective equilibrium. For instance, logic-guided transitions can clash with heuristics-guided ones, and in the long run the former are bound to win in terms of purely epistemic justification. Alternatively, the purely internal development of mathematics might change our naïve intuitions about infinity, sets, part-whole relations and the like.

The wide considerations concern the success of the application of the basic package and its derivatives. The basic package, together with its derivatives, plays a paramount role in the cognition as a whole and receives its share of justifiedness from the coherence and success of the whole. This is, famously, the Quinean line on logic and mathematics: they are to be accepted because they ground our best overall theory, in particular physics and cognate sciences (Quine thinks this is the only justification and rejects the immediate-intuitional kind). The immediate-intuitional and the narrow coherentist kind would be lame without the wide one: immediate self-evidence is phenomenologically hardly distinguishable from simple firm conviction (such as a fanatic about any kind of subject matter might have), and coherence itself is measured by the items from the package, so that it would be circular without an independent support.

The internal reasons (obviousness, narrow coherence, and wide theoretical success) are reasons to believe that many basic items are reliable, justified in the external sense. The naïve cognizer starts with obviousness and the impossibility of imagining things otherwise. It takes considerable reflection even to start doubting the deliverances of intuition and the cogency of basic belief-transitions. For the naïve cognizer the obviousness guarantees truth and reliability. The further step is theoretical justification. The reflective cognizer systematizes her intuitions, reflects about her belief-transitions, and critically judges the applications. It is the task of psychology and of the history of logic, mathematics, and physics to describe and explain the actual advance from mere reasoning to meta-cognition and reflection on reasoning strategies and intuitions. Theoretical considerations then may buttress the initial 'feeling' that the basic package is reliable.

The answer briefly sketched here combines some elements of traditional empiricism with some elements of traditional apriorism. It takes over from empiricism its naturalistic motivation: all cognition and all facts about cognitive structures are to be explained naturalistically, in terms of the interaction of cognitive mechanisms with the physical environment.[4] It agrees with the apriorist in going beyond individual learning and in taking the phenomenology of the situation as basically correct and justifying, but in a weak and fallible way.

One last word. I have criticized relativists-pragmatists, with a keen awareness that a rationalist has a lot to learn from them. They have made the cognitivist challenge more graphic and persuasive by casting it in an exaggerated fashion as a threat to rationalism. I have tried to argue that, in fact, it is no threat; it should be welcomed as an opportunity to enlarge the Classical Picture, taking into account the diversity of cognitive media and the biological underpinnings of human cognition. If the project succeeds, the rationalist should be thankful to his relativist-pragmatist opponent for having given him the opportunity and having reminded him of the urgency of a project that might otherwise have seemed too obvious to be undertaken.

APPENDIX

Theory and Observation

1. The Bold and the Modest Claims

1.1. Is Observation Autonomous?

In this appendix I shall look at one particular issue that is of direct relevance to the debate between the relativist and the rationalist, and continue the discussion of Churchland's views. It is the issue of the relation between theory and observation in science. In the first part we discuss Churchland's views, and in the second we consider an important and influential view – put forward by Dudley Shapere – which comes close to some of Churchland's central theses and improves upon them.

The basic question concerns the autonomy of observation and, at the level of cognitive capacities, of perception. Let us look at a famous example. Suppose that two otherwise similar persons diverge in their beliefs on some particular matter of fact; for instance, one believes that the sun revolves around the earth (geostatic hypothesis), and the other believes that the earth revolves on its own axis and around the sun (heliostatic hypothesis). Suppose they both watch the sunrise. Will they see the same thing? Would their visual experience be the same?

Yes, answers the philosopher whom we shall call the 'autonomist.' She is a philosopher who thinks that differences in belief do not influence seeing itself. To put it in a slightly more sophisticated fashion, she holds that there is a level of perceptual experience that is autonomous in respect of beliefs, particularly theoretical beliefs. The autonomist in our example claims that both persons have *the same visual experience.* Although this experience might be differently 'coloured' by expectations and emotions, it is the same visual experience of being presented with the sun moving upward.

No, answers the holist philosopher who thinks that seeing and believing, observation and theory form a whole in such a way that beliefs influence seeing, and that the two are inseparable. In the standard astronomical example, the holist would claim that what the first person sees is different ('subjectively') from what the second person sees in the same situation. *There is no visual experience common to both situations.*

How is the contrast between the autonomist and the holist relevant to the relativism/rationalism debate? If perception (observation) is inseparable from theory, theories cannot be tested by independent means. What scientists produce are *epistemic wholes* made of a more theoretical part plus theory-laden 'data.' Scientists with widely divergent theoretical beliefs, that is, divergent conceptual frameworks, command divergent epistemic wholes, which cannot be tested and compared on the background of neutral observational data. Further, the more theoretical part of the epistemic whole, its 'conceptual framework,' is justified and acceptable relative to its database, but the database is acceptable relative only to its conceptual framework. Combine this thesis with the idea that there are different conceptual frameworks, and you have a kind of justificational relativism: a statement, including a perceptual statement, can be justified only within a whole, and there is no justification independent of a particular framework. To quote a relativist, Gonzalo Munevar (whom Churchland approvingly mentions in *NP*): 'it should become apparent that an observational language will not be neutral between radically different theories because there can be no "preferred frame of reference." This I call the Principle of Relativity of Perception ... I must be clear that the principle does *not* say that *all frames* are on a par, but only that several *may* be – thus we cannot assume that ours is *the* representation of reality' (1981, 27 emphasis in text). *Obviously, holism is a natural position for a relativist to adopt.* The rationalist is much more comfortable with the autonomist stance. If there is a level of perception that is (at least comparatively) autonomous, and if human perceptual apparatus is rather uniform across cultures, then one may hope that people with widely divergent cultural and theoretical background will agree about statements geared to that level (e.g., 'This long, thin thing has moved a bit'). There will be no relativity at this low level. The rationalist is, of course, not committed to a blind trust in such statements. 'The sun has moved a bit' is decently observational, but it is false. It is not the truth of observational statements but consensus about them that matters for him. If the theory corrects observation statements, in the sense of showing that a statement registers only apparent movement, or position, or size, then this is done uniformly for all observers, and this uniformity is what matters for the rationalist. Of course, the rationalist might try to square his views with holism, if holism proves to be true, but the marriage of holism and rationalism is an uneasy one (see Newton-Smith's (1981) chapter on theory and observation, for an interesting attempt at matchmaking).

The famous defender of holism and the father of the whole tradition, N.R. Hanson, has proposed the astronomical example we mentioned, dramatized by the historical setting (1965, 10ff.) and Churchland has followed him very closely in his first book (1979). We are invited to picture the situation at the very birth of the heliocentric-heliostatic hypothesis, when the early pioneers like Copernicus, Kepler, and Galileo (or his hero Salviati) were defending the new heretical doctrine. Again, picture a champion of a doctrine watch the sunrise in the company of her opponent. Do both see the same thing or not?

Let us agree that every believer in the geocentric (and geostatic) hypothesis sees the dawn the way Tycho or Simplicio do: they see the sun moving (rising) and the horizon as static, so they see *the apparent motion of the sun*. What about a champion of the heliocentric and heliostatic hypothesis, Kepler or Salviati-Galileo? There are two possibilities:

A. The champion of the heliocentric hypothesis does not see the apparent motion of the Sun. She has performed a Gestalt-switch, a mini-revolution in ways of seeing, and now sees the moving horizon and a fixed sun (holistic hypothesis).
B. The champion of the heliocentric hypothesis sees the apparent motion of the sun (the same as his opponent), but her conclusions from what she sees are different (autonomistic hypothesis).

On the commonsensical level, the hypothesis (B) seems more plausible. People today accept the heliocentric story, but they still speak about the sun's rising, and no one feels seasick when watching the sunrise from his home, as one presumably would if one really saw the horizon sinking down.

The Holists, however, have endorsed the hypothesis (A): 'Kepler and Galileo see a static sun' (Hanson 1965). Presumably, Galileo's beliefs shape his vision, and he simply does not see the apparent motion. Some people might find astronomical examples unpersuasive, because they do not involve active intervention on the part of the scientist. So let us also introduce an example concerning a simple experiment. Oersted had been the first to show that electrical currents deflect magnetic needles. His experiment (performed at the Copenhagen University in spring 1820) consisted in letting the current pass through a wire situated above a compass needle. When the angle between the wire and the needle is right, the needle moves. Imagine, now, that a group of people of different scientific education (some lacking any such education) is watching the experiment and commenting. I suppose that the following comments would be tolerable (although the last one is admittedly anachronistic):

'The long thin thing has moved round a bit.'
'The needle has rotated about 45 degrees.'
'The magnetic needle has rotated about 45 degrees.'
'There is a force acting on a magnetic needle and making it move.'
'The magnetic needle has moved under the impact of the force, owing to the energy from the current.'
'The magnetic needle has moved because of the magnetic field created by the current.'

I presume that everyone will agree that the order of comments indicates a hierarchy of knowledge – one needs only his eyes to be in a position to make the first comment, some elementary-school geometry to make the second, a little bit of physics for the following two or three comments, and some high school physics for the last one. The initial comments are more 'observational,' the last ones more 'theoretical.'

What we want to know is whether there is a level at which Oersted and his opponent will be able to agree on what they see, independent of what they might believe. The holist says, 'No' (or, if pressed hard, claims that such a level, if it exists, is informationally impoverished and therefore insignificant). The autonomist says, 'Yes, there is such a level,' and the judgment characterizing it would be something like: This long, thin thing has moved a bit.'

Let us now take a closer look at positions and arguments. The specific aim is to discuss the contribution of Paul Churchland in so far as it enters the relativism/rationalism debate. However, matters are somewhat complicated. Churchland himself seems to have modified his opinions in the course of time, and it is almost impossible to appreciate the motives and the consequences of his changing views outside the wider context of the debate. Therefore, I shall present this wider context in the briefest outline.

1.2. The Bold Claim: Holism

Consider, first, the original, pronounced, and bold version of holism. It is represented by Hanson, Kuhn, and Feyerabend, and by the early work of Churchland himself (1979), although Churchland is not explicit on all the points in question. (For example, whereas Hanson, Kuhn, and Feyerabend insist on the existence of radical perceptual-conceptual changes, he prefers to talk more liberally about 'expanding our perceptual consciousness,' where 'expanding' seems to denote retaining what we had and adding much more, rather then discarding our initial perceptions.)

I shall call the Bold Claim of the holist:

Our perception is shaped by our beliefs in such a way that the two are inseparable. To use a term fashionable in cognitive psychology, perception is 'penetrable' by beliefs.

The inseparability claimed by the holist is a serious matter. It is not only that observers (when they say things such as 'The needle has moved under the influence of an electromagnetic field') are not immediately aware of combining two distinct components – this the autonomist gladly acknowledges. The claim is that perception and belief are welded together, so that no amount of analysis can distinguish the components.

If we take observation in science to be dependent upon or even constituted by perception and if we translate 'systematic beliefs of scientists' into 'theories,' the debate about beliefs and perception translates into debate about theory and observation. The immediate consequence of the holistic claim is that there is actual theory-induced divergence in perception to be found in the practice of science: *Observation is theory-laden. There is no theory-neutral observation.*

The theory-ladenness of observation is the counterpart of (if not the same thing as) the penetrability of perception by beliefs. The thesis plays an explanatory and a normative role in holistic theories. It is taken to explain actual and important episodes in the history of science. In particular, it should account for the relatively swift and encompassing nature of 'scientific revolutions.' The idea is that the pioneers (such as Copernicus or Galileo) perform a Gestalt-switch, a radical change in view, including a perceptual change. This gives birth to the new paradigm. The new paradigm is then divulged as a whole; the disciples, the Vivianis, the Torricellis, learn at the same time a new theory and a new way of looking.

The thesis also has normative consequences, since it suggests – as we mentioned at the outset – that justification has to be holistic. In Churchland's words, 'human knowledge is without propositional or judgmental foundations. That is, there is no special subset of the set of human beliefs that is justificationally foundational for all the rest' (1979, 41).

It does not seem obvious that our astronomical beliefs penetrate our perception and influence the way we see the sun in the morning, or that people with different theoretical backgrounds perceive the movement of the needle (in Oersted's experiment) in different ways, especially that one can misperceive the situation and see the needle as not moving simply because one believes that the needle should not be moving. Therefore, the Bold Claim needs some stage setting and a lot of argument.

One strategy is mellowing the hard facts and using the slippery slope trick: show some examples and then argue that even astronomical or simple experimental situations involve contamination by theory. For example, at the beginning of the famous chapter on observation in his *Patterns of Discovery* (1965), Hanson invokes the issue of what one sees when looking at a prepared slide under the microscope. One microbiologist sees in the cell before her a cluster of foreign matter; another sees a cell organ. It is clear that in such cases the differences in skill, in attention, and in what one is looking for might influence what one sees, although Hanson does not even bother to argue that point. Hanson then suggests that this activity is analogous to watching the sunrise. (I hasten to enter a disagreement: in the sunrise situation one does not need any professional skill to notice that the angular distance from sun to earth has increased, and no professional skill will make one see the horizon moving down.) In the same line one finds the argument from ambiguous pictures. The holist invokes divergence in the ways ambiguous patterns are disambiguated – someone's rabbit is another's duck. He goes on to claim that this is the normal situation in science, invoking Roentgen, microscopes, and the like. Finally, the holist invokes the role of language, which she sees as both formative (linguistic relativity) and evidential.

Holists have been drawing much support from constructivist theories of perception. Some well-established psychologists, such as Richard Gregory, have advocated a general holism about perception, which has been grist to the mill of the holist in the philosophy of science.

Let me finally mention a more sophisticated argument, the one from the character of belief-content. Paul Churchland, in his *Scientific Realism and the Plasticity of Mind,* has offered an interesting strategy in defence of the Bold Claim. He starts from sensory states and treats perception as 'exploitation of sensory information.' A sensory state can have two kinds of content. It has objective (correlational) content, given by its normal correlation: a sensation is objectively of *X* if it normally occurs when something in the perceiver's environment is *X*. A sensory state has subjective content if it prompts the suitable immediate judgment, for example, a state has subjective content that this is warm if it would prompt the immediate judgment 'This is warm.' The official formulation of the condition is that a state is subjectively a sensation of *X* if and only if under normal conditions the perceiver's characteristic non-inferential response to any sensation of such a kind is some judgment to the effect that something or other is *X*.

Churchland claims that learning some relevant theory can induce drastic, or as he would say, 'sensational,' changes in our perception. (The title of the relevant chapter in his book is 'The Expansion of Perceptual Consciousness.') This happens in the following way. The usual sensations, for instance, of warmth and coldness, are subjectively about warmth and coldness. Being about temperature and since temperature is mean kinetic energy, however, they reliably indicate the mean kinetic energy and reliably detect subtle changes of energy level. Now you are ready to 'expand your consciousness.' You have only to start thinking in terms of kinetic energy, and you will switch from subjective sensation of warmth and coldness to the subjective sensations of the novel parameters, those of kinetic energy (I translate Churchland's notation in the way he indicates): 'The point is that the sensations mentioned are objectively of the novel parameters cited in exactly the same sense in which they are objectively of the more familiar parameters of common sense. As potential objects of observation, therefore, those novel parameters await nothing more than the same conceptual attention we currently squander on the primitive and chimerical categories of the common sense' (1979, 26). The same holds for other kind of sensations: 'And let us not forget our olfactory and gustatory sensations , for our nose and mouth comprise an analytical chemical laboratory of admirable scope and sophistication. These provide the sensational resources for recognizing a wide variety of compounds, molecular structures/ shapes/sizes, and chemical situations. Were our enthusiasm for the analytic, the descriptive, and the explanatory to equal our enthusiasm for the narrowly aesthetic, these organs would render manifest to us much more of the immediate environment's constitution than they do' (ibid., 27).

These remarks can be taken in two ways. Taken in the conservative way, they claim the following. If we learned some more physics and chemistry, and paid more attention to what we have learned, we would still have the same sensations, but we would know that they indicate to us important physico-chemical parameters. The soup would taste the same, but we would know about the chemical ingredients in it. I take it that these claims are true and banal. They are like the following claim: if you knew that this new book in front of you is about spies, it would still look the same to you, but you would know that you are looking at a book about spies. The autonomist can accept such claims without ado, and without inconsistency. Taken in the revolutionary way, the remarks claim that by learning chemistry you expand your *perceptual* consciousness. The world begins to *look* to you, *taste* to you, and *smell* to you differently. All that is demanded for such a revolution is theoretical learning and a change in attention. I think that this is the intended reading. Indeed, in the sequel to the remarks quoted, Churchland speaks about 'our capacity for enhanced perception' (ibid.). This revolutionary stance of course, is, unacceptable to the autonomist.

These are practical consequences of the Bold Claim. It is time to scrutinize the Claim's credentials and to attempt some criticism.

1.3. The Bold Claim: Defending the Autonomy of Observation

A critique of holism and a defence of the autonomy of observation need not rest content with the commonsensical assurance that we all do see the sun rising, and that people confronted with a moving needle see it moving regardless of their scientific or even their general cultural background. It can evoke psychological theorizing, the history of science, and the basic facts about the structure of argumentation in science. Let me give a brief sketch of each line of defence.

Recent trends in cognitive psychology tend to stress the relative autonomy of basic perceptions. David Marr has persuasively argued that perception of shapes and movement is independent of data from memory – what are commonly called beliefs and opinions. Memory is accessed only in cases when data are ambiguous, not in the normal run of things. He offers an explanation in terms of the autonomy of basic-level perceptual processing and of the independence of basic-level perceptual mechanisms. The terms of art for such autonomy are 'modularity,' 'encapsulation,' and 'impenetrability.'

In more technical terms, in Marr's view (as aptly summarized by L.M. Vaina 1990, 49–91), vision starts with an intensity array containing two types of information: the intensity changes and the local geometry. This information is then used by low-level mechanisms to produce a 'description' of an image in terms of simple, low-level symbolic assertion, called the raw primal sketch. The next representation is a full, primal sketch, which 'makes explicit object boundaries or contours, shadows, changes in texture, and specular reflexions, obtained by using geometrical reasoning on the earlier descriptions and some limited higher-level knowledge' (ibid., 54). Still further, we get the representation of the geometry of visible surfaces, and so on, all the way to the full, conscious, visual experience that tells us what the world is like. Each submechanism has access to a limited amount of stored knowledge – and the full store of the memory is available only at the latest stage of processing.

Jerry Fodor has presented a detailed defence of the autonomist view built upon the modularity thesis (1984, 23–43), so I suggest that the reader who is interested in psychological details consult his paper[1]. Psychology gives initial support to the idea of the autonomy of observation. There are considerations from history and from the structure of science, however, which need separate discussion.

Let us start with the paradigmatic example, the one from astronomy. The holist's claim that pioneers of the heliostatic hypothesis saw a static sun is, in the first place, a historical statement, not simply a nice metaphor. There is a matter of fact about what the pioneers of the heliocentric view saw, and the defender of the Bold Claim is committed to the actuality of theory-induced perceptual divergence at important junctures of the history of science, together with a wide divergence between different epochs of that history. Further, the particular matter of fact is not an indifferent example – Galileo is not merely another John Doe.[2] It is part and parcel of the holistic picture of scientific change that it is not theory alone that is being transmitted from the pioneers to the followers, but novel ways of perception and novel practices (this is what makes it exciting to talk about paradigms instead of mere theories). If there is no novel way of perception, characteristic for the pioneers – if Galileo sees the same scene Tycho does – then there is no novel way of seeing that they could transmit, and the story about whole paradigms instead of theories becomes somewhat shaky. (Remember that planetary astronomy is the touchstone of the holism debate, because here the tremendous and revolutionary shift concerned directly visible objects in contradistinction to the comparable shift brought about by quantum physics; so if the holist story does not work here, it will work nowhere else).

Did Galileo see the *real* movement of the earth, and was he *not able to see the apparent movement of the sun?* The answer is a clear 'No.' Galileo saw the same scene Tycho saw. We know this is so from his writings. In the 'Second Day' of his *Dialogues* he speaks about apparent movement. His hero, Salviati, invites his interlocutors to take the following as a 'principle of their theorizing': whatever movement is ascribed to the earth, it is 'necessary for it to remain *completely unperceivable*' (*'del tutto impercettibile'*) for the inhabitants of the earth who partake in this movement. Furthermore, it is necessary that this movement be 'represented as common to all other visible bodies, who lack this movement, being separated from the Earth.' If there is a visible movement common to all visible heavenly bodies, therefore, it can result either from the movement of the earth, or from the movement of the 'the rest of the universe.' 'In both situations one would see the same appearances' (*'medesime apparenze'*) (*I Dialoghi*, 112). The crucial phrase is 'the same appearances.' Galileo is explicit in claiming that advocates of both theories see the same appearances.

Not only do we have Galileo's direct and clear testimony. The sameness, or resistance of appearances, is not a hindrance to the theory, but is, in his opinion, an additional piece of evidence for the theory. Things look exactly as they should if the heliostatic theory is true. The fact that all heavenly bodies seem uniformly to revolve around the earth supports, in Galileo's opinion (as in ours too), the hypothesis that it is in fact the earth that moves. To put it in a nutshell: *The correct theory wins because it explains the appearances, not because it transforms them.* Similarly, no one demands of optical theory that it make us correct the apparent size of objects viewed under the microscope – amoebas do not appear very small because we know they are very small. Nor do viruses under electronic microscopes appear smaller than amoebas under optical ones because we know that the viruses are even smaller. The correct theory explains why they look as they do, and if they did look different, that would tell against the theory, not in favour of it.

This is a good point to address an argument made by Churchland against the relevance of the modularity of perception to the theory/observation debate. Fodor has argued that perception is modular, that perceptual apparatus has some hardwired 'presuppositions' concerning visual geometry, and that the output of the perceptual module is theory neutral. Churchland strikes back: 'If an observation judgment does have such presuppositions, its theory-laden character will in no way be reduced by hardwiring those presuppositions into the process by which the judgment is produced, and by closing the process to all contrary information. If everyone is a hopeless slave of the same hardwired theory, then what we have is a universal dogmatism, not an innocent Eden of objectivity and neutrality' (*NP*, 258). But this is not the issue. Everyone's perceptual apparatus is so hardwired that everyone watching the sunrise perceives the apparent movement of the sun. This appearance is neutral in relation to the relevant astronomic theory; no matter who is right, Tycho, Galileo (or, for that matter, Einstein), the appearance remains the same. This appearance is 'objective' in the modest sense of intersubjectively valid, repeatable, and checkable. This is all the autonomist rationalist needs and hopes for – a common basis from which to start, not to end.

The talk of 'hopeless slavery' is in this context misplaced and positively misleading. Modularity entails not intellectual slavery, but perceptual bondage; Galileo went beyond appearances and explained them in the same breath.

Let us now take a look at the example involving experimentation and consider the way in which the experiment is conceived and normally explained to a beginner. In order not to repeat myself, I shall change the vocabulary a little and agree that to make an experiment is to put questions to Nature (as Fodor in his more recent paper on theory and observation, 'The Dogma That Didn't Bark' [1991], enjoins us to do). The problem of theory and observation then translates into the following one: how do we find out whether and what Nature has answered?

Although Oersted was interested in the ultimate unity of things and wanted to show that all forces are, in fact, one and the same force, his question put to Nature was a more modest, but still a theoretical one:

TQ: Nature, please tell me whether the electrical current produces a force that can act upon a magnetic needle?

Given his set-up, it was in only one fashion that Nature could have answered, namely, by moving or not moving the needle (nodding her head or not). Therefore, the first thing to find out is whether the needle has moved or not. This is the observational question:

OQ: Did this thing move?

The movement (or lack of the movement) of the needle carries all the information there is. In actual fact, Nature has nodded in response to the question.

The perception of the movement of the needle ('this long, thin object here'), sufficient for an answer to OQ, seems to be quite independent of any knowledge of physics or philosophy of nature. The movement could have been seen by a three-year-old child, by an aboriginal who thinks the needle is a kind of insect and has a soul, and by Oersted's intellectual opponent who believes in the disunity of the world as working hypothesis. It could have been registered on the piece of paper, and deciphered by Oersted's granddaughter; it could have been (except for some contingent details) digitalized, fed into the computer, and saved in its memory.

The situation looks dramatically different when we pass to the question 'Why?' The three-year-old, the aboriginal, Oersted, and the disunity-champion will give widely divergent answers depending on their capacities, knowledge, interests, and so forth. Unfortunately, in order to know whether Nature has answered the original theoretical question, TQ, one has to pass through the answer to the Why question (one has to interpret Nature's nod).

The most important fact about further investigation is that the interlocutors have to agree, step by step, about low-level theories in order to agree about the final answer to TQ (first, that the long, thin object is an inanimate thing, a needle; then, that it is magnetic; then, that some force has to act on the thing if it is suddenly to move; further that there is an electrical current in the wire, etc.). There is *an important order of reasons.* Let us look at this order.

The simplest comments on the movement of the needle that we have listed above seem to involve no theory worth mentioning. Less simple are low-level 'theories,' such as commonsensical beliefs about magnets and magnetic needles. Low-level theories are *separable*: believing that something is a needle is separable from believing that it is magnetic. Therefore, the disagreement is, *as a matter of fact, localizable*. Further, it should be localized, and still further, it is in real debates mainly local. For example, relativists often invite us to picture ourselves discussing advanced science with a member of a quite different culture. But if you disagree with someone about whether needles have souls, you will probably not discuss electromagnetism with him. Your disagreement is about what a typical needle is, and this disagreement can be settled largely without appeal to Maxwell's theory. Conversely, if you have reached the stage at which you can meaningfully discuss electromagnetism, you are past an abundance of low-level theories, and certainly past the stage at which the possibility of needles' being ensouled is a serious issue. This simple, historical matter is often forgotten.

It is sometimes said that if you start at a low-level, the gap between the raw, low-level data and the theory will be too big to bridge, but this objection underestimates the power and plausibility of low-level theories. There is an important continuity linking the comments we have listed, and the essential part of learning elementary physics is to learn the facts and principles allowing one to pass from one level to another. The hierarchy from more observational towards more theoretical knowledge follows this order of reasons. The separation of observation in a strict sense from theoretical interpretation-extraction follows the lead of the dramatic difference between noticing a movement of a thin object and guessing at why the object moved. If there is a distinction to be made, this is the most natural – in fact, the only natural – point.

I shall not address here the holist's arguments from ambiguous patterns, except for a brief comment. First, the process of disambiguating ambiguous data follows the same pattern of ascent from low-level theories to higher-level ones. Second, the most important form of observation in mature science is measurement. What is measured, however, are not vague, holistic patterns. Typically, the decision confronting the observer (a human or, for that matter, a computer) is a binary decision: did the needle go past this mark – yes or no? Did the counter click? Does this curve cross zero within this interval? The road towards reducing observation to such decisions is the main road of the development of experimental technology, which starts from the 'world of approximation' and ends in the 'universe of precision,' as Koyré has phrased it. It is hard to imagine how the commitment to a theory can radically transform one's vision so that its victim does not see the simple movement of a needle.

These commonsensical remarks can be corroborated by well-known episodes from the history of science. If observation were theory-laden, the greatest disagreements about observation would take place when the clash in predictions concerns two widely divergent complexes of theories, two 'paradigms,' for example, when a young and revolutionary paradigm is being introduced and its predictions are tested. The counter-examples are famous episodes such as the discovery of black-body radiation, the ultraviolet catastrophe, and the Michelson-Morley experiments.

Black-body radiation has ultimately suggested to physicists that at the basic level of nature, physical processes run not in a smooth, continuous fashion, but in 'quantum jumps.' The contrast to classical physics is clear and dramatic. Under such circumstances, the holist view would predict a wide disagreement about observation – in fact, the widest possible. The defenders of the traditional view, on the holist hypothesis should simply have stuck to the verdict of 'I can detect no radiation,' or 'I hear no clicks from the counter,' whereas the quantum revolutionaries literally should have seen the light (the black body glowing with radiation confirming their theory). Of course, nothing of the sort happened.

The same holds for the ultraviolet catastrophe and the experiments surrounding the advent of the theory of special relativity. Although the results of all observations listed have been of utmost importance, overthrowing the whole of classical physics, there has been no substantial disagreement about observation. The important disagreements have arisen about the relevance – how much does the observation prove? This is precisely what the non-holistic theory predicts. The data are sacrosanct – the best place to drive the wedge is the data-theory link, and in actual fact this is where scientists attempt to drive it.

Philosophers oriented towards 'tough science' and inimical to speculations sometimes allege that the observation-theory distinction is a product of an obsessive fear of scepticism on the part of their tender-minded colleagues. They should notice, however, that the dramatic difference between observing a movement, and presenting a theory to account for it is certainly not a product of anybody's philosophical obsessions. It is a commonplace. Further, the *observational* agreement about, say, black-body radiation in the face of fundamental theoretical differences is a fact of the history of science that cries for explanation, not a philosophical invention.

Let us look now at the argument from content. Notice, first, that there is no place in the Churchland scheme for perception proper, only a place for sensations and full-blown beliefs. Sensations owe their subjective content to beliefs: what you believe is what you feel or see, and the beliefs form a seamless whole. How persuasive is this idea when tested on examples? Remember the case of warmth versus kinetic energy. Churchland has recommended that his reader expand her consciousness by learning some thermodynamics and rearranging her attention by turning it away from the common-sense conceptual framework and concentrating on the scientific framework. It is not clear that a change of belief (theory) would induce any change in 'feeling.' On the contrary, the sensation remains stubborn, which is easy to show precisely in the example of warmth. One of the most important differences between the scientific story in terms of kinetic energy and the everyday story is that where the everyday story – presumably based on perception – introduces a polarity of warm against cold, the scientific story allows only degrees of the same thing, kinetic energy. The polarity warm/cold has to do with physiology of our temperature detectors. Thus, a good test of the holist stance would be the following: if a person were to adopt the scientific story as her deepest belief, would she still be judging the temperature of the environment in terms of the warm/cold contrast, or would she judge an ice cube to differ from a hot, iron cube only in degrees of the same property?

Most of us have at some point learned that temperature is kinetic energy. I do not recall any change in the perceived contrast of hot (warm) objects and cold ones. The reader should, of course, judge for herself or himself, but it would be strange indeed if people lost the warm/cold contrast simply by virtue of being taught some physics. Paying attention, even practising, would hardly diminish the felt contrast between a warm stove and ice-cream.

Furthermore, the warm/cold contrast is a kind of *perceptual contrast* ostensibly characterizing things, not feels. It is not my feel of ice that is cold, but the ice itself. Please remember that we are talking of 'subjective content,' and the subjective content of the feel of cold is that of cold things. Therefore, Churchland cannot argue that the 'feel' itself has no intentionality, no content apart from accompanying beliefs. It does have a content characterized at least by the warm/cold contrast, and that contrast seems to be resistant to change of theory or belief. Thus, Churchland's hypothesis fails on the simplest test, the one explicitly suggested by him as his paradigm example.

The argument from content also fails with visual experience. Although Galileo firmly believed that the sun does not move, his subjective visual content was still that of 'moving sun.' No amount of theory can contravene the basic observation. If the argument seems to have any force, it derives from confusion between the objective and the subjective sense of 'seeing.' Given that what Galileo sees is objectively the scene in which the earth rotates and the sun is static, one can inadvertently pass to the conclusion that somehow Galileo must be able to see subjectively the same thing, the more so because his beliefs go in the right direction, and he is willing to say: 'Lo, the earth has just moved another bit!' But this judgment of his remains inferential; it cannot, by sheer force of belief, be turned into immediate judgment expressing and describing his visual experience.

Let us now take stock. The Bold Claim of the holist is incompatible with the data on the modularity of perception. It misrepresents the history of science. It misrepresents the actual disagreements in science and gives the wrong prediction about the pattern of acceptability of observational data.

1.4. *The Modest Claim: Educability*

Holism, as proposed by Hanson and defended by Churchland in his first book, was a bold doctrine. Its boldness attracted attention and made it the focus of much debate, especially when Kuhn and Feyerabend used it to support quite radical claims.[3] Such bold claims did not turn out to be very plausible, however, so various authors have tried to hedge them in various ways.

The most influential recent modification is due to Paul Churchland himself, in his 1989 book, *NP*. We shall call the modified proposal the 'Modest Claim.' It revises the original, bold proposal at its two sore points. First, it gives up the instant penetrability of relevant perceptions by theory: 'Who ever claimed that the character of a scientist's perception is changed simply and directly by his embracing a novel belief?' (*NP*, 263). Well, Churchland did. Remember that for 'expanding your perceptual conscience' you just have to learn new facts, that is, embrace a novel belief and pay sufficient attention to it. (Of course, I do not insist. If Churchland wants his earlier remarks to be taken the Modest Way, I have no objection, but I shall try to show that modesty makes the Claim toothless).

The relativist-pragmatist proponent of the Modest Claim reminds his reader that it is possible to train people's perceptual apparatus and to cultivate their perceptual capabilities. This should be done within the community, 'learning their nonstandard observational vocabulary from birth, in an ongoing *practical* setting where no other idiom is even contemplated' (*NP*, 263). (According to Churchland, he was always claiming only this much). The penetrability is replaced by educability. The paradigm case is musical training: 'Everyone knows that the "ear can be trained," as we say, to sustain these remarkable and nonstandard perceptual capabilities. But the existence of trained musical perception is a straightforward existence proof for the possibility of theoretically-transformed perception in general' (ibid., 269). The proponent of the Modest Claim thus will try to base his holism on such a weaker basis. Since the musical examples do not seem to be particularly relevant to the history of science, however, and the application to the spectacular changes, such as the heliocentric revolution, is out of the question, the revision must go further. What is now appealed to are communities with perceptual and linguistic practices quite different from ours, where people are trained in a vocabulary radically different from the one our children learn. In fact, Churchland turns to imaginary exotic communities, and carries out thought experiments involving them .

This introduces the second important characteristic that distinguishes the Modest Claim from the Bold Claim. The Modest Claim concerns the alternatives that are possible, mainly only *merely possible.* It argues for the contamination of observation by theory from the *possibility of radically different communities, and in generally radically different situations* from those we are familiar with. Of course, these communities are not identical to the community in which our science has evolved. We may imagine the proponent of the Modest Claim to plead as follows: 'It may be that as a matter of fact the scientific community shares enough low-level beliefs, and that people as a matter of fact share enough of perceptual equipment to be able to reach consensus on most scientific issues. But we must aim at full generality and look at possibilities. Might it not happen that the two communities do not share even the most basic ways of identifying objects, of 'cutting the world up,' in such a fashion that their respective observations diverge as much as do our theories?' To summarize, the Modest Claim introduces two important revisions of the original proposals, educability instead of instant penetrability (no penetrability by beliefs only) and a possibilist strategy, presupposing the epistemological relevance of mere possibilities.

1.5 The Modest Claim: Discussion

Let us first note that even the Modest Claim does not vindicate the intended point of the Galileo-Brahe example. One would expect, if the Modest Claim were true, that after three centuries people will finally come to see the sun as static. Again, the prediction of the Modest Claim fails. The moral seems to be that the perception is *not indefinitely plastic.* But more is to be said.

A better look at Churchland's defence of the Modest Claim reveals that he is arguing mostly for *improvability*. Is improvability relevant? Suppose that your sight might improve so much by study and practice that you are able accurately to estimate angular measures of movement. You look at the needle in the Oersted experiment and say: 'Look, the needle has moved 1/195 π radians.' Does this statement invalidate the more primitive claim: 'The needle has moved'? Does it turn the more primitive claim into a theoretical claim? Of course not. One must admit that with better eyesight one might notice a movement where previously one noticed none. But measurement in real science is not dependent on idiosyncrasies of an experimenter's visual acuity in such a drastic fashion. After all, why not use a lens?

If the actual improvement is not so crucial, the potential improvement can be only less than important. In short, improvability is largely irrelevant to the debate. The holist needs the possibility of reorganization, not of mere refining in order to clinch his point. It is extremely difficult to think of any intellectual change the result of which could be added to our native sensory apparatus so as to undo the clear perception of movement, as required in the Galileo example or in the Oersted example. Certainly, Churchland has provided none. Generally, the simple observations needed in standard science are observations of the location or instrument readings that reduce to recognition of simple configurational facts ('the pointer is to the left of the line number 3'), where there simply is very little chance of spectacular reorganization of what is seen.

There is one further problem. I note (with dismay) that Churchland goes on to invoke his argument from content about potentialities for the change of perception, even after he has abandoned the idea of instant penetrability, or rather has denied that he ever held it. But what may the argument now be? Remember that the argument in its relevant, revolutionary guise started from the premise that perception is objectively about physical parameters (kinetic energy, electromagnetic waves of different wavelengths, chemical patterns, etc.). It then introduces the idea that our perception can become subjectively about the same matters, if only we learned the relevant portion of science and applied it.

Churchland has denied that he ever held that simple theoretical learning can change our perception. His new idea is as follows: 'In fact, we begin to become such mutants or aliens ourselves when we change our sensory modalities by augmenting them with unusual instruments, such as phase-contrast microscopes, deep-sky telescopes, long-baseline stereoscopes, infrared scopes, and so forth. And the metamorphosis is completed when, after years of professional or amateur practice, we learn to see the world appropriately and efficiently with these new senses' (*NP*, 259). The new way to expand our perceptual consciousness, therefore, is to use deep-sky telescopes, infrared scopes, and so forth. Is this all the argument from content reduces to?

Let us agree that all these apparatuses supplement and expand our senses. A microscope allows us to look at an amoeba or a virus. The autonomist accepts this fact and views the situation in the following way: when one observes a virus (or a photograph of one, to be more realistic), one sees a pattern of lines and shades. One is taught to discriminate relevant configurations, that is, to treat them as figure, against the background of irrelevant noise. One is also told that the configuration is (represents) a virus. Everyone with normal eyesight is capable of seeing the pattern of lines and shades, and this seen pattern is *theory neutral*. (But one needs a theory to build a microscope! Well one needs one to build ... binoculars, and one can use ... it to look at people without making either people or what you see theory dependent.) We are back at square one.

Worse still, the effort to extend our senses with the help of technology points to a defect in the holist's position. The need for such extensions shows what everyone knows, namely, that a theory itself will not perform the miracle and would not change our perceptions in the requisite way; we have to act on sense organs and extend their power. But, if the *only* way drastically to change one's perception is to *modify sense organs* (by using technological extensions), then perception must be resistant and modular. It changes dramatically only when the sensory input changes dramatically. Perception covaries with sensation (not with beliefs). This is precisely what the autonomist predicts.

So much for the problematic facts. Now the issue of the impact of the Modest Claim must be addressed in the wider context.

The first thing to be noticed about Churchland's possibilist strategy is that it removes the debate from the central concerns of philosophy and history of science. The main arguments employed by Churchland concern distant possibilities, distant in the sense that the history of science is not affected by them. They deal in exotic (imaginary) communities in which children are trained in observational ontologies widely different from ours, in science fiction and in thought experiments. This is far removed from the worlds of Galileo, Tycho, or Planck, with whom proponents of the Bold Claim were concerned, and it is hard to see how Churchland's conclusions might legitimately influence the philosophy of science. His conclusions are simply of no avail to a defender of paradigm incommensurability, or related Kuhnian or Feyerabendian claims, unless the defender can show that the exotic communities are, in fact, the real, historical communities of our scientific tradition – a task that goes far beyond Churchland's explicit and argued statements. The possibilist strategy is relevant for the general theory of knowledge, in the way in which Cartesian thought experiments (Demons or Brains-in-a-Vat) are, and it belongs there, not in the context of debate about actual scientific practice.

I want to argue for this line of criticism in more detail. Therefore, the issue of what remains of holistic claims and ambitions when the Bold Claim is replaced by the Modest Claim must be addressed. We should be wary: Churchland speaks as if his claim proves that observation is 'inseparable' from theory; in reading him, therefore, we should bear in mind that all that can be legitimately meant by 'inseparability' is that our present perceptual input might have been shaped by the aggregate (total) impact of our early training. (In the context of the Bold Claim, inseparability meant that perceptions change as theory changes). This is what 'inseparability' reduces to in the context of the Modest Claim (I shall continue to use quotes to mark this weak sense of 'inseparability').

Can the weak notion ('inseparability,' which is, in fact, educability) perform the task for which the strong (literal, Hansonian) notion was harnessed? This question is relevant even if Churchland himself does not intend his notion to perform the job – since he uses the term 'inseparability' and talks as if he has succeeded in proving that there is no theory-neutral observation, philosophers and scientists might be lured into thinking that Churchland has finally provided the (respectable and functioning) tools to vindicate the traditional holist approach, with its attendant suite of incommensurability, and so on. Thus, we the following question must first be addressed: If Churchland's Modest Claim were true, could it perform the classical job of defending holism and supporting relativism?

Let us again use the Oersted example to make the search for an answer more vivid. Remember that the anti-holistic picture of the situation includes the following ideas. There is a hierarchy of descriptions and explanations of what is going on in the experiment. Some processes and some properties are inferred at a very high theoretical level (properties such as having a vector potential of such-and-such a kind). This inference is based on the acceptance of statements of the lower level. At the lowest level of statements we have claims, such as 'This long, thing has moved,' which represent what we directly observe. The scope of the consensus follows the descending line of the hierarchy (the lower the level of the statement, the more consensus it gets), and consensus about the observational statement is quite universal: upon inspection anybody will agree that the long thing has moved. Given Oersted's situation, the low-level descriptions are much more reliable than the high-level ones – in fact, the high-level hypothesis that the current will act on the needle is tested by the observation and confirmed by the movement of the needle.

Suppose that the Modest Claim is true. That is, suppose that perception is educable, that long training could result in the refinement of perception, and even in some rearrangement in what is perceived. Further, suppose that it is psychologically possible that there might exist a community with a completely different vocabulary, practices, and ideology, the members of which do not share our 'observational ontology' (e.g., who do not experience 'the flow of time' and who perceive things naturally in terms of the four-dimensional space of Special Relativity). How would that possibility reflect on our understanding of Oersted's experiment?

First, we have already said that the mere improvability of perception (seeing more distinctions, smaller and slower movements) does not threaten the existing, non-refined datum. A gross movement of the needle cannot be conceptualized away by using a different conceptual scheme, nor can it be made invisible by more refined perception.

Second, the hierarchy of reasons remains untouched. The statement about the long object's moving remains more certain and more popular (in terms of consensus) than the statement about the vector potential. There is *nothing at all in the epistemic organization of the hierarchy that is being threatened by the Modest Claim.*

Third, the mere possibility of an alternative ontology does not threaten the credentials of our ontology. The methodological principle of conservatism dictates that the scientist should not undertake drastic revisions unless it is absolutely necessary. A fortiori, the scientist should not give up her ontological framework solely because a different community using a different framework is imaginable. To see this, suppose that Oersted's opponent, the disunity-champion, argued from such a distant possibility: 'Look, there must be a possible world harbouring a scientific community that does not have the notion of "movement" and the notion of "a long, thin object" in its ontology. A member of such a community would not see that the needle has moved. So your experiment is invalidated.' Of course, Oersted would have been right in dismissing such a complaint as unfair and void.

Even if (by a quirk of irrational weakness) we conceded that outlandish possibilities are relevant to actual science (against the third point just made), it would be hard to formulate a really threatening alternative ontology, for instance, a four-dimensional one poses no such threat – the change of spatial coordinates is simply translated into different language. 'The movement of a long, thin thing' is so resistant simply because it is ontologically undemanding. How much 'observational ontology' do you need to have the experience of a long, thin object moving? Well, you need at least three-dimensionality and some gestalt-principle of common destiny – shapes and edges moving together belong to the same spatio-temporal configuration – nothing more. The grouping by common destiny belongs very probably to native human sensory apparatus. On the other hand, if seeing things in three dimensions is already counted as 'theory,' then holism becomes almost vacuous – simply call anything 'theory,' and then any cognitive state is of the same kind as any other.

Even if the Modest Claim were true, it would leave the relative certainty of different levels from high-level theory to observation unchanged; that is, it would not threaten the hierarchical structure of actual scientific practice, and, most strangely, it would leave untouched everything we said about the experiment from a non-holist standpoint.

The only way for the Modest Claim to become relevant for the debate about the actual history and practice of science would be to incorporate some evidence that the educability of perception plays a significant role in science (as it certainly does in music and painting), more specifically, that the differences in the ways scientists' perceptions have been educated have played a major role in the history of science. Churchland has done nothing to present such evidence. Furthermore, since observation in most relevant parts of advanced science concerns measurement readings and nothing like artistic perception, it is doubtful that the evidence will be forthcoming.

What about more traditional and more general holistic claims, such as incommensurability and Gestalt-switches? There is no need to stress that nothing in favour of incommensurability of actual theories follows from the mere possibility of there being exotic communities holding theories incommensurable with ours.

Finally, giving up instant penetrability of perception deprives the holist of an important model for theory change: the Gestalt-switch model according to which the scientific revolutionary (Kepler, Galileo) induces in his pupils a sudden change of perception, so that almost at once they 'see the world differently.' The Modest Claim enjoins us to revert to the less spectacular traditional picture: the revolutionary teaches his new interpretation and explanation of data, and the interpretation is accepted, among other things, because it explains better the same data which the old theory did not explain so well.

It seems then that the Modest Claim is unfit for the job the holist wants it to perform. One might wonder how the relatively slight change from the Bold Claim to the Modest Claim could render the claim so toothless. The mere shift from instant penetrability to educability does not seem to entail consequences about the very principles of science. The secret lies in the fact that educability completely changes the focus of the debate. The idea of instant penetrability of perception by theory encourages the view that people of different opinions will have wildly different perceptions of the same things. The idea of educability reduces the specific impact of theories and thereby renders implausible the view that purely theoretical differences induce perceptual divergence. In order to counterbalance this weakening, the holist has to revert to distant possibilities, thereby excluding himself from the debate about actual science.

1.6. Perils and Promises

Of course, the proponent of the Modest Claim is not automatically responsible if the Modest Claim is something of a failure in the context of the traditional debate about theory and observation. The proponent might have his own agenda, different from the traditional debate. Therefore, we turn now to Churchland's explicit statement of his agenda. He proposes the following picture: 'If observation cannot provide a theory-neutral access to at least some aspects of reality, then our overall epistemic adventure contains both greater peril, and greater promise, than we might have thought' (*NP*, 255). Well, 'greater peril' sounds bad enough, but Churchland does not say what the peril consists in. Thus, there is no need to insist. The promise is more interesting: 'The first and perhaps the most important consequence is that we must direct our attention away from foundational epistemologies ... direct contamination with (higher) theory is probably incompatible with foundationalism. A second consequence is that our current observational ontology is just one such ontology out of an indefinitely large number of alternative observational ontologies equally compatible with our native sensory apparatus And a third consequence is that, since some theoretical frameworks are markedly superior to others, the quality of our observational knowledge is in principle improvable' (ibid.). The greatest part of the promise is only tangential to the topic of this book, so I must be brief in discussing it.

Let me start from the third consequence, improvability. The improvement goes in directions largely irrelevant for science, but relevant for art and enjoyment, such as listening to music, or some sports, such as target shooting. Experimental technology has made science long since independent of outstanding prowess in visual acuity or subtle hearing-and-listening capacities.

The second consequence has already been discussed. If the term 'observational' is to cover properties like mean kinetic energy, then any ontology is observational. 'Ontological relativity' seems then to reduce to the idea that there is an ontology entailed by every comprehensive theory. Classical particle mechanics comes with an ontology of particles and forces: Maxwell's electrodynamics with an ontology of fields; genetics with an ontology of genes. But this is only a consequence of what a theory is: a set of interconnected statements about some domain of discourse (kings, cabbages, etc.). Of course, the relevant situation is the one in which different comprehensive theories speak about the same domain, or what seems to be the same domain (cabbage vs. cabbage cells, or contact forces vs. fields). But this really serious question, and the attendant issues of intertheoretic reducibility, are left untouched by the simple idea that there might be different 'observational' ontologies. If forces reduce to fields, or if cabbage reduces to cabbage-cells, then there is no clash between cabbage-ontology and cell-ontology, or between forces-ontology and fields-ontology. But nothing in the plurality of theories and their immanent ontologies points in the direction of irreducible plurality, let alone serious ontological relativity. In particular, this is an issue independent of the theory/observation distinction, and holism about observation contains no promise and no peril in this domain. (What is still worse, Churchland is a fierce reductionist in his philosophy-of-science moments. For him, therefore relativity should be apparent, rather than real.)

If 'observational' is closer to the everyday understanding of the term, then it should be pointed out that the basic ontology of three-dimensional things moving in space and enduring in time seems to have *no serious observational* rival. It has not been dislodged on the observational level even by very powerful rivals, such as general relativity, or by quantum physics. This means not that it is accurate, or true, but only that it is very resistant. Notice that technological extensions of our senses (sophisticated microscopes and telescopes, CT-scanners, etc.) change nothing in this respect. We still see stars as dots, portions of tissue as coloured patches, and so forth.

The third consequence is supposed to be the anti-foundationalist one. It does work against the radical, fanatical foundationalist who claims infallibility for all perception. But such a foundationalist is a straw man. Real foundationalists are more subtle. Foundationalism typically treats perceptual contents (states, propositions, data) as sufficient to justify the corresponding belief in the states of affairs represented, for instance, 'this looks red' justifies (prima facie, inductively, defeasibly) 'this is red.' Accepting purely subjective perceptual content (like 'this looks red') is always justified.

Where does the fact pointed out by Churchland that perception is shaped by various factors enter the story? It does not deprive common-sense judgments of their prima facie justification. If something looks red to me, I am prima facie justified in believing that it is red, regardless of the exact nature of the process that shapes my perception. Churchland himself is quite enthusiastic about human powers of sensory discrimination and about senses very reliably indicating the almost exact values of sophisticated physical parameters. Now, if my sensory apparatus is good enough to justify beliefs about the exact state of mean kinetic energy of the air molecules in the room (as he enthusiastically claims), why is this same sensory apparatus not good enough to justify the simpler belief that the room is tolerably warm? By his own lights, Churchland should be more of a foundationalist.

Alternatively, the plasticity of our sensations might be taken to undercut the justification of the pure 'judgments of appearance,' such as 'the room seems warm to me.' But this line of attack forgets that foundationalism is (traditionally) a present time-slice theory. It enjoins us to start from the output of perceptual capacities that we now have, regardless of the history of the capacity. It tells me that if I now feel warm, I am justified in believing that I now feel warm. The fact that I might have felt different had I been brought up in an entirely different community is totally irrelevant.

The third 'consequence,' therefore, is far from being established as following from the Modest Claim. Even if it did follow, however, this would not represent much of a revolution in epistemology. Foundationalism is no sacred cow, and coherentist alternatives to foundationalism are very popular nowadays.

It is ironic that the coherentist alternative would also be at a loss with the Modest Claim. Coherentists are not such antagonists of observation as one might think (if one had not read coherentist literature with particular attention). They think observation is not enough for justification, but most of them go to great lengths to enssure some kind of privileged status to observation. Remember Quine: his 'web of belief' comes closest to the outside world at the observational periphery. Davidson gives observational statements privileged status, because they are supposed to be caused by the events they are about. More recent coherentist epistemologies, such as that of Bonjour, take pride in claiming that a coherentist is able to give the observation the privileged status it deserves.

Thus, the Modest Claim would be somewhat homeless in the epistemological environment if it had the consequences Churchland alleges it has. It is doubtful, however, that any important consequences would follow from the claim that perception can be modified under some circumstances. The Modest Claim is simply a truism posing as a revolutionary discovery.

2. The Return of the Bold Claim

2.1. Introduction

In the last decade the format of discussion has been spectacularly altered by a new approach to scientific practice. The new approach takes its start from the view that observation (in the widest sense of the word) concerns information – that it is, in fact, a process of gathering and extracting information that is there, in the observed events and processes, to be picked up, registered, and preserved. Within this informational framework the Bold Claim has come to new life.[4] Let us look at an example.

Hanson's famous example from planetary astronomy, which we used to introduce the issues, can be translated into informational terms: the astronomer registers the apparent movement of the planets (the registration can be done by mechanical means, as well). The apparent movement is caused by the position of the earth and by the real movement of the planets, so it carries information about the real movement. Since this movement is causally dependent on gravitational forces, it carries information about the action of gravitational forces. Thus, the data registered by the astronomer carry information about the action of gravitational forces.[5]

The information-theoretic approach seems promising and fruitful. The pioneering figure in this line of information-oriented views of observation is Dudley Shapere, whose paper, 'The Concept of Observation in Science and Philosophy,' published in 1982, deserves to be taken as the starting point in any discussion of the issue.[6] I shall also briefly mention his more recent paper 'Rationalism and Empiricism: A New Perspective' (1988). Shapere offers a more up-to-date example – the solar neutrino experiment. The neutrinos travel from the sun to the earth, they are captured in tanks of cleaning fluid (perchlorethylene) located in a deep mine to shelter them from other particles. The neutrinos are practically not interfered with, so they carry unadulterated information directly from the sun's interior. Of course, some rare interactions do occur, and one needs considerable physical theory to calculate the probabilities of each specific kind of interaction. Once a neutrino has been trapped in a tank of cleaning fluid, its presence is detected by its effects on the fluid: a neutrino would be captured and a radioactive nucleus would be formed. Radioactive nuclei are then detected in the standard way, thanks to their own radiation. The information-theoretic story is as follows: neutrinos carry information directly from the sun, and this information is being detected by counters registering the eventual decay of a radioactive nucleus. In the words of Shapere's own summary description: 'But then there is the question of how to test the theory under consideration; and that consists in a *theory of transmission and a theory of an appropriate receptor of that information.* Again the application of prior ideas is crucial: the ways in which energy is transmitted from its birthplace (according to the theory of the source) in the solar core to us are spelled out in terms of certain background information, as are the kinds of apparatus that will be appropriate for receiving that energy here on earth and interpreting it as information, evidence, concerning what goes on in the source of that energy or information, the centre of the sun' (1988, 307; emphasis in text). Shapere also mentions in passing a third observational situation, in which the scientist is looking at dots or lines on a photograph, seeing them as images, for example, of stars or of the elementary particles moving through magnetic fields. I shall freely use all three examples.

The heart of the new approach is the notion of observation as reception of information. Shapere's crucial definition is as follows: '*x* is directly observed (observable) if: (1) information is received (can be received) by an appropriate receptor; and (2) that information is (can be) transmitted directly, i.e., without interference, to the receptor from the entity *x* which is said to be observed (observable) and which is the source of information' (1988, 10). Receptors are detecting instruments – tools such as counters, or even substances for the capture of elementary particles. Given that current physics recognizes four fundamental types of interaction (electromagnetic, strong, weak, and gravitational), receptors will be devices capable of detecting instances of any of them. Shapere stresses the role of mechanical registering devices and computers in observation in advanced science – no human agent has to be present in order for observation to take place. Information is an objective commodity, emitted by objects: 'There turn out ... to be four fundamental types of interaction through which objects emit information' (Shapere 1982, 32), namely, those we have just listed above. In this influential paper (1982) Shapere addresses a great number of issues. Besides formulating the information-oriented view itself, he is mainly interested in showing that epistemology of science should separate the treatment of observation from the discussion of perception. The problem of theory-ladenness is perhaps only the third on the list of Shapere's priorities, so he is very sketchy and moreover somewhat ambivalent about the issue.

I shall therefore proceed as follows: first, I shall outline what I think are the two most important questions about the observation-theory distinction within the informational context. I start from the worry that the information-theoretic approach might give some new ammunition to the holist. I shall then distinguish two strands in Shapere's approach to the observation-theory distinction and isolate the more radical, holistic strand for further consideration. Finally, I shall try to show that the arguments for holism that might be gleaned (distilled, fabricated) from Shapere's paper are not valid. I shall not spend any time on conjecturing how close Shapere himself is to the radically holistic line. In the more recent paper (1988) he comes close to abjuration of most holist tenets. Of course, if our refutation is correct, and if he has in fact been such a holist, the refutation will bear against him too.

2.2. *Two Questions about Theory and Observation*

The information-theoretic line as presented by Shapere, broadens the meaning of the term 'observation' and 'observational situation.' It not only divorces observation from perception, but introduces the idea of an observation situation as encompassing the flow of information from its source to the receiver. The traditional question about separability of theory and observation must be adapted to this very broad framework.

I would like to distinguish two questions that are successors to the traditional one. Within the broad framework, one can perhaps distinguish what belongs to the external world up to and including the immediate impact of the world on the cognitive agent – the flow of information in nature or laboratory – from what is going on inside the cognitive agent (human or computer). Then, when looking inside the 'head' (or the CPU) of the cognitive agent, one can distinguish different things she is doing – some more primitive and immediate, some more theoretical.

Let us introduce the corresponding questions by a simplified example. An experiment in a Wilson cloud chamber will typically involve the passage of elementary particles through the chamber, their being photographed, then the photographs' being 'read' by a human or computer 'reader,' and their being interpreted to yield relevant data. Within the information-theoretic framework, one can distinguish two problems concerning such an experiment, and generally the inner structure of scientific practice.

The first question is as follows:

1. Can we and should we distinguish two processes – the first taking place in a laboratory and outside the cognitive agent leading to the photograph, that is, ending with the finished photograph; the second, internal to the cognitive agent, starting with the intake of photographed data by the scientist (or computer) and ending with a proposition (utterance or printout) to the effect that the experiment shows such and such a hypothesis to be acceptable? If the answer is yes, one might call the first process the process of information gathering, or registering, and the second the process of cognitive extracting of information .

In general terms, the first problem concerns *the separability of information transmission from the process of extraction of information.* Can the two be separated in the proposed way? Is this separation meaningful and epistemologically fruitful? Does it cut the practice of science at its joints? The positive answer suggests the distinction between the physical process of transmission and a cognitive process of extraction, including recognition, interpretation, and other kinds of theoretical elaboration. The negative answer amounts to holism about information gathering and processing.

Let us now focus more narrowly on the extraction of information. Here, we face a second and familiar problem, our question (2):

2. Should we distinguish a 'primitive,' pre-theoretical phase of extraction of information from the properly 'theoretical' phase? In the context of our example, the pre-theoretical phase would end up in a description of the photo in terms of dots and streaks, and the theoretical phase would deal in electrons, their paths, and the like, issuing in the proposition about the hypothesis tested in experiment.

In general, the second problem concerns – within the cognitive part – *the separability of the pre-theoretical from the properly theoretical phase of the extraction of information.* It seems that this second problem is more akin to the traditional (Hansonian) problem of the relation between observation and theory. The negative answer to this second question is precisely Hanson's and Churchland's holistic answer.

The negative answer to both questions constitutes a radically holistic stance, with which we shall be occupied in this chapter. The radical holist goes a step further than Hanson does. Not only is the cognitive process of extracting information a holistic structure in which one cannot and should not distinguish the contribution of theory from the contribution of simple intake of data (registration or perception), as Hanson and Churchland claimed, but the whole 'observation situation,' including manipulation of the observational set-up and the processes taking place in it, is theory-dependent and therefore theory-laden.

2.3. Isolating the Holistic Strand

Let us look now at Shapere's approach. He does not put his questions in quite the same way as we did, nor does he distinguish the two questions we have asked, at least not explicitly. (My justification for forcing the framework of questions (1) and (2) upon his text is that such a framework makes the choices the philosopher of science faces clearer than does general talk about 'observation.')

Shapere certainly accepts a weak version of theory-ladenness of observation (I shall look at it presently), but it is not clear how much farther he would go in the same direction. Concerning the problem I have distinguished as question (2), his stance seem to be clearly in favour of non-separability of pre-theoretical and theoretical stages. There is only one stage in mature science, and this is the highly theoretical one. The proposed 'pre-theoretical' stage is an artefact created by philosophers obsessed with sceptical doubts.

Concerning our question (1), he does not offer clear-cut answers (as noted, he does not seem to distinguish the questions exactly as we proposed to do it). His ideas on information gathering can be interpreted in at least two different ways. Read in the first way, he only says that in an 'observation situation' taken very broadly, theory plays an important role: providing for the instruments and the set-up in general and providing knowledge needed for the interpretation of registered information. The observation is 'theory-laden' in this broad and innocuous way (meaning simply that it is necessary to employ background theoretical information in doing science). This is, in fact, Shapere's official meaning of 'theory-ladenness,' and he is explicit about his dislike of the term itself: 'The employment of background information in science – indeed the necessity of employing it – has been termed by some philosophers the 'theory-ladenness' of observation. Putting the fact in that way has led to a great deal of perplexity' (1982, 39).

All this is clearly compatible with the separability of information gathering from the more theoretical stage of information processing, which includes interpretation. If this is what Shapere had in mind, and some passages do point this way, we cheerfully agree. We note at this point that Shapere is no supporter of relativism, and that he explicitly criticizes the Feyerabendian tradition. In his more recent paper, when discussing the importance of 'background ideas' that support an experiment, he is quite explicit about a fundamental point: that the data of science have scientific value that is 'independent of – not determined by – those background ideas' (Shapere 1988, 309).

The second way is the holistic way. Read in this manner, Shapere claims that that theory is somehow involved already in the process of registration, and that there is no stage of the whole process that is exempted from the grip of the theory. At least one competent reviewer, James Robert Brown, takes Shapere to be a holist in the above described sense, and, of course, this fits perfectly with Shapere's holistic stance on the question (2) of the separability of the pre-theoretical stage of extraction from the theoretical stage.[7]

My purpose here is not the exegesis of Shapere. I am concerned only with the radical holistic approach itself, and I wish to argue against it. I do not wish to saddle Shapere with such holism. I shall invent a persona, therefore, embodying the radical and bold holistic streak in Shapere's paper, and call him simply the Holist. The Holist takes

Shapere's remarks to contain arguments for a negative, holistic answer to questions (1) and (2).

2.4. *The Debate*

2.4.1. Introduction

We may picture the Holist as claiming the following: 'The new picture of observation makes it much more dependent on theory than the old one. In this new picture, there is no naked eye, to be isolated from the rest – there is only the continuous process of information transmission and gathering, and much of the process is of our making, especially in an advanced science. The set-up is begotten from theory, and the theory dictates what counts as being observed. The habits of scientists follow this dictate – they freely speak about observing neutrinos, or the interior of the sun, without bothering to speak about visual impressions, of dots on their photographs and the like.' In fact, Shapere's paper does provide fuel for such discourse. In order to underscore this fact, then to show how a move from a general information-theoretic framework to the specific radical holistic alternative within it could be effected, and finally to criticize it, I shall stick closely to Shapere's formulations. I shall picture the Holist as taking Shapere's statements as a starting point and interpreting them as yielding arguments for holism.

I was able to distinguish three possible lines of argumentation for holism that might take Shapere's statements as starting points. One line is actually Shapere's and concerns his answer to question (2) – it deals with the vocabulary of science – and I shall present it as the last one. The two other lines deal not with words, but with things themselves. They are not in Shapere's text, but easily can be read *into* it.

2.4.2. The Argument from the Set-up

The Holist might try to use the following remark made by Shapere to concoct an argument in favour of inseparability: 'We have seen, in the case of the solar neutrino experiment, the pervasive role played by what may be called "background information." It should be clear that this observation-situation could never have been set up had that background information, or a very large part of it, not been available' (1982, 39). Taking this idea as a premise, the Holist might conclude that the importance of theory in setting up the observation makes theory somehow present in the observation itself. He would, in fact, take 'dependence on theory' to be transitive: if the observational set-up is dependent on theory for its existence, and if what is observed depends on the set-up, then what is observed depends on theory.

The remark about the importance of background information is sound. There is no legitimate way, however, for the Holist to use it for his purposes, to prove the inseparability of observation from background knowledge, because *the fact that the observational set-up is dependent on theory for its existence does not entail that processes taking place in the set-up themselves are theory laden*. To show this we might start from an analogy: in order to build a dam that regulates the flow of a river, considerable engineering knowledge is needed. This does not make the flow of the river theory-laden or inseparable from the builder's knowledge, or theoretical in any way. The river flow is a natural, causal process, regardless of how the water dam was produced.

The point is perfectly general and applies to any manipulation of natural processes (from cooking to the explosion of an H-bomb); the theory does not enter into the causal process, no matter how much of it one needs to build the set-up regulating the process. Applied to the observational set-up, the point remains valid. In order to observe fingerprints one needs some elementary knowledge of detection techniques. This does not make looking at fingerprints theoretical, nor does it make fingerprints themselves theory-laden. Remember the solar neutrino experiment detailed by Shapere. The neutrinos travel from the sun to the earth, and they are captured in tanks of cleaning fluid. The neutrinos are practically not interfered with, so they carry the unadulterated information directly from the sun's interior. Of course, some rare interactions do occur, and one needs much physical theory to calculate the probabilities of each specific kind of interaction. The presence of a neutrino in the tank is detected by its effects on the fluid: a neutrino would be captured and a radioactive nucleus would be formed. Radioactive nuclei are then detected in the standard way, thanks to their own radiation. As mentioned above, the information-theoretic story asserts that neutrinos carry information directly from the sun, and this information is being detected by counters registering the eventual decay of radioactive nuclei.

A large amount of theory is needed to generate the idea of trapping neutrinos in cleaning fluid tanks, and more theory (and a lot of money) to detect them by their effect. (In Shapere's words: 'But without such ingredients as weak interaction theory, experimental information about reaction rates, the theory of stellar structure, knowledge of the properties of rare gases, the technological capabilities of existing proportional counters, and so forth, the experiment would not only have been impossible to perform; it would have been, in the most literal sense, inconceivable' (1982, 39).) The passage is concerned with history, describing the prerequisites (theoretical or monetary) of observation. *But the process of information transmission and registration is a purely physical process.* No theory intervenes on the long journey of neutrino from the sun to the earth. There is no theory (or money) sitting in the tank waiting for the neutrino. The interaction with cleaning fluid is a perfectly non-theoretical one, and the counter is simply registering the product of the decay of radioactive nuclei.

In general, a causal flow in a set-up is independent of the history of the set-up – two identical set-ups originating in different ways will produce the same kind of causal flow. Given that the builders' knowledge (background information) is part of the history of the set-up, it is irrelevant to the causal flow within it. The mistake of the Holist has been to have overlooked this fact.

2.4.3. The Argument from Determination by Theory

The next argument can be read from Shapere's statement itself, if one slightly forces the idea of 'specification': *'specification of what counts as directly observed (observable), and therefore of what counts as observation, is a function of the current state of physical knowledge, and can change with changes in that knowledge'* (1982, 11; emphasis in text); 'what counts as "observational" in science is "laden" with background information' (ibid., 42). Presumably, the statement applies to the situation in which there is a physical process leading from the source to the receiver, and in which we may then ask what is being observed by the receiver.

The statement about specification can be read in two (incompatible) ways.

1. Current physical knowledge at time *t enables us to know* what is (as a matter of fact) being directly observed.

This is the realist way. The notion of observation employed is perfectly objective, in the sense that the notion of information received in observation is completely objective. In this sense, an aboriginal looking at a Wilson cloud chamber is observing the motion of electrons, because the information about electrons is contained in what he registers. He does not know, however, that he is receiving information about electrons, because he lacks the requisite physical knowledge. The first way is useless to the Holist (and perfectly acceptable to us). He cannot argue from it to the theory-ladenness of observation, because here the theory intervenes *outside* the observation process – it determines not what is being observed, but only what one knows about things one observes.

The Holist will be more interested in the alternative, rather anti-realist way:

2. Current physical knowledge at time *t makes it the case* that something is being observed, and *determines what is being observed.*

According to this proposal, it is the physical theory that makes (or partly makes) the information received by the photographic plate of the Wilson cloud chamber into information about electrons. (Maybe it even makes photographic plates into appropriate receptors.)

The proposal is precisely what the Holist needs. The question is whether he can have it, given his other views about observation.[8] Remember that the Holist is committed to the information-oriented view of observation and to Shapere's definition of observation. In this view, information is something emitted by objects, and observation is detection of interactions. For our Holist, therefore, the observation boils down to the process in which the information transmitted is being registered by an appropriate receiver, mechanical or human.

The question now is: Given that the transmission and registration are natural, causal, lawful processes, how can knowledge determine anything about them? Human knowledge does not give prescriptions to Nature, nor does it dictate to Nature its laws. To see the impotence of knowledge in this regard, consider an observation situation centuries ago: an old-style chemist observes with her naked eye changes in the colour of a flame. The current knowledge tells her that she is watching the process of phlogiston release – 'Lo and behold, the firewood is now releasing more phlogiston than before.' If the knowledge then current dictated what was being observed, and what information was being transmitted, it would dictate the conclusion that our chemist is observing phlogiston release and that the information normally carried by the light from the flame was, centuries ago in the heyday of the phlogiston theory, information about phlogiston release. Obviously, the theory dictates what we count as observation, and, if true, it reveals what is being observed, but it does not make a process into observation, nor does it determine its object.

It seems, then, that the Holist's argument is wrong headed. Any apparent plausibility it might have derives from the confusion between the realist and the anti-realist reading of Shapere's initial statement. Read in the realist way (science tells us what we observe), it is perfectly plausible but useless to the Holist; read in the anti-realist way (science creates what we observe), it is useful to the Holist but extremely problematic.

2.4.4. The Last-Ditch Defence

The Holist can now retreat to something like the following claim: 'By observation I do not mean simply the process of registration (the way from source to the receiver), but the wider process that leads to the formation of scientists' beliefs (i.e., a process issuing in beliefs or statements like "An explosion is going on at such and such a point on the observed heavenly body"). In this process, which extends from the source all the way to the final belief state, the role of the background theory is paramount. It is the background theory that makes the scientist's perceptual state into the state of observing an explosion on the distant heavenly body – it is in this sense that current physical knowledge dictates what is to count as observed.' The Holist is hereby proposing a very wide notion of observation, which encompasses the route source → receiver → beliefs and explicitly introduces into his picture the segment of the process that starts from registration and ends with belief state. Moreover, he locates the impact of background theory precisely at this segment.

This really seems like a desperate move, since the Holist has now almost given up the holistic assumptions. He is offering a picture of the process segmented precisely as proposed by the non-holist in his answer to question (1) concerning the separability of information gathering (through registration) from information extracting (out of the registered material). The 'observation situation' is divided in two, and it is plausible to suppose that the first part, from the source to the receiver is a non-theoretical and non-mental process governed simply by the laws of physics, whereas the second part, from the receiver to the belief, is partly theory driven, consists in interpretation, and depends on the agency of computing or generally cognitive devices, mechanical or human.

At this juncture the reformed holist might question our assumption that the tail part of the process (the part from registration to belief) has an epistemically relevant structure. He might enjoin us to take as a paradigm case a situation in which the incoming data are converted almost automatically into beliefs (or their counterparts in computer memory in the case of processing performed by computer). Suppose that an astronomer is taking in the counter-reading and without reflection saying, 'Oh, here goes another explosion.' The Holist (in his reformed guise) might ask us to take this as a central case and to accept the following interpretation – there is no epistemically significant process going on from the intake of counter-reading to the formation of belief – the intake is at the spot converted into observing the explosion, and the vocabulary the scientist is using testifies to this fact.

We now approach our question (2): the separability of a more receptive and more primitive phase of information processing from the phase in which the advanced theory actively intervenes.

2.4.5. An Argument from Scientific Vocabulary

At this juncture the explicit viewpoint of Shapere coincides completely with that of the Holist. Shapere discusses the set-ups in which a camera (photon receptor) is attached to the relevant piece of experimental equipment (telescope in one case, spectroscope in another, Wilson chamber in yet another). Dots, lines, and streaks appear on the photograph. He argues persuasively that dots and lines do not become relevant to science until they have been shown to be images of something and until they have been shown to constitute information. He enjoins us to look at the series: speck – dot – image – image of a star (or smudge – streak – spectrum – spectrum of a star). He then characterizes his opponent as claiming that 'we take as our starting point the perceptual analogues ... of these dots, streaks or lines, and try to see how we could pass from them, without use of any "background information" whatever, in the rightward direction of the sequence.' He notices, correctly in my opinion, that such a passage is impossible, but he then jumps to a much stronger claim: 'But in fact we do not begin with dots (or specks, or sense-data) and add those further ingredients to make an inference, *we use the vocabulary that is strongest given what we know* in the sense I have detailed. We *begin* by calling the mark an image of the star, and *it is when specific reasons for doubt arises* ... that we *withdraw* our description to the more "neutral" (with respect to the alternatives) level of speaking of it *only as an image* (of something)' (1982b, 47). He mentions that such points will be familiar to readers of criticisms of the sense datum and related theories, and, indeed, the passage is reminiscent of Austin's arguments in *Sense and Sensibilia.*

Notice that Shapere (and the Holist) admit the existence of the 'more "neutral" (with respect to the alternatives) level of speaking.' He claims only that the advanced vocabulary is not obtained by starting from the more neutral one and adding the relevant pieces from background theory. 'We' are supposed to start with advanced vocabulary, and 'retreat' to the 'neutral' one only in special cases. It is not true, however, that scientists retreat to the vocabulary of spots and streaks only when reasons for doubt arise. The retreat is necessary for learning the vocabulary and for explaining why the statements couched in the advanced vocabulary are taken to be true.

The novice learns about observation by being confronted with spots and streaks. 'See, this dot is the image of a star.' 'See, this streak is the image of a condensed vapour cloud.' 'Why did it condense?' 'Well, it was ionized because such and such a particle has passed through it.' This kind of conversation is normal and necessary in the learning process. The novice cannot start with an advanced vocabulary, or she would not recognize dots as images. But this kind of talk incorporates many presuppositions, most important, the following:

- The novice is able to recognize spots and streaks independently of advanced physical theory. This point is banal but is essential for any further progress.
- The occurrence of spots and streaks can be interpreted in terms of their immediate cause. The interpretation is not problematic, and it grounds the seeing of dots as produced by light (or streaks as produced by condensed vapour).
- This immediate cause is lawfully connected with some more remote cause, say, passage of some elementary particle. The novice must learn about this connection in order to interpret the streak as the image of the moving elementary particle.

Thanks only to the truth of these presuppositions, the interpretation gives grounds for believing certain statements about what is being observed, couched in a highly advanced vocabulary, to be true. Thus, behind the ease and routine in the use of an advanced vocabulary, one can discern a structure of reasons and grounds, allowing and justifying the use of the vocabulary. The advanced vocabulary is not justificationally self-sufficient; it demands recognition of spots and streaks, low-level explanations and interpretations for its smooth functioning.

Suppose that any element in the structure breaks down. For example, it turns out that there was no ionization process in the chamber. In this case, watching the photo would not be observing the path of an elementary particle. It is the validity of interpretation, backed by the theory, that makes us confident that we are observing the path of the elementary particle.

Let us now very briefly look at the issue of relevance. Shapere correctly observes that dots and lines do not become relevant to science until they have been shown to be images of something and until they have been shown to constitute information. His very formulation, however, points to a two-stage process, consisting of the perception of dots and lines as the first stage and of 'showing that they are images of something' and that they constitute information as the second stage.

Shapere (and the Holist), however, presents his point in a very misleading fashion, claiming that dots or lines are, as such, irrelevant to science. He might as well have said that pointer readings are 'as such' irrelevant to science. If 'as such' is supposed to mean 'in isolation from theory' and 'irrelevant' means 'useless,' then we may assent, but this is not a very strong claim, and it does not entail that dots or lines, when interpreted with the aid of background theory, cannot play a crucial role in science. A car is 'as such,' meaning without gasoline, irrelevant for the purpose of reaching your destination – this means only that you have to put gasoline in it, not that cars are 'gasoline-laden,' so that gasoline is 'inseparable' from the car, or that you start by buying car-plus-gasoline from the factory, or that knowing anything about cars is irrelevant for driving, and you can forget about cars and worry only about gasoline.

Shapere further confuses two issues: the sufficiency of perceptual input and the separability of perception from advanced theory. He is irritated by the philosopher's question, 'How is it possible to obtain knowledge ... by beginning with perception and without any beliefs ... whatsoever?' But this question is irrelevant for the issue. If it is the case, as Shapere claims, that cognition cannot start from mere perception, this still does not entail that perception is not distinct from 'surrounding' theoretical beliefs. We can have both perception as distinct from theory, and theory and perception working together in producing good science. But this is precisely the traditional picture.

I shall end with a more general criticism of the view that one cannot distinguish relevant justificational structure behind the statements of the physicists. If observation were theory laden in the sense that observations always carried the whole relevant theory with them, the greatest disagreements about observation should take place when two 'paradigms' clash, especially, when a young and revolutionary paradigm is being introduced. In such cases the strongest vocabulary available within the first paradigm is certainly radically different from the strongest vocabulary of the second one, and there is no uncontaminated level at which to describe the results of observation.

The counter-examples are the discovery of black-body radiation, the ultraviolet catastrophe, and the Michelson-Morley experiments accompanying (if not initiating) the most spectacular 'paradigm change' in the history of modern physics. Although the results of relevant observations have been of the utmost importance, overthrowing the whole of classical physics, there was no interesting disagreement about observation itself. In itself this fact should make one suspicious of the holistic thesis.

Important disagreements might arise about relevance: how much does the observation prove? This is precisely what the non-holistic theory predicts. The data are sacrosanct; the only place to drive the wedge is the data-theory link, which is where everybody attempts to drive it. This motivates at least the distinction between more and less observational beliefs, the objects of the former being treated as phenomena by the latter.

To return to the original holistic motivation, the argument from the parlance of the physicists offers no comfort to the Holist and misrepresents the actual structure of scientific debate.

So much for Shapere and the Holist. To return to the Holist alone, we have seen that his last-ditch defence will not work. Even if he accepts the distinction between the natural, interactional process leading to the registration and the cognitive process leading to the fixation of belief, and he tries to save the holistic nature of the latter, he will find no credible support in the practice of science.

3. The Anti-Holistic Alternative

The information-theoretic approach to scientific practice seems promising to many philosophers and scientists, but Shapere presents the elements of this approach with some holistic overtones. I was worried about these overtones: can it be that an information theorist is committed to holism? In reply to this worry, I have sought to isolate the holistic strand and discuss it in its stark form (the Straw Holist). The upshot of the discussion has allayed the worries: *the information-theoretic approach does not offer any good ground for holism about observation.*

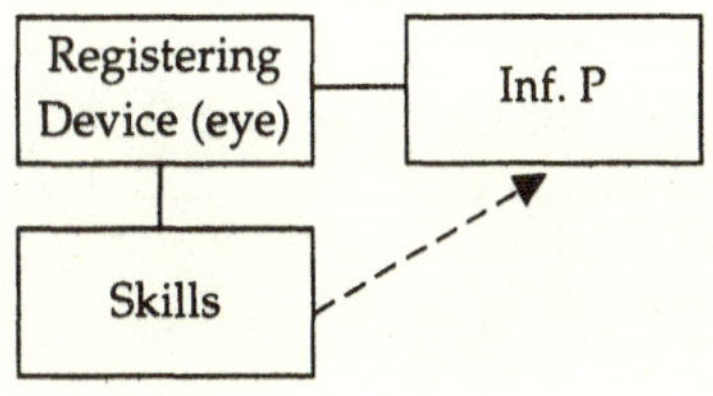

FIGURE A.1
Perception of the movement of light points

The result entails the possibility and even the plausibility of an alternative – a non-holistic information-theoretic approach to observation. As of now, its plausibility is established only negatively, by pointing out the mistakes (or even absurdities) of the Holist.

Let me now briefly sketch a positive alternative, without trying to defend it. The positive alternative gives affirmative answers to the two initial questions. First, the process of information transmission and registration is separable from the process of extracting information by human or computer. Second, the process itself of extracting information can be divided into stages – on the more primitive stages no advanced theory intervenes (this is the 'perceptual,' strictly observational phase), whereas on more advanced stages theory intervenes and plays a crucial role in extracting information. I hope that Shapere would agree with much of the positive alternative.

To revert to the classical astronomical example: since the action of gravitational forces causes the movement of the planets, the movement carries the information (Inf. F) about forces. The real movement viewed from the earth looks like a revolution about the earth, our apparent movement of the planets, so the apparent movement carries information (Inf. M) about the real movement. In order to extract this information (Inf. M) one needs the heliocentric theory. Finally, to the naked eye, the apparent movement looks like movement of light points on a dark vault; so the perception of movement of light points (Inf. P) carries information (Inf. A) about the apparent movement of the planets. In order to have the perception of movement of light points (Inf. P), one needs no theory; innate spatial skills are sufficient. Thus, this perception would be a good candidate for a purely non-theoretical, narrowly observational item. See figure A.1.

For each further step some theory is needed. Some folk astronomy

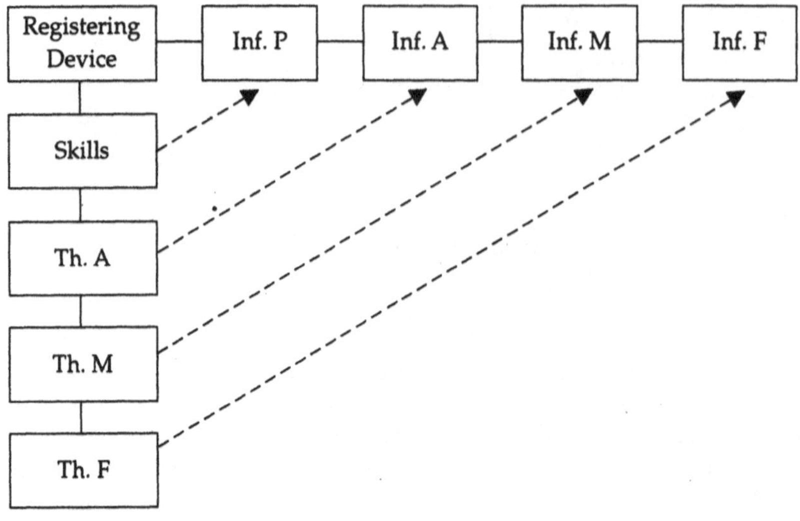

FIGURE A.2
Perception of the movement of light points with theory

('Look, these spots are distant big objects') is needed to pass from light spots to the apparent movement of planets (extracting Inf. A). Call this theory, Th. A.

As remarked, heliocentric theory (Th. M) is needed to extract Inf. M about the real movement of planets. The Newtonian law of universal gravitation (Th. F) is needed to pass to Inf. F concerning forces. Newtonian astronomers, interested in gravitational effects, will use the vocabulary formed by the theory of gravitation (Th. F) when interpreting data that carry Inf. F concerning forces. Their interpretation will rest, among other things, upon the heliocentric presupposition (Th. M) and upon direct evidence (Inf. P and Inf. A). See figure A.2.

The picture can easily be applied to the solar neutrino example as well. The state of the counter carries information about the events in the tank, the events in the tank carry information about neutrinos, and neutrinos carry information about events in the sun. For each advanced stage the physicist needs a corresponding theory.

The structure of the picture is simple. The horizontal line stands for the process of information transmission, which is a natural, causal process. It carries no theory and no interpretation. The process marked by a vertical column of skills plus theories (Th. A to Th. F) is cognitive – perceptual, computational, representational. It consists of a preliminary, narrowly observational phase issuing in simple perception, and of advanced, theoretical stages in which the registered data are interpreted, and, when the interpretation is successful, the information is being extracted from the registered data.

The vertical, cognitive process can also take place in the computer. One can distinguish simple registration of data from their processing – the first corresponding to a strictly observational phase and the second to the intervention of a theory.

The positive anti-holistic picture perfectly fits into the informational framework and makes sense of the customary procedure, namely, to apply increasingly advanced theories – in a stepwise procedure – to the deciphering of observational data.

Notes

Chapter 1. Philosophy and Cognitive Science

1 For a general overview of the domain see (Bogdan 1993). It is still a matter of controversy whether folk-psychology is a theory, a protopsychology (as claimed, for instance, by Paul Churchland and Partricia Smith Churchland), or simply practical wisdom (as claimed by, e.g., K. Wilkes), that is, whether it is more like a cookbook or more like a theoretical treatise. The other current controversy concerns the status of introspection in the formation of people's knowledge of themselves (see Gopnik 1993; Goldman 1993).
2 For an overview see Lycan (1986, chap. 4).
3 See Marr (1982). We roughly follow the apt summary in Vaina (1990).
4 For a very interesting challenge see Devitt and Sterelny (1989).
5 For a good brief introduction see Smith (1990).
6 For example, Barsalou (1987) has shown that prototypes might not exist as stored items, or at least not stored in a fixed manner, but are constructed ad hoc when the need arises. Subjects use different criteria of typicality depending on the context, for example, similarity to a central tendency in a more detached and theoretical context, and appropriateness to the goal in a more practical goal-derived context (Barsalou 1987, 106). Worse, mere linguistic context can change the perception of relevance: 'For example, when *animals* is processed in the context of milking, *cow* and *goat* are more typical than *horse* and *mule*. But when *animals* is processed in the context of riding, *horse* and *mule* are more typical than *cow* and *goat*' (Barsalou, reporting the work of Roth and Shoben 1987, 106).
7 The prototype view has now a strong competitor: the view that concepts are theory dependent. Susan Carey (1985) and Frank Keil (1987) have shown that already at an early age, children ascribe properties to animals on the bases of

their (primitive) proto-theories, not primarily on the bases of perceptual similarity. Discussions between advocates of the two views continue.

8 For example, you watch a car hanging over a cliff in a very unstable position; you then mobilize your rule concerning unsupported objects, and, in the absence of any information to the contrary, you conclude that it will fall. (Movies often play at defeating such conclusions in unexpected ways – something happens and James Bond's car simply flies off.)

9 Thanks to the anonymous referee whose remarks have tempered my optimism about the solution.

10 A good way to do it is in terms of consistency. Suppose that John knows that the object in front of him is unsupported. Nothing in the appearance suggests that the object cannot fall. Thus, it is consistent to assume that it will fall. This is precisely the content of the default rule, which can be written in the following way, taking CONS to mean 'it is consistent that':

$$\frac{\text{UNSUPPORTED }(x) : \text{CONS FALL }(x).}{\text{FALL }(x)}$$

The conditions stated above the line are called 'prerequisites' of the default, and the conclusion below the line is called its 'consequent.' In the Jane example the prerequisite is twofold: the event that is a party is a party-with-Jane, and it is consistent to assume that the party event will be fun. The new information concerning the arrival of Jane's boyfriend makes it inconsistent to suppose that the party will be fun. Therefore, the step to the consequent is blocked.

11 I shall follow the version discussed by Stich (1990, chap. 1). The pioneering paper is Wason (1968).

12 See Cosmides (1989).

13 For an excellent discussion concerning the discovery of continental drift see Solomon (1992).

14 See Fodor and Pylyshyn (1988).

15 Rummelhard and McClelland (1986, 34).

16 The introductory literature on learning is easy to find. When learning about connectionism, I have found very useful the beginners guide by Orchard and Philips (1991). More knowledgeable readers can find interesting general discussion in Hanson and Burr (1990).

17 Ramsey has been an ally and a close collaborator of Stich, so that his classification is supposedly not biased against relativistic views. (Let me mention here that I am indebted to him for the conversations on relativism we had at Lake Bled in Slovenia in summer 1993.)

Chapter 2. Epistemology: The Classical Picture

1 For Plato, see White (1976); for Descartes, Williams (1978).

2 For a general introduction to the area consult the excellent book by Kirkham (1992).

3 The term 'verisimilitude' has acquired a technical, precise meaning in the hands of K. Popper. It is used by him and by I. Niiniluoto in conjunction with the classical correspondence theory of truth for theories (see an account and bibliography in Newton-Smith 1981, 52ff). Some recent authors have attempted to sever its link with the truth of theories, still retaining links with the truth of empirical observations (see Zamora Bonilla 1992).

4 The proponents of 'apparent truth' as the epistemic goal (see Foley 1987) claim that it is enough for achieving epistemic merit that the enquirer has looked for and accepted the apparent truth – her best estimate of what is true. The issue is very complicated, but fortunately the matters we discuss are so general that we may rest content with asking the proponent of apparent truth that he would advise the enquirer. Of course, he cannot give the advice, 'Forgo the truth and seek apparent truth!' because the only way for the enquirer to seek apparent truth is to seek what he himself takes to be the truth. The advice should therefore be: 'Seek the truth!' This places the proponent of apparent truth in the camp of truth-advocates for all purposes relevant to our debate.

5 Of course, this brief mention fails to do justice to the subtleties of the issue. For fuller treatment and bibliography see Kirkham (1992, chap. 3) and Haack (1976).

6 For an excellent defence and analysis of the 'ought implies can' principle in epistemic matters see Taylor (1990).

7 A good overview of the state of the problem is Kitcher (1992). The single most important opus that has arisen as a neoclassicist response to the problem is that of Alvin Goldman. For a very readable and enjoyable introduction see his (1993); the more advanced works are (1986) and (1992).

Chapter 3. Relativism-Pragmatism

1 Since this passage was written, Churchland has published a new book, *The Engine of Reason, The Seat of the Soul: A Philosophical Journey into the Brain* (Cambridge, Mass.: MIT Press, 1995).

2 In the appendix, I discuss the somewhat tangential issue of independent tests of the truth of our theoretical beliefs, given that this issue also appears persistently in the relativistic literature.

3 I also don't know whether people are generally able to follow such advice, if this is indeed relativist-pragmatist's advice. Take an example: Jack is supposed to form a belief that uranium is violet for a practical reason, because this will help him seduce Jane, whom he desires ardently. He is also supposed not to care whether 'Uranium is violet' is true, and especially not to enquire whether it is true, but to form belief on romantic and erotic grounds. The advice is neither simple nor self-evident. (In the polemical part I shall have more to say about this issue. Simple but awkward questions arise, a propos the example, with deliberate choice of beliefs. How many people can do it? Could you come really to believe that a metal is of such-and-such colour without having the slightest indication that this is really so, only on the strength of the practical consequences of holding such a belief? Could you train yourself in this direction? How do you start the training? For a criticism of pragmatism along these lines see Heal (1990), and for a discussion of believing at will see Scott-Kakures (1994).

Chapter 4. The Idea of Truth-Intolerance

1 Remember the shorthand introduced in chapter 2 on the Classical Picture. If the representational medium is such that the state couched in it can be true or be false, then the medium is *truth-tolerant*, and, if not, it is *truth-intolerant* (where 'truth' is taken as representing truth-or-falsity). Those who prefer second-level talk about a state's being capable of assessment in terms of truth, or along the truth dimension; are invited to translate my shorthand into their preferred talk: a state is truth-tolerant if it can be assessed along the truth dimension; if not, it is truth-intolerant.

2 A reader sympathetic to Professor Churchland's work might accuse me of exaggerating isolated claims that he makes and turning his theory into a caricature (I am using the title 'Professor' to indicate that we discuss now the views of a person, not simply the dead letter in his book). I have two kinds of apology to make, and then I shall offer an extended argument for my approach. First, I think that a great deal of the appeal of Professor Churchland's work resides in his revolutionary claims. He writes as if he wanted to show that the results of neuroscience demand a complete upheaval of epistemology. Now, if this is merely exaggeration and rhetoric, his claims would be philosophically much less interesting. Second, even if one day Professor Churchland came to renounce his revolutionary stance, or even if it turned out that he never was, in his heart, a revolutionary, the stance would remain interesting in itself. The revolutionary stance deserves to be reconstructed in its pure form and discussed or criticized as such. (If you don't think these views are really those of Professor Churchland, bear with me and consider

them in themselves, no matter who actually holds them). Personally, I do not think that presenting the stance in the pure form amounts to any injustice towards Professor Churchland.

3 David Armstrong (1973, chaps 1 and 2), David Lewis (1983), Brian Loar (1982), Fred Dretske (1981), Donald Davidson (1980), and a host of their followers.

4 If we were allowed at this point to introduce the value of truth in the discussion, we would offer the following reason for this particular predilection for states generating true theories-in-the-book. In theory building we are interested in representations that represent the way the world is. But any such representation will either succeed in doing so, or fail, and then it will be either true or false. This creates a strong presumption in favour of the usual view, namely, that theories do have truth-value. The revisionist could of course claim that his idea of representation is a non-standard one, that representation in his sense does not really represent, but this claim then shifts the burden of argument upon him.

Chapter 5. The Non-Sentential Media

1 I have heard the reply from Dan Sperber (at my talk at CREA, Paris, in December 1994).

2 Let me briefly consider an objection, which has been raised in discussion by M. Engel.

Objection: Maybe truth is not so important for maps as it is for sentences. A very distorted map can still be useful, and a very distorted but simple and readable map can be more useful than a correct but complicated, too detailed, and illegible map.

Reply: Sometimes false information is useful, because of some fortuitous coincidence or happenstance. In these cases false sentences and distorted maps are equally useful.

Most often, however, a distorted map is the one that distorts certain relations and keeps others straight. Suppose you travel from A to C, and you have to pass through B in order to reach C. The amount of time you need is not of great concern to you. Then, a map that correctly represents the order A–B–C is just right for you; even if it happens to misrepresent distances it will be all right. Moreover, if you travel by some main highway, you do not need to know the exact direction – as long as you keep going roughly towards north you will reach C. But in all these cases, the map is useful because it correctly represents what is essential – it is true where it matters (for further discussion of the analogies between maps and theories look at the fascinating lecture by Bas Van Fraassen (to be found in the Proceedings of the Philosophy of Science Association, 1993).

Finally, for the last clause of the objection: there is no relevant difference between maps and theories in respect of a trade-off between accuracy and simplicity; a simple but somewhat rough presentation of, say, the Theory of Relativity will be much more useful for a general reader than a very accurate, super-sophisticated, and completely hermetic presentation.

3 Many pictures are, in these respects, similar to maps. The sitter's family and critics complaining about lack of portrait likeness treat the portrait as a false representation of the sitter. Critics often notice such lack of similarity. For example, Gombrich (1982) notes that the portrait of Masaryk by Kokoschka misrepresents Masaryk's face by widening the distance between his nose and his chin) implying of course that there is a matter of fact about relative distances, which is misrepresented by the painter. (Some misrepresentations are admired for aesthetic reasons; some are not). Similarly, in the case of photographs: when the policeman at the border complains that the passenger's face is clean shaven in the passport photo, and that the passenger has meanwhile grown a beard and moustache, he can rightly claim that the actual photograph misrepresents the passenger as much as a false description would.

4 Churchland gives an example of maps in so-called Brodman's areas: 'These areas or subareas of these areas are of further interest because several of them plainly constitute topographic maps of some aspect of the sensory or motor periphery, or of some other area of the brain. For example, the neighbourhood relations holding between the cells in a given layer in the visual cortex at the rear of the brain correspond to the neighbourhood relations holding between the cells in the retina from which they receive inputs' (*NP*, 81).

5 It has been shown that maps reorganize themselves even in adults; after a nerve section or amputation of a digit, the relevant area does not react to stimulation, but within the following months the representations of the adjacent digital areas expand and approach each other.

6 For example, the tactile field of a mouse's vibrissae 'maps into the same subtectal region as do the forepaws and ears' (Schoene 1984, 256), subtectum being the neural substrate onto which the spatial values from the various modalities are projected.

7 Gallistel (1990) offers much more sophisticated examples of cognitive maps, but since he is more a classical computationalist, we are not going to use his examples against Churchland – we want to meet Churchland on his own connectionist ground.

8 Thanks to a referee of the University of Toronto Press for making me aware of the necessity of making these remarks.

9 'The position is not essential for representation,' our opponent might insist. False. The relevant operations on position coordinates are those in the vector space, which are defined on components of vectors, that is, essentially over structure.

10 For example, the position of *P* carries the message that John is 4 feet high, and this message either is true or is false. For the coordinate system of decent dimensionality (i.e., of countably many dimensions), the information in the position of the point is only equivalent to the list of sentences, one for the projection of the point on each axis. All the systems we shall encounter will be of this kind

11 It can be a spatial parameter: for instance, it can code for the direction or distance of a distal goal. If it represents, say, a flower, as being reachable in so many steps, then this representation is true if the flower is so many steps away from the animal, and false if it is not. The more subtle the state-space representation, the more ways there are in which it can turn out to be true or to be false. A possibly true proposition is coded at every coordinate axis. (State-space representations are routinely used for calculation in physics. No one supposes that therefore the relevant portions of physics are incapable of being true or false.)

12 Up to this point I have simply assumed that unconscious, subpersonal beliefs or belief-like states and the representational structures that support them can be assessed for their truth-value, and I have argued that one can extend the assessment from propositional representational structures to non-propositional ones. It is time to discharge the assumption. Why would any one think a structured representation figuring in the brain of a living creature indicating some mundane state of affairs to which it appropriately corresponds should not be regarded as capable of being true or false? One reason, in fact the only one I was able to find in the literature, is as follows: 'The moral is that it is not enough to explain the possibility of false indication that we impute correspondence relations on the basis of natural facts, however salient those facts may be. The correspondence relations must be associated somehow with the practice of assertion or claim making, a false proposition being the content of a false assertion' (Forbes 1989, 544). The argument is invalid. First, it begs the question against the naturalist. If it is stipulated that there is no truth without assertion, then of course the creatures devoid of capacity to produce speech acts cannot have any kind of states that represent or misrepresent the world. This stipulation is implausible for frogs and unbelievable for chimps. But since the anti-naturalist would hardly be

moved by such examples, it is better to argue on the basis of imaginary situations.

By the report of our space crew, Solitarians appear to be extremely intelligent creatures. They rarely communicate with each other, and when they do, it is by simple commands, never by assertions. A Solitarian lives quite isolated and passes its time in constructing ingenious machines, compared with which our most sophisticated devices are children's toys. It seems that they have an innate mathematical ability quite beyond ours and a gift for engineering. They are good at games. After watching our boys play chess for ten minutes, a Solitarian has mastered chess and is now able to beat any terrestrial chess champion.

Our opponent should admit that Solitarians do not have beliefs, that their thoughts are never true or false, because there is no practice of assertion or claim-making among them. 'But maybe the whole story is incoherent?' This remains to be shown. 'Well, if the Solitarians could be brought to make assertions, they would claim many things.' But so would chimps. If by 'associating' you mean ascribing in a fanciful way, I can associate frogs' behaviour with what I would say if I liked to eat flies. If you stick to the condition that the creature must actually be able to make assertions, then you have to deny to Solitarians any ability to represent/misrepresent their surroundings.

It is better, then, to accept that assertion is only one among many, although the most convenient, means to convey belief content. It is no transcendental condition. The missing element that perhaps should be added to correspondence to obtain a belief-like state is that the representation has to play an appropriate functional role in simple cases, the role in guiding behaviour.

13 It is a pity that Churchland doesn't state in what sense the configurations are supposed to be incommensurable. He says only that incommensurable configurations are incompatible. Are any two incompatible configurations incommensurable? That would trivialize the notion, reducing it to mere difference. A configuration representing the letter 'A' by that criterion would be incommensurable with the one representing 'B,' or 'C.' What has to be added to mere difference in order to obtain incommensurability? Not having dimensions in common cannot be the missing element. The configurations in the activation space that do not have dimensions in common are not incompatible; therefore, by the criterion, they are not incommensurable. Churchland claims that neurocomputationalism gives new life to the Feyerabendian program. It is difficult to judge the claim if such a crucial notion as incommensurability is not clearly translated into the neurocomputational vocabulary.

14 The debate starts with Fodor and Pylyshyn (1988) and continues in a long series of papers. Let me mention Clark (1991, 1993), Rey (1991), Smolensky (1991), Van Gelder (1991), Garson (1994), Hadley (1994), McLaughlin (1993a, 1993b), De Vries (1993).

15 See Clark (1991). Horgan and Tienson have presented their views in their work (1989, 1991, 1992a,b, 1993, 1994).

16 Churchland's cryptic remarks shift the burden to the critic who has to reconstruct alternative readings of his proposal. Let us therefore take a close look at his statement of why an activation can be wrong: 'It may be wrong because the situation confronted is not a member of the class of situations that will reliably activate *A* from almost any perspective, even though it happened to activate *A* on this occasion' (*NP*, 220). Call the class of situations that reliably activate *A* from almost any perspective 'class of reliable *A* activators,' in short, RAA. Call the target situation *S* and the network *N*. The alternatives are as follows.

1. *The Intended Alternative*: *S* is a member of a non-trivial RAA, and *N* activates *A*. (e.g., in *S* there is a typical, clearly visible barn, and *N* activates barn-prototype). Happy ending. The activation of *A* is not wrong and is presumably correct.

2. *The Idiot*: *N* outputs the same prototype *A* in response to any input vector. Thus, every situation is an RAA. *N* is, by Churchland's criterion, never wrong, since it outputs *A* only for members of RAA.

Churchland might respond that *N* is not a well-trained network. This response, however, places an unexpected burden on the notion of 'well-trained network,' and it is hard to see how the notion could carry such a burden if 'not giving wrong answers' is not built into the notion itself. But if 'not giving wrong answers' is built into the notion of being well trained, then of course the notion of well-trained network cannot serve to explicate the notion of wrong answer. (The same result occurs if one takes a roundabout way and defines the content of the prototype by what normally causally prompts its activation. This brings into play the host of semantic notions with which Churchland does not want any traffic.)

3. *The Privileged Point of View*: *S* is not a member of RAA, *S* is an *A*-situation, and *N* activates *A* on the grounds of information acquired from a singular vantage point; for example, a soldier recognizes the rifle of the enemy (*S*) skilfully camouflaged in the bushes by the momentary glitter, visible from one vantage point, only in a split second. The situation *S* would not activate the 'enemy'-prototype (=*A*) from any other perspective, so *S* is not member of RAA; it is an enemy-situation, therefore an *A*-situation, and the soldier was lucky to have a vantage point on the situation. Was the activation of

'enemy'-prototype wrong? Certainly not. It was a paragon of epistemic virtue of the soldier. By Churchland's criterion, however, the situation's not being in RAA, the soldier's response was simply wrong.

4. *The Lucky Guess*: *S* is not in RAA; *S* is an *A*-situation, and *N* by happenstance activates *A*. (The enemy is well hidden in the bushes, but there is no glitter of the rifle. Our soldier simply looks in the direction of the bushes and out of the blue thinks, 'There is the enemy.')

Churchland's criterion says that the activation was wrong. Thus, he does not have the means to distinguish wrong-false (which the activation is not, since the thought is true) from wrong-unjustified (which it is), and that his notion is closer to wrong-unjustified.

5. *The Understandable Mistake*: No living soul can distinguish the replicant (*S*) from a human being (*A*). The replicant situation *S* is in RAA, and *N* activates *A*.

By our lights *N*'s diagnosis is false (no replicant is a human being) but understandable and justified. By Churchland's lights it is not wrong. He has no means of judging its falsity, and no wish to do so.

6. *The Common Inaccuracy*: Remember that the network that has learned the 'dog,' 'cat,' and 'bird' prototype, has been presented with Alfred the wolf (*S*), and has activated the dog-prototype (*A*). *S* is in RAA (since the network would classify Alfred as a dog from any relevant perspective).

By our lights the answer is wrong-false, and it is unclear whether it is wrong-unjustified (it depends on the stringency of one's criteria of justification). By Churchland's criterion it is not wrong. Churchland's criterion would be tolerable as a rule-of-thumb concerning justification, although it is a bit primitive and not at all revolutionary, were it not for the Vantage Point cases. As matters are, it yields confused and counter-intuitive judgments. Given that right and wrong should be categories of some importance, this is indeed crippling. Whatever Churchland's intentions, it seems from the characterization of his notion of 'wrong' that the means he has shown that he has at his disposal are very far from being sufficient to ground a serious epistemology.

17 I have heard this view in discussion from my colleague and friend Vanda Bozicevic, and the idea seems natural, since Churchland is, in other contexts, an eliminativist.

18 Could an instrumentalist, a non-Churchlandian relativist, avail herself of the opportunity, and accept this line of defence? Hardly. *Qua* epistemologist she must account for the vicissitudes of theory building, no matter what opinion she has about the ontological commitments of given theories. She cannot do so by using a grey-box model that ignores theories altogether.

19 Of course, one can say that the network has skill in finding out about flight, but this then trivializes the issue, since knowledge-how in this sense is not opposed to knowledge-that.

20 Compare Hume on miracles: either an event qualifies for being a miracle by being extremely improbable – but then we should not believe that it took place – or it is believable given our background knowledge – but then it is no miracle.

21 Compare the argument by Horgan and Tienson (1992b). The relevant recent literature encompasses Pollack (1990), Van Gelder (1990, 1991), Smolensky (1990), Hadley (1994), and Niklasson and Van Gelder (1994).

22 Besides the general idea that connectionist systems do not support truth/falsity, Churchland has a specific argument for the irrelevance and unattainability of truth, the one we quoted in subsection 2.1 of this chapter. Remember: 'For one thing nothing guarantees that we humans will avoid getting permanently stuck in some very deep but relatively local error minimum. For another, nothing guarantees that there exists a possible configuration of weights that would reduce the error messages to *zero* ... And for a third thing, nothing guarantees that there is only *one* global minimum. Perhaps there will in general be many quite different minima, all of them equally low in error, all of them carving up the world in quite different ways ... These considerations seem to remove the goal itself – a unique truth – as well as any sure means of getting there. Which suggests that the proper course to pursue in epistemology lies in the direction of a highly naturalistic and pluralistic form of pragmatism' (*NP*, 194; emphasis in text). The argument is repeated in Churchland's recent paper on Feyerabend (1993). The danger to which the argument points is familiar – like a shortsighted hill climber descending from a mountain, who is merely following the line of the steepest descent, the system can end in a hole (local minimum) instead of reaching the foot of the mountain (the global minimum). This danger is not particular or fatal to the connectionist learning – other systems that learn have analogous problems, and connectionist systems have ways to cope with the problem, for example, initiating periodic reshuffling, which can propel the system away from the local minimum.

Please note that the general thrust of the argument is incoherent with the supposition that representations in the network do not admit of truth/falsity. In the second point, the one about reduction of error message, the 'error message' is interpreted as a sign of untruth or falsity. But if network-states are hospitable to falsity, they should be hospitable to truth. In general, the move from 'It is difficult to attain the whole truth' to 'One should not aim for true theories' is unjustified and somewhat irresponsible. (Compare the move from 'It is impossible to attain perfect harmony in family life' to 'Do not try to live with the members of your family as harmoniously as possible.')

Let us nevertheless consider the remarks, in isolation from the rest of Churchland's views. To the dismay of their maker, the three remarks can be translated into more conventional language:

1. Nothing guarantees that humankind will avoid getting permanently stuck with a super-theory that is locally satisfying – gives excellent predictions and retrodictions, is simple and elegant, and so on, but is such only in relation to particular kinds of situations and parameters. Our best theory might be parochial and false.
2. Nothing guarantees that there is a perfect and infallible global theory.
3. Nothing guarantees the uniqueness of ideal global theory. Theories are underdetermined by data and by normative requirements, so that there might be more than one optimal theory, each complete and virtuous in its own way, and each carving the world in its own way.

I cannot see that the 'connectionist' formulation adds much to the traditional formulation of the traditional worries. Let us look at the worries themselves. The first worry does not tell against realism and the value of truth, just makes one less optimistic about attaining the whole truth. The second worry is quite difficult to assess. In its connectionist formulation it is liable to be taken in a technological sense: given actual networks there is no error-free configuration. In this sense its content is probably true, but there is no reason to be worried: we knew all along that we are not infallible, nor shall we become such. If we take it in a principled sense, appealing to God's-eye view, it needs much more arguing than is offered by Churchland. Why is it, in principle, impossible that a network (infinite if needed) should yield error-free messages?

The third worry is the most serious one. It has been debated since Duhem and Quine, and I cannot here enter the principled debate. However, I claim that Churchland is in no position to present the worry the way he does, for several reasons. First, the worry does not entail that there is no final truth of the matter about the world. The worry does entail that there might be several equally justified theories (the deepest minima within our reach). Thus, if the worry is real, that might entail that the final truth might not be within our reach: we might end up with a theory that is thoroughly justified, but is still false. This is generally admitted by realists (and sometimes even taken to define realism). The worry, however, leaves open the more optimistic possibility that various optimally justified theories (all the deepest minima) are compatible. Second, the connectionist variant adds nothing new to the classical debate, only a nice spatial state-space picture of the problem; so a fortiori it does not add any new support to the relativist view. Also, it is completely misleading to present the emergence of the problem as somehow dictated by the recent discoveries of neuroscience, or to imply that neuroscience has generated it. Remember our general aim in the book: to find out whether the new results of cognitive research give some new grounds for relativism-pragmatism.

23 The notion has been proposed in Karmiloff-Smith (1992).

24 For dissenting views see other papers in the 1993 volume of *Mind and Language*.

25 Let me note the affinities with recent structuralist views as expressed, above all, by Michael Resnik, who sees 'mathematics as a science of patterns' (1981).

26 The general idea behind the answer seems to be explanation-as-unification: something is explained by being brought in line with a more general pattern common to many special cases.

27 If an etiological prototype is anything like an account of an event in terms of its etiology, it can certainly go wrong, assigning wrong typical antecedents to the event. Some such prototypes do not, and these are (roughly) true.

28 Let us check this in order. (a) Graded membership: To return to the cyanide example, suppose that the link cyanide-edibility is only 75 per cent strong (whatever way the prototype theorist takes the strength). This is more than enough to condemn the representation as being dangerously wrong. The moral is that probabilistic (or fuzzy-membership) considerations only hedge the main point, but neither obstruct nor evade it. The probabilistically weighted prototype can misrepresent the world as much as a non-probabilistic one would. (b) Default structure: Default 'knowledge' can be as correct or incorrect as any other (e.g., 'Cyanide-laced food is edible, if it is not rotten'). Nothing in the mechanics of default reasoning undercuts the truth-dimension. (c) Non-sentential representation: If one can non-sententially represent the information that cyanide is edible, this representation will be as false as the corresponding sentence. In general, the nature of representational medium is immaterial, as long as the information carried is the same. Mentally-neurally represented theories carry the same information that is carried by sententially represented ones (otherwise the former would not generate the later). Therefore, if the theory-in-the-book carries true information, the mentally-neurally represented one should carry it too. (d) Holistic character: Holism does not preclude truth, as already argued in the previous chapter. The same holds for issues addressed by the Stability Argument of the previous chapter. The hypothesized ad hoc character of prototypes (Barsalou) may be of interest for the dynamics of non-stable 'knowledge,' but

it can hardly be relevant for its truth. (Whether you believe something on only one occasion, or for your whole life, is irrelevant for its truth or falsity.)

29 For example, the prototype for 'metal' will not be the everyday prototype of solid mass of metallic colour resembling lead or gold, but a prototype of specific type of molecular structure (and distribution of electrons in outer shell) and the like. The prototype associated with lasers will have nothing to do with SF-movies (as many everyday prototypes of laser have) but will concern inversions in population of atoms – more atoms in an upper state than in a lower.

30 One further illustration of the point with the help of an example given by Churchland himself, who claims that the connectionist framework is particularly suitable for accounting for conceptual change, or, as he prefers to call it 'conceptual redeployment.' One of his parade examples of 'conceptual redeployment' is the unification of optics and electrodynamics. We follow his exposition. Maxwell's formulas summarizing the relations between electric and magnetic fields entailed the existence of a wave-like electromagnetic disturbance, spreading out from any oscillating charge. The velocity of disturbance is dictated by electrical and magnetic properties of the medium. Now, a calculation with given values for the atmosphere yields as a result the number that corresponds to the known velocity of light: 'This extraordinary coincidence invited an attempt to see further optical phenomena as facets of oscillatory electromagnetic phenomena' (*NP*, 238). It turns out that the electric and magnetic properties of transparent substances dictate their refractive indexes. It is easy to see from the example how complex is the (presumed) detection of similarity between two theoretical prototypes. The electromagnetic and the optical prototype were not, at first glance, structurally similar. What prompted their identification was that they yielded the same numerical values for some calculations. The abstractness and precision of calculations played the crucial role in the recognition of 'similarity.' In order to support the recognition the prototypes have to be abstract and precise, to contain equivalents of Maxwell's laws, and to enable calculations with them (which means considerable field theory, differential equations, and the like).

One might wish to add to the list of examples quantum mechanics. Its predictive power is due to its enormously complicated mathematical apparatus. Nothing simpler will yield accurate predictions in the domain. If, in the heads of scientists, quantum mechanics is represented by quantum prototypes, then the prototypes must have the requisite mathematical complexity. Such prototypes seem very close indeed to theories-in-the book.

31 Let me briefly mention one last possibility (pointed out to me by my col-

league N. Smokrovic). The relativist-pragmatist might take prototypes to be truth-tolerant when couched in some (e.g., sentential) media, and truth-intolerant when couched in the connectionist medium. This is, however, an extremely implausible view. First, we have seen that connectionist networks are not truth-intolerant in themselves, and there is no reason why a truth-tolerant representation type, implemented in a truth-tolerant medium, would yield a truth-intolerant result. Second, if the view is taken to mean that the same prototype changes its receptivity to truth/falsity by changing its medium, it is almost self-refuting. The sameness of a prototype across media can consist only in the sameness of its semantic content, and the sameness of content entails the sameness of receptivity to truth-falsity by any notion of semantic content. If it is taken to mean that some prototypes, that is, 'sentential' ones, are truth-tolerant, but some, precisely those that are couched in connectionist medium, are not, then the 'sentential' prototypes are essentially different from connectionist ones, and the pragmatist is left with the enigma: How can the truth-intolerant connectionist prototype of a theory account for the essentially different 'sentential' one, corresponding to the same theory written down in a book?

32 See, for example, Tractatus 2.17., 2.221, 2.222, 4.01. 4.014, 4.016., and for a recent discussion Carruthers (1989, chap. 15).

33 For an introduction to the issues see, for instance, Pollock (1986).

34 Compare chap. 2, n3.

35 There might be a small wrinkle in the story (and a grain of truth in Churchland's picture of the situation): if human minds are complete connectionist systems and nothing else, then the process of understanding and discovery might be less logical than expected, at least in the narrow sense of logic. This, however, need not upset even the most traditionalist epistemologist – the process of discovery, the actual hitting upon the right idea, was always considered to be somewhat messy. What counts for the traditional epistemologist is the ability of the Sophisticated Enquirer to put her reasons in a decent form, to effect a rational reconstruction and offer a good logical justification for her discovery. This the connectionist Sophisticated Enquirer can, by supposition, do.

36 For example, A. Clark claims that the 'flash of insight' is best understood in terms of connectionist processing:

> 'We might point to Stephenson's (allegedly) watching his kettle boil and conceiving the idea of the steam locomotive, or someone's studying the behaviour of thermodynamic systems and conceiving the ideas behind PDP. These aspects of scientific discovery have two prime characteristics, which should by now attract our attention.

> The flash of insight is typically fast. The idea just comes to us, and we have no conscious experience of working for it.
> The flash of insight involves using rather abstract perceived patterns in one domain of our experience to suggest ways of structuring our ideas about some other apparently far removed domain.
> In the light of these characteristics it is not absurd to suggest that some PDP mechanism is operating in such cases.' (1989, 140)

The proposal is in keeping with the story about similarity of prototypes told by Churchland and briefly summarized in the preceding chapters.

37 The proponent of the muddy Venn diagrams offers an expert opinion: 'This model is easier to grasp than any axioms or rules, and does as well. (There are in fact deep theorems to show that we have here in essence the most general model of probabilities, provided the mud can be fine enough).' (Van Fraassen 1989, 161).

38 If you care about art, compare the dilemmas of the epistemologist faced with newly discovered cognitive techniques with the dilemmas of the art critic faced with newly invented artistic techniques: One day spray-can painting comes to supplant brush painting. The enthusiasts (the Churchlands of art criticism) proclaim the death of art criticism as we know it: 'The traditional art critic has been a judge of the brush stroke. The new and revolutionary technique has brought a completely new notion of artistic achievement into play ... and so on.' The art critics strike back and propose three levels of assessment: First, one can still ask the question about the overall effect of a painting painted with a spray can, in abstraction from details about the spraying, they respond. This is the globally oriented assessment. Furthermore, spraying is not without its predecessors. Spraying reminds one of pointillist techniques on one side, and of Pollock's drippings on the other. Is the revolutionary artist presenting us with a process that follows the same implicit norms that were followed by pointillists or by Pollock? This is the global structure-oriented assessment. Finally, one can judge a particular round of spraying in the same way one can judge a particular set of brush-strokes. This is the local assessment. The proposal of the art-theoretician comes very close to what we are going to propose.

39 A quote: ' He (De Jong) also defined a measure of robustness of performance over a range of environments and demonstrated by experiment the robustness of genetic algorithms over the test set' (Booker, Goldberg, and Holland, reprint 1993, 830).

40 To test the commonsensical intuitions notice that the situation is relevantly similar to meeting an 'obviously brilliant' Martian, having no idea about how he performs his feats – the right attitude is one of epistemological praise

for the results and biological curiosity about the method, and this is precisely what reliabilism recommends.

41 When the set of alternatives is more variegated and concerns various possible values for the given parameter, the system gives as its output the maximum-likelihood set of values for the unknowns.

42 Concerning deductive inferences, the work done by Gaerdenfors and his collaborators (e.g., Gaerdenfors 1993) shows that they are not out of reach for connectionist systems. The informal idea behind it (Gaerdenfors, personal communication, June 1993) is the following: Let the system move from one local minimum (attractor, relatively stable state) to another. Let the initial minima represent premises, and the final minimum the conclusion. The movement itself is of a connectionist kind (not just implementation of classical routine), but very stable and reliable. Then we can abstract from the process features and concentrate on the global movement. This, then, is classical inference.

43 As noticed by the anonymous referee for the Press, this train of thought has some resemblance to Fodor and Pylyshyn's argument (1988).

Chapter 6. The Value of Truth

1 *P*-situations are simply situations in which it is the case that *p*. I remain uncommitted as far as the exact ontology of situations, propositions, or states of affairs goes.

2 See Bigelow and Pargetter (1990, chap. 1).

3 The original Socratic argument is found in *Theatetus*, 162a. For the discussion see, for instance, Burnyeat (1990) and Siegel (1986).

4 I have been mostly impressed by finding such attitudes to truth in some promising young scientists, and I am still puzzled, after long conversation with them, how their holding attitude is possible. But this may simply show the limits of my ability to empathize.

5 Elisabeth List of Graz University has pointed out to me that this strategy actually presupposes the pragmatist's contention that epistemic virtue is ultimately to be grounded in usefulness. I agree that the strategy does this, and it seems to me that it is precisely for this reason that it is efficient against the relativist-pragmatist: it turns his weapons against him. In the book I leave it open as to whether there are alternative possibilities for defending the Classical Picture.

6 I shall postpone the discussion of one of Stich's arguments against the instrumental value of truth – I shall call it Semantic Argument, since he puts much

weight on it – which presupposes his semantical views, until the next chapter, after the presentation of the semantical issues.

7 Consequently, I shall disregard the situations in which there is nothing the agent can do about her condition (e.g., being terminally ill) and in which the only relevant role of belief is bringing one into some emotional state. It is extremely unclear how to value such emotional states. Further, although the pragmatist might plausibly suggest that it is better for the helpless person not to know the sad truth, this is not advice he can give to the person in question.

8 A belief is a means-end-belief if it is about means to the given end. Sometimes they are called 'instrumental beliefs,' but I shall avoid this usage lest someone accuse me of surreptitiously importing instrumental value into definition of relevant beliefs.

9 'But you can fail to know that the door is unlocked, and falsely believe that it is locked, so you stay in the room.' Of course, but this only shows that false means-end-beliefs are harmful.

10 I leave aside the realism-instrumentalism issue. If highly theoretical statements are useful because they are conservative, not because they are true, then they fall out of the scope of discussion.

11 For example, I need thirty-six pencils, and they are sold by the dozen. Therefore, I decide to buy three dozen. If my premises are true, there is no way I can lose. (No possible world in which things go wrong in such a way that three dozen yields thirty-four items). Or, I want a boiled egg, and at normal altitude I put it in boiling water (No nomically possible world in which things go wrong).

12 An example from the literature: Commenting on Wittgenstein, Crispin Wright invites us to consider a tribe of tile makers whose arithmetic is incoherent and by our lights false. They might still be successful: 'Imagine a benign demon who protects the contractor's tribe from the consequences of their incoherent arithmetic by swiftly tailoring the facts and/or their apprehension of them to meet their conclusions' (Wright 1980, 310). In other words, when the contractor produces the wrong number of paving stones, the builder conveniently miscalculates.

13 I recommend the definition of coincidence due to D. Owens: 'A coincidence is an event which can be analyzed into constituent events whose nomological antecedents are quite independent of each other' (1992, 13ff.).

14 A participant in a discussion about this chapter (at Collège Internationale de Philosophie, Paris) has argued for the ultimate pragmatic equality of false and true beliefs by opposing my claim that every non-coincidentally successful false belief can be replaced by a necessarily successful true one

with the symmetrical claim: 'For every successful true belief one can find a false one which would equally well do the job.' Although the symmetry is nice, it does not establish the equality in the last resort. Push comes to shove when a policy is to be chosen and recommended. The truth-follower advises the enquirer to find out how things are in order to succeed ('Find out which mushrooms are really poisonous and which are edible'). The truth-critic cannot advise the enquirer to form a belief that would coincidentally do the same job, since the enquirer would not know what to look for.

15 Elliott Sober makes the similar point against Stich in his excellent article (1985, 172). I extend it to the relevant counter-factuals.

16 Let me briefly comment on one more mixed case. Devitt offers a purported counter-example to the explanatory value of truth: 'That truth is unnecessary to explain success can be brought out with the help of Putnam's Twin Earth example. Twin-Earth Ralph would be just as successful here as Ralph. The fact that his beliefs are about Twin-Earth Fraser, not Fraser, would be irrelevant to his success in dealing with the latter' (1987, 37). Let us then imagine the particular interaction crowned with success: 'Hello, Mr Fraser,' says Ralph. 'Can you lend me your bicycle please?' Ralph gets the bicycle. Ralph has false indexical beliefs about who the man is ('This man is Fraser,' where Ralph's token of 'Fraser' refers to Twin Earth Fraser). Ralph has, however, a lot of true beliefs (some of them implicit): 'This is the man called Fraser.' 'If I say "Hello, Fraser," this man will start talking to me.' 'This man has a bicycle.' 'This man is disposed to lend me his bicycle.' The truth of the last two beliefs certainly is essential for Ralph's success. Thus, Ralph succeeds partly because he has (a lot of) true beliefs. His false beliefs also help, the result of coincidence (it is a coincidence that the man who is not Twin Earth Fraser reacts exactly the way Twin Earth Fraser would, and this coincidence is part of the Earth-Twin Earth set-up).

Devitt also makes the curious remark that brain-in-the-vat Ralph would be successful despite the falsity of almost all of his beliefs. I am unable to make sense of the remark; it is utterly mysterious to me what success of a brain-in-the-vat consists in. A referee has hinted at the possibility that being successful is simply being satisfied with what one takes to be one's life. The brain-in-the-vat has no real accomplishments in the outside world, only imaginary ones. But if imaginary accomplishments count as much as real ones, then we should separate two issues: first, do true beliefs help one actually to do what one wants to do, and second, do true beliefs help one towards imaginary accomplishments? The second issue is nowhere prominent in the relativist-pragmatist writings – probably with good reason: people are in general not satisfied with imaginary accomplishments, and philosophers would hardly take a Daydreamer's Guide as a guidance to epistemology.

17 There are deeper problems about such induction. How does one assess situations as similar? To see the problem consider the most elementary example, the choice of 'perceptual strategy.' In a noisy environment, it is better to rely on sight than on sound when communicating or trying to figure out the details of what is happening in order to get what one wants. (This holds for such otherwise quite diverse situations as a take-off at the airport, a dance in a disco, a battlefield, an old-fashioned factory, and a well-isolated room with a record player playing Wagner at maximum volume.) Why? The obvious explanation is that sight will here produce more *true* perceptual beliefs than sound, and that you will be able to act on those beliefs. The Truth Ignoring Policy blocks this explanation. But why would anyone count as relevantly similar the situations listed, unless one is already concerned with reliability (i.e., truth-generation) of sight vs. hearing? Almost the only common denominator of such situations is the level of sound, and this level affects the success, not directly, but through reliability of perceptual process, which is a truth-linked criterion. If one rejects this criterion, one has to have separate, inductively established recipes for each environment and each particular goal (e.g., communicate visually in the disco, at the airport, in the battlefields), without any reasonable explanation, except that it has worked in the past (God knows why). Further, such recipes are very rigid: if airplanes were to take off silently, or our friend started listening to Wagner at very low volume, the preference for sight over hearing might loose its rationale, in a manner utterly unpredictable from the standpoint of the Truth Ignoring Policy of the relativist-pragmatist. This suggests that the relevant classification of situations is truth oriented – whether or not they offer such and such opportunities for getting accurate information – and this classification reverts to truth-goal. Remember that we are interested in success-generating cognitive strategies. However, if you take any taxonomy that does not classify situations by informational opportunities (which counts hearing Wagner at high and low volume together and places the loud take-off together with the quiet take-off, not together with listening at loud volume to Wagner), there is practically no chance that a global correspondence between such a non-truth-oriented taxonomy of situations and the success of particular belief-forming strategies. A direct correspondence between types of strategy and types of situations – cutting across truth-generation – would indeed be a miracle. But since the relativist-pragmatist rejects the mediation of truth, he must rely on such miracles.

On the veritistic approach, the link between different circumstances and differential reliability of strategies is straightforward, if contingent, as is the link between true belief and the success of action. No miracles are needed.

18 To get the feel of the conjecture at work, consider briefly how it counters the basic assumption of James's famous pragmatist argument for the existence of god. *James*: If I believe that there is a god, my life will be meaningful. Therefore, in case of insufficient evidence, I should believe there is a god. *The agnostic*: Suppose, there is no god. Either your life would be meaningful or not. If it would be meaningful, then god falls out. You should believe then that such-and-such a life is meaningful independent of whether or not god exists and you should attempt to live such a life (the conjecture that a true sentence will get you all that a false sentence promises to deliver). If it would not be meaningful, then your believing that there is god does not make it meaningful. In other words, the job is done by (purportedly true) belief: I can lead a meaningful life.

The agnostic's answer further suggests that neither James nor anyone else can rationally use the argument in the first person, since one would then have to confront the question about one's own belief in the meaningfulness of life independent of the existence of god. (Or claim: My life would be meaningful even if god does not exist, but I do not believe it). Thus, there is no chance that the rational agent might persuade herself to become a believer by the pragmatist argument.

19 The following remark is so naïve that I am hiding it in the notes, but I did hear it in discussions: 'There are no true means-end-beliefs.' *Answer*: Means-end-beliefs are simply a variety of causal beliefs, specifying actions as causes. If you allow causal beliefs, how do you weed out means-end-beliefs? If you disallow true causal beliefs, you imply that nothing causes anything, or if it does, no one can know it. In the first case, nothing is useful for any purpose. In the second, all that is left is complete scepticism.

20 It would have been more understandable if the critic claimed one of the following: 'Beliefs thought to be true are not reliably useful'; or 'There is no truth, so there are no true beliefs to be useful.' The first claim is at least plausible if you think that many people are poor judges of truth and hold many false beliefs (and of course hold them to be true). The second, anti-realist claim questions not the link truth-utility, but the availability of the first member of the link, and it belongs elsewhere. Notice, however, that our relativist *does not* profess to limit himself to the first claim or to endorse the second. He does claim that real truth (not apparent truth) has no instrumental value, and he is ready to grant that there are true beliefs, but takes them all to be useless.

21 Usefulness comes close to being what Mackie calls an INUS condition for

attaining the goal = insufficient but necessary part of an unnecessary but sufficient condition (1965).

22 Remember Bond and Goldfinger?

23 This point might have far-reaching epistemological consequences. Epistemic justification is sometimes presented as a kind of ultimate deontic requirement (like moral justification in the Kantian tradition), neither needing a grounding in needs and interest nor admitting of it. Such presentation is then also used to weaken or even sever the links between justification and truth (Chisholm and Pollock are good examples). Our point shows that justification alone is practically of slight relevance and lends direct support to the truth-centred view of justification, the view that justification is important as our best indicator of truth.

24 The philosopher who has done much to further this line of enquiry is Hartry Field (1986).

25 Similar considerations hold for most explanations by relational and supervenient properties. Jane, four feet tall, likes Jim (five feet tall) and John (six feet tall) and dislikes Peter (three feet, 8 inches tall). Simple explanation: Jane likes men taller then herself and dislikes those less tall. A relational property (being taller than oneself) gives a more general explanation than any of the micro-explanations invoking particular properties that ground in each case the relation of being taller than Jane. If you prefer physics to stories about Jane, take explanations invoking conservation principles, in contrast to micro-explanations of the same phenomena detailing particular interactions.

26 The lesson concerns the indeterminacy of folk-psychological concepts and of philosophical ideas that rely on such concepts.

27 This has been missed in the critical literature. Barry Lower (1993) in his otherwise excellent critique of Stich concedes to Stich that his different TRUTH(*, ...,*) predicates might clash over some issues, and he thereby concedes that they are in competition. S. Jacobson in his criticism accepts that there is an issue of choice between TRUTH(*, ...,*)s and tries to argue that we have the right to choose the one we want (1992, 340), thus conceding to the pragmatist exactly what he needs. K. Bach doubts that Stich can define TRUTH* without appealing to truth (1992, 22); for Stich, however, TRUTH* just is our truth, the one grounded in our causal-functional mode of reference – that is the whole point.

28 The example is Davidson's.

29 The examples suggests a generalization of the usual truth scheme: let p^* stand for the truth conditions of 'p' when 'p' is interpreted according to the

REFERENCE* scheme, and the attendant INTERPRETATION* function. Then the following holds: '*p*' is true* iff *p**. Much more work is to be done in order to clarity the behaviour of the truth-predicate in various schemes. I suspect that truth is a higher-level property, supervening upon various realizations, and I hope to elaborate the hunch.

30 Stich's formulation is as follows:

> Whatever the explanation, it is clear that our intuitions do not result from a systematic and critical assessment of the many alternative interpretation functions and the various virtues that each may have. One way or another we have simply inherited our intuitions: we have not made a reflective choice to have them. Those who find intrinsic value in holding true beliefs (rather than TRUE* ones, or TRUE** ones ...) are accepting unreflectively the interpretation function that our culture (or our biology) has bequeathed to us, and letting that function determine their basic epistemic value. In so doing they are making a profoundly conservative choice; they are letting tradition determine their cognitive values without any attempt at critical evaluation of that tradition. (*Fragmentation*, 245)

and further:

> The conservatism entailed by the idiosyncratic nature of the interpretation function is of a rather different kind. There are endlessly many functions mapping mental states to truth conditions (or propositions or possible states of the world). In this bristling infinity of functions there is one that is singled out by common sense as providing the 'real' truth conditions for mental states, in contrast with the TRUTH-CONDITIONS*, the TRUTH-CONDITIONS**, and all the other variations on the theme. But if, as we have been assuming, it is the causal/functional interpretation function that is sanctioned by intuition, then it is not a particularly simple or natural function. Rather, it is something of a hodge-podge, built from a more or less heterogeneous family of strategies for fixing the reference of terms and another family of strategies for transmitting reference from one speaker to another. What distinguishes acceptable groundings and transmissions is not that they share some common natural property, but simply that they are found to be acceptable by commonsense intuitions. (Ibid., 119)

31 The interlocutor might now protest: 'Look, the difference between TRUTH-*c* and TRUTH-*d* is so insignificant that our intuition yields an unusual verdict. We should look at more exotic interpretation functions, and then it will become obvious that enquirers with goals defined in terms of those functions are certainly pursuing different epistemic goal than we do.' Suppose then

that you meet members of the Martian academy, capable of speaking English. They explain to you that they want to know about members of a certain natural kind *K*, whether they have an important property *P*, which is very important according to their biology. You ask them about the kind *K*, and they explain that there is a very complicated way of identifying certain natural kinds and of referring to them, which is far beyond your grasp (until you have learned a lot about Martian science), but that he sincerely believes that the predicate '*K*' stands for a very definite natural kind. He seems to be very much taken up with his task, and keeps talking about bits of evidence that point to the possibility that *K*-items have *P*. He informs you that the whole system of referring to objects and kinds in Martian is essentially different from that in the languages of Earth. Now, if the fellow seems sincere to you, would you not say that he is after the truth about *K*? What possible relevance for the question whether he is a truth-seeker could his exotic way of referring to *K* have? On the other hand, we could justifiably expect the Martian fellow to admit that our ways of referring and our interpretation function, TRUTH* (or TRUTH-*c*), are not in themselves an impediment to our cognitive enterprise.

32 W. Lycan (1991) argues for the choice of the entrenched truth-predicate because it would be costly to do otherwise. But this is exactly what the relativist needs: an argument that the only reason we have to cherish truth is a pragmatic one. I think that the proper response is on the descriptive side to deny that we exercise any choice in the matter, and on the normative side to say that there is nothing interesting to choose, since the would-be alternatives are epistemically neutral.

33 Some defences that I have heard at various conferences have appealed to the alleged necessary intentionality of belief: a belief that *p* entails belief that *p* is true (if the believer has the concept of truth and is reflective enough). The relativist-pragmatist answer would be to question the need for such a strict notion of belief: why not work with shmeliefs that have a functional role similar to that of belief, but are not representationally tied to any particular state of affairs? I have avoided this aprioristic line in general, to meet the relativist-pragmatist on his own naturalistic ground.

34 One point of his discussion about biology is to show that 'there *may* be lots of diversity in the population, and for lots of different reasons'; 'There is a great diversity among contemporary humans with respect to the language(s) they speak and understand ... the first step is to note that, in light of what is little known on these matters, it is entirely possible that the cognitive mechanisms subserving inference are similar in important ways to the cognitive mechanism underlying language comprehension'; 'The exist-

ence of innate inferential strategies is an entirely open, empirical question, as is the extent to which a person's inferential strategies are shaped by his or her cultural surroundings' (*Fragmentation*, 73, 69, 72). The issue of diversity is addressed in chapter 7, section 2, on relative and absolute grading of cognitive strategies.

35 I am stressing Stich's stronger formulations, not to caricature his view in order to attack it more easily, but because they bring into the open what the relativist-pragmatist really needs. The cautious formulations simply do not support his attack on truth.

36 *Fragmentation*, 99.

37 Stephen J. Gould (1989) offers an impressive account of the role of randomness in evolution. His picture of evolutionary change is guided by the idea that in the initial stages there is a great diversification – an idea he documents by the spectacular example of the Cambrian fauna found at the Burgess Shale and reconstructed by H. Whittington and his collaborators. The diversity is then drastically reduced by catastrophes that decimate the extant species. Who survives such catastrophes is a largely contingent matter. He urges upon the biological and paleontological community the distinction between rules of survival at normal times and completely different rules valid in periods of catastrophic changes. How does this affect our argument? It is obvious that the intelligence and the reliability of the cognitive apparatus of our distant ancestors are rather impotent in the face of epidemics, earthquakes, and droughts on a continental scale. They belong to the instruments of survival under normal circumstances – as also do the strong jaws of carnivores or the pincers of Gould's proto-scorpions. None of these protects one against a viral epidemic or earthquake, and all presumably have been selected for in normal circumstances. No more is required for our argument. (This is a variation on the 'necessary and sufficient conditions' theme, this time in paleontological clothing: intelligence might not be sufficient for survival, but it is an important contributory cause.)

38 The classic critiques of Panglossian optimism about evolution are Gould and Lewontin (1979) and Lewontin (1984).

39 The thesis aligns itself with a moderate evolutionary optimism that sees optimality as a supporting factor, not a factor that dictates acceptance, or to use Kitcher's formulation: 'Functional descriptions which are backed by optimality analyses receive substantially higher prior confirmation than those that are not backed by optimality analyses' (1987, 80). Of course, not being a biologist, I cannot offer the precise, not to mention quantitative, data that would be needed for a final biological decision (of the kind Kitcher discusses in the article quoted), but only general plausibility considerations. I find very

congenial the critique of Stich by Eliott Sober (1985). He also stresses the fact that variability of environment favours reliability, and points to the importance of 'generalist' strategies valid over a wide range of environments.

40 Being a non-specialist, I list as my best source the issue of *Scientific American* on 'Life, Death and the Immune System' (Sept. 1993), in particular, the papers of C. Janeway, 'How the Immune System Recognizes Invaders,' and of P. Marrack and J.W. Kappler, 'How the Immune System Recognizes the Body,' in the same issue.

41 The point has been forcefully drawn to my attention in a conversation with William Ramsey.

42 For further, rather impressive evidence of the social sophistication of apes – documented for four species: Pan troglodytes, Pan paniscus, Macaca mulatta, and Macaca arctoides – one can with pleasure consult and read de Waal (1989).

43 For the enlarged discussion of the issues of social intelligence and the importance of reliable 'mind-reading' see Whitens' anthology (1991).

Chapter 7. From Truth to Virtue

1 For an interesting discussion of the issue, coming close to the relativist-pragmatist position, but not endorsing it, see Hooker (1994).

2 Compare Richard Boyd's pronouncements on the centrality of theoretical knowledge (1990, 184).

3 For a recent discussion of the strategy see Stein (1994).

4 See Goodman (1983), Cohen (1981), and Stein (1994).

5 Philosophical sportsmanship suggests that even such possibilities be taken into account, since they are readily imaginable (see an interesting discussion in Levin 1988, where the consideration is placed in an appropriate setting). A naturalist should resist the suggestion in the present context, where it draws attention away from what is to be realistically expected and places a heavy and undeserved burden upon the shoulders of the rationalist, thereby giving an unfair advantage to the relativist.

6 See, for example, *Fragmentation*, 147.

7 For instance, G. Harman, one of the most radical critics of the traditional assumption in favour of logic, claims that it is sometimes rational to retain contradictory beliefs if one has 'no time or ability to trace the source of inconsistency' (1986, 17).

8 Historically, the formulation has been traced to Locke's idea that the probable argument is 'such as for the most part carries truth with it' (*Essay*, Book IV, chap. 15).

9 For his arguments see Cohen (1981, 1986) and the debate published in the same issue of *Behavior and Brain Sciences*.

10 See Gigerenzer (1991), Gigerenzer, Hoffrage, and Kleinbolting (1991), and Kornblith (1993).

11 Churchland has a way of surprising his critics. I was told by a reliable source that he is taking precisely the route of Peircian-Putnamian anti-realism. I am afraid that he will have to revise some of the main claims of 'neurocomputational perspective': that connectionist representations are truth-intolerant (since Peirce-Putnam anti-realist 'truth' is as much propositional as the classical one, so intolerance for one entails intolerance for the other), that there is an irreducible plurality of 'schemes' of things, and in general he will have to become absolutist-rationalist like Peirce and Putnam. Notice, though, that in his discussion with Putnam (Churchland 1992a) he abides by his rejection of 'classical truth and reference.'

12 See Nye (1972).

13 The other well-known example is the biological discourse concerning genes.

14 Perhaps Quine was right that the indeterminacy vanishes within a translator's mother tongue, but I do not wish to go into the issue here.

15 It is bad to concentrate on frogs and bugs. For some diversity, read Gallistel's *The Organization of Learning* (1990), on beautifully precise and determinate spatial maps in invertebrates. Primitive representations *can be* determinate, and this is enough. Thus, we have it, bugs have it, why should *T* not recognize it?

16 Needless to say, I prefer Churchland the realist to Churchland the no-truth theoretician.

17 'You have read too much into the word "grasp,"' our opponent might say. No, the word *'grasp'* is unimportant; the stress is on 'the real.' The realist claims that we do have an access to the real through our theories. The details of description of the mode of access are immaterial: grasp, or information gathering, or simply representing as opposed to mis-representing are equivalent in this highly general context.

18 If a philosopher says that he accepts that our representations represent the real as it (deeply) is, but that he would not like to use the word *true* in this context, let him invent a word, say 'shrue.' A theory is shrue if it allows us to grasp reality (as it is – to represent it otherwise is not to grasp it). A representation forming part of a shrue theory representing that the snow is white is shrue if it shows us the snow as it really is, namely, white. Generally, '*R*' is shrue iff *R*. Then, shruth is the goal of cognition, common to different cognizers, and capable of grounding non-relativistic norms. The relativist loses.

19 Our conclusion is perhaps another up-to-date variant of the Socratic rational-

istic turning of the tables against the relativist that we have mentioned at the beginning of Part Three The original argument is to be found in Plato's *Theatetus* (170a–171d). For a rather recent commentary and bibliography see Burnyeat (1990). The most thorough discussion of the classical reductio argument built on Plato's idea and its importance in the contemporary context is found in Siegel (1986). Although I think that it is valid, I am not discussing the classical reductio argument, since, as it stands, it is neither attractive nor persuasive to the philosophical naturalist, and I have nothing original to add to it.

Conclusion

1 The expression 'primitively compelling' stems from the work of Christopher Peacocke (1992).
2 For example, *Philosophical Investigations*, I, paras. 218–19.
3 I find myself in broad agreement with views of philosophers such as Collin McGinn (1993), George Rey (1993), John Pollock (1993), and Robert Nozick (1993). Important year indeed, 1993!
4 Peter Carruthers (1992) claims that this is the very essence of classical empiricism.

Appendix

1 For detailed criticism of Churchland on neurological grounds see Gilman (1992).
2 My colleague Z. Sikic has made me aware of the John Doe line of defence against historical evidence.
3 I must add that I have often encountered in discussions the view that Kuhn and Feyerabend did not, in fact, endorse or defend the holistic thesis. According to this view, Kuhn and Feyerabend speak about 'perception' metaphorically, meaning 'understanding' or 'grasp'; when they say that a revolutionary 'perceives' a thing in a novel way, they mean simply that she understands it in such a way. I am not interested in the exegesis of Kuhn and Feyerabend, but I think that the ideas of global paradigm change and of incommensurability lose coherence and prima facie plausibility if they are not supported by the holistic stance on theory and observation. In fact, if Kuhn and Feyerabend accepted at least the relative separation of theoretical and observational statements, they also would have to accept that different theoretical traditions (or cliques of particular paradigm fans) might have shared observational commitments at some level. But this view does clash with a lot of their pronouncements.

4 The cognitive-psychological underpinnings of the informational approach stem mainly from the work of J.J. Gibson. The best general philosophical presentation of information-based epistemology is Fred Dretske (1981).

5 For a detailed and persuasive information-theoretical story about this particular matter, see W. Harper's series of papers on Newton, especially 'Consilience and Natural Kind Reasoning,' in Brown and Mittelstrass (eds) (1989), and references therein.

6 Shapere (1982b); unfortunately, since I was not able to get a copy of the journal, all the quotations are from the preprint. I apologize to the reader, and I thank Mr M. Edman for having sent me the preprint.

7 J. Brown also gives in a brief remark (what I think is) the correct diagnosis of what goes wrong with the holist's argument: 'It is *our conception* of which processes are observations that is theory-laden, not the processes themselves' (1989, 171).

8 Can Shapere himself have it? Can he maintain it together with his other views? He thinks that theory-ladenness as he takes it does not undermine realism. But realism seems to go ill with Thesis of Determination. If current knowledge determines which things are registered, and which information is present in the registration, then one should talk rather about construction than about registration.

References

Agnoli, F., and D. Krantz (1989) 'Suppressing the Natural Heuristics by Formal Instruction.' *Cognitive Psychology* 21, 512–29.

Alston, W.P. (1993) 'Epistemic Desiderata.' *Philosophy and Phenomenological Research* 52, 527–51.

Anderson, J.R. (1980) *Cognitive Psychology and Its Implications*. San Francisco: Freeman.

Armstrong, D. (1973) *Belief, Truth and Knowledge*. Cambridge: Cambridge University Press.

Bach, K. (1992). 'Truth, Justification and the American Way.' *Pacific Philosophical Quarterly* 17, 16–20.

Barsalou, L.W. (1987) 'The Instability of Graded Structure: Implications for the Nature of Concepts.' In *Concepts and Conceptual Development*, ed. U. Neisser. Cambridge: Cambridge University Press.

Barwise, J., and J. Perry (1981) *Situations and Attitudes*. Cambridge, MA: MIT Press.

Bechtel, W. (1990) *Connectionism and the Future of Folk Psychology*. Publications of the ZIF, No. 39. Bielefeld, Germany: ZIF.

Bechtel, W., and A. Abrahamsen (1980) 'Beyond the Exclusively Propositional Era.' *Synthese* 82, 223–53.

Bigelon, and Pagette (1990) *Science and Necessity*. Cambridge: Cambridge University Press.

Bogdan, R. (ed.) (1993) *Mind and Common Sense*. Oxford: Blackwell.

Booker, L.B., Goldberg, and J.H. Holland (1989) 'Classifier Systems and Genetic Algorithms.' *Artificial Intelligence* 40, 1–3. Reprinted in *Readings in Knowledge Acquisition and Learning*, ed. B.G. Buchanan and D.C. Wilkins. San Mateo, CA: M. Kaufmann, 1993.

Boyd, R. (1990) 'Realism, Conventionality and "Realism About."' In *Meaning and Method*, ed. G. Boolos. Cambridge: Cambridge University Press.

Braithwaite, R.B. (1974) 'The Predictionist Justification of Induction.' In Swinburne (ed.).
Brown, J.R. (1989) *The Rational and the Social*. London: Routledge.
– (1991) 'Illustration and Inference,' In *Picturing Knowledge*, ed. B. Baigrie. Toronto: University of Toronto Press.
Brown, J.R., and J. Mittelstrass (eds) (1989) *An Intimate Relation*. Dordrecht: Kluwer.
Byrne, R.M.J. (1989) 'Suppressing Valid Inferences with Conditionals.' *Cognition* 31, 61–83.
Byrne, R.W., and A. Whiten (eds) (1988) *Machiavellian Intelligence*. Oxford: Clarendon Press.
Burnyeat, M. (1990) *The Theatetus of Plato*. Indianapolis: Hackett.
Carey, S. (1985) *Conceptual Change in Childhood*. Cambridge, MA: MIT Press.
Carruthers, P., (1989) *Tractarian Semantics*. Oxford: Basil Blackwell.
– (1992) *Human Knowledge and Human Nature*. London: Routledge.
Cheng, P.W., and K.J. Holyoak (1985) 'Pragmatic Reasoning Schemes.' *Cognitive Psychology* 17, 391–416.
Cheng, P., and L.R. Novick (1992) 'Covariation in Natural Causal Induction.' *Psychological Review* 99.
Churchland, Paul M. (1979) *Scientific Realism and the Plasticity of Mind*. Cambridge: Cambridge University Press.
– (1986) 'Some Reductive Strategies in Cognitive Neurobiology.' *Mind* 95, 279–309.
– (1989) *A Neurocomputational Perspective: The Nature of Mind and the Structure of Science*. Cambridge, MA: MIT Press (cited as *NP*).
– (1992a) 'Activation Vectors versus Propositional Attitude: How the Brain Represents Reality.' *Philosophy and Phenomenological Research* 52, 417–24.
– (1992b) 'A Deeper Unity: Some Feyerabendian Themes in Neurocomputational Form.' In R.N. Giere (ed.).
– (1993) 'Evaluating Our Self Conception.' *Mind and Language* 8, 211–22 (Special Issue, 'Eliminativism').
Churchland, Patricia S. (1986) *Neurophilosophy*. Cambridge, MA: MIT Press.
Churchland, P.S. and T.J. Sejnowski (1988) 'Neural Representation and Neural Computation.' In *Neural Connections and Mental Computation*, ed. L. Nadel. Cambridge, MA: MIT Press.
Clark, A. (1989) *Microcognition*. Cambridge, MA: MIT Press.
– (1991) 'Systematicity, Structured Representations and Cognitive Architecture: A Reply to Fodor and Pylyshyn.' In Horgan and Tienson (eds).
– (1993) *Associative Engines*. Cambridge, MA: MIT Press.
Clark, A., and A. Karmiloff-Smith (1993) 'The Cognizer's Innards: A Psychologi-

cal and Philosophical Perspective on the Development of Thought.' *Mind and Language* 8, 487–519.
Cohen, L.J. (1981) 'Can Human Irrationality Be Experimentally Demonstrated?' *Behavior and Brain Sciences* 4, 317–70.
– (1986) *The Dialogue of Reason*. Oxford: Oxford University Press.
Commons, M., S. Grossberg, and J. Staddon (eds) (1991) *Neural Network Models of Conditioning and Action*. Hillsdale, NJ: Lawrence Erlbaum.
Cussins, A. (1993) 'Nonconceptual Content and the Elimination of Misconceived Composites.' *Mind and Language* 8 (Special Issue, 'Eliminativism').
Davidson, D. (1980) *Essays on Actions and Events*. Cambridge: Cambridge University Press.
Davies, S. (ed.) (1992) *Connectionism: Theory and Practice*. Oxford: Oxford University Press.
De Vries, W. (1993) '"Who Sees with Equal Eye Atoms or Systems into Ruins Hurl'd."' *Philosophical Studies* 71.
de Waal, F. (1989) 'Peacemaking among Primates.' Cambridge, MA: Harvard University Press.
Devitt, M. (1987) 'Does Realism Explain Success?' *Revue Internationale de Philosophie* 41, 29–44.
Dretske, F. (1981) *Knowledge and the Flow of Information*. Cambridge, MA: MIT Press.
Dummett, M. (1978) 'Truth.' In *Truth and Other Enigmas*. London: Duckworth.
Edwards, S. (1993) 'Formulating a Plausible Relativism.' *Philosophia* 22, 63–71.
Elster, J. (1983) *Sour Grapes*. Cambridge: Cambridge University Press.
Etchemendy, J. (1990) *The Concept of Logical Consequence*. Cambridge, MA: Harvard University Press.
Evans, J. St B. (1989) *Bias in Human Reasoning: Causes and Consequences*. Hillsdale, NJ: Lawrence Erlbaum.
Field, H. (1978) 'Mental Representation.' *Erkenntnis* 13:1; also in *Readings in the Philosophy of Psychology* 2. Cambridge, MA: Harvard University Press.
– (1986) 'The Deflationary Conception of Truth.' In *Fact, Science and Morality*, ed. G. Macdonald and C. Wright. Oxford: Basil Blackwell.
Fodor, J. (1981) *Representations*. Cambridge, MA: MIT Press.
– (1983) *The Modularity of Mind*. Cambridge, MA: MIT Press.
– (1984) 'Observation Reconsidered.' *Philosophy of Science* 53, 23–43.
– (1991) 'The Dogma That Didn't Bark.' *Mind* 398, 201–20.
Fodor, J., and Z. Pylyshyn (1988) 'Connectionism and Cognitive Architecture: A Critical Analysis.' *Cognition* 28, 3–71.

Foley, R. (1987) *A Theory of Epistemic Rationality.* Cambridge, MA: Harvard University Press.

Forbes, G. (1989) 'Biosemantics and the Normative Properties of Thought.' *Philosophical Perspectives*, vol. 3, ed J.E. Tomberlin. Atascadero, CA: Ridgeview.

Gaerdenfors, P. (1993) 'Non-monotic Inferences in Neural Networks.' Unpublished manuscript.

Gallistel, C.R. (1990) *The Organization of Learning*. Cambridge, MA: MIT Press.

Garson, J.W. (1994) 'No Representations without Rules.' *Mind and Language* 9, 25–37.

Gibson, K.R. (1990) 'New Perspectives on Instincts and Intelligence.' In *Language and Intelligence in Monkeys and Apes – Comparative Developmental Perspectives*, ed. S.T. Parker and K.R. Gibson. Cambridge: Cambridge University Press.

Giere, R.N. (1990) 'Evolutionary Models of Science.' In *Evolution, Cognition and Realism*, ed. N. Recher. CPS Series in Philosophy of Science. Washington, DC: University Press of America.

– (ed.) (1992) *Minnesota Studies in the Philosophy of Science*, vol. XV, *Cognitive Models of Science*. Minneapolis: University of Minnesota Press.

Gigerenzer, G. (1991) 'From Tools to Theories: A Heuristic of Discovery in Cognitive Psychology.' *Psychological Review* 98, 254–67.

Gigerenzer, G., U. Hoffrage, and H. Kleinbolting (1991) 'Probabilistic Mental Models: A Brunswikian Theory of Confidence.' *Psychological Review* 98, 506–28.

Gigerenzer, G., and K. Hug (1992) 'Domain-Specific Reasoning: Social Contracts, Cheating, and Perspective Change.' *Cognition* 43, 127–71.

Gilman, D. (1992) 'What's Theory to Do ... with Seeing?' *Philosophy of Science* 43.

Glenberg, A., and M. McDaniel (1992) 'Mental Models, Pictures and Text: Integration of Spatial and Verbal Information.' *Memory and Cognition* 5.

Goldman, A. (1986) *Epistemology and Cognition*. Cambridge, MA: Harvard University Press.

– (1992) *Liaisons*. Cambridge, MA: MIT Press.

– (1993a) *Philosophical Applications of Cognitive Science.* Boulder, CO: Westview Press.

– (1993b) 'The Psychlogy of Folk Psychology.' *Behavioral and Brain Sciences* 16, 15–28.

Gombrich, E.H. (1982) *The Image and the Eye*. Oxford: Phaidon Press.

Goodman, N. (1983) *Fact, Fiction and Forecast*, 4th ed. Cambridge, MA: Harvard University Press.

Gopnik, A. (1993) 'How We Know Our Minds.' *Behavioral and Brain Sciences* 16, 1–14.

Gould, S.J. (1989) *Wonderful Life*. New York: Norton.

Gould, S.J., and R.C. Lewontin (1979) 'The Spandrels of San Marco and the Panglossian Paradigm.' Reprinted in *Conceptual Issues in Evolutionary Biology,* ed. E. Sober. Cambridge, MA: MIT Press.

Graham, G. (1991) 'Connectionism in Pavlovian Harness.' In Horgan and Tienson (eds).

Haack, S. (1976) 'The Pragmatist Theory of Truth.' *British Journal for the Philosophy of Science* 27.

Hadley, R.F. (1994) 'Systematicity in Connectionist Language Learning' *Mind and Language* 9, 247–72.

Hanson, N.R. (1965) *Patterns of Discovery.* Cambridge: Cambridge University Press.

Hanson, S.J., and D. Burr (1990) 'What Connectionist Models Learn: Learning and Representations in Connectionist Networks.' *Behavioral and Brain Sciences* 13, 471–518.

Harman, G. (1986) *Change in View.* Cambridge, MA: MIT Press.

Hatfield, G. (1991) 'Representation and Rule-Instantiation in Connectionist Systems.' In Horgan and Tienson (eds).

Haugeland, J. (1985) *Artificial Intelligence: The Very Idea.* Cambridge, MA: MIT Press.

Heal, J. (1990) 'Pragmatism and Choosing to Believe.' In *Reading Rorty,* ed. Alan Malachovski. Oxford: Basil Blackwell.

Heil, J., and A. Mele (eds) (1993) *Mental Causation.* Oxford: Basil Blackwell.

Hesse, M. (1986) 'Is There an Independent Observation Language?' In *The Nature and Function of Scientific Theories,* ed. R. Colodny. Pittsburgh: Pittsburgh University Press.

Holland, J., K. Holyoak, R. Nisbett, and P. Thagard (1986) *Induction: Processes of Inference, Learning, and Discovery.* Cambridge, MA: MIT Press.

Hooker, C.A. (1994) 'Idealisation, Naturalism, and Rationality: Some Lessons from Minimal Rationality.' *Synthese* 99.

Hookway, C., and D. Peterson (eds) (1993) *Philosophy and Cognitive Science.* Cambridge: Cambridge University Press.

Horgan, T., and J. Tienson (1989) 'Representations without Rules.' In *Philosophical Perspectives.* Vol. 17, ed. J.E. Tomberlin. Atascadero, CA: Ridgeview.

Horgan, T., and J. Tienson (eds) (1991) *Connectionism and the Philosophy of Mind.* Dordrecht: Kluwer.

– (1992a) 'Cognitive Systems as Dynamical Systems.' *Topoi* 11, 27–43.

– (1992b) 'Structured Representations in Connectionist Systems?' In S. Davies (ed).

– (1993) 'Level of Description in Nonclassical Cognitive Science.' In Hookway and Peterson (eds).

– (1994) 'Representations Don't Need Rules.' *Mind and Language* 9, 1–24.

Horwich, P. (1990) *Truth*. Oxford: Basil Blackwell.

Humphrey, N.K. (1988) 'The Social Function of Intellect.' In Byrne and Whiten (eds).

Jacobson, S. (1992) 'In Defense of Truth and Rationality.' *Pacific Philosophical Quarterly* 73, 335–45.

Johnson-Laird, P.N. (1983) *Mental Models*. Cambridge: Cambridge University Press.

– (1994) 'A Model Theory of Induction.' *International Studies in the Philosophy of Science* 8, 5–30.

Johnson-Laird, P.N., and R. Byrne (1991) *Deduction*. Hillsdale, NJ: Lawrence Erlbaum.

Johnson-Laird, P.N., and P.C., Wason (eds) (1979) *Thinking Readings in Cognitive Science*. Cambridge: Cambridge University Press.

Kahneman, D., P. Slovic, and A. Tversky (eds) (1982) *Judgement under Uncertainty: Heuristics and Biases*. Cambridge: Cambridge University Press.

Karmiloff-Smith, A. (1992) *Beyond Modularity: A Developmental Perspective on Cognitive Science*. Cambridge, MA: MIT Press.

Keil, F.C. (1989) *Concepts, Kinds and Cognitive Development*. Cambridge, MA: MIT Press.

Kirkham, R.L. (1992) *Theories of Truth*. Cambridge, MA: MIT Press.

Kitcher, P. (1992) 'The Naturalists Return.' *Philosophical Review* 101, 53–114.

Kyburg, H. (1970) *Probability and Inductive Logic*. London: Collier-Macmillan.

Langley, P., H.A. Simon, G.L. Bradshaw, and J.M. Zytkow (1987) *Scientific Discovery – Computational Explorations of the Creative Processes*. Cambridge, MA: MIT Press.

Levi, I. (1983) 'Who Commits the Base Rate Fallacy?' *Behavioral and Brain Sciences* 6.

Levin, Janet (1988) 'Must Reasons Be Rational?' *Philosophy of Science* 55, 199–217.

Lewis, D. (1983) *Philosophical Papers I*. Oxford: Oxford University Press.

Loar, B. (1982) *Mind and Meaning*. Cambridge: Cambridge University Press.

Lower, B. (1993) 'The Value of Truth.' *Philosophical Issues, 4, Naturalism and Normativity*. Atascadero, CA: Ridgeview.

Ludwig, K. (1994) 'Dretske on Explaining Behavior,' *Acta Analytica* 11, 111–24.

Lycan, W.G. (1986) 'Tacit Belief.' In *Belief*, ed. R. Bogdan, Oxford: Oxford University Press.

– (ed.) (1990) *Mind and Cognition*. Oxford: Basil Blackwell.

– (1991) 'Why We Should Care Whether Our Beliefs Are True.' *Philosophy and Phenomenological Research*, 203–7.

Maffie, J. (1990) 'Naturalism and the Normativity of Epistemology.' *Philosophical Studies* 59, 333–49.

Marr, D. (1982) *Vision*. New York: Freeman.

McGinn, C. (1993) 'Logic, Mind, and Mathematics.' In *Dennett and His Critics*, ed. Bo Dahlbom. Oxford: Basil Blackwell.

McLaughlin, B.P. (1993a) 'The Connectionism/Classicism Battle to Win Souls.' *Philosophical Studies* 71, 45–72.

– (1993b) 'Systematicity, Conceptual Truth and Evolution.' In Hookway and Peterson (eds).

McLaughlin, B.P., and J. Fodor (1991) 'Connectionism and the Problem of Systematicity: Why Smolensky's Solution Doesn't Work.' In Horgan and Tienson (eds).

McNamarra, J. (1986) *The Border Dispute*. Cambridge, MA: MIT Press.

Medin, D.L. (1989) 'Concepts and Conceptual Structure.' *American Psychologist* 12.

Millikan, R.G. (1993a) 'On Mentalese Orthography I.' In Millikan, *White Queen Psychology and Other Essays for Alice*. Cambridge, MA: MIT Press.

– (1993b) 'On Mentalese Orthography II.' In *Dennett and His Critics*, ed. B. Dahlbom. Oxford: Basil Blackwell.

Munevar, G. (1981) *Radical Knowledge*. Indianapolis: Hackett.

Neal Radford, M. (1992) 'Connectionist Learning of Belief Networks.' *Artificial Intelligence* 56, 71–113.

Neander, K. (1991) 'Functions as Selected Effects.' *Philosophy of Science* 58, 168–84.

Newton-Smith, W. (1981) *Rationality of Science*. London: Routledge.

Niklasson, L.F., and T. Van Gelder (1994) 'On Being Systematically Connectionist.' *Mind and Language* 9, 288–302.

Nisbett, R., and L. Ross (1980) *Human Inference: Strategies and Shortcomings of Social Judgment*. Englewood Cliffs, NJ: Prentice-Hall.

Nisbett, R., and T. Wilson (1977) 'Telling More Than We Can Know: Verbal Reports on Mental Processes.' *Psychological Review* 84, 231–59.

Nozick, R. (1993) *The Nature of Rationality*. Princeton: Princeton University Press.

O'Keefe, J. (1989) 'Computations the Hippocampus Might Perform.' In *Neural Connections, Mental Computations*, ed. L. Nadel, L.A. Cooper, P. Culicover, and R.M. Harnish. Cambridge, MA: MIT Press.

Orchard, G.A., and W.A. Philips (1991) *Neural Computation*. Hillsdale, NJ: Lawrence Erlbaum.

Osherson, Daniel N., and E. Smith (eds) (1990) *An Invitation to Cognitive Science*. Cambridge, MA: MIT Press.

Owens, D. (1992) *Causes and Coincidences*. Cambridge: Cambridge University Press.

Peacocke, Christopher (1992) *A Study of Concepts*. Cambridge, MA: MIT Press.

Peirce, C.S. (1955) *Philosophical Writings of Peirce*, ed. J. Buchler. New York: Dover.
Plantinga, A. (1993) *Warrant and Proper Function*. Oxford: Oxford University Press.
Plunkett, K. (1993) 'Making Nets Work Hard.' *Mind and Language* 8.
Pollack, J.B. (1990) 'Recursive Distributed Representations.' *Artificial Intelligence* 46, 77–105.
Pollock, J.L. (1986) *Contemporary Theories of Knowledge*. London: Hutchinson.
– (1989) *How to Build a Person: A Prolegomenon*. Cambridge, MA: MIT Press.
– (1992) 'Rationality, Function and Content.' *Philosophical Studies* 65.
– (1993) 'The Phylogeny of Rationality.' *Cognitive Science* 17.
Putnam, H (1981) *Reason, Truth, and History*. Cambridge: Cambridge University Press.
Pylyshyn, Z. (1973) 'The Role of Competence Theories in Cognitive Psychology.' *Journal of Psycholinguistic Research* 2, 21–50.
– (1980) 'Computation and Cognition.' *Behavioral and Brain Sciences* 3, 111–32.
Quine, W.v. O. (1970) *Philosophy of Logic*. Englewood Cliffs, NJ: Prentice-Hall.
Ramsey, W. (1994) 'Do Connectionist Representations Earn Their Explanatory Keep?' *Mind and Language* 12, 34–66.
– (1996) 'Rethinking Distributed Representations.' *Acta Analytica* 14, 9–25.
Ramsey, W., S. Stich, and J. Garon (1990) 'Connectionism, Eliminativism and the Future of Folk Psychology.' *Philosophical Perspectives* 4.
Resnik, M. (1981) 'Mathematics as a Science of Patterns: Ontology and Reference.' *Nous* 15, 529–50.
Rey, G. (1991) 'An Explanatory Budget for Connectionism and Eliminativistm.' In Horgan and Tienson (eds).
Rips, L. (1983) 'Cognitive Processes in Propositional Reasoning.' *Psychological Review* 90, 38–71.
– (1989a) 'Similarity, Typicality and Categorization.' In *Similarity and Analogical Reasoning*, ed. S. Vosniadou and A. Ortony. Cambridge: Cambridge University Press.
– (1989b) 'The Psychology of Knights and Knaves.' *Cognition* 31.
Rosch, E. (1978) 'Principles of Categorization.' In *Cognition and Categorization*, ed. E. Rosch and B.B. Lloyd. Hillsdale, NJ: Lawrence Erlbaum.
Rosenberg, J.F. (1990) 'Connectionism and Cognition.' *Acta Analytica* 6, 33–46.
Rumelhart, D., and J. McClelland (1986) *Parallel Distributed Processing: Essays in the Microstructure of Cognition*. Cambridge, MA: MIT Press.
Salmon, W. (1974) 'The Concept of Inductive Evidence.' In Swinburne (ed.).
Schaller, H.N. (1990) 'Solving Constraint Problems Using Feedback Neural Networks.' In *Parallel Processing in Neural Systems and Computers*. ed. R. Eckmiller, G. Hartmann, and G. Hauske. Amsterdam: Elsevier.

Schmitt, F. (1992) *Knowledge and Belief*. London: Routledge.

Schoene, H. (1984) *Spatial Orientation*. Princeton: Princeton University Press.

Schyns, P.G. (1991) 'A Modular Neural Network Model of Concept Acquisition.' *Cognitive Science* 15, 461–508.

Scott-Kakures, D. (1994) 'On Belief and the Captivity of the Will.' *Philosophy and Phenomenological Research* 54, 77–104.

Searle, J. (1990) 'Consciousness, Explanatory Inversion, and Cognitive Science.' *Behavioural and Brain Sciences* 13, 585–642.

Sejnowski, T.J., and C.R. Rosenberg (1987) 'Parallel Networks That Learn to Pronounce English Text.' *Complex Systems* 1.

Shafir, E., and A. Tversky (1992) 'Thinking Through Uncertainty: Nonconsequential Reasoning and Choice.' *Cognitive Psychology* 24, 449–74.

Shapere, D. (1982a) 'Rationalism and Empiricism: A New Perspective' *Argumentation* 2.

– (1982b) 'The Concept of Observation in Science and Philosophy.' *Philosophy of Science* 49, 485–525.

Shastri, L., and V. Ajjanagadde (1993) 'From Simple Associations to Systematic Reasoning: A Connectionist Representation of Rules, Variables and Dynamic Binding Using Temporal Synchrony.' *Behavioral and Brain Sciences* 16, 417–94.

Siegel, H. (1986) 'Relativism, Truth and Incoherence.' *Synthèse* 68, 225–59.

Simon, H., and J. Larkin (1987) 'Why a Diagram Is (Sometimes) Worth Ten Thousand Words.' *Cognitive Science* 11, 65–99.

Smith, E.E. (1990) 'Categorization.' In Osherson and Smith (eds), vol. 3.

Smolensky, P. (1989) 'Connectionist Modeling: Neural Computation / Mental Connections.' In *Neural Connections, Mental Computations*, ed. L. Nadel, L.A. Cooper, P. Culicover, and R.M. Harnish. Cambridge, MA: MIT Press.

– (1990) 'Tensor Product Variable Binding and the Representation of Symbolic Structures in Connectionist Systems.' *Artificial Intelligence* 46, 159–216.

– (1991) 'The Consitutent Structure of Connectionist Mental States: A Reply to Fodor and Pylyshyn.' In Horgan and Tienson (eds).

Sober, E. (1985) 'Panglossian Functionalism and the Philosophy of Mind.' *Synthèse* 64, 165–93.

Solomon, M. (1992) 'Scientific Rationality and Human Reasoning.' *Philosophy of Science* 59, 439–55.

Stadler, E. (1983) 'How Are Grammars Represented?' *Behavioral and Brain Sciences* 3, 391–402.

Stalnaker, R. (1984) *Inquiry*. Cambridge, MA: MIT Press.

Stampe, D. (1977) 'Towards a Causal Theory of Linguistic Representation. In *Midwest Studies in Philosophy*, vol. 2, ed. P. French, T. Ehling, and H. Wettstein. Minneapolis: University of Minnesota Press.

Stein, E. (1994) 'Rationality and Reflective Equilibrium.' *Synthèse* 99, 137–72.

Stich, S. (1983) *From Folk Psychology to Cognitive Science*. Cambridge, MA: MIT Press.

– (1985) 'Could Man Be an Irrational Animal?' *Synthèse* 64, 115–35.

– (1990) *The Fragmentation of Reason*. Cambridge, MA: Bradford Books, MIT Press (cited as *Fragmentation*).

– (1991a) 'Do True Believers Exist?' *Proceedings of the Aristotelian Society.*

– (1991b) 'The Fragmentation of Reason: Precis of Two Chapters.' *Philosophy and Phenomenological Research*, 97–201.

– (1993) 'Naturalizing Epistemology: Quine, Simon and the Prospects for Pragmatism.' In *Philosophy and Cognitive Science*, ed. C. Hookway, and D. Peterson. Cambridge: Cambridge University Press.

Stove, D.C. (1986) *The Rationality of Induction*. Oxford: Oxford University Press.

Suppe, F. (1988) 'A Nondeductivist Approach to Theoretical Explanation.' In *The Limitations of Deductivism*, ed. A. Grunbaum and W. Salmon. Berkeley: University of California Press.

Swinburne, Richard (ed.) (1974) *The Justification of Induction*. Oxford: Oxford University Press.

Taylor H., and B. Tversky (1992) 'Descriptions and Depictions.' *Memory and Cognition* 20.

Taylor, J.E. (1990) 'Epistemic Justification and Psychological Realism.' *Synthèse* 85.

Taylor Parker, S. (1990) 'Why Big Brains Are So Rare.' In *'Language' and Intelligence in Monkeys and Apes – Comparative Developmental Perspectives*, ed. S. Taylor Parker and K.R. Gibson. Cambridge: Cambridge University Press.

Thagard, P. (1990) 'Concepts and Conceptual Change.' *Synthèse*. 82, 255–74.

Tomberlin, J.E. (ed.) (1989) *Philosophical Perspectives, Action Theory and Philosophy of Mind*, vol. 3. Atascadero, CA: Ridgeview.

– (1990) *Philosophical Perspectives, Action Theory and Philosophy of Mind*, vol. 4. Atascadero, CA: Ridgeview.

Ullman, Shimon (1979) *The Interpretation of Visual Motion* Cambridge, MA: MIT Press.

Vaina, L. (1990) 'What and Where in the Human Visual System: Two Hierarchies of Visual Modules.' *Synthèse* 83, 49–91.

Van Benthem, J. (1989) 'Reasoning and Cognition.' In *Research Directions in Cognitive Science: European Perspectives*, vol. 2, ed. H. Schnelle. Hillsdale, NJ: Lawrence Erlbaum.

Van Fraassen, B.C. (1989) *Laws and Symmetry*. Oxford: Clarendon Press.

Van Gelder, T. (1990) 'Compositionality: A Connectionist Variation on a Classical Theme.' *Cognitive Science* 14, 355–84.

– (1991) 'Classical Questions, Radical Answers: Connectionism and the Structure of Mental Representations.' In Horgan and Tienson (eds).

Villanueva, E. (ed.) (1990) *Information, Semantics and Epistemology.* Oxford: Basil Blackwell.

Wagner, Steven J. (1993) 'Truth, Physicalism and the Ultimate Theory.' In *Objections to Physicalism*, ed. Howard Roginson. Oxford: Clarendon Press.

Wason, P.C. (1966) 'Reasoning.' In *New Horizons in Psychology,* ed. B.M. Foss. Harmondsworth: Penguin.

White, N.P. (1976) *Plato on Knowledge and Reality.* Indianapolis: Hackett.

Whiten, Andrew (1991) *Natural Theories of the Mind – Evolution, Development and Simulation in Everyday Mind Reading*. Oxford: Basil Blackwell.

Williams, B. (1978) *Descartes*. Harmondsworth: Penguin.

Wright, C. (1980) *Wittgenstein on the Foundations of Mathematics*. London: Duckworth.

Zamora Bonilla, J. (1992) 'Truthlikeness without Truth: A Methodological Consideration.' *Synthèse* 93.

Index

Abrahamsen, A., 32, 48, 64, 65–6, 67, 102–3
Agnoli, F., 19–20, 206–7
Ajjanagadde, V., 31, 99
argument from intolerance, 160, 164
argument from omission, 161, 166, 167
Aristotle, 6, 59, 200, 213, 214
Armstrong, D., 46, 301
assessment, 19, 35, 44, 52, 55–7, 67, 74, 81, 92, 99, 101, 103, 109, 116, 120, 121, 124, 127, 130, 132, 169, 192, 193, 197, 204, 206, 211, 214, 224, 225, 280, 283, 292, 299

Bach, K., 298
Barsalou, L., 11, 277, 289
Bechtel, W., 32, 48, 64, 65–6, 67, 71, 102–3, 119
Berkeley, G., 6, 192
bias, 16, 18, 19, 23, 150, 195, 203–8, 210
Bold Claim, 237–41, 248, 251, 252, 255, 258
Booker, L.B., 122, 292
Boyd, R., 302
brain, 13, 21, 22, 25, 44, 45, 64, 67, 68, 73, 75, 77, 83–4, 87, 89, 94, 100, 102–4, 107, 118, 131, 174–8, 282, 283
brain-in-the-vat, 295
Braithwaite, R.B., 201
Brown, J.R., 4, 79, 84, 220, 263
Burnyeat, M., 293, 304
Byrne, R., 23, 24, 176, 179, 180, 181, 208, 209

Carruthers, P., 289, 302
causal relevance, 152
Cheng, P., 204, 209, 210
Chomsky, N., 8, 9, 203
Churchland, P.M., 1, 4, 5, 22, 28, 31, 35, 36, 42, 48, 50, 52, 56, 60, 64, 66, 67–70, 74–9, 83, 84, 86–94, 96–112, 114–19, 121, 123, 124, 126, 217, 219, 221, 223–6, 233–40, 242, 246–52, 254–8, 262, 277, 280–2, 284–8, 290, 292, 303, 304
Churchland, Patricia, 91, 210
Clark, A., 91, 105, 285, 289, 291, 292
Classical picture (of cognition), 37–9, 42–6, , 48, 49, 52, 53, 55, 60, 63, 116, 118, 120, 127, 128, 130, 132, 135–7, 149, 168, 170, 177, 185, 186, 198, 218, 223, 227, 232, 280, 293

cognitive styles, 51, 52, 58, 135, 187, 203, 205, 208, 227
cognitivist challenge, 232
cognizer,10, 11, 40, 42, 51, 53, 58, 82, 89, 107, 120, 121, 130, 132, 135, 136, 167, 173, 174, 188, 190, 201, 228, 230–2, 303
Cohen, L.J., 203, 205, 302, 303
coherence, 51, 80, 87–90, 116, 124, 126, 127, 132, 231, 232, 303, 304
coincidence, 146, 147, 148, 151, 172, 174, 177, 281, 290, 295; definition of, 294
comparability, 52, 55, 56, 58, 60, 135, 187, 188, 189, 193, 195, 196, 202, 227
competence, 8–10, 18, 19, 26, 194, 203, 205, 206, 207, 208, 210
concept, 10, 11, 12, 24, 27, 29, 30, 97, 105, 106, 109, 111, 277, 290; of evidence, 130; of justification, 197; of truth, 163, 200
conceptual analysis, 41, 49, 108
conceptual scheme, 64, 217, 218, 253
conjunction task, 16
Copernicus, N., 235, 237
correspondence, 42, 68, 72, 76, 78, 82, 93, 108, 109, 110, 113, 116, 166, 279, 283, 284
curiosity, 38, 157, 158, 179, 181, 191, 293
curious, 137, 168, 179, 295
Cussins, A., 219

Dalton, C., 59, 213
Darwin, C., 59, 215
Dascal, M., x
Davidson, D., 46, 96, 258, 281, 298
Davies, M., x
De Vries, W., 285
de Waal, F., 180–1
demon, 52, 144, 146, 170, 193, 203, 292, 294
descriptive pluralism, 52, 58, 60, 64, 135, 187, 194, 195, 196, 203, 208, 211, 227
desire, 38, 41, 78, 93, 143, 148, 149, 280
Devitt, M., 138, 152, 154, 155, 230, 277, 295
Dretske, F., 281, 305
Dummett, M., 200

Ebbinghaus, J., 6
Einstein, A., 36, 173, 215, 220, 243
Elster, J., 150
enquiry (inquiry), 4, 5, 20, 69, 166, 170, 177, 186, 199, 220, 298
epicycles, 182
epistemic justification, 76, 231
epistemic virtue, 42, 44, 49, 59, 116, 118, 132, 185, 190, 288, 295
epistemology, 3, 5, 36, 37, 38, 39, 42, 45, 46, 50, 58, 73, 86, 87, 88, 93–5, 108, 118, 119, 124, 128, 129, 132, 186, 225, 228, 257, 260, 282, 288, 289, 298; information-based, 305
error message, 86, 87, 88, 287
Etchemendy, J., 199, 200
evaluative, 44, 119, 121, 140, 187
Evans, G., 19, 20, 206, 208
evidence, 4, 7, 11, 13, 18, 20, 64, 79, 83, 90, 100, 108, 112, 113, 115, 128–32, 174, 178–80, 182, 195, 201, 203, 204, 209, 219–21, 229, 232, 242, 254, 259
evolution, 1, 20, 21, 34, 57, 162, 168, 169, 170–3, 177, 182–5, 189, 194, 226, 229, 301

false belief, 93, 145–7, 151,152, 294, 295, 297

Feyerabend, P., 48, 64, 88, 121, 237, 248, 252, 263, 284, 287, 304
Field, H., 298
fitness, 20, 21, 54, 165, 169, 170, 171, 172, 174, 177–84
Fodor, J., 91, 241, 242, 243, 278, 285, 293
folk-psychology, 30, 71, 87, 88, 108, 185, 218, 223
functional, 22, 32, 65, 73, 77, 84–6, 128, 140, 160, 177, 284, 298–300
Forbes, G., 283
Frege, G., 118, 213

Galileo, G., 79, 235, 237, 241–3, 247, 249–51, 254
Garon, J., 97, 99, 101
Garson, J.W., 285
Gibson, J.J., 305
Gibson, K.R., 175, 176, 177
Giere, R.N., 36, 114, 169, 212
Gigerenzer, G., 204, 205, 209, 303
Gilman, D., 305
Glenberg, A., 77
goal(s): communicative 76; cognitive, 5, 36–44, 47, 49, 51–4, 65, 82, 121–2, 126, 135–45, 160, 162–9, 177, 185–7, 189–91, 193, 195–7, 199, 200, 202, 211–15, 227, 228, 277, 283, 296, 299; comparable, 195, 196, 202, 228; practical, 56–9, 65, 68–70, 82, 87–9, 93, 147, 149–53, 175
Goldman, A., 123, 275, 279
Gombrich, E.H., 284
Goodman, N., 194, 302, 312
Gorgias, 47, 53,216
Gould, S.J., 301

Haack, S., 279
Hadley, R.F., 285, 287
Hanson, N.R., 98, 235, 237, 238, 248, 252, 258, 262, 278
Harman, G., 302
harmony theory, 126
HEALTH (*...), 165–6
Heider, Fritz, 16
Helmholtz, H., 7
heuristic, 15–19, 22, 23, 44, 81, 193, 195, 202, 204, 206, 207, 211, 228–31
holism, 30, 32, 96, 100, 102, 117, 234, 235, 240, 242, 249, 252, 254, 256, 260, 261, 263, 264, 272, 289
holist, 11, 32, 86, 94–9, 105, 107, 234–8, 241, 245–8, 250–2, 254, 255, 260, 262–4, 268, 272, 273, 275, 289, 304, 305
Holland, J., 81
Hooker, C.A., 302
Horgan, T., 91, 285, 287
Hume, D., 46, 106, 193, 197, 287
Humphrey, N.K., 177, 179–80, 181–2

incommensurability, 89, 210, 252, 254, 284, 304
incomparability, 52, 56, 189, 227
Indifference Thesis, 170, 172, 176, 179
inference, 7, 13, 14, 19, 20, 31, 41, 43, 68, 125, 170–2, 194, 195, 200, 201, 205, 209, 252, 269, 293, 300
inferential, 31, 57, 84–5, 129, 147, 169, 171–3, 178, 183, 193, 194, 207, 239, 248, 301
inquiry. *See* enquiry
intelligence, 3, 6, 8, 43, 174, 176, 177, 179, 180–3, 301, 302
irrational(-ity), 18, 19, 38, 47, 63, 158, 166, 199, 203, 206, 208, 216, 231, 254
isolation assumption, 56, 57, 188, 189, 191

Jacobson, S., 298
Johnson-Laird, P., 17, 23, 24, 80, 195, 204, 205, 207, 208
Jutronic, D. x

Kahneman, D., 16, 17, 19, 195, 206
Karmiloff-Smith, A., 105, 289
Kekule, F.A., 118
Kepler, J., 102, 112, 235, 254
Kirkham, R.L., 279
Kitcher, P., 114, 230, 279, 301
knowledge, 4–9, 11–14, 18, 19, 22, 23, 30, 32, 35, 37, 39, 41–3, 45, 48, 56, 64–8, 80, 81, 87, 88, 95, 97, 100, 102–5, 110–13, 117, 120, 125, 142, 144, 145, 155, 181, 184, 186, 188, 189, 199, 204, 209, 212, 223, 230, 236–8, 241, 244, 245, 252, 256, 263, 265–8, 271, 287, 289, 302
Krantz, D., 19, 206
Kuhn, T., 102, 110, 237, 248, 252, 305

Langley, P., 216
Laudan, L., 42
law, 40, 46, 102, 112, 122, 126, 144, 145, 147, 162, 185, 193, 197, 215, 218, 224, 267, 268, 270, 274, 290
Leslie, J., 192
Levi, I., 205, 302
Lewis, D., 14, 281
logic, 12, 14, 16, 23–5, 41, 42, 48, 57, 68, 80, 114, 120, 126, 128–31, 163, 164, 192, 196, 199–202, 207, 209–11, 213, 230, 291, 302
logical link, 142, 143
Lower, B., 298
Lycan, W.G., 7, 277, 300

Machiavellian intelligence, 179, 181
Main Argument, 52, 58, 138, 157, 162, 168, 187, 194
map, 22, 63, 64, 74–8, 81–5, 94, 108, 109, 113, 125, 137, 158, 159, 161, 163, 166, 185, 209, 218, 281, 282, 303
marginal cognitive utility, 178
Maxwell, C., 100, 245, 256, 290
McDaniel, M., 77
McGinn, C., 304
McLaughlin, B.P., 91, 285
McNamarra, J., 207
Medin, D.L., 10
medium, 6, 21, 63–5, 67, 70, 71, 75, 76, 79, 80–2, 85, 110, 113–15, 120, 220, 221, 224, 282, 291–3
Mellor, H., x
Mendel, 59, 213, 214
mental model, 23, 24, 80–2, 207
mind, 5, 10, 13, 16, 21, 30, 44, 45, 47–9, 54, 64, 67, 73, 75, 84, 94, 100, 118, 126, 132, 137, 142, 192, 195, 208, 209, 212, 213, 217, 229, 230–2, 246, 248, 252, 263, 291
Modest Claim (about theory and observation), 233, 248–9, 251–5, 257–8
Munevar, G., 234
mutation, 20, 148, 171

natural kinds, 224, 300
natural selection, 169–71, 182, 183, 189
naturalism, naturalistic, 4, 45, 46, 184, 198, 205, 219, 222, 224, 227, 302, 304
Neander, K., x
Newton, I., 4, 40, 42, 59, 118, 190, 213–15, 235, 274, 279, 305
Newton-Smith, W., 4, 40, 42, 213, 214, 235, 279
Nietzsche, F., 41, 46
Niiniluoto, I., 279

Niklasson, L.F., 287
Nisbett, R., 16, 17, 195, 205
nomic, 100, 144, 145, 234, 235, 238, 243, 273, 294
norm, 37, 42, 43, 48, 52, 55, 58, 59, 77, 126, 135, 136, 187, 196, 205, 227, 292, 304
normative, 16, 41, 43, 44, 46, 48, 53, 58, 94, 139, 206, 207
Novick, L.R., 204, 210
Nozick, R., 185, 229, 305

observation, 50, 64, 68, 88, 100, 122, 141, 181, 212–15, 218, 233–43, 245–56, 262–8, 270–2, 279, 304, 305
observation-theory distinction, 260
Oersted, H.C., 236, 238, 243, 244, 250, 252, 253

perseverance, 18, 195, 211
Plantinga, A., 45
Plato, 38, 47, 213, 279, 304
pleiotropy, 21, 171, 174
Plunkett, K., 289
policy, 54, 57,145–8, 151, 153, 191, 297, 298
Pollack, J.B., 287
Popper, K., 55, 212, 279
possibilist pluralism, 194
proof, 12, 15, 79, 119, 130–2, 144, 153, 173, 184, 189, 249
proper function, 173, 174, 177, 178
prototype theories, 12
Ptolemy, Claudius, 100, 118
Putnam, H., 217, 293, 303
Pylyshyn, Z., 9, 91, 278, 286, 291

Quine, W.O., 46, 48, 96, 192, 231–2, 258, 288, 303

radical descriptive pluralism, 52, 60, 227
Ramsey, W., 29, 30, 97, 99, 101, 278, 302
rational, 4, 5, 10, 18–21, 23, 38, 41, 42, 44–50, 50, 54, 55, 59, 63, 67, 68, 79, 90, 101, 108, 113, 115, 117–21, 124, 127–32, 136, 137, 139, 144, 145, 147, 149, 151, 157, 158, 161, 166, 168–70, 172–4, 177, 179, 182–94, 197, 199–201, 203–6, 208–16, 219, 220, 225, 227–9, 231–6, 243, 250, 254, 297
rationalism, 45, 232
rationality, 21, 23, 45, 47, 118, 124, 169, 177, 186, 187, 197, 199, 205, 208, 212
reasonable, 9, 49, 118, 127, 132, 148, 163, 167, 174, 180, 199, 201, 219, 296
reasoning, 6–20, 22–4, 28, 38, 49, 53, 55–8, 73, 75–7, 80–1, 87, 98, 107, 111, 117, 118, 120, 125–8, 131, 140, 142, 145, 147, 150, 152, 155, 158, 183, 187, 192, 193–5, 199, 203–11, 220, 228, 230, 231, 232, 241, 289, 305
reference, 5, 47, 53, 111, 138, 139, 153, 158–61, 163, 164, 167, 170, 190, 197, 199, 208, 219–21, 234, 296, 298, 299
Reid, T., 46
reliability, 35, 82, 117, 122, 123, 126, 128, 132, 137, 144, 168, 169, 170, 172–4, 178, 183–6, 188, 191, 193, 197–201, 229–32, 296, 297, 301, 302
reliable, 7, 20, 23, 31, 36, 43, 78, 87, 118, 122, 123, 137, 149, 153, 154, 169, 170, 172, 173, 178, 183, 184, 189, 192, 197, 198, 200, 207, 218, 229, 230, 231, 232, 253, 285, 293, 302, 303
Resnik, M., 289
Rey, G., 91, 285, 304
'right-wing' and 'left-wing' epistemologies, 44–5, 122–3

Rips, L., 12, 111, 207
Rosch, E., 10, 11
Rosenberg, J.F., 128, 129, 130
rule, 59, 75, 117, 127, 130, 184, 286, 292; connectionist, 127, 128; of inference, 9, 13–15, 21, 22, 27, 59, 80–2,106,126, 127, 129,131, 132, 195, 199, 200, 207–9, 228, 229, 230, 278, 294
Russell, B., 45, 65, 116

Salmon, W., 200, 201
Salviati, F., 235, 242
Schaller, H.N., 125
Schyns, P.G., 109, 110
science, 3–5, 14, 18, 21, 36–9, 42–5, 48, 49, 51–3, 58, 64, 68–70, 73, 77–9, 93, 95, 101–5, 110–13, 115, 118, 132, 141, 188, 190, 192, 205, 212–19, 222–4, 226, 227, 231, 233, 237, 238, 240, 241, 244–6, 248–51, 254–6, 260–4, 266, 268, 269, 271, 272, 280, 289, 300
scientific realism, 48, 68, 190, 217, 226, 227
Scott-Kakures, D., 280
Seager, W, x
Searle, J., 10
selection task, 17, 19, 23, 206
semantic, 19, 24, 26, 30, 32, 41, 67, 71, 72, 75, 82, 91, 95, 96, 97, 99, 100, 113–15, 117, 120, 123, 137, 138, 152, 157, 158, 161–8, 200, 208, 219–23, 229, 285, 291, 293, 294
Shafir, E., 207
Shapere, D., 233, 259, 260, 262–9, 271–3, 305
Shastri, L., 31, 99
Siegel, H., 293, 305
Simon, H.A., 59, 79, 212, 215, 216
situation-relativity, 187, 191
Slovic, P., 17
Smith, E.E., 277, 289
Smokrovic, N., x
Smolensky, P., 125, 127, 285, 287
Sneed, J., 114
Sober, E., 295, 302
Solomon, M., 278
Sousa, R. de, x
Sperba, D., 281
Stalnaker, R., 72
Stanic, M., x
state-space, 32, 34, 35, 83–4, 87, 96, 283, 288
Stein, E., 203, 302
Stich, S., 4, 5, 20, 42, 48–56, 58, 70, 97, 99, 101, 136, 138, 146, 149, 152, 153, 157–73, 184, 186, 189, 190, 194, 195, 197, 203, 205, 211, 213, 215–17, 225, 226, 278, 293, 295, 298, 299, 301, 302
Stove, D.C., 202
success, 3, 5, 6, 33, 35, 36, 53, 54, 58, 59, 68, 78, 87, 91, 92, 98, 112, 117, 122, 139, 140–7, 149–57, 162, 168–72, 180–2, 184, 187, 189, 190, 192, 197–9, 201, 209, 211–14, 218, 219, 221, 223, 225, 229, 231, 232, 261, 275, 294–7
Suppe, F., 114
survival, 152, 153, 162, 169, 172, 184
Swinburne, R. 201

Taylor, H., 77
Taylor, J., 281
Taylor Parker, S., 177
teleological, 190
Thagard, P., 105, 106
theories-in-the-head, 67, 73, 78–9, 87, 98, 100, 103, 104, 110, 117, 224, 291
theories of syntax, 8, 9
theories of thinking, 16, 18, 19, 23, 24;

harmony theory, 125; prototype theory, 111–13
theories of vision, 7
theory, scientific, 50, 64, 88, 94, 96, 97, 101, 114, 115, 232–75, 279, 283, 284, 288, 290, 291
Tienson, J., 91, 285, 287
truth, 14, 19–21, 24, 38–43, 49–55, 58, 59, 63–76, 81–4, 86, 88–104, 107–13, 115–21, 132, 135–71, 173, 174, 177, 178, 182, 184–8, 191, 193, 194, 196–201, 209, 212–14, 216, 218–28, 230, 232, 234, 270, 279, 282, 285, 290, 292, 296, 297, 299, 301–3; —centred epistemology, 59, 94, 108, 228, 298, 300; —goal 52, 54, 68, 69, 135, 138, 177, 187, 191, 199, 214, 227, 228, 281, 289, 298; —(in)tolerance, (in)hospitality, 39, 43, 61–5, 71, 73–5, 82–4, 90, 91, 94, 95, 97, 99, 101, 102, 107, 108, 111, 113, 116, 119, 135, 282, 289, 293; —value (true/false), 14, 66, 67, 73, 94, 108, 115; value of, 38, 39, 40, 71, 138, 139, 140, 144–8, 151–4, 157, 169, 173, 174, 192, 193, 227
Tversky, A., 16, 17, 19, 195, 206, 207
Tversky, B., 77

Vaina, L., 7, 241, 277
van Benthem, J., 199
Van Fraassen, B.C., 225
Van Gelder, T., 285, 287
veritistic, 39, 149, 169, 213, 299

Wagner, S.J., 219, 222, 296
warrant, 31, 123, 154
Wason, P.C., 279
White, N.P., 279
Whiten, A., 176, 179, 180, 181
Williams, B., 279

Zamora Bonilla, A., 279

www.ingramcontent.com/pod-product-compliance
Lightning Source LLC
LaVergne TN
LVHW090804070826
844660LV00022B/1077

* 9 7 8 1 4 4 2 6 5 7 7 0 0 *